YANKEE WARHORSE

YANKEE WARHORSE

A BIOGRAPHY OF Major General Peter Osterhaus

Mary Bobbitt Townsend

UNIVERSITY OF MISSOURI PRESS
COLUMBIA

University of Missouri Press, Columbia, Missouri 65211
Printed and bound in the United States of America

First paperback printing, 2021

Cataloging-in-Publication data available from the Library of Congress

ISBN 978-0-8262-1875-9 (hardcover : alk. paper)
ISBN 978-0-8262-2252-7 (paperback : alk. paper)

∞™ This paper meets the requirements of the American National Standard for Permanence of Paper for Printed Library Materials, Z39.48, 1984.

Design and composition: Kristie Lee
Typefaces: Adobe Garamond and Bernhard Modern

Frontispiece: Osterhaus monument on the Vicksburg battlefield. (Author's collection)

For my mother,
Elizabeth Osterhaus Bobbitt,
with love

Contents

Foreword

PETER J. Osterhaus has long deserved more attention from historians and students of the Civil War than he has received. He was, in many ways, the best example of disinterested ethnic patriotism in the conflict. An important division commander in the Army of the Tennessee, especially during the Vicksburg and Chattanooga campaigns, Osterhaus contributed greatly to many Union operations from the start of the war in Missouri until the capture of Mobile, Alabama, in April 1865. He held commands that ranged from the Twelfth Missouri to the Fifteenth Corps and earned the respect of his superior officers because of his dependability, energy, and resourcefulness as a campaigner. Subordinates enjoyed relating colorful stories of his unique German American mode of expression, but when it was necessary to drive deep into enemy territory or face the foe on the field of battle, they knew this gifted commander could be relied on to help engineer success. Osterhaus based his war career on military ability, not ethnic favoritism, and he won the respect of his associates and men alike because of that stroke of integrity.

Any good biography of Osterhaus would be a breath of fresh air, but it is particularly delightful that this one was written by a direct descendant of old Peter Joe. Mary B. Townsend had already retired from a career as a hospital nursing executive when she contacted me several years ago, based on a handful of articles about Osterhaus and the men he commanded that I had written a long time before. She had an idea to write a full-fledged biography of her great-great-grandfather. There are many amateur historians working in the Civil War field, producing self-published books that probably should never have been written, so I was initially hesitant to endorse Mary's effort. But her enthusiasm and drive carried her through the sometimes tedious job of researching and writing a book, and led her to develop skills as a historian and writer. The end result, I am proud to see, is a first-rate biography of a significant general in the Union army.

There are many new views of Osterhaus in this volume, and Townsend very ably summarizes them in the Introduction. He was not a Prussian but a West

German liberal whose life was upset by participation in an anti-Prussian revolution in 1849. Townsend provides much detail heretofore unknown about his participation in that revolution, which brought him to the United States in time to understand the issues surrounding the great sectional conflict. Osterhaus, like most German Americans, sided with the North, risking the welfare of his large family by devoting his time and energy to the military effort to save the Union. He lost his wife to illness just before the Chattanooga campaign, but only briefly interrupted his service in the field to make arrangements for his children and later to marry his sister-in-law. Townsend has ably brought the personal aspects of Osterhaus's life to readers, despite the comparative lack of letters, diaries, and other personal accounts written by the general.

Osterhaus's service to the United States did not end with Appomattox. He held an important command in Mississippi during the early days of Reconstruction, and served as U.S. consul in Lyon, France, for many years. Ironically, Osterhaus spent the last years of his life in his native Germany, passing away a short time before his adopted country declared war on his native land in World War I.

This biography is part of a new wave of interest in the history of German American involvement in the Civil War. Several editions of significant primary material have appeared, including Joseph R. Reinhart's translations of letters from soldiers that appeared in German-language newspapers, *Two Germans in the Civil War: The Diary of John Daeuble and the Letters of Gottfried Rentschler, 6th Kentucky Volunteer Infantry* and August Willich's *Gallant Dutchmen: Civil War Letters from the 32nd Indiana Infantry.* Walter D. Kamphoefner and Wolfgang Helbich also edited selections from 343 letters dealing with the Civil War era that are housed in a German archive and published them as *Germans in the Civil War: The Letters They Wrote Home.* Recent studies of German Americans in the war include Martin W. Ofele's *German-Speaking Officers in the U.S. Colored Troops, 1863–1867* and Christian B. Keller's *Chancellorsville and the Germans: Nativism, Ethnicity, and Civil War Memory.*

It is encouraging that the new literature on German American involvement in the Civil War is diverse, giving equal weight to western and eastern theaters of operations, and bringing to light resources in Europe. It has also gotten away from the old emphasis on excessively praising the Germans and now takes a hard look at problems and weaknesses, as well as extolling accomplishments. There are healthy signs that historians are taking the story seriously as an important area of study.

This biography of Osterhaus fits well into the new literature, for Townsend has conducted extensive research to illuminate her subject's life in both Europe and the United States. She does not portray him as a superman, saint, or military genius but analyses his strengths and weaknesses in a balanced way, despite her direct lineal connection to the general. The book is a mixture of good history and familial devotion that charms and teaches at the same time. Finally, the old general has received his due.

Earl J. Hess
Stewart W. McClelland Chair in History
Lincoln Memorial University

Acknowledgments

I GIVE MY deepest appreciation to my own true love, Michael J. Townsend, who supported me every step of this journey with his encouragement and feedback. Among his many other talents, he is a consummate editor and thoughtful critic.

This book would not have been written had not Earl J. Hess, coauthor of *Pea Ridge,* encouraged me to go forward with the project. He patiently read my overabundant first draft and gave me sound advice throughout the long process. Thank you again, Earl. All remaining mistakes are strictly my own.

My thanks to the historians of the National Park Service who willingly shared their files and expertise: Terry Winschel from Vicksburg, Jeffrey Patrick from Wilson's Creek, Steve Black from Pea Ridge, and James Ogden from Chickamauga and Chattanooga. Thanks also to Dr. William G. Piston, coauthor of *Wilson's Creek,* who spent a day showing me the Wilson's Creek battlefield from an expert's perspective. Brig. Gen. (Ret.) Parker Hills helped me understand the terrain and tactics on the several Vicksburg-campaign battle sites.

I was fortunate to have the services of the superb research librarians at the Beaverton, Oregon, Public Library and the Temecula, California, Public Library, who made long-distance research possible through the Interlibrary Loan System. Out of hundreds of requests, they found all but one.

Thanks also to the family members and friends who have made contributions to this book: Olivier Richard located and translated German material. François and Monique Richard researched Osterhaus's stay in Lyon, France. Eugen Deubner offered information on Osterhaus's descendants in Europe. Matt and Emmanuelle Richard Welch helped me establish a Web site on Osterhaus (www.pjosterhaus.com) and did some sleuthing in Karlsruhe. George Osterhaus provided family history in the United States. Dale Hargrave provided a family picture of Osterhaus. Axel Steuerwald translated a key German document for me. Special thanks to Scott Kline, geographer and fire marshal among his other talents, who created the maps in this book.

Finally, thanks to Clair Willcox, Sara Davis, and Annette Wenda, editors at the University of Missouri Press, for their considerate encouragement and support.

YANKEE WARHORSE

Introduction

PETER Joseph Osterhaus, major general of Volunteers for the Union army in the American Civil War, rightly referred to himself as "an utterly unknown person—*homo novus*." This remains true today, despite the fact that Osterhaus, an exiled leader from the 1848 rebellion in Germany, enjoyed a meteoric military career in America. Working as an accounting clerk in St. Louis as the war began, he joined up immediately and rose from the rank of private to brigadier general in just a year. During his years of service to his adopted country he played a significant role in several of the major turning points of the war, led fifteen thousand men on Sherman's March to the Sea, served as the military governor of Mississippi during the early days of Reconstruction, and represented the United States in consular positions in Europe after the war. Recognized by his superiors, loved by his officers and men, he could rightly be called the "Yankee warhorse" for his many solid contributions to the Union war effort in the West. Yet his accomplishments were underreported even in his day, and even less is known about him now. The little that has been written about him, apart from some excellent essays, has often been inaccurate.[1]

How did Peter Joseph Osterhaus acquire his skill as a military leader? Historians have credited both his Prussian military heritage and his training at the prestigious Berlin Military Academy. Actually, neither of these assumptions is completely accurate. His birthplace, Koblenz, had only recently come under Prussian rule as capital of the new Rhine Province ceded to Prussia in 1815. He grew up in a nonmilitary family and moved as a young adult to the southern duchy of Baden. True, he did have some Prussian military training, but just the obligatory year of officer's training that the Prussians required of all young men. He also had experience in warfare, but as a rebel on the barricades of Mannheim, not on a formal battlefield. What he did have was a keen interest in military matters, a lively intellect, and the ability to adapt. He was schooled by his experience early in the American Civil War, and he learned well.

Osterhaus had been a U.S. citizen for six years when the Confederates attacked Fort Sumter. Less than a week later, he enlisted as a private in the Union army at the advanced age of thirty-seven. The army was delighted to have him.

From a standing U.S. Army of fewer than twenty thousand, President Abraham Lincoln quickly had to mobilize a huge new force made up almost entirely of untrained and overenthusiastic civilians, bringing with them little idea of what it meant to fight or to lead effectively. In this crisis the government was desperate for leaders with military experience. In addition to his Prussian military training and his brief battle experience, Osterhaus was able to offer his new country his ability to speak and to write English. These were desirable skills for commanders of volunteer units, particularly heavily German-speaking units, and not surprisingly his men elected him major almost immediately. He advanced to colonel within a few months, forming his own regiment. Like many other German revolutionaries with previous military training, Osterhaus was a superb molder of new soldiers. But unlike the case with most of his compatriots, who rarely rose above regimental command as the war progressed, his performance in the field would soon earmark him for advancement to higher levels.

Even though Osterhaus was little known by the general public, he soon made a name for himself within the army. From the earliest days of the war, his superior officers recognized Osterhaus as an energetic, dependable leader, often assigning him temporary commands at a higher level than his rank would indicate. He led a division throughout most of the war, advancing temporarily to corps command for part of that time. Along the way he won the praise of Generals Grant, Halleck, Frémont, McClernand, Curtis, Hooker, Logan, and Sherman for both his reliable performance in battle and his capable leadership on campaign.[2]

Osterhaus was the only man in the Union army present at both the first military action in the West, the capture of Camp Jackson in St. Louis, and the last official Confederate surrender of the war, Kirby Smith's surrender finalized on May 26, 1865, which he had the honor of signing. Between those signal events, Osterhaus fought in most of the decisive western campaigns along a fifteen hundred–mile front, including Wilson's Creek, Missouri; Pea Ridge, Arkansas; the several battles around Vicksburg, Mississippi; the three battles of Chattanooga, Tennessee; several battles of the Atlanta campaign; the march to Savannah, Georgia; and the final battle of the war at Fort Blakely, near Mobile, Alabama. In particular, Osterhaus's steady performance at Vicksburg, Chattanooga, and Atlanta, major turning points in the war, contributed more to those Union victories than he was given credit for in the press. Besides his best-known battle contributions at Pea Ridge and Chattanooga, he also fought countless smaller day-to-day skirmishes throughout the long campaigns.

"Osterhaus was never more jolly or at home than on the battlefield," remembered one of his officers. He stood out from the other volunteer officers in his understanding of both tactics and logistics, even though his careful field preparation led to the criticism by later historians that he was unduly cautious in battle. All agreed, though, that his skill for the placement and utilization of field artillery in battle was better than that of most of his peers in the volunteer army. Of his major battles, in only one, at Ringgold Gap, Georgia, facing Patrick Cleburne, was he clearly bested. In nearly every other major contest his actions contributed significantly to a Union victory.[3]

Osterhaus spoke English with a heavy accent, providing great stories for his men to pass around the campfire. He was actually quite fluent, and he was especially known for his accurate, cogent intelligence reports and detailed, if enthusiastic, operations reports. However, the prejudices of the day against German immigrants did impact him, particularly in his dealings with Southern citizens, who were convinced that the German soldiers were much worse pillagers than other "Yankees." He was often the most visible German to blame, yet there is no evidence that he condoned or encouraged plundering any more than his peers.

In addition to steady leadership in battle, Osterhaus excelled as point man on major troop movements, operating independently to locate the best routes and to feel out the enemy. For the first two years of the war he honed these skills in sometimes obscure assignments that provided him the practical field experience that the more quickly promoted officers lacked. Nathaniel Lyon first utilized his skill in leading the advance at Boonville, Missouri, in that first official battle of the western theater. The next summer, Samuel Curtis assigned him command of the forward Union outpost deep inside hostile Arkansas. That grueling experience was his last taste of the war's backwaters, but not his last experience leading the advance.

In the spring of the following year U. S. Grant relied on Osterhaus to discover a way across the Mississippi River below Vicksburg for the entire Union army. Later, during the Vicksburg siege, Grant trusted Osterhaus to guard his rear from Joe Johnston's Confederate reinforcements and then, once Vicksburg had fallen, used him to lead one arm of the advance on Jackson. In the fall Grant again chose Osterhaus to spearhead the Army of the Tennessee's campaign to relieve William Rosecrans, trapped at Chattanooga. In 1864 William T. Sherman assigned him command of the Fifteenth Corps on the March to the Sea. His final battle contribution was to coach the inexperienced E. R. S. Canby through the siege and capture of the forts at Mobile Bay.

His men and officers admired Osterhaus as a fighting general who led from the front and took care of his troops. While they approved his willingness to act forcefully when needed, such as he did at Ringgold Gap, they were also confident that he would not needlessly sacrifice their lives, as he showed them at Port Gibson and Vicksburg. Although he was remarkably approachable, the German insisted on proper camp discipline and regular drills, making it his business to have the men well prepared for combat. The overall result of his stewardship was a lower casualty rate than many of his peers.

Of the nearly two hundred thousand German-born or -descended Union volunteer soldiers who served in the American Civil War, only a dozen officers born and raised in Germany achieved the rank of general; of these only three were appointed major general, Volunteers before the war's end. Two of the three, Carl Schurz and Franz Sigel, were both promoted by President Lincoln because of their political influence rather than because of their military exploits. The third, Peter Joseph Osterhaus, was by far the best and most experienced field officer of the three. Even so, there was a considerable wrangle between Sherman, Grant, and Lincoln over his appointment, due in great part to the politics of his peculiar situation. Osterhaus expected to be judged solely on the merits of his performance in battle, but that did not happen for a number of reasons.

Like many others of all ranks, Osterhaus did not emerge from the war unscathed: early on he contracted malaria and dysentery and was later wounded in the Vicksburg campaign, both incidents causing physical problems that plagued him throughout the war and for the rest of his long life. And he lost his beloved wife on the eve of the Chattanooga battles, hurriedly leaving his five bereft young children in the care of friends while he returned to battle.

After the war Osterhaus was appointed military governor of Mississippi during the first six months of Reconstruction, finding himself somewhat flummoxed by the myriad, nearly insoluble problems of the South as the country began to reunite. Then he became the U.S. consul to Lyon, France, representing his neutral country during the Franco-Prussian War. Later he regained his German citizenship, established a business in Germany, and then served for a time as U.S. vice consul in Mannheim, neatly combining his dual citizenship in the one position. After the turn of the century, Osterhaus returned to America twice, where he was belatedly honored as one of the last surviving Union major generals of the Civil War.

Despite his war-related ill health, Osterhaus lived to see the first two years of World War I unfolding sixty miles from his childhood home in Koblenz. Always an avid student of history and current events, he must have been astonished at how warfare had changed by this time. Perhaps fortunately, Osterhaus died in January 1917, at the age of ninety-four, before his two beloved countries were at war with each other. Ironically, his family was divided by the conflict, like many families had been fifty years before during the Civil War.

From the glimpses of Osterhaus afforded by the material written both about him and by him, several conclusions about his character seem reasonable. He was a man who saw things mostly in absolutes: he had strong opinions about the proper duties of a citizen and lived his life by them, even when his ideals put him at risk for being in the minority, arousing prejudice, or being actively persecuted. He felt that a citizen should be loyal to a government that represented his values and that all men should leap to serve such a government in time of war, regardless of personal agendas.

Osterhaus's personal code of conduct was based on valued military comportment in what was one of the last wars led from horseback, where individual effort was more important to the outcome than the devastating weapons developed in the twentieth century. No qualities were more important to him than honesty, bravery, and energy, traits that he himself demonstrated over and over during the Civil War and that he admired in others. He prized loyalty to his friends and to the leadership of the country and resisted joining in public criticism of acts with which, quite possibly, he privately disagreed. Osterhaus accepted the fact that he could go only so high in the army, based on his outsider origins, and was very satisfied with having achieved the rank of major general of Volunteers before the end of the war.

All of these traits make him appear to be larger than life, which, of course, he was not. He could be stern, rigid, and implacable to his enemies, including civilians. He didn't have great respect for the capabilities of black people. He had little feeling for the subtleties attendant to bringing a rebellious people back into the Union. And he probably loved waging war a bit too much. But by becoming intensely engaged in four historic armed conflicts in his more than ninety years, Peter Joseph Osterhaus was truly a man of his turbulent times, one who deserves to be better known to our generation than he is.

Several factors contributed to Osterhaus's obscurity, beginning with the scant media coverage of the western campaign, especially throughout the first years of the war. Osterhaus's immigrant status probably reduced his coverage as well; he was seen as a "Prussian" general commanding German units, although in fact he commanded men of all backgrounds. Aside from the wildly enthusiastic German-language newspapers in the Midwest, there was not much press interest in covering foreign units, which had gained a frequently ill-deserved reputation for being unreliable in battle, at least in the East.[4]

Second, throughout the war Osterhaus served under commanders who were controversial, including John Frémont, Franz Sigel, John McClernand, Joseph Hooker, and E. R. S. Canby. The first three traded on their political influence to get their appointments. They ultimately roused the contempt of the Union army high command for various reasons: Frémont was accused of chaotic management, Sigel was plainly incompetent in battle and was finally removed, and McClernand, although a competent field officer, could not avoid crossing swords with U. S. Grant. Of the West Pointers, Joseph Hooker had failed at Chancellorsville and was trying to retrieve his damaged reputation when Osterhaus served under him, and Canby was moving too slowly to suit Grant in the final campaign of the war when Osterhaus was sent to help. Of all Osterhaus's commanders, only Black Jack Logan, another political general, and O. O. Howard, a dour West Pointer, were held in high regard by the Union top command. Osterhaus managed to find a way to work with all of these disparate superiors without attaching himself to their often unpopular political causes; however, his contributions were often ignored because of his commanders' failures. This phenomenon continued in later years, as historians tended to reflect a West Point bias in judging the performance of field generals and to denigrate the contributions of those labeled as "political" generals.[5]

Finally, and perhaps most important to Osterhaus's obscurity, was his own reticence. Unlike many other officers, including his German-born compatriots, he did not believe in campaigning for fame or promotion in either the ethnic or the national press, and in later years consistently declined requests to write his memoirs. "He fights the battles of his Country and asks for no one to applaud him," said one of his peers. All that survive of his personal writings are his short account of the war, one year of his diary, and a few letters to his son, a circumstance that forces later judgments about his personality, attitudes, and values to be inferential at best. His accomplishments, however, are a matter of record.[6]

Chapter 1
Before the War

PETER Joseph Osterhaus, later so adept a military leader, was born into a decidedly unmilitary family in Rhine Province, a new province created and awarded to the kingdom of Prussia in 1815 after the defeat of Napoléon. His father, Josef Adolf Oisterhusz, was a self-made, prosperous contractor in the city of Koblenz. Oisterhusz and his wife, Eleanora Kraemer, a local butcher's daughter, had three sons. Eldest was Anton Heinrich, who later joined his father in his business as an architect and contractor. Next came Peter Joseph, who was born on January 4, 1823. The youngest by six years was Lorenz Joseph Adolph. As were most people in the southern German duchies, the Oisterhuszes were Catholic. Although Josef Oisterhusz was of Dutch ancestry, he and Eleanora decided to change the spelling of their sons' surname to the German version, Osterhaus.[1]

Aside from three years in Rotterdam, young Joseph, as he preferred to be called, grew up in Koblenz, an ancient city on the Rhine, with a busy father and a mother who died when he was only fifteen. He was a lanky boy, reaching six feet, two inches, with auburn hair and freckles, a broad forehead, and piercing blue eyes (later he would sport a magnificent red mustache and goatee). At some point in his youth he learned to ride and to swim, both skills that would stand him in good stead in later trials, but his main love was academics, at which he excelled. During this period he developed the lifelong interest in world history and politics that led to his dreaming of becoming a professor of history at the university. Even though this was not to be, people in later years recognized Joseph for the scholar that he remained at heart and for his quick intelligence and wide-ranging interests, particularly in politics and world affairs. Like many other young men of his time in the German kingdoms along the Rhine, Joseph became a romantic intellectual who dreamed of a united, constitution-governed German nation to replace all of the existing duchies and kingdoms that were loosely connected by a German confederation that kept power squarely in the hands of the nobles.[2]

Unfortunately for Joseph, his father failed to appreciate the value of Joseph's ambition to become a historian. Clearly seeing no need for a university education in order for a man to be successful, he steered his middle son into business, just as he did his other sons. At his father's insistence, when Joseph was seventeen he began a three-year business apprenticeship, perhaps in connection with the family business. At the end of his apprenticeship there was still the matter of his military obligation to settle before Joseph could find a job and move on with his adult life. The Prussian army required all twenty-year-old men to serve on active duty for a period of two years followed by service in the *landwehr* (reserves) until the age of thirty-nine, with a short annual training obligation. (Osterhaus's obligation for active duty was cut to one year because of a technicality.)[3]

Osterhaus joined a Koblenz-based *jaeger* outfit, Regiment no. 29 of the Third Rhine Infantry, and began the only formal military training that he ever received. His yearlong instruction prepared him somewhat for service as an officer, although the quality of instruction was considered inferior to the three-year formal officer's training program taught at the Prussian Berlin Military Academy and elsewhere in the German kingdoms. Yet even in the short course, Prussian officer training emphasized strict personal discipline, precision in drills and maneuvers, and the values of patriotism, obedience, and honor that Osterhaus took with him throughout his life. The *jaeger* regiment Osterhaus joined was a light infantry unit: men both lightly armed and trained for rapid movement who operated as skirmishers in advance of the regular infantry. The army had begun to modernize by the time of Osterhaus's service in 1844, so besides the interminable drilling he learned to use the latest basic equipment in artillery and small arms, including the new breech-loading rifle. He was an apt and interested student; many of the principles taught during this year he put to great use later in the United States.[4]

By the time Osterhaus enlisted in 1843, soldiers were frequently used in lieu of the inadequate civilian police to put down local unrest. Osterhaus watched with dismay as the army's brutality in quelling civic disturbances and its contempt for the people escalated through the 1840s. He could not have easily reconciled the army's "enthusiastic" cruelty and oppression of the lower classes with his own developing ideas of individual rights in society. When his compulsory active-duty year was up at the beginning of 1845, Osterhaus was appointed second lieutenant of the Twenty-ninth Reserve Regiment stationed in Neuwied, on the Rhine, about five miles north of Koblenz, with the requirement of one or two weeks of training each year. Now came the critical decisions about the rest of his life: Should he go into business with his father, as his older brother had? Did he have the stomach to continue serving in the oppressive Prussian army, even as a reserve officer? His next move seems to have answered both of those questions. He decided to leave Rhine Province for another duchy in the German

Confederation, a loosely organized group of dozens of Germanic duchies and kingdoms both small and large formed in 1815 after the fall of Napoléon.[5]

During his army days, Osterhaus was certainly exposed to evidence of state oppression in Prussia-controlled Koblenz. However, he knew that in the non-Prussian southern duchies, accustomed until recently to twenty years of enlightened Napoleonic rule, the governing nobles' influence was less intrusive. As Osterhaus was making decisions about where to establish his career, it was only logical that he thought of the southern duchy of Baden, both for its business possibilities and for its more open political climate. Mannheim, Baden's largest town, was located near the confluence of the Neckar and Rhine rivers at the far northwest corner of the duchy. The ancient and liberal University of Heidelberg, exuding German romanticism, was nestled in the wooded hills a few miles up the Neckar. Besides the beauty of the place, Osterhaus can't have been immune to Baden's heady political climate. The Badeners hated Prussia but had a great deal in common with, and admiration for, their liberal neighbors in France and particularly Switzerland. Unlike in Prussian territories, in Baden dissidents could still voice liberal opinions despite the looming presence of army regiments of the grand duke of Baden that were permanently stationed at Mannheim.[6]

In April 1845 Osterhaus traveled to Mannheim seeking work and stayed two months, enjoying the liberal atmosphere. At the end of this time, having entered into a partnership with Carl Nestler and Company, which specialized in haulage, he returned to Koblenz to formally resign from the army and make his move permanent. He had served in the Prussian *landwehr* just six months. Once settled in Mannheim, Osterhaus lost no time establishing himself in business. During this period he also began courting his future wife, Matilda Born, who was the daughter of a notary in Kreuznach, a town across the Rhine about halfway between Mannheim and Koblenz.[7]

The year 1847 was a momentous one for Osterhaus. He married twenty-two-year-old Matilda on August 26, and presently she announced that she was expecting their first child. Professionally, he became a member of the Mannheim Trade Conference in September. Shortly thereafter he was awarded citizenship of Mannheim, having already been made a citizen of Baden. Although he was considered a foreigner, these achievements showed that he had begun to be accepted in Baden society. At the age of twenty-four, Osterhaus was well on his way to a full and productive life in his thriving new land. Unfortunately, events started escalating that would ultimately have Baden revolting against the rest of the German Confederation by mid-1849.[8]

In 1847, when Joseph Osterhaus and his friends discussed nationalism over their beer, Friedrich Hecker was the name mentioned most often. Hecker was a young, radical Baden state assemblyman who spoke out eloquently for a united German nation governed by a constitution, a concept that threatened the entitlements of the nobles. This idea was rapidly gaining more and more supporters, among them Osterhaus. With revolutionary fervor already at a boil in Baden, as it was throughout the rest of the German Confederation and Europe, Osterhaus was riveted by telegrams that arrived from France on February 23, 1848, trumpeting a massive people's revolt in Paris. Three weeks later the German Confederation's ruling body bowed to the rising pressure and issued an invitation for all German states to send representatives to a new national assembly to revise the confederation's constitution to include more citizen rights. Hecker was an obvious choice to represent Baden.[9]

Even before the National Assembly met, Baden had taken the lead in liberalizing its own governing body, and early in March the new state assembly had moved quickly to require that all Badener men capable of bearing arms be formed into citizens' armies. By mid-March the city council of Mannheim had established its own citizens' army, inviting Hecker to lead it. The first officer to step up to join him was law student Franz Sigel, late a second lieutenant in the Baden state army. Osterhaus's business partner, Carl Nestler, was also appointed a leader in the Mannheim contingent, and since Osterhaus had had some officer's training, he no doubt took a leadership role as well and probably met Sigel and Hecker for the first time during this period. Meanwhile, Joseph and Matilda Osterhaus became parents of their first child, Eleanor, and tried to get on with some semblance of a normal life through the rest of 1848 while they closely followed the unfolding activities of the National Assembly meetings in Frankfurt.[10]

In December Osterhaus also met Lorenz Brentano, a moderate who was both prominent in the National Assembly and the revolutionary leader in Baden after the now exiled Hecker left for America. Osterhaus and Brentano were elected majors of the two battalions of the Mannheim citizens' army, Brentano for his political power and Osterhaus for his military training. Brentano would prove to be not much help with things military, preoccupied as he became in revolutionary activities; Osterhaus in effect ran both battalions. In many cities the citizens' army was somewhat of a joke, unruly and poorly trained and equipped. Most guard units had no practical value except for social events and patriotic parades, but Mannheim's was one of the few more active units that would actually have a role in the coming revolt, due, in part at least, to Osterhaus's preparations.[11]

The rejection of the new constitution by the largest German states in early 1849 infuriated liberals throughout the confederation. In April and May the people of Baden and the surrounding states of Bavaria, Hesse, Württemberg, and Rhenish Prussia all rose against their governments, in some cases, particularly in Baden, joined by sympathetic state soldiers. In most of these revolts the Prussians and other state troops declared martial law and restored order without meeting much organized resistance. Only in Baden and the Bavarian Palatinate across the Rhine did the resistance continue for any length of time, and eventually Baden stood alone.[12]

In the middle of this chaotic period, Joseph Osterhaus and his wife also struggled with personal tragedy: the death of little Eleanor, only ten months old. Matilda was again pregnant, her baby due to arrive in August, and her safety must have preyed on Osterhaus's mind as he weighed the extent of his participation in the unfolding events. Although he treasured his family, demands for his military skills were escalating. As he would later in America, Osterhaus put the cause above his own family's needs and plunged into revolutionary activities. On May 13, 1849, the Baden revolution suddenly began: Brentano and his state committee forced the grand duke of Baden into exile at Strasbourg, where the next day the duke issued an urgent appeal to the confederation for help to quell the rebellion. Initially, the bloodless coup seemed to have been easier than the revolutionaries had anticipated. From its hopeful beginning to its ignominious end, the Baden revolt lasted only six weeks but must have seemed much longer to those who endured it.[13]

Once Brentano and his state committee had taken control of Baden, events began to move rapidly. On May 9 Osterhaus was one of a committee of twelve formed for the arming of the citizens of Mannheim. On May 15 the Mannheim municipal council appointed him head of the citizens' army and military coleader of the city, together with Col. Franz Baron von Roggenbach, commander of the Baden state army's Second Dragoon Regiment (mounted infantry) stationed there. Apparently, this coappointment was a safety measure to ensure that the dragoons remained loyal to the revolutionary government in case of armed conflict. Osterhaus's citizens' army remained under the control of the city council. Roggenbach shortly decamped for Prussia, and after the Mannheim city council conducted an unsuccessful search for a native Badener commander to replace him, Osterhaus agreed to lead both the citizens' army and the Second Dragoons. Osterhaus now held de facto military control of Mannheim, by its location surely the first target of any Prussian invasion, but gaining control of his new citizen-soldiers was a different matter. Less than half were combat-prepared. Uniforms, arms, and equipment were scarce, organization chaotic.[14]

As new military commander in Mannheim, Osterhaus had trouble with his fractious command almost immediately. On May 24 he issued a public order that revealed both his frustration and his politics, headlined "A Public Announcement by the Commanding Officer of the Citizens' Army of Mannheim": "The lack of attendance of soldiers to both exercise and watch duties is causing me to urgently remind everyone once again of the importance of the strict fulfillment of their citizen's duties. It is my belief that I can expect the fulfillment of these duties all the more, since in doing so we will prove to the enemy that our declarations to the old government were more than a mere justification for opposition, but the will of the people to overthrow the enemies of its freedom."[15]

There is no doubt that Joseph Osterhaus took Baden's new military decrees seriously, since later treason charges against him listed his arming of a corps of incoming Dutch freedom fighters, leading the Second Dragoon Regiment into treason (that is, in support of the revolutionary government), and disarming some of his citizens' army to reassign the arms to all unmarried men who had completed their mandatory military training. However, because he was in a hybrid position over both the citizens' army and the Baden army dragoons, he had a problematic chain of command. Did he report to his old coleader Brentano and the Baden state revolutionary government as leader of his regiment of state troops, or was he still accountable to Mannheim's conservative municipal council for the citizens' army, or both?[16]

The command structure became more complicated when Brentano appointed Johann Phillip Becker as commander-in-chief of all the state's local militias except for the Baden state army units. This new command was lumped all together under the title of "National Guards." Becker set up headquarters in Mannheim, and quickly got about the business of trying to make an army of these eager but mostly untrained men. But that would include only half of Osterhaus's units. The Baden army units, including his, were to be led by the commander in chief and minister of war, Karl Eichfeld, whose personality was described as "dreamy and retiring."[17]

Dreamy or not, Eichfeld and Becker needed to get organized quickly, because by May 16 the grand duke's appeal for help had already resulted in the rapid mobilization of the Hessian state army, in coalition with other armies, including the Prussians. These trained troops began to gather north of the Neckar River to put down Baden's revolt. Only two weeks after the initial revolt, the commanders of this threatening force declared martial law in large parts of northern Baden, including Mannheim, imposing the penalty of death for carrying arms or acting against the ducal government.[18]

Mannheim swarmed with activity as battle loomed. The key to defense of the city was control of the bridges over the Neckar and the Rhine rivers. Guards and artillery were posted at each bridge, and the Rhine itself was patrolled by river steamers commandeered for the purpose by the revolutionaries. Guards were also posted at the railroad station. Logically, Osterhaus in his role as military commander of the city should have directed this activity, but due to the confused command structure this may not have been the case. What is known is that he ordered an artillery unit to be established and started drilling the men. He also took charge of supplying the batteries at the rivers with ammunition.[19]

National Assemblyman Franz Raveaux clarified Joseph Osterhaus's ambiguous chain of command somewhat on May 29 by formally entrusting him with sole military command of Mannheim, based on Raveaux's belief that Osterhaus was absolutely dependable in his support of the revolutionary government. (The Mannheim local council made that appointment unanimous a week later by naming twenty-six-year-old Osterhaus colonel of the Mannheim citizens' army.) Raveaux's action was certainly timely, because that very day, in the midst of an oppressive heat wave, Osterhaus was in military control of Mannheim as he watched new commander-in-chief Sigel jauntily lead four thousand volunteers out of town on an ill-advised foray to the north against Hessian troops. Sigel's troops, a disorganized bunch of untrained units with unskilled commanders, were quickly routed and fled back to Heidelberg, nearly prostrate with the heat and the shock of actual battle. Sigel, mortified at not being able to control his men, tendered his resignation to the state committee, and it was accepted.[20]

In mid-May the revolutionary assembly had sent a delegation to America to implore Hecker to return to lead Baden, since Brentano was not interested in a permanent assignment as head of the new government. But events would not wait. Three weeks after the delegation left, when Hessian troops crossed the Neckar River and were spotted a few miles northeast of Mannheim, civilian anxiety grew intense. The new government leadership seemed to be faltering; absent Hecker, the people were even beginning to long for the return of the grand duke. Meanwhile, on June 13, Hecker left his farm in Illinois for Baden to heed the call of the people.[21]

On June 12 Baden and the Bavarian Palatinate across the Rhine appointed Gen. Ludwig von Mieroslawski of Poland as virtual military dictator of both of the duchies, giving him overall command of the rebel armed forces, including the National Guard, which had been leaderless since Sigel stepped down. Mieroslawski promptly brought back the popular Sigel as his second in command and immediately went to Mannheim to take charge, superseding Osterhaus's latest commander after only a week. That should have clarified Osterhaus's command structure, but the city fathers did not necessarily agree to relinquish command over their citizens' army, as events would show. With more than sixty thousand allied Prussian and Hessian troops massing to the north, Mieroslawski organized his line of twenty thousand volunteers so that it ran west to east from the left bank of the Rhine at Ludwigshafen through its right-bank neighbor, Mannheim, to end near Heidelberg.[22]

When the first allied attacks began, Mieroslawski was not nearly finished with building defensive works in front of both Mannheim and Heidelberg or with making preparations to barricade or destroy all bridges on the Neckar and Rhine rivers. Early on June 15 a Prussian division drove straight at Ludwigshafen, forcing rebel troops through the town and across the barricaded bridge into Mannheim. While Mieroslawski and Osterhaus watched the fighting across the Rhine from the Mannheim side, the enemy spotted them as well, and the

Prussian artillery fire was so accurate that an enemy artillery canister landed under the rebel general's horse. Fortunately for him, it was a dud.[23]

This battle was Osterhaus's first exposure to shelling and live small-arms fire, and he soon realized the artillery's value in a fight. As the Bavarian Palatinate's rebels raced to safety over the Mannheim bridge, already partially destroyed by the Badeners, the Prussians began bombarding Mannheim from trenches along the west side of the river. But Osterhaus's batteries and riflemen immediately returned fire from behind cotton bales on the Baden side, and over the hours that followed, Osterhaus's rebel artillery surprisingly had the best of it. The Prussians finally withdrew from Ludwigshafen several days later. However, that engagement was the end of any rebel resistance in the Palatinate. As of June 18, Baden was utterly on its own.[24]

Back when the attack began, with battle raging on several fronts, Mieroslawski ordered the Mannheim bridges destroyed, and he detached Baden troops from Mannheim to support the struggling rebel line east of the city, leaving Osterhaus and his National Guard units behind to continue the firefight against the Prussians across the Rhine. Not only did Osterhaus's men hold the line, but the other rebels succeeded as well in driving back the more experienced northern attackers all along the front, stunning the leading citizens of Mannheim, who had fully expected the rebels to be beaten.[25]

Their defeatism landed the good burghers in a lot of trouble, for on that first day of fighting, as they heard the sounds of battle all around the city, members of the Mannheim city council got cold feet, imagining what would happen to them when the soon-to-be-victorious Prussians tried to enter the town and found the bridges destroyed. So, in spite of Mieroslawski's orders to the contrary, they ordered the citizens' army to stop destroying the new bridge across the Neckar River. When Mieroslawski returned from the battlefield that evening, he found that the work on the bridge had been halted. Furious, he immediately declared martial law, thus eliminating any further annoyances from the council.[26]

Where was Osterhaus when all this was going on in his jurisdiction? Was he even aware that the city council had overridden Mieroslawski and had ordered Osterhaus's citizens' army to protect the bridges from destruction? If so, Osterhaus was clearly in a spot, with crucially conflicting orders to follow. If he had obeyed the council that had appointed him, he would have had to order his men to interfere with destruction of the bridges against Mieroslawski's orders. Perhaps the most plausible explanation is that Osterhaus indeed was aware of the council's order and countermanded it but the citizens' army refused to obey him. His surprise resignation a few days later supports this theory. However, because the evidence is scanty, Osterhaus's part in this affair remains unclear.[27]

Osterhaus remained at his post in Mannheim during the next military action, which occurred some miles to the south on June 21. In that battle the rebels fought bravely against the larger enemy force, initially doing quite well. But during the height of battle the rebel cavalry commander, a Colonel Beckert, late of the Baden state army, abruptly signaled his horsemen to do an about-face from the middle of the line and caused the entire cavalry to beat a disorganized retreat, quickly followed by the collapse of the suddenly unsupported artillery and the green infantry. This was an unexpected disaster from which the revolutionaries never recovered.[28]

The next morning, June 22, the mutinous Beckert and his dragoons under Major Thomann moved quickly from Heidelberg to Mannheim, drumming up antirevolutionary support in both towns. Later that day, having consulted with the weaseling Mannheim municipal council, Thomann crossed the still-open Neckar bridge and invited the Prussian army to come into Mannheim and take the city. Realizing that the cause was lost, Joseph Osterhaus had already resigned from his command and was going home to his pregnant wife when a friend warned him that there were Prussian soldiers in his house waiting to arrest him. From that moment on, he was a fugitive.[29]

Prussian troops scoured the towns for revolutionary leaders and sympathizers, throwing them in prison when caught. Osterhaus was not the only one who succeeded in evading them; all of the top leaders got out in time. At last there was only Franz Sigel to lead the ragged remainder of the rebel army across the Rhine into Switzerland around July 15, just as Friedrich Hecker finally arrived in Strasbourg from America, ready to take over the now-defunct revolutionary government. The final capitulation of the rebels on July 23, 1849, occurred at the fortress at Rastatt, where they had barricaded themselves, waiting in vain for Sigel to return and save them, as he had promised. Carl Schurz, a nervy nineteen year old who would later be instrumental in Osterhaus's military career, escaped from Rastatt through the sewers at the denouement.[30]

The Prussians were ruthless in punishing the revolutionary leaders they captured, executing large numbers and imprisoning others for long terms on charges of treason. But their main targets were the actual ringleaders of the last phase, including Joseph Osterhaus. Knowing how his heavily pregnant wife was likely to be treated by the conquering army, Osterhaus probably arranged to extricate her and took her with him. As he recalled fifty years later, Osterhaus enlisted the aid of a friendly steamer captain to cross the Rhine River and then the help of a sympathetic coach driver to effect his escape. Instead of heading directly south to France and safety, Osterhaus traveled north to Kreuznach, where Matilda's family lived, perhaps to assure himself that they would see to her and also to get some traveling money.[31]

The Prussians continued to hunt for Osterhaus, charges of treason having been filed against him on June 28. His route after Kreuznach is not known in detail, the authorities searching for him concluding that he had gone from there to England. But in fact he borrowed the passport of one of his brothers in Koblenz and swam two rivers while making his way to Strasbourg, France. Osterhaus was next seen in Nancy at the end of July in the company of one of Friedrich Hecker's brothers-in-law, Karl Eisenhardt (both men were considered important fugitives). Probably trying to catch up to Hecker, now gone to ground, they went back to Strasbourg, but Hecker had left for Paris the day before the final surrender at Rastatt.[32]

On August 4 Osterhaus, Eisenhardt, and another of Hecker's brothers-in-law arrived in Paris and left for Le Havre the same night, having again missed Hecker by a few days. Hecker and his family had been forced into hiding in Paris and later Le Havre because of the French government's willingness to extradite accused criminals back to Prussia. The Heckers and relatives except for Eisenhardt booked passage for America and embarked with relief on August 11. Osterhaus, however, took a chance and stayed in hiding in Le Havre, waiting for Matilda to give birth and join him. Her baby, Anna, was born on August 29, and mother and tiny infant were on their way a short time later. Osterhaus had booked second-class passage for the three of them on the ship *Argo,* and they left Le Havre around October 1. With no advance planning, Osterhaus now suddenly had to make a life for his little family in a foreign land. Matilda was never to see her home or family again.[33]

Besides Hecker's brother-in-law Karl Eisenhardt, two other exiles from the revolution were also traveling in second class on the *Argo.* In contrast to the vast majority of German émigrés who had had some choice about leaving their homeland, all four of these men had been forced to leave as political exiles. None knew his precise legal status at this point; Prussian prison sentences were not handed down until the following year. Like the others, all that Osterhaus knew was that his hard-earned Baden citizenship had been revoked and that he was wanted by the authorities. He later learned that he had been sentenced in absentia to four years in prison for treason. Baden offered exile in lieu of jail time for political criminals, but they still would have had to serve any remaining time, had they returned. Osterhaus finally received a full pardon on July 8, 1857; ironically, by then he had also been awarded U.S. citizenship.[34]

The few new German émigrés who had actually participated in the European revolutions of 1848–1849 were known as the "Forty-Eighters." The German American press, which had closely followed the revolution, now kept the public informed as to the arrival of their heroes. Men like Lorenz Brentano, Friedrich Hecker, and Franz Sigel discovered that they were well known in the German American community before they even set foot in the United States. Sigel, in particular, was lionized for his perceived heroism in the revolution. Not so Osterhaus, whose brief stint as military commander of Mannheim was eclipsed in the press by Sigel's exploits.[35]

When the Osterhaus family landed in New York on November 6, 1849, they faced yet another thousand miles of travel with winter fast approaching. They were headed for Belleville in St. Clair County in southern Illinois, an established German American enclave not far from St. Louis. Although they had no relatives there, they knew that Friedrich Hecker had settled there, as had his two brothers-in-law who had accompanied Osterhaus in his flight across France. Surely during those long days in hiding in Le Havre, Osterhaus was encouraged to join the others in the rich American heartland known to Germans as the Rhineland of America; he was confident of a welcome there. Little Anna, in motion for almost her entire life, was finally able to lay her head in a permanent bed sometime before the end of 1849. Shortly after they arrived in Belleville, Joseph Osterhaus celebrated his twenty-seventh birthday.[36]

The newly arriving Forty-Eighters, although a vastly disparate group in terms of political ideology, religion, and social class, were as a whole somewhat different in demographics from the other German émigrés: typically more educated, more idealistic, and less able to support themselves by the blue-collar jobs available to newcomers. It was a good thing that Osterhaus's father had insisted on a business education; many of the professors and other professionals who came to the United States either died penniless or went back to Europe, unused to having no support from family wealth and unable to pursue their professions in the United States. With his business education and experience plus his command of English, thanks to his solid prep-school education, Osterhaus could realistically hope to find employment in some business capacity if he could make the right connections.[37]

Greeting the Osterhaus family on their arrival in Belleville was Gustave Koerner, an earlier émigré who became perhaps the most influential German American in Illinois. Koerner, later an important influence in Osterhaus's military career, had welcomed Hecker and helped him buy a farm, and he noted with satisfaction the coming of Osterhaus and his family, along with Hecker's sisters' families. Koerner was a moderate who later became lieutenant governor of Illinois and enjoyed the ear of Abraham Lincoln. He admired Osterhaus, leading one to infer that Osterhaus was also a moderate in his political and social opinions. Osterhaus had no shortage of opinions and loved to argue, but preferred doing so in his own home rather than in the public arena favored by many of his fellow Forty-Eighters.[38]

Once having established a toehold in their new country, the Forty-Eighters made an impact on American society and German American thought far greater than their numbers would have predicted. Although some returned to Europe when restrictions were lifted, most found a way to fit into their new country, often as physicians, journalists, educators, or lecturers. When Franz Sigel immigrated a few years after Osterhaus, he worked in New York as a language tutor and fencing instructor, playing piano in German clubs in the evenings. In the Midwest, Carl Schurz moved rapidly into politics from a Wisconsin base, becoming U.S. senator from Missouri a few years later. Osterhaus became a merchant.[39]

By the spring of 1850, Osterhaus had opened his own store, serving the largely German community of Belleville. The family lived above the store on the unpaved main street along with a merchant about Joseph's age and a young woman who may have been a live-in servant. Since he was able to capitalize a new store with a census valuation of one thousand dollars so soon after he arrived, Osterhaus was apparently financially trustworthy. There is no information about where he got the money, but it may have been a combination of his own savings rescued by Matilda before she left, loans from either her family or his, and loans from Belleville associates or banks. Even though most of Osterhaus's clientele was undoubtedly German-speaking, he clearly knew English before he arrived. Although he would always speak the language with a thick accent, his clear and fluent writing later also helped his military career.[40]

Given the preponderance of German American families living in the Belleville area, Osterhaus had a rather soft landing for a refugee, making many lifelong friends and later leading the sons of many of them in the American Civil War. Joseph and Matilda lived over the store for nearly two years, and their first son, Hugo, was born there in 1851. But with Matilda's fourth pregnancy, quarters were clearly becoming too small to accommodate both the family and the entertaining that they enjoyed. So they moved a few miles east to the little town of Lebanon, also in St. Clair County, where Adolphus (Otto) was born in December 1852. There they stayed for the next eight years, during which time they welcomed three more children, Alexander, Emma, and Karl, and lost little Adolphus, date and cause unknown.[41]

Again, Osterhaus was off to a good start at establishing himself in a new community. He had his first and only brush with American politics when he was appointed postmaster of Lebanon, a patronage position. He probably got the job as a result of supporting Democrat Franklin Pierce, who won the presidential election of 1852, but it may have simply been a result of knowing Gustave Koerner. Two years later Osterhaus proudly received his citizenship papers for his new country. His courtly manners and agreeable personality made him popular with the other Forty-Eighters, his home becoming a social center for that group where they probably sang or played chess as well as arguing about events of the day. As always, politics was a blazing hot topic.[42]

The axis of German American settlement in Illinois was a few miles east of St. Louis, running between Belleville and Lebanon. In the early 1850s most of the immigrants in both southern Illinois and St. Louis were Democrats because of that party's support of immigrant rights. Both groups also opposed slavery, if for different reasons, but found that their party did not. Because of the slave issue, in both communities German Americans began increasingly to shift to the new Republican Party just then being formed, and Osterhaus probably moved over then as well. During the campaign of 1856, among the Democratic orators whom Osterhaus no doubt heard in Belleville trying in vain to convince their ethnic neighbors to support presidential candidate Stephen Douglas instead of Republican John C. Frémont were Congressmen John A. Logan and John A. McClernand, both of whom would become Osterhaus's commanders during the war.[43]

The year 1856 was a good one for postmaster and new American citizen Joseph Osterhaus, who had every reason to be satisfied with his new country and his progress. He had by now sold the store and was building a distillery in Lebanon valued at forty thousand dollars. The highlight of the year occurred when he and Matilda were invited as leading citizens to attend a dinner in honor of prominent Illinois Republican Abraham Lincoln, who was most likely in town to give a speech in support of Frémont. Matilda sat next to Lincoln; he recalled her later as "a delightful German woman who spoke very little English." Undoubtedly, Lincoln won the Osterhauses over on this occasion by his usual warmth and simplicity; Osterhaus always spoke of him highly.[44]

If 1856 was a good year for the Osterhauses, the next year was an entirely different matter. When Democrat James Buchanan was sworn in as president in 1857, Osterhaus was immediately ousted as postmaster because he had switched to the Republican Party and had supported Frémont for president. Thus ended a dependable source of family income. Later in the summer the first major national stock market crash and panic started a several-year depression throughout the country. Five thousand businesses and banks failed nationwide; one was the Belleville bank. Osterhaus lost the distillery. How the family survived financially for the next two years is not known, but clearly they had to scrimp. In September 1860 the census taker found them still living in Lebanon, Osterhaus working as a clerk. The couple had no live-in help, unusual for that day for a family with five little children under the age of ten. When the prospect of a job in St. Louis came up in late 1860, Joseph and Matilda had little choice but to leave their congenial friends and make the move to the big city.[45]

Bustling St. Louis was a bigger city than any the Osterhauses had lived in before, with paved streets, gas streetlights, and a streetcar line. Its German population alone was twice the size of Mannheim. The city was rapidly changing: Northern businessmen were moving in and establishing new enterprises, challenging the political dominance of the Southern hierarchy. They also brought with them Northern views on slavery that were not welcomed by the city's powerful. New Yorkers George Pomeroy and William Benton, owners of the large wholesale dry-goods store that hired Osterhaus as an accountant, were just such Northern businessmen.[46]

Osterhaus had found a dwelling on Gratiot Street between Broadway (Fifth) and Sixth, at the northern edge of the large German American community. Just a block to the west on Gratiot began a neighborhood of mansions owned by wealthy slave owners, and a block farther on loomed the dome of McDowell's Medical School. Although there were some elegant homes on his block, given his financial constraints Osterhaus's new home was most likely a four-family row house, a big change for active youngsters used to playing in a yard of their own.[47]

Although Osterhaus had brought his family to a slaveholding state, there were few slaves in the city, and by living in a German American neighborhood perhaps the children were not directly exposed to slavery. His own first experience with slavery occurred on his way to his new job. His streetcar route took him north on Broadway past the courthouse square, where on the courthouse steps he could see an appalling spectacle: humans being sold like animals in a slave auction. Nearer the harbor, he saw a sign reading "James Skinner, Dealer in Slaves." His outrage, coupled with his strong beliefs about the responsibilities of a conscientious citizen, would not let him ignore this abomination in the days to come.[48]

The Forty-Eighters that Osterhaus now joined in St. Louis were men who defied simple description. Coming from many walks of life, claiming allegiance to various duchies rather than a common German identity, all they really had in common was the shared experience of the revolution. Although he was a Forty-Eighter by definition, Osterhaus likewise did not fit into any stereotype. In a group with many freethinking socialists, he was a Catholic liberal. Unlike many of them, he was not outspoken publicly on the issues of the day; his leadership would be best expressed later on the battlefield, not the stump. Osterhaus also had to find his place in the larger rancorously divided German American community. For years there had been heated disagreements between German Catholics and Lutherans, old guard and new Forty-Eighters, on everything from the separation of church and state to slavery. An atypical Forty-Eighter, Osterhaus likewise did not mesh comfortably with the previous immigrants because he was actively proabolition and had become a Republican.[49]

The intense internal dissent in the St. Louis ethnic community must have been a bit of a surprise to Osterhaus. And coming as he did from a predominantly German American small town, "nativism," active antagonism against immigrants by the rest of the citizens, must also have been a new experience, but one he was to encounter many times. The old-guard "natives," Southern by sympathy and family connection, resented the huge influx of newcomers and reacted with anger against "damned Dutch" foreign habits, ridiculing their soft caps, beards, and heavy accents. As the decade ended, concerns about nativism and the potential spread of slavery to the new states west of Missouri gradually led the internally divided St. Louis German Americans toward a common political agenda and voice.[50]

A catalyst for this movement was the radical German-language press in St. Louis, dominated in the midfifties by Heinrich Boernstein's newspaper, *Anzieger des Westens.* Besides the usual Forty-Eighter-style social criticism, his paper could be depended upon to be full of Republican-leaning, antislavery, antinativist political rhetoric. The flamboyant Boernstein, later to be Osterhaus's first commanding officer in the Civil War, was instrumental in swaying local German American opinion away from the conservative Democrats and toward the new Republican Party, despite reservations about some of its nativist members. Other prominent Forty-Eighters got involved as well, including Franz Sigel, who recognized that the center of German American political power was in the Midwest and moved from New York to St. Louis in the late 1850s on the invitation of another Forty-Eighter, Dr. Adam Hammer.[51]

By the time Osterhaus arrived in St. Louis, the unusual coalescence of German American opinion in the city and to a lesser extent other parts of the Midwest, opposing nativism and supporting preservation of the Union, made German Americans a power to be reckoned with in the presidential election of 1860. Encouraged by their eloquent political leaders, Gustave Koerner, Franz Sigel, and Carl Schurz, among others, the German Americans were able to control a bloc of delegates at the Republican National Convention and were almost certainly a factor in winning the presidency for Lincoln against an opposition split on the issue of slavery.[52]

With the election of Abraham Lincoln coming shortly after Osterhaus's arrival in Missouri, he was immediately caught up in the events that within a few months would lead to the outbreak of civil war. He was appalled as Southern states began to secede from the Union, starting with South Carolina in December. How could Americans throw away the precious national unity that the Germans had fought for in vain in their own revolution? And it looked as though his own state might follow her sisters out of the Union. The majority of Missouri's citizens were on the fence: they opposed secession for either economic or military reasons but would not condone any Federal military aggression or interference that trampled Missouri's state rights or individual freedoms, including the freedom to own slaves. For most German American Missourians, though, abolition was just as important as states' rights, and preservation of the Union was paramount. Not surprisingly, they and Osterhaus were staunch Unionists.[53]

Now the possibility of war was on every mind. If conflict were to start, the resource-rich border state of Missouri would be a great prize for either side, particularly with St. Louis being a key port on the Mississippi River. And the plum in St. Louis was the largest Federal arsenal west of the Mississippi, located in the German American section of town. Missouri partisans believed that whoever controlled the arsenal would control the city and thus the state. Guarded at the time by just four U.S. soldiers and a few officers, the arsenal held a rich cache of arms and munitions, including sixty thousand rifles and field pieces.[54]

For the next few weeks, control of the arsenal and its contents was the focus of machinations by both sides, the Unionists led by U.S. Congressman Francis P. Blair Jr., the most powerful Republican politician in the state, and the secessionists by Missouri governor Claiborne Fox Jackson. Blair, having cemented a coalition between the German American leaders and the Northern business leaders in St. Louis, began secretly arming and drilling men in a private militia known as Union Clubs in order to protect the arsenal until Federal reinforcements could be secured. He and his coalition began raising money privately to arm the militia, a major contributor being Osterhaus's new employers: the dry-goods firm of Pomeroy and Benton.[55]

Osterhaus joined one of Blair's Union Clubs, meeting secretly late at night at the home of Dr. Adam Hammer, a Mannheimer and friend of Friedrich Hecker's who had served as a military surgeon for the Baden rebels before being exiled. Hammer's particular Union Club consisted of students from his medical school. Osterhaus came to his home late at night to teach the rudiments of soldiering to these young would-be soldiers, trying to muffle the noise of their guns thumping on the floor by scattering hay around. Since Hammer's home was only about six hundred yards from the arsenal gate, it would be a logical base for mounting an early response to any secessionist incursion there, a fact that obviously wore on Hammer's nerves. A contemporary recalled that during one of these secret drill sessions the jumpy Hammer heard a noise and grabbed for his revolver, which the cooler Osterhaus calmly took away from him.[56]

In addition to the Union Clubs, the German American Turner Club of St. Louis swore support for the Union and made military drilling mandatory for its several hundred members, asking militarily trained Forty-Eighters, including Franz Sigel, to train them. There was another group drilling in St. Louis as well: shortly after the New Year a new secessionist militia called the Minute Men was formed. In contrast to the secrecy of the Union Clubs, the Minute Men drills were defiantly public, and they began parading openly through the streets, engaging in shouting matches with their pro-Union opposites. Minute Men headquarters, rumored to have a cannon in the front hall, was the Berthold mansion, just a mile from the Osterhaus residence, which must have made both Matilda and Joseph a bit uneasy.[57]

With the Minute Men parading in the streets, the German American Union Clubs began to drill openly as well. In contrast to the well-supplied and stylishly uniformed secessionists, the Union Club men wore civilian clothes, and many had to drill using sticks for rifles. When they did venture on public parade, Osterhaus and his fellow countrymen had to endure taunts and insults from the hostile onlookers for their sloppy drilling. Turning them into soldiers might be difficult, but turning them into implacable foes of the secessionists would not.[58]

Soon two hundred Federal troops arrived from Fort Riley, Kansas Territory, to control the arsenal. They were commanded by Capt. Nathaniel Lyon, an ardent abolitionist from New England, who immediately and unofficially began to organize the drilling of the Union Clubs as well. St. Louis was in a highly excitable condition, with crowds gathering on the sidewalks at the drop of a rumor. No Unionist felt safe; German Americans were attacked and their homes robbed, making the location of the Osterhaus residence close to the edge of the ethnic community a realistic worry for them. Franz Sigel quit his job as school superintendent in February and enlisted in a private militia as a second lieutenant, but Osterhaus, however much expertise and heart he knew he had to offer his new country, had a lot to consider before he could do the same, not least of his concerns being how he would support his family.[59]

At the time of Fort Sumter, April 12, 1861, Governor Jackson was in St. Louis consulting with the commander of the St. Louis Militia District, Gen. Daniel M. Frost, and other prominent secessionists to figure out how to seize the arsenal for the state militia. While they were still in discussion, on April 15 President Lincoln issued a call for seventy-five thousand state militia for three months' service to suppress any parties who obstructed Federal law, and informed Jackson that Missouri's contribution would be four militia regiments. In line with his state's neutral posture, Jackson fired back a bitter refusal. He then acted legally to convene two regiments of the Missouri Volunteer Militia in St. Louis for the period May 6 to May 11 for their yearly routine drill and muster.[60]

This potential threat caused Lyon and Blair to feel a new urgency to officially muster in the volunteer troops for the Union that Governor Jackson had so adamantly refused to provide. The Union Club and Turner volunteers, including Joseph Osterhaus, had already been organized into companies and partial regiments by Lyon, from whom Lt. John M. Schofield gradually mustered four regiments of volunteers into the U.S. Army and provided them with arms. After that, another regiment of volunteers and five regiments of Home Guards for the protection of the city were formed and armed, or about ten thousand men in all. Then Lyon secretly shipped his remaining guns over to Governor Richard Yates in Illinois, essentially emptying the arsenal within the week.[61]

Thirty-eight-year-old Joseph Osterhaus signed up as a private in the Second Missouri Volunteers, effective April 15, and slipped into the armory on April 24 to be officially sworn into the U.S. Army by Schofield. Matilda must have been somewhat reassured by the fact that he was only committed for three months. Undoubtedly swaying Joseph's decision to join up, Pomeroy and Benton continued to pay his wages after his enlistment, as a patriotic gesture. This was not uncommon: in the German American community support for the volunteers was high. Continuation of salaries, gifts of company flags, and offers of free meals, beer, and cigars were some of the perks frequently extended to the new soldiers.[62]

Although native-born Americans and Irish and French immigrants were all represented in the first four St. Louis volunteer regiments, the Second and Third Missouri Volunteer Infantry regiments were almost all German Americans. The many older Forty-Eighters who enlisted may have seen the war as their last hurrah, the last opportunity to strike a blow in support of the national state they had failed to achieve in the homeland. Their European military training led to assignments in artillery, engineering, and training, but although they were effective in whipping the new recruits into shape, few made it very far in the ranks of leadership. Only 2 percent of officers in the Union Volunteer Army were German American, as opposed to 9 percent of volunteer troops overall. By the end of the first year of the war, just seven, including Osterhaus, would be either acting or appointed generals.[63]

By April 27 the men of the first four volunteer regiments had elected their commanding colonels: for the First Regiment, Frank Blair; for the Second, fire-breathing editor Heinrich Boernstein; for the Third, Franz Sigel; and for the Fourth, Nicholas Schuttner, with Dr. Adam Hammer as his lieutenant colonel. Although Boernstein had served in the Austrian army, only Sigel of the group had significant military command experience, and that as a rebel. Boernstein's Second Missouri consisted of twelve companies; Osterhaus joined Company B Rifles, as distinguished from Company B Infantry. Being relatively new in town, Osterhaus did not know many of the men in his new company. Most were several years younger than he; the average age for immigrant volunteers was twenty-seven. When Osterhaus joined the company, Otto Schadt, the elected captain, immediately resigned his position and recommended Osterhaus for the post. Schadt, who had been an ensign in their former Prussian regiment, felt uncomfortable taking precedence over his old lieutenant. Osterhaus immediately set to work intensely drilling his new recruits morning and afternoon, and in the evenings teaching his officers (two lieutenants, four sergeants, and eight corporals) the rudiments of leadership. There was not a moment to lose: their initiation to flying bullets would take place just two weeks later.[64]

Osterhaus, sporting a "bristling beard and mustache which protruded from his face like a megaphone," had a distinctive style in leading drills: one of the men recalled that he had a "voice like a trumpet, and sometimes gave his orders in German and sometimes in English, both of which languages he spoke very well." Since there was no uniform method of military training mandated this early in the war, Osterhaus was able to develop his own methods that reflected his European training. In contrast to other volunteer officers, he was reasonably up-to-date on the latest techniques that West Pointers had borrowed from Europe during the 1850s, much of which had originated with the Prussians.[65]

Lyon, unofficially elected general by the volunteers, was likewise frantically busy mustering, organizing, training, housing, and supplying his new army, already two-thirds the size of the whole Regular Federal Army at that time. Meantime, he managed to keep his eye on the impending encampment of General Frost's state militia, a provocation he did not intend to let pass. To foil Jackson's plan to encamp his militia on the bluffs overlooking the arsenal, Lyon stationed the Second Missouri Volunteers, including (now) Captain Osterhaus and his Company B Rifles, on the heights on the spacious grounds of the Marine Hospital, where they could see both the river and the arsenal less than a mile away over the fields and scattered houses.[66]

Frost's backup choice for the state militia campsite was a park called Lindell Grove, located to the west of town, a bit past the city limits. On May 6 the encampment, named Camp Jackson after the governor, was convened for six days according to state law. But although the U.S. flag flew over the camp, its temporary streets were named after new Confederate president Jefferson Davis and General P. G. T. Beauregard, a clue to the sentiments of many of those encamped there. Many Unionist militia men attending became uncomfortable and resigned during the week. Therefore, the actual number encamped in the grove fluctuated from day to day, but by all accounts it numbered somewhere under a thousand men, only about a tenth of Lyon's new forces. Frost would have been foolish to attempt to attack the fortified and well-manned arsenal, which in any case was now empty of weapons. However, Lyon and Blair wanted to capture Camp Jackson anyway, mostly as a way to control Jackson, whom Lyon considered to be a traitor only biding his time to act against the Union. On the evening of May 9, Lyon and Blair, despite shaky legal grounds, convinced the Lincoln-sanctioned Committee of Public Safety, made up of the mayor and other prominent Unionist citizens, to agree to their plan to take Camp Jackson the next day, arguing that it could be done without a gun being fired.[67]

Although the military action at Camp Jackson was at the least rash and probably wrongheaded, one has to admire Lyon's logistical achievement. Up most of the night, by morning he had succeeded in drafting a plan to move Federal troops from seven different locations through crowded and in some places hostile city streets over varying distances such that they all convened on the target at the same time. This actually worked, no mean feat given the lack of experience of his new soldiers and their leaders, and the units all arrived at Lindell Grove shortly after three o'clock. Frost was well aware of Lyon's approach, and in fact had expected something like this for days. Still, Frost couldn't believe that Lyon would try an action so patently illegal and irregular.[68]

In an unusually perfunctory (for him) account of the events of May 10, Joseph Osterhaus wrote, "The Camp with all men, materials etc. was taken, and the prisoners of war escorted by my Command to the U.S. Arsenal, when they were placed in Custody." The actual events were far more complicated than this would suggest. Osterhaus, clearly a competent and approachable leader in the eyes of the men, had been elected major by the Second Missouri Volunteers three days before and now commanded a battalion of both of its rifle companies, more than three hundred men and officers. Although the men were still without uniforms, as they formed up Osterhaus had reason to hope that his battalion would give a soldierly account of themselves on the long march through the city streets. He couldn't know it at the time, but two of his later commanders would observe him in his first military assignment for the U.S. Army.[69]

Shortly after noon on that cool spring day, civilian Ulysses S. Grant was standing across from the arsenal gate in the crowd that watched the new Union Volunteers and Regulars move off toward Camp Jackson, led by Nathaniel Lyon on horseback. The regiments, including Major Osterhaus's battalion leading the Second Missouri, marched up Carondalet and Broadway past his home corner of Gratiot Street, bayonets flashing, his oldest son, Hugo, probably watching in the crowd. The excitement was electric all over the city. Cheers in the German American neighborhoods changed to boos and insults as the men moved into the center of town and turned west on parallel streets toward Lindell Grove.[70]

As he deployed his men at Lindell Grove, Osterhaus was astonished at the size of the excited crowds, including women and children, that surrounded the camp. When they heard of the troop movement they had gathered even before Lyon's men arrived, some bringing picnic lunches, others armed with pistols and other weapons to help defend their Southern boys against the "damned Dutch." They crowded around the entrances to the camp, on both sides of the streets, and on nearby hills, buildings, and rooftops. Two interested bystanders on Olive Street near the grove were civilians William T. Sherman and his seven-year-old son, Willie.[71]

General Frost, surrounded as he was by this much larger force, after an angry exchange of notes with Lyon prudently had his men stack arms, and the Missouri State Militia thus became prisoners for no reason except that they had obeyed the legal summons to attend annual camp. As Lyon had predicted, no shots had been fired, but soon the angry crowd was surging into the campground among the prisoners. Sensing the ominous mood, Lyon grandly offered to parole the militia men then and there in order to avoid a clash between his untrained troops and the potential mob. But at this juncture Lyon's admirable planning broke down. Unexpected by him, only about ten militia men took him up on his offer, most figuring that in accepting parole they would admit some sort of wrongdoing. Thus, Lyon was stuck with hundreds of prisoners but with no viable plan to control them. His only option was to march them the six miles back through the hostile crowds to the arsenal, where in fact he had made no plans to either house or feed them properly, but at least there they would be behind guarded walls.[72]

His last-minute strategy for the march was to sandwich the prisoners between single files of Blair's First Missouri and Boernstein's Second Missouri, the other units remaining to guard the camp. Boernstein lined his men up behind the First Missouri, Major Osterhaus's rifle battalion again leading, with a large number of prisoners between them. Behind them the mob closed in, filling the street. During the long delay while they were forming up at the east end of camp at the head of Olive Street and Lyon was back in the camp deploying the Third and Fourth Missouri as guards, Osterhaus could hear a military band playing the national anthem and "Yankee Doodle" over and over at the head of the column. But the band could not completely drown out the curses and catcalls from the incensed crowd on all sides as their gallant boys were being lined up to be led away.[73]

Once the column finally moved out at around five thirty in the afternoon, it had gone only a short distance before it was halted once more in a long delay, perhaps as long as an hour. The crowd was becoming more hostile by the minute against the Volunteers, saving their worst venom for the German Americans. Now shouts were accompanied by stones, bricks, and dirt clods, which the men endured without reacting. Sigel's regiment was at the other end of Camp Jackson, guarding the western gate, when a gunshot rang out from the crowd. In the melee that followed, a captain of the Third Missouri was hit in the leg by friendly fire (dying of his wound two weeks later). Many of Sigel's men thought that their compatriot's wound was caused by a citizen's bullet, and after firing in the air, the excited new soldiers fired several shots directly into the crowd. Said one of Sigel's men, this "started a general fusillade, we volunteers shooting more at each other than at the crowd of citizens gathered at the east end of the camp."[74]

At about the same time, more shots were fired from the surrounding crowd into the marching formation stalled on Olive Street. Colonel Boernstein reported that the Second Missouri was halted next to a building under construction when "shots came from the building, from the trees and from the camp fence, and bullets went whistling past our heads." Two soldiers fell dead where they stood. Now general firing commenced, finally spreading into the ranks of the Second Missouri. Sherman in his memoirs recalled that a drunk fired a shot into Osterhaus's men, wounding a soldier. Return fire was initially aimed over the heads of the civilians, but then, Sherman wrote, "The fire ran back from the head of the regiment toward its rear, and as I saw the men reloading their pieces, I jerked Willie up, ran back with him into a gulley which covered us, lay there until I saw that the fire had ceased, and that the column was again moving on."[75]

Osterhaus and the other regimental officers immediately tried to quell the firing, but the inexperienced and angered troops didn't respond immediately. When the firing stopped, at least fourteen civilians had been killed, including women and a babe in arms, and at least another forty had been wounded. About a dozen Volunteers and Regulars were killed or wounded, and the state militia lost three killed. Then, with the band still blithely playing on as they had throughout the shooting, the First and Second Missouri finally resumed their long march with the prisoners back to the arsenal, arriving at dark without further incident. After dropping off his share of prisoners at the arsenal, Osterhaus took his hungry and thirsty battalion back up the hill to their Second Missouri quarters at the Marine Hospital, only to endure a night of heavy rain in their leaky tents as they mulled over the day's startling events. In the morning the captured state militiamen, rethinking their moral positions after a night of sleeping on straw in overcrowded quarters with no food or water, accepted parole and were released.[76]

Lyon's action at Camp Jackson had the city swarming like a kicked anthill. That night mobs formed in the streets, particularly along Broadway, intent on doing harm to the "damned Dutch." One of the mob leaders was Dr. Joseph McDowell, head of the medical school just down the street from the Osterhaus home, whose school was forced to close later that year when the Federal authorities converted it into the infamous Gratiot Street prison. Osterhaus was certainly very anxious about his family during this time, but without doubt Matilda prudently kept all of the children inside. After a rash of shootings over the next several days, the city settled into an uneasy peace.[77]

Although the capture of Camp Jackson played an important part in securing Missouri for the Union, the immediate repercussions were not ones that Nathaniel Lyon had anticipated. Predictably, citizen reaction to the capture of Camp Jackson, the first military action in the West after Fort Sumter, was sharply divided along partisan lines. Like other Unionists, Joseph Osterhaus thought the capture of Camp Jackson highly important because it would confine the military clashes on the Mississippi River to mostly Confederate soil. That particular outcome held a personal interest to him, for he was loath to subject Matilda and his five young children to the trials of a war-torn city while he was elsewhere. St. Louis was in enough turmoil as it was.[78]

Secessionists condemned what they called the "Camp Jackson Massacre." They believed that the firing on civilians was unprovoked, except by some benign name-calling, and painted the German American troops in particular as monsters. They were absolutely incensed that Federal troops had so blatantly trampled on their state's right to have a militia. Many, if not most, of the numerous fence riders, far from supporting Lyon's action, were so outraged that they wound up in the secessionist camp. One of the most prominent of these was former governor Sterling Price, who accepted Governor Jackson's offer to lead the new secessionist Missouri State Guard (MSG) and went on to campaign for the South throughout the war.[79]

That the state was indeed secured for the Union was not a foregone conclusion the day after the Camp Jackson affair as Lyon moved to deploy his forces to guard the approaches to the city. On May 16 he ordered Major Osterhaus and his rifle battalion with the rest of the Second Missouri to guard the highest point in North St. Louis against any rebel incursion. Establishing his first independent camp on the heights between Bremen Avenue and Hyde, Osterhaus placed his two artillery pieces to cover the North Missouri Railroad tracks and the Mississippi River. Able to see his family only sparingly, he spent the next few weeks training his new battalion in skirmishing techniques and the use of the new Enfield and Springfield rifles. There was little enough preparation time available. The war in the West was starting to intensify, and his new battalion would hit the road on its first extended campaign less than a month after Camp Jackson.[80]

Chapter 2

The Trans-Mississippi Campaigns of 1861 and 1862

READY or not, Maj. Joseph Osterhaus and his rifle battalion left St. Louis on their first campaign on June 13. His men were clad in multicolored uniforms made or donated by various civilian volunteer groups; there were not enough shoes, blankets, or tents to go around. But at least the men of the Second Missouri began their first campaign in relative comfort, traveling the first leg by train, then boarding steamers for the rest of the ride into the capital, Jefferson City, where Gen. Nathaniel Lyon hoped to capture Gov. Claiborne Fox Jackson and Gen. Sterling Price. When the battalion arrived on the morning of June 16 itching for battle, they were disappointed to find the American flag flying over the capitol building high on the hill. Lyon had already taken possession of the deserted capital without a fight.[1]

Jackson and Price were now reported to be gathering a thousand Missouri State Guard recruits at Boonville, so Lyon pushed on up the Missouri, taking Frank Blair's First Missouri, Osterhaus's battalion of riflemen from the Second Missouri, Capt. James Totten's Company F, Second U.S. Artillery, and several companies of Regulars, seventeen hundred men in all. Ten miles below Boonville, the Union commander spotted an enemy battery partially hidden on the bluff ahead, so he decided to disembark his little force on the south bank and go ahead on the river road. At this point, he needed skirmishers to feel out the enemy's position. Turning to Major Osterhaus, he asked him if his battalion, now three companies strong, could skirmish. After all his training efforts, Osterhaus was able to reply that they certainly could, so Lyon sent them on ahead. Thus, Osterhaus led the advance of the first Union attack in Missouri's first official battle of the war. The rebel force was not nearly as big as Lyon had been led to believe. Rumored at up to a couple of thousand men, it really amounted to fewer than five hundred, led by Jackson's reluctant nephew, West Point graduate Col. John Marmaduke. Marmaduke knew it was hopeless to pit his hastily gathered

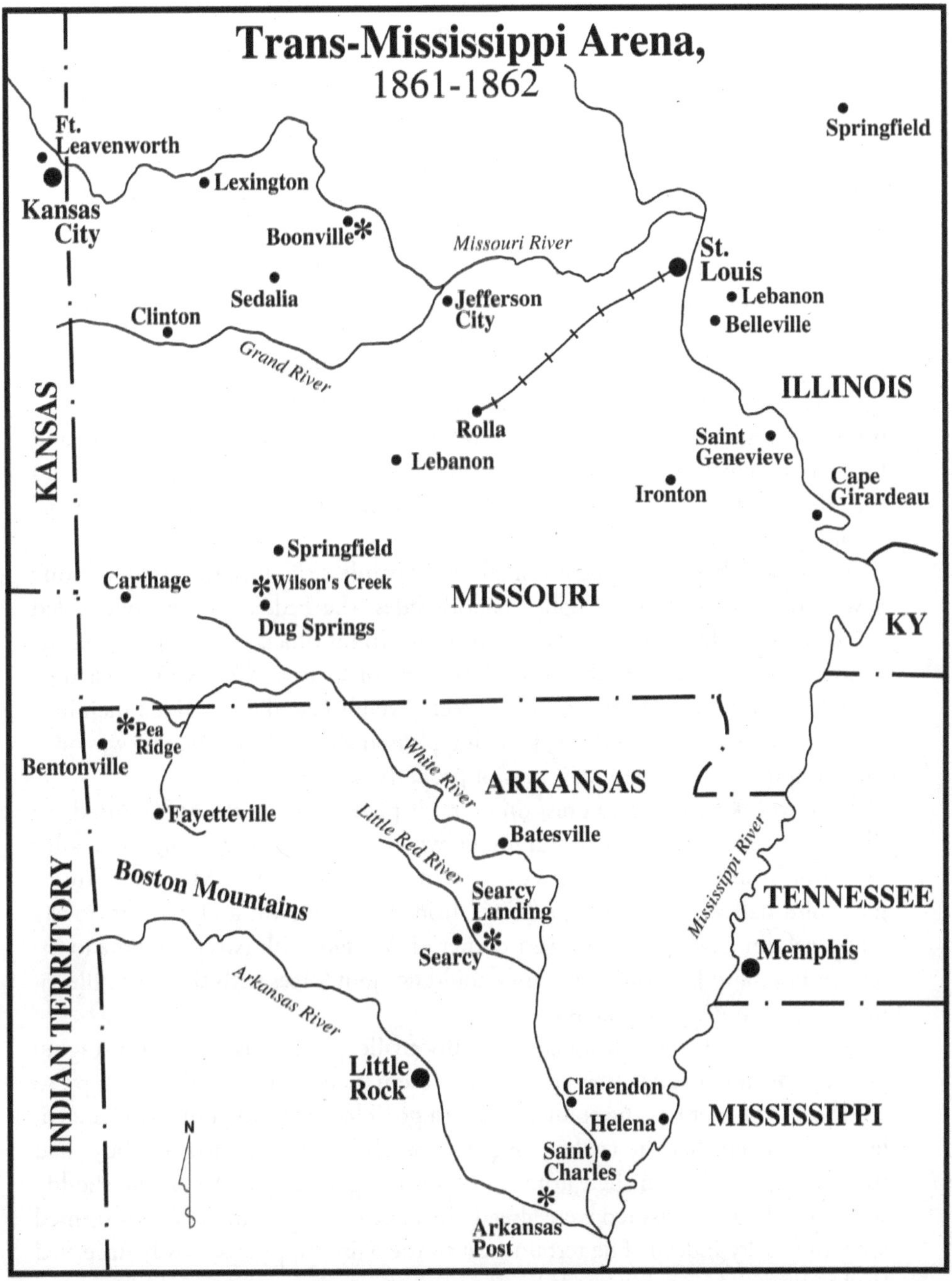
Trans-Mississippi Arena,
1861-1862
Ft. Leavenworth
Kansas City
Lexington
Boonville
Missouri River
St. Louis
Springfield
Lebanon
Belleville
Sedalia
Clinton
Jefferson City
Grand River
ILLINOIS
KANSAS
Rolla
Lebanon
Saint Genevieve
Ironton
Cape Girardeau
Springfield
Wilson's Creek
Carthage
Dug Springs
MISSOURI
KY
Pea Ridge
Bentonville
White River
ARKANSAS
Fayetteville
Little Red River
Batesville
Mississippi River
Boston Mountains
Searcy Landing
Searcy
TENNESSEE
Memphis
INDIAN TERRITORY
Arkansas River
Little Rock
Clarendon
Helena
MISSISSIPPI
N
Saint Charles
Arkansas Post

and ill-equipped few hundred recruits against two thousand or so better-trained and -equipped men with artillery support, but his uncle insisted on a fight.[2]

After two miles of cautious advance, Osterhaus's men found themselves under enemy fire for the first time in real battle. They found Marmaduke's small force spread out on both sides of the road on a slope near a brick farmhouse. As the rebels opened up, the Union troops prudently responded by lying flat on the ground to shoot and reload. This tactic, as it turned out, demoralized and disgusted some of the untrained rebels, who were expecting the traditional shoulder-to-shoulder line. One later accused the Federals of not fighting fair. If lying low to shoot did not seem fair, what happened next was completely unacceptable. Captain Totten briskly wheeled his battery to the front and opened fire, soon joined by heavy firing from both flanks of Union infantry. Not only did the artillery land nine-pound shells in the MSG lines, but two balls also penetrated the brick house, driving the family into the cellar and the rebels out the back. Soon Marmaduke's wavering men fell back over the brow of the hill to protect themselves from the shelling, where they stood their ground briefly and fired another volley. But then the steady Union firing broke their resolve, and they fled. In twenty minutes it was all over, with Marmaduke making it official by ordering a retreat.[3]

The skirmish at Boonville was a relatively painless training exercise for Lyon's new army. Casualties were light on both sides, the Federals losing two killed and nine wounded, the MSG about the same. In his official report of the battle, Lyon was well pleased with the performance of Osterhaus's skirmishers: they were "thrown forward with excellent effect." Major Osterhaus had led men into battle for the first time, and besides being pleased with his own men he was once again impressed by the effectiveness of properly used artillery.[4]

Lyon was determined to press on with his plan to scatter the MSG and drive the rebels from the state once and for all, which would require a tough trek after Price southward across the plains of western Missouri. He had Maj. Sam Sturgis meet him halfway with an equal force from Leavenworth, and had previously sent Sigel directly to the southwest corner of the state with two regiments to intercept Price and Jackson so that they could not join forces with Ben McCulloch, just over the border in Arkansas.[5]

As the Federal troops headed out of Boonville, Osterhaus's battalion singing German drinking songs, the crowds gave them a cheerful sendoff, as happy to see the last of them as the soldiers were to go. That euphoria quickly changed, however. Given that the farthest one-day march that Osterhaus's city boys had thus far experienced in their army careers was eight miles and that the shoddy shoes they had been issued were already in shreds, the grueling marches seemed long and rocky indeed. The terrain west of the Mississippi was mostly unsettled land with very few rough roads for the wagons, creating logistical dilemmas on a daily basis, if not from the ravages of weather, then from enemy raiders. As

Osterhaus immediately discovered, the clay roads could change overnight from choking dust to knee-deep mud. His green soldiers had to learn survival skills by trial and error on their first march; inevitably, they would suffer more than on later treks.[6]

Osterhaus, in order to lead effectively, was finding that he had to adapt much of what he had learned in Europe to conditions as he found them here in this open western country. Not only were distances much greater and battlefields in rougher terrain, but the men themselves were certainly different from the obedient European conscripts and haughty Prussian officers he had dealt with before. His ten years in his new country had given him an appreciation for the western American volunteer that newer German immigrant officers, fresh off the boat, could not hope to match. Although his first commands in the Civil War were of mostly German American soldiers, by early 1863 Osterhaus would have command over a broad variety of western Americans, many of whom were self-sufficient homesteaders and farmers used to personal hardship. Western men seemed by nature and experience much less formal and more inventive in emergencies than their Union compatriots to the east, unlikely to stand on ceremony or to tolerate fools. Spit and polish was simply not important to them; informality and approachability garnered more respect, as long as they were combined with strong leadership.[7]

In a speech after the Vicksburg campaign of 1863, Osterhaus summed up the contrast between European armies and his American troops this way: "We need no Prussian red tape Lieutenants in this country—no armies as Europe has them! We need an army of citizens,—men who love their country, men whose highest ambition is, after war is over, to be again free American citizens." Contrary to the showy entourages of some of his Prussian counterparts, Osterhaus eschewed pomp at the expense of his troops. "It is entirely against my Rule to ask fatigue parties for personal purposes," he wrote in late 1861, when he discovered that his men had been detailed to build a corral for his headquarters. In leading these citizen-soldiers, Osterhaus managed to be both approachable and strict when required. Whether his style of leadership was effective would soon be tested in a major battle.[8]

By comparison, Franz Sigel, who had enjoyed a much more prominent role in the German revolution than Osterhaus, seemed unable to adjust to situations that deviated from the Prussian military textbook, a shortcoming that severely limited his usefulness in the Civil War. He came across to his officer peers as a grandstander rather than a good team player. Although he continued to be loved and admired by the German American public and his soldiers throughout the war, he quickly lost the respect of the American commanders, who saw him as a loner who would plunge into battle unprepared and then be forced to retreat. By war's end he had been sidelined due to his shortcomings in strategy and leadership.[9]

Halfway through the march, as Lyon rendezvoused with Sturgis, he received urgent word that Sigel, now at Carthage, was in danger of being annihilated by the MSG. Lyon immediately acted to try to rescue Sigel's command from capture. Ordering loads lightened and equipment abandoned, he set his column on a hideously difficult forced march. After only two hours of rest, Lyon's leading elements covered the next fifty miles in only thirty hours, Osterhaus with Sturgis's brigade bringing up the dusty rear. This last stretch was brutal, a march all day through fierce heat and thick dust with no food but hardtack and precious little water, followed by a night march through a pitch-dark wood in hilly, rough country. Rest stops were brief, no blankets needed. Men suffering from the heat and dehydration dropped by the wayside by the hundreds. At one point, several officers were said to have approached Major Osterhaus, imploring him to go to Lyon for relief. His blunt reply was, "You must excuse me, gentlemen, but that is not my business." If accurate, this rather cold response is also an interesting commentary on Osterhaus's idea of leadership. When left to it, he would do anything in his power for the well-being of his men. But when the circumstances required it, he could follow the toughest orders implacably. That was all very well, but one man summed it up for many of the three-month enlistees when he said, "I wish I had stayed at home and sent my big brother."[10]

Instead of pursuing Sigel as he retreated from Carthage, the MSG continued south to meet up with McCulloch on July 6, proceeding fifty miles southwest of Springfield to get themselves organized. When Lyon's exhausted Federal column finally stumbled into camp near Springfield to join Sigel, the MSG had already been in their own camp for a week, with McCulloch and five thousand more Confederates just across the Arkansas border. Lyon had failed to prevent a junction of his foes; in fact, his campaign thus far had actually driven them together. Both of the opposing armies were in dire straits with regard to supplies. The Federal troops "were almost naked, without shoes, and without coffee and sugar, compelled to depend on the countryside" for food and fodder, which they often had to buy with their own money, if any. There were not enough tents for protection against the brutal sun, no clothing or other needed supplies waiting for them when they reached Springfield. Food was a problem, half rations and sometimes even quarter rations being the usual fare. Fresh water from wells and springs was soon tapped out; tainted creek water began making the men sick. Some began to die of fever. For most of the men, their three months' enlistment was up on or before July 28, and for many, that day couldn't come too soon.[11]

With the others, Osterhaus was ordered to keep all his tired men on the alert, ready to move out at a moment's notice. This meant that they had to sleep in all of their gear with their guns at their sides. Lyon's three-month enlistees were fed up with the poor conditions and were also very worried about their families and farms with harvest fast approaching. Not surprisingly, despite Lyon's pleas, two thousand of his soldiers left for home on July 24, the day their enlistments were up. Osterhaus had more luck with his men, whose enlistments were also up that day. He noted with satisfaction: "The term of enlistment (3 months) expired on this date but I succeeded in prevailing on my men to remain with me through the then imminent collision with the rebels, and was thus enabled to participate in the battle of Wilson's Creek." Clearly, he was spoiling for a fight; neither he nor his men wanted to go home without striking a blow at the enemy.[12]

On July 31 Osterhaus was elated when he was notified that Gen. John C. Frémont, newly appointed commander of the Department of the West, had appointed him colonel and authorized him to raise a three-year regiment. Understandably, Frémont was concerned about the future of the department, with most of his force mustering out after three months, and immediately upon his arrival in St. Louis he had begun making plans for raising the new army he would need, starting with "educated officers who had seen service," like Osterhaus. Not wanting to miss the impending battle himself, Osterhaus instead sent several recruiting officers from his battalion back to St. Louis to get started finding the thousand men his new regiment would need. One of these recruiters was his old Prussian compatriot Capt. Otto Schadt. Schadt's Company A was led in the upcoming battle by his first lieutenant, August Guentzel.[13]

After three weeks in camp, food, fodder, and time were running out for Southerners Sterling Price and Brig. Gen. Ben McCulloch as well. It was either fight or go back to base. Figuring that the barely trained, barely equipped new soldiers were about as ready as they were going to get under the circumstances, on July 31 the two rebel leaders headed toward Springfield with eleven thousand men. They were divided into three cohorts: Price and his Missouri State Guard, Brig. Gen. N. B. Pearce with a division of Arkansas State Troops, and McCulloch with his Confederate brigade made up of units from Arkansas, Texas, Louisiana, and Kansas.[14]

Learning of the rebel movement, on August 1 Lyon decided to move his fifty-eight hundred men forward out of Springfield to meet them, despite the poor condition of his command. His hope was to defeat the three columns heading his way one at a time, beginning with McCulloch, before they could combine against him. On August 1, after the worst of the heat of the day had passed, Osterhaus and the others marched toward Cassville, where McCulloch was thought to be. The march was excruciating: they fought choking dust a foot deep that coated everyone, turning their sweat to mud and making them unrecognizable to each other except by voice. With the temperature over a hundred degrees, the lack of shade and water to relieve their intolerably dusty mouths, and already weakened by dehydration from illness and ten days on half rations, many dropped by the wayside. Late that evening they camped at Dug Springs, seven miles from the leading elements of McCulloch's forces, who were camped at Cane Creek. The next day Osterhaus watched from a distance as the advance units of the two armies met in a brief skirmish at Dug Springs, repeated the following day after the aggressive Federals pursued the MSG now backpedaling advance three miles farther to the Curran Post Office. At that point, Lyon, now twenty-four miles from Springfield, had reached the end of his tenuous supply line and decided to abort the mission. What they did not know was how close they had come to being pounced on: McCulloch had set a surprise night attack in motion to catch Lyon at Curran. Fortunately for Lyon, his troops were almost back to Springfield before the bulk of the rebels arrived on the scene. Realizing they had missed the opportunity, the Confederates followed along slowly, and on August 6 all three rebel columns encamped at Wilson's Creek, about ten miles south of Springfield.[15]

By August 9 Lyon was becoming very depressed because of his intolerable situation: his army was outnumbered and ill-equipped and -fed, with no hope of supplies or reinforcements in the offing. But instead of retreating, he decided to surprise the Confederates with a fierce attack. Then, before they could recover from it, the Federals would slip away to Rolla. That afternoon he called his officers to his quarters, issuing orders for them to prepare to leave that evening and surprise the rebel camp early the morning of August 10. One soldier recalled that Osterhaus and the others smiled, shook hands all around, and had a drink, toasting the decision to fight "like men who were about to engage in a game the result of which was already determined in their favor."[16]

Although the volunteers were as eager to fight as their leaders, the last difficult days had shaken their confidence in their officers, and Osterhaus's small battalion was not immune. According to a German American newspaper report, the night before the battle an anonymous soldier posted a sign in Osterhaus's camp saying, "We cannot go into battle with such field officers." Perhaps the sign was posted by the men of Company A, resenting the fact that Osterhaus sent their experienced captain to St. Louis on a recruiting assignment when to their minds he should have been there to lead them into battle. But Osterhaus himself had never led in a full-scale battle; the same was true of his eight officers. Since that was a common situation among the Volunteer units, something else must have stirred the men up to an unusual pitch to have them post such a sign. It would thus be interesting to know what Osterhaus told them as he rallied them before battle, because whatever it was, they were inspired to hold their own under fire and gave a fine account of themselves and their battalion, as did their commander.[17]

At about six that evening, Col. Franz Sigel and his brigade of 1,200 headed out of Springfield to circle behind the rebels, while Osterhaus's battalion waited impatiently just outside town with Lyon's three remaining brigades. About dusk Lyon ordered his excited command west toward battle. The battalion led by "that sturdy veteran" Major Osterhaus marched to its favorite German song, and the other units bellowed the other camp ditties that usually accompanied their marches. Maj. Sam Sturgis's First Brigade had the advance, leading with

Capt. Joseph B. Plummer's battalion of three companies of U.S. Army Regulars, followed by Osterhaus's battalion, then Capt. James Totten's Battery F. (Aside from Osterhaus's battalion, the only other volunteer unit in Sturgis's brigade was one of the two cavalry companies.) Osterhaus's battalion consisted of three companies, each at that point a good deal under its nominal strength: the total for all three, calculated from his own casualty report, was only 182 men and officers. (Osterhaus's battalion was not included in the official casualty report of the battle.) From the Second Missouri he had Company A, led by 1st Lt. August Guentzel in Capt. Otto Schadt's absence, and Company C under Capt. Herman Bendel. He also listed a Company D (Rolla) under a Capt. Bowen.[18]

Wilson's Creek was to be "the hardest fought field which I had occasion to witness during this whole war," according to Osterhaus years later. Casualty rates for both sides were among the worst of the entire war, creating literally a "Bloody Hill," as it was afterward called. Osterhaus would be in the thick of the battle from the first shot to the last: he led his skirmishers going in and formed the rear guard leaving the field after the battle. In between, his small band held both the Union's vulnerable right and left flank positions at key moments in the day. He and his Missourians had wanted a fight; perhaps they got more than they bargained for.[19]

Lyon's plan of attack was to surprise the rebels, rapidly rolling up their camp from the north end and, with luck, panicking them into fleeing before they could get organized. Sigel, a mile south and unable to communicate directly with Lyon because of the intervening enemy, was to attack when he heard Lyon's artillery firing. The plan depended on Lyon advancing rapidly, exploiting surprise, and driving the fleeing rebels from their camps into Sigel's trap across their escape route south down the Telegraph Road. As the sky began to lighten with approaching day, Osterhaus and the other officers assembled their men quickly and silently for the final march into battle. Their way led south across a shallow valley and up over a spur that stood between them and Oak Hill that overlooked the Confederate camp beyond. They were soon spotted by rebel foragers out early who saw the column of Union troops quietly pouring across the valley, Lyon immediately deployed Plummer's First U.S. Battalion on the left and Osterhaus's battalion out to the right as skirmishers. This vanguard fanned out and moved rapidly forward three hundred yards ahead of the column of infantry.[20]

Col. James Cawthorn, whose Southern cavalry brigade was camped in the ravine just east of the spur, sent a mounted patrol of three hundred to the top of the spur with orders to quickly spread out to delay the enemy advance until the Confederates could get organized. When he saw the Southerners moving into position along the spur, Lyon had Totten's artillery fire a few rounds as the Federal skirmishers moved forward as fast as they could over the rough ground. Quickly driving back Cawthorn's outmanned patrol, Osterhaus's and Plummer's

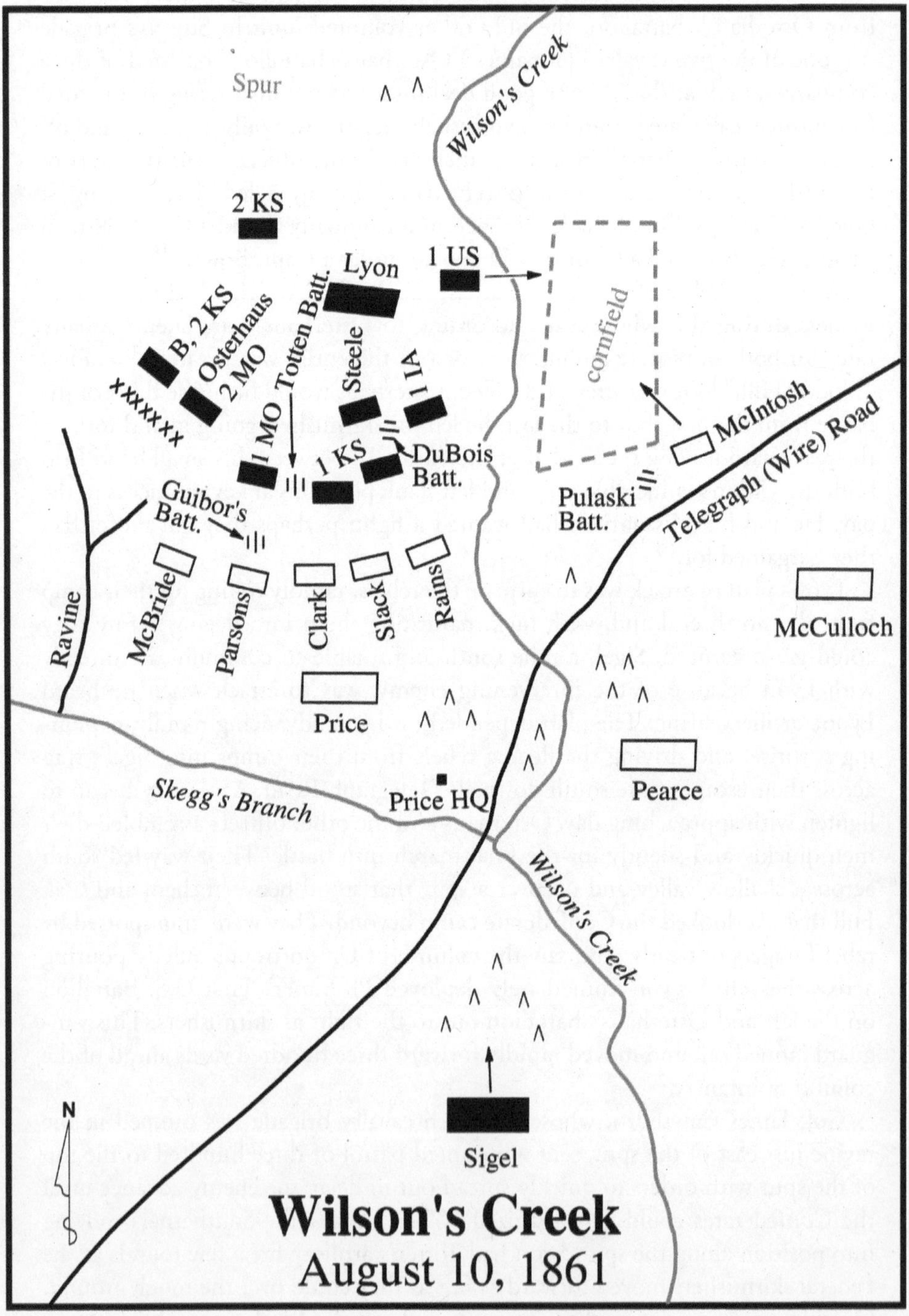

Wilson's Creek
August 10, 1861

Modern view of Osterhaus's position at the top of Bloody Hill, looking toward Price's headquarters near the house. (Author's collection)

skirmishers and the First Missouri crested the spur around five o'clock. Across the next ravine they spotted the rest of Cawthorn's men, about six hundred, now dismounted and defending the last hill (Oak Hill itself) before the main rebel camp. Lyon again ordered Osterhaus's battalion forward on a flanking movement to the right and Plummer off to the left. Osterhaus led his skirmishers as rapidly as possible through the brush-filled ravine between the spur and the top of Oak Hill, together with the First Missouri driving back Cawthorn's force. Just as the Federal skirmishers gained the crest of Oak Hill Osterhaus surprised Col. Benjamin A. Rives's rebel cavalry camp three hundred yards to the west of him and, with Totten's battery, immediately opened fire, scattering the men and capturing most of their horses. By about six o'clock, Lyon stood with Osterhaus and the other officers atop the hill, glasses trained at the Confederate camp aswarm with activity along Wilson's Creek at the bottom of the slope.[21]

As the rest of the Federal column moved up to the line, Osterhaus and his battalion now formed the Union right flank next to a large ravine that cut into the southwestern crest of Bloody Hill, charged with protecting the blue line from any efforts to turn it from that direction. Against the Union's two regiments plus Osterhaus's battalion, about seventeen hundred men in all, Sterling

Price was quickly assembling about thirty-one hundred men, mostly Missouri State Guards, with four field pieces. Price formed them running east to west at the southern base of the hill, gradually adding more to the left of his line by regiments as they got organized.[22]

In his official report, Osterhaus stated that he had to deal immediately with an impending rebel cavalry attack on his right flank:

> At that time my attention was attracted by a noise, apparently caused by the movements of a large body of mounted men in front of my position, but entirely out of my view. My command being in my opinion rather a little too far ahead of the column already, I rode back to General Lyon to make him the proper report, and to suggest the order to proceed toward the supposed column of the enemy. The General gave me the order and sent some troops [probably Company B, Second Kansas] to support me. I advanced with my command in double quick, and arrived at the edge of a valley just in time to see at least one thousand men, cavalry, advancing undoubtedly with the intention to flank our right. The whole force was in the very best range for my Minie rifles. I fired into them about six times by battalion fire, and most effectively; the report of my fire attracted the attention of the gallant commander of the artillery on my left, Capt. Totten, who detailed immediately two of his guns to my assistance. A few rounds of canister did fearful execution in the enemy's ranks, and in a short time he disappeared totally from the battle field. Our right was secured.

The fact that Osterhaus repaired to Lyon directly for direction, instead of to his brigade commander, is consistent with how Lyon personally directed the battle: brigade command was essentially ignored. Observing the effect of his orders, Osterhaus was gratified that his incessant drilling paid off: using a series of simultaneous volleys on his command, Osterhaus was able to maintain control of his wildly excited green troops so that they would more carefully aim their shots than had they been firing independently.[23]

About seven thirty Price tried to turn Osterhaus's flank. At that moment, next to Osterhaus, Col. George L. Andrews of the First Missouri was preparing a charge south down the hill to try to take out Capt. Henry Guibor's Battery that was causing great damage in his front. Now seeing the new Confederate threat on his flank, Andrews aborted his charge, angling the right end of his line so that it faced west to connect with Osterhaus's battalion. Supported by two of Totten's guns, this force faced Gen. James H. McBride's six hundred MSG, formed in the shadow behind a slight elevation at the base of the hill, while the rest of Andrews's First Missouri had their hands full against a determined assault in their front by Gen. Mosby M. Parsons's full division. As McBride's troops gained the top of the low elevation, they were immediately pummeled by Osterhaus's battalion and the rest of the Union right and Totten's artillery, driving them down behind the elevation. But then, collecting themselves, the

Southerners scrambled across the elevation and gradually moved up the slope of the now bloody hill against Andrews and Osterhaus. There were no fewer than three separate charges and countercharges in this assault. The toll on Federal Missourians was severe, even though Lyon had sent up more elements in support. When Colonel Andrews of the First Missouri, wounded in the action, eventually made a fighting retreat over the crest of Bloody Hill, McBride pulled back his Confederates as well, receiving orders to move to another part of the field. Although losing ground, Osterhaus's battalion of the Second Missouri and elements of the First Missouri had once again prevented the Southerners from turning the Union flank.[24]

In the first of several odd lulls in the fighting, Osterhaus and the other officers realigned and steadied their units. To these new soldiers, their first battle experience was overwhelming: "The artillery fire was as fast as any one could count and the roar of musketry was incessant." Orders simply could not be heard. The smoke was so thick that they couldn't see a hundred yards ahead. Neither side having erected barriers or dug trenches, their only refuge from flying bullets and artillery canister was to lie low or hide in the patchy brush. The green Union recruits desperately needed cool leadership to guide them through the utter chaos they were experiencing. As more and more of the Union officers were killed or wounded, including three of Osterhaus's own eight, Osterhaus joined Lyon, staff officers Maj. John Schofield and Capt. Gordon Granger, and the other remaining line officers in personally rallying the Federal troops whenever they wavered, no doubt Osterhaus exhorting them in both German and English.[25]

It was now nine o'clock, nearly three hours after the battle had started in earnest. Relative positions had not changed: the Union army still held Bloody Hill, while the Confederate army still threatened its southern slope. During a lull, both Price and Lyon took stock of their tactical situations and redeployed their troops. The Confederate commander decided to stop trying to turn Osterhaus's beleaguered right flank and instead concentrate on smashing up the middle to take out the artillery in order to drive Lyon off the hill. As part of his plan he withdrew McBride's division and Guibor's Battery from his left and placed them closer to the center of his line, reducing the pressure against Osterhaus. Anticipating that the Confederate movement would increase the pressure on Totten and the volunteer battery of Lt. John Du Bois on his left flank, Lyon ordered Osterhaus along with Captain Frederick Steele's battalion of Regulars and Company B of Plummer's battalion to shift their commands toward the Union center and left to cover the artillery.[26]

Osterhaus, having farther to move than the others, was still in the process of crossing his men from the Union right flank to the batteries as Price's second major assault began. Extremely heavy fighting swelled all along the line. Arriving near the center of the line, Osterhaus saw that Totten was covered by Steele's battalion and the First Iowa, so he decided to move farther left to support Du Bois, positioning his battalion just to the right of that battery. Lyon, having suffered two wounds during this assault, gathered himself to go back to the fray just as Osterhaus came up. Osterhaus reported, "I arrived [near Du Bois] at the moment when our noble General Lyon led a battalion of the Iowa troops in person towards the enemy: my position was partly masked by the Iowa's leaving me no chance to assist them."[27]

Osterhaus and his men had to wait about twenty minutes near Du Bois's Battery while room was made for him in the front line. About this time Capt. Henry Guibor's rebel battery, on high ground to the west, was lobbing in shells in a concerted effort to silence Du Bois's Battery, and Osterhaus and his men had to endure the nerve-wracking, earsplitting bombardment for what seemed like an eternity, as Osterhaus mildly put it, "suffering a good deal from the enemy," while they waited to move up. Once on the line, Osterhaus most likely had Andrews's First Missouri on his left. At about this time, according to Andrews's battle report, Osterhaus's battalion and Lyon, leading the First Iowa, saved the battered First Missouri from a rout under a fierce Confederate attack. Shortly thereafter, Osterhaus saw General Lyon personally leading a battalion of Second Kansas troops in a charge toward the enemy. Then Osterhaus was too busy to watch, himself leading a charge of his greatly reduced battalion: "The Confederate sally threatened Du Bois' Battery greatly; my supporting battalion was therefore ordered to charge and by its resolute move checked and drove back the Enemy thereby securing for the battery an advanced position," he reported. During Osterhaus's charge, the already wounded General Lyon took a fatal bullet in the chest, becoming the first Union general to die during the war. Osterhaus later said, "We could drive back their assaults, but could not shield our General Lyon against the enemy's ball. He fell a martyr soldier in a good cause."[28]

The battle raged on at close quarters for another half hour, but the superior Union weapons began to tell. Osterhaus reported, "We came rather close together, the enemy was very strong, but my men had better arms." Even so, Du Bois described the underbrush as so thick in his front that enemy troops were able to sneak within twenty yards of his guns before they were spotted and repulsed, making Osterhaus's infantry support indispensable for defending his gunners. Osterhaus noted that it had been a pretty long fight, although it was now only ten o'clock. The fully committed Federals were getting battle weary, but Pearce had three fresh Arkansas regiments that had not even seen action at this point. For their next assault the Confederates would put about five thousand troops on the Confederate line.[29]

General Lyon had been dead a half hour, but Maj. Sam Sturgis was only just now finding out from Lyon's aide, John Schofield, that as the only remaining brigade commander he was suddenly the senior commander on the field. As on the Confederate side, particularly among Price's officers, the toll of Union officers in this battle was severe. And no one knew where Sigel and his command were. During the lull, Sturgis called the few remaining officers, including Osterhaus, into council. The situation was grim. Not only were they outnumbered, but they were also getting low on ammunition, including artillery shells, and most men had not been able to fill their canteens since leaving Springfield nearly twenty-four hours before. If Sigel did not appear, there was no way the Union army could do any more than it had already done. With Sigel the Federals might yet have a chance to push the Confederates into full-scale retreat, but definitely not without him.[30]

At that moment, the Union commanders spotted a column flying an American flag approaching from the area where Sigel's guns had been last heard to the south. As the line advanced closer and started up the hill, Du Bois ordered his men to hold fire, thinking the column was Sigel's men at last. Suddenly, a battery started firing from behind the approaching line, and the Federals realized that they had been fooled once again by the lack of distinctive uniforms. Rather than Sigel, it was Pearce's fresh Arkansas regiments who had finally joined the battle in what would be Price's third and most ambitious assault. Osterhaus's tiring battalion and the remnants of the battered First Missouri were on the spot once more to hold the Union left flank. They and Du Bois's guns outlasted the Confederates for the last time and silenced the rebel battery as the whole line held firm in the fierce, if uncoordinated, half-hour-long assault. Price, realizing that the attack would not prevail, once more withdrew downslope.[31]

It was now eleven thirty. With more of his regiments and batteries reporting that their ammunition was almost gone, Sturgis took advantage of the latest lull to withdraw the Union forces from Oak Hill altogether, sending Du Bois's battery, supported by Osterhaus's battalion, to the spur about four hundred yards to the rear to cover the withdrawal. Steele's battalion stayed on Bloody Hill until the last units had marched off, repelling one last rebel charge. Then he withdrew as well, passing Du Bois and Osterhaus on the spur. Half of Du Bois's guns were disabled, so the gunner asked Osterhaus's battalion to stay behind to cover him while he made repairs and exchanged a few more shots with the Pulaski Light Battery. About then the rebels, cautiously advancing once more to the crest of Bloody Hill, discovered that the Federals had left the field, and, spying Du Bois and Osterhaus on the distant spur, let out a roar of victory as they stood atop a vacated battlefield.[32]

Then the little Union force was reluctantly on its way back to Springfield, not pursued. Osterhaus's band was significantly smaller than when they had started out: besides his three officers, he reported forty enlisted men killed or wounded, for a total of 24 percent, one of his heaviest percentage losses during the war. Sturgis was still debating whether to withdraw all the way to Springfield or to wait for news of Sigel when an officer from the German's brigade rode in and reported the total rout of Sigel's command. When they reached Springfield they found Sigel, who had made it back to town ahead of them, accompanied by just one officer. He reported that his green troops had panicked under several Southern cavalry charges and could not be rallied. Osterhaus's opinion of his compatriot's performance is not recorded.[33]

No sooner had the Federals withdrawn from the field than the arguments began about who won the battle. Osterhaus summed it up for the Union position: Sturgis had given the order to withdraw *after* the rebels had retreated down the hill. "The United States soldiers lost during this fierce encounter not an inch of ground" to an enemy three times their size. The Confederate reports, on the other hand, described the Federals as being driven fleeing from the field. Perhaps judging who won the battle in terms of who was driven from the field was not as relevant in this case as was how well the Federals had accomplished Lyon's purpose for fighting in the first place: hitting the Confederates hard enough to make good the escape to Rolla of his outnumbered army. This his army succeeded in doing.[34]

Osterhaus and the other young officers who survived their first major combat at Wilson's Creek had many valuable lessons to absorb: the importance of field position, the problems arising from difficulty in communicating between separated commands on the field during battle, the value of individual leadership in rallying faltering troops, and the use and effectiveness of artillery in defense and in combined attack. Osterhaus was particularly struck by the inadequacy of protection that open terrain provided for troops going against rifles. He was well aware of the European changes in military strategy evolving as the superiority of the rifles over muskets became clear, but now he had seen the actual effect of this new weapon for himself.[35]

Once back in Springfield, Major Sturgis turned the command over to Colonel Sigel, who conferred with Osterhaus and the other officers, then ordered preparations for immediate retreat to Rolla, to begin before dawn the next morning. The march was marred by a more or less open revolt against Sigel by most of the officers, who complained about his inept and insensitive handling of logistics. A few days from Rolla, Major Sturgis again took over command, supported by most of the other officers. Notably, Osterhaus did not sign the letter sent later by the officers to Maj. Gen. Henry W. Halleck covering their potentially mutinous actions in this matter. Osterhaus either was not asked for his views or declined to make them known. This was an early example of his prudence in avoiding political controversy, exercised consistently for the length of the war. However, Osterhaus could not fail to learn a great deal from Sigel's mistakes on this march. In his own future marches he was meticulous in rotating the lead from day to day and in ensuring that all of his command's basic needs were addressed evenhandedly.[36]

On August 17 Osterhaus led his small cohort into Rolla, where new uniforms and other needed supplies awaited, too late to be of help. Also waiting for him there was a letter from General Frémont ordering him immediately to St. Louis to assume the command of his new regiment, described as "nearly completed." Leaving his battalion in the charge of the senior captain as ordered, Osterhaus boarded the first available train and headed for home.[37]

With Frémont's three-month regiments evaporating and Sterling Price's Missouri State Guard still threatening the western part of the state, Frémont desperately needed volunteers for the three-year enlistment called for in President Lincoln's latest appeal. In appointing Osterhaus, Frémont very likely was counting on the belief that ethnics would be more likely to volunteer for units led by ethnics. Once back in St. Louis, Osterhaus threw himself into recruiting and training hundreds of inexperienced civilians, since he was to have only a month before they were sent into the field as soldiers and officers. Contrary to Frémont's assurances that his regiment was all but completed, Osterhaus discovered that only three companies of the ten that he needed had been formed so far, two of these traveling from Belleville to join before he had even returned from the front. To attract prospects, his recruiter, Capt. Otto Schadt, touted not only the bond of German ethnicity but also Osterhaus's own growing reputation and recent performance. Many who had seen Osterhaus in action at Wilson's Creek elected to follow him, including about a third of the still healthy men from his former battalion and others from the Third and Fourth Missouri and the First Iowa. These formed what Osterhaus judged to be "a solid stock of officers and Men" around whom to build the regiment.[38]

But Frémont was right: ethnicity did count. Ninety-two percent of Osterhaus's Twelfth Missouri Volunteers were born in Europe, making the regiment one of the most "quintessentially German" units in the army during the Civil War and one in which most of its members spoke only their native language. By the end of August Osterhaus had signed up five companies, and four others were mustered in before the regiment left for the field on September 19. According to army policy, Osterhaus would remain an acting colonel until the final company in his new Twelfth Missouri Volunteer Regiment was in place; this did not occur until December. Meanwhile, Osterhaus selected his officers from the men he knew in the Belleville companies, his rationale not so much cronyism as practicality. The fact that he knew these men, and they him, allowed him to establish a mutual respect as the basis for the protracted process of teaching them how to be good officers, a much harder task than training infantry.[39]

As soon as men were mustered in at Concordia Park they began an intensive period of what the energetic, "dashing" Colonel Osterhaus described as "the instruction of the men in their military duties, to drill and discipline them and to promote the state of their efficacy for the field generally." This program and its lasting effects on the men were best described by the captain of Company B, Frederick Tell Ledergerber, later a major in the Twelfth:

> The fact that our regiment almost always received the honored position of being sent first whenever the enemy was near was due to the discipline that Osterhaus introduced. He was the master in it. . . . The officers had to keep their own traits under control and didn't dare commit any blunders themselves. . . . (He always gave the orders in English, the spicy part in German.) As a result there was a spirit in his exercise that always spread throughout his entire command within a short time. . . . Also, every soldier and officer in the regiment felt that we had made a good impression. We got "esprit de corps" that never left us. On the other side, he was always diligent to see that every soldier got his proper rations.

Because of his own European training, Osterhaus understood the elements of effective military command better than a new civilian commander could be expected to. He respected army organization and rules rather than resisting them, and conveyed the expectation to his men and officers that they would do the same. He also sincerely respected his men, and praised them whenever he could with an affection that was clearly returned.[40]

In the midst of Osterhaus's intense preparations, the sublimely disorganized Frémont diverted him and another German-speaking officer to escort around the area Prince Napoléon, cousin to Napoléon III of France. (Although the contemporary press listed Osterhaus as Frémont's aide-de-camp, this public relations assignment was no doubt temporary, given Osterhaus's other priorities.) Napoléon's aide found Osterhaus and his cohort to be "quite distinguished and very moderate," noting that they seemed embarrassed at the exaggeration and U.S. Army–bashing indulged in by the other German-speaking officers milling around Frémont. Osterhaus here again clearly distanced himself from German American military politics.[41]

On September 19 Osterhaus received orders to take the Twelfth Missouri to Jefferson City, where Frémont, impressed with what he knew of Osterhaus, immediately assigned him to command the Second Brigade of Sigel's Third Division, even though he was still technically only a major. Here ended Osterhaus's brief direct command of his beloved Twelfth Missouri, which went on to distinguished service in the war, eventually being mustered out after the fall of Atlanta in 1864. Under his new orders, Acting Colonel Osterhaus's command now consisted of three regiments: his old Twelfth Missouri, the German American Seventeenth Missouri, and the Forty-fourth Illinois, about half German. These approximately three thousand men were joined by a battalion of the Third Missouri, four hundred strong, and two German-led batteries, each with six field pieces, that would see much service under him: Capt. Martin Welfley's

Missouri Battery and the Fourth Ohio Battery under Capt. Louis Hoffmann. Osterhaus was delighted to discover that the Fourth Ohio was made up mostly of cannoneers who had been with him in the 1848–1849 revolution at Baden. A few days later Sigel added a cavalry unit, the Benton Hussars. Osterhaus also acquired an assistant adjutant who would be with him for most of the war: the bilingual, hard-drinking Capt. William E. Gordon, a Scot who had been educated in Württemberg. This new command was a huge increase in responsibility for Osterhaus, but without any time to get organized he had to take them all on the road again in pursuit of Price.[42]

The next day, September 28, they were off, probably by train, to Sedalia, where Sigel had established Third Division headquarters. There they stayed two weeks before heading toward Springfield after Price, a delay that was fine with Osterhaus, who clearly needed more time to organize himself and his new brigade. Frémont, once at his new headquarters in Springfield, was working on a plan of attack against Price's and McCulloch's forces when President Lincoln, unhappy over a host of issues, decided to replace him. On the evening of November 2, when Frémont informed his stunned key officers that he had been relieved, Sigel immediately offered to resign in support, while Osterhaus silently ground the point of his scabbard into the gravel. As Lincoln had feared, the news of Frémont's ouster stunned and angered the Pathfinder's many avid German American admirers. More important, the German American soldiers, who were recruited with the promise that they would fight under Frémont, were near mutiny.[43]

After their first shock, Sigel and Osterhaus had quite different responses to the news. Squarely at odds with Sigel and other influential Forty-Eighters, Osterhaus decided to back the government's position, agreeing with his old Belleville friend Gustave Koerner that the German reaction had been overemotional and would soon die out. This must have been a difficult decision for him, given that Frémont had been instrumental in Osterhaus's promotions, supported by Sigel. Yet Osterhaus clearly saw himself as a professional soldier rather than a political appointee, and his decision here was once again to keep out of the politics of command. By this stance Osterhaus earned the respect of some of the nonethnic officers and perhaps helped to dampen the sparks of mutiny among his men and officers.[44]

With Frémont's ouster, the army headed back to Rolla, offensive forgotten. When Osterhaus arrived he found that Maj. Gen. Henry W. Halleck, an old West Pointer and most recently an extremely successful California lawyer, had taken Frémont's place. Halleck was known as an excellent administrator, a talent that would be sorely needed to achieve order out of the chaos that Frémont had left behind. He was also opinionated, especially about the relative competence and value of politically appointed officers versus those from his own school, West Point. His opinions now and in his later role as general in chief of the Union army would influence Osterhaus's career several times in the future.[45]

The day after Halleck's appointment Sigel repaired to St. Louis for a month's medical leave, leaving now Acting Brigadier General Osterhaus (still technically only a major) in temporary command of the entire Third Division at Rolla. He found his hands very full: the mostly German American soldiers and officers in his command still seethed about their hero Frémont's inexplicable dismissal on the eve of battle at Springfield and still believed that they had to have Frémont or Sigel in command in order to win. Col. Grenville Dodge noted that Osterhaus was the only German American officer who "took no part in the feeling and sentiment" among his men. Despite the unpopularity of his position, Osterhaus held to it and now, with Sigel absent, defused the men's anger by ordering frequent drills, parades, guard duty, and inspections to try to keep them busy as well as to improve their small-arms skills. Osterhaus's main military assignment during this period was enemy surveillance, a new role for him. Sterling Price had moved his camp, and Halleck at headquarters in St. Louis needed to figure out his intentions. Osterhaus's extensive intelligence reports marked the first time his comprehensive and thoughtful writing appeared in the *Official Records*.[46]

As Sigel's absence dragged on, Halleck became very concerned about the lack of overall leadership for the ten thousand mostly German American troops at Rolla, which included both Sigel's and Hungarian Alexander Asboth's divisions. Aside from Sigel, no one at Rolla held sufficient rank to take overall command. Political and practical considerations overrode Halleck's usual inclination to favor West Pointers as he mulled promoting a foreigner, either Osterhaus or Asboth, to brigadier general to command at Rolla. Deciding that perhaps Osterhaus was the better of the two, Halleck requested his appointment on December 16. Congressional approval was required for the appointment, a process that usually took some time; meanwhile, on December 19 Joseph Osterhaus was pleased to receive as expected his formal commission of colonel of Volunteers.[47]

Halleck appointed fifty-six-year-old West Pointer Brig. Gen. Samuel R. Curtis to command the newly created District of Southwest Missouri, including the troops at Rolla, and gave him a simple but exciting assignment for a man with little combat experience: to eliminate the threat of Sterling Price, who was definitely a thorn in Halleck's side. When Sigel heard of Curtis's appointment, he was terribly upset that he had been passed over for promotion, feeling strongly that he himself deserved the appointment for his outstanding experience and performance as well as his seniority. He took his case to the newspapers, and finally resigned from the army in a huff on December 31. Over the next month, rumors of a pro-Frémont cabal among Sigel's German American officers so spooked Halleck that he privately urged the delay of any promotions of German

Americans, including his own nomination of Osterhaus. Thus, Sigel's public tantrums had a direct impact on Osterhaus, who was one of the officers Halleck thought were "fully committed" to this rebellious faction. Although this view was mistaken, Osterhaus's promotion to brigadier general of volunteers was circumspectly put on hold despite his solid performance in the field.[48]

Newly appointed commander Curtis was concerned about the Third Division's reaction to the news of Sigel's sudden resignation, hearing rumors of "a mutinous murmor [*sic*] in the ranks" and of some discussion among the officers about whether they should resign also in support of Sigel. The very day of the resignation Curtis took Osterhaus on rounds through Sigel's division to gauge the men's mood. To his relief Curtis found the camps quiet and the officers in good humor. He attributed this to Osterhaus. He wrote to Halleck, "He seems to be a leading spirit in that Division and I think his good sense will lead him to act wisely and assist me in preserving the good order of this command." When Sigel's resignation was subsequently not accepted, he took another twenty-day leave while his case, with its attendant national uproar, was hashed over in Washington. While Sigel was gone, not returning to Rolla until the end of January, Osterhaus once more had command of the again unsettled Third Division, now with his new commander Curtis's full confidence.[49]

He would not have long to wait for his first challenge. Orders came on January 4 to prepare to march at a moment's notice. Just over a week later Osterhaus took a brigade on the advance through wind and snow in pursuit of Price. Curtis had already sent Col. Eugene A. Carr south with a cavalry reconnaissance in force to pin down the location of Price's army and to harass his foraging expeditions. But Carr felt too pressured to hold this position, and Halleck ordered Curtis to reinforce him immediately with infantry and then to go after Price with his entire command. Curtis ordered Osterhaus forward with a brigade of three regiments, two cavalry battalions, and two batteries; the rest of Curtis's divisions would follow in stages.[50]

In his instructions to Osterhaus, Curtis also added a personal comment that warmed Osterhaus's heart: "General Halleck writes that your name has been presented for promotion, which I hope you may continue to deserve and ultimately secure." (This note was written two weeks before Halleck recommended that Osterhaus's promotion quietly be put on hold.) Halleck was uneasy that Curtis had only German commanders to choose from for leading the advance out of Rolla, and particularly reluctant to use Sigel's division because of its reputation for looting, but in his note to Osterhaus Curtis seemed to imply that he expected Osterhaus would reward his confidence in him by controlling his men.[51]

That proved difficult. The men soon ran short of rations, some imprudently having thrown away their despised hardtack at Rolla. One soldier wrote to his family that Osterhaus "did all in his power" to keep them from unofficially bagging hogs and cattle along the route, but they succeeded in augmenting their rations in spite of him. Plundering seemed to be commonplace. Wrote a soldier in the Thirteenth Illinois, "The only place we have passed untouched, and from which we have not levied contributions on our march, has been a graveyard." There is no evidence that this activity was condoned by Osterhaus; in fact, he frequently issued orders forbidding it. In one incident he was too late to keep the men from eating hundreds of pounds of bacon stolen from a smokehouse, but he issued scrip to the owner and deducted the bacon from the soldiers' future rations. But he now had to control his column through no fewer than seventy-nine officers, not all of whom shared his views. When Osterhaus joined Carr at Lebanon, Carr as senior took command of the forward post pending Curtis's arrival a few days later. He wrote Curtis on January 26, somewhat contradictorily, that Osterhaus had a fine brigade drill but that "discipline is still very bad." Mentioning plundering in his next sentence, he did not directly accuse Osterhaus's Germans of looting, although his implication was clear.[52]

One of the last of Curtis's army to arrive at Lebanon was Franz Sigel with his remaining two brigades. Curtis and Sigel were on polite but distant terms, their staffs and camps having little to do with each other. Having established a good working relationship with Curtis in the intervening weeks, Osterhaus may not have been overly delighted to see his old commander return. Curtis spent the day after Sigel's arrival reorganizing his army into four small divisions sorted by ethnic considerations. Sigel was officially in command of the First Division but also had overall wing command of both the First and Second, made up of mostly immigrants from Illinois and Missouri. Below him, Colonel Osterhaus officially had command of the First Brigade of the First Division, but also took acting command of the whole First Division, consisting of the Twelfth and Seventeenth Missouri; the Twenty-fifth, Thirty-sixth, and Forty-fourth Illinois; Welfley's Missouri Battery; and Hoffmann's Fourth Ohio Battery. Hungarian Brig. Gen. Alexander Asboth led the much smaller Second Division, composed of two infantry regiments, two cavalry units, and two batteries. The Third and Fourth Divisions were primarily native-born troops led by Col. Jefferson C. Davis and Col. Eugene Carr. None of the regiments was at full strength, what with sickness and detachments for guard duty along the supply road. Curtis would eventually offer battle with 10,250 troops in all.[53]

In Lebanon, as Osterhaus began organizing his new units during weather "variable as the capricious temper of a lunatic . . . but always with more or less mud," Curtis issued draconian orders limiting supplies and equipment to be taken on the upcoming forced march toward Springfield, to commence on February 10: only six days of rations and no tents, despite the freezing weather. The night before, Osterhaus read the orders to his brigade, closing with "a touching appeal to our patriotism," perhaps to offset the effects of the hardships sure to follow. By February 12 they were camped eight miles from Springfield, where a brisk skirmish of the Union advance guard with a regiment of rebels seemed to indicate that Price would give battle the next day. Long before dawn, Osterhaus took the First along with the other divisions arrayed in line of battle toward Springfield. The excited men listened expectantly for the first sounds of firing, but they were disappointed. Price had skedaddled during the night, burdened with a long supply train of as much of his winter camp as he could salvage on short notice.[54]

Curtis pushed his cavalry on through the town that same day in pursuit of Price, who was headed past the old Wilson's Creek battlefield on the Telegraph Road on his way into Arkansas to meet up with Ben McCulloch's command. Over the next days, Osterhaus's and Asboth's divisions brought up the rear of Curtis's column and could only listen in frustration from a distance to the sounds of continued small engagements as Curtis's cavalry drove Price across the state line into Arkansas, nipping at his rear guard and picking off his trailing supply wagons. Late the evening of February 17, Price led his flagging soldiers into Cross Hollow, Ben McCulloch's winter headquarters, twelve miles south of Little Sugar Creek on the Telegraph Road. Pressure from Curtis forcing them to burn their winter camp structures and extensive stores, McCulloch and Price hit the road south once more on February 19. The same day, in a freezing rain that froze their ragged clothing stiff, Curtis with Osterhaus's and Asboth's divisions moved west to Osage Springs to try to flank the Confederates, but they were too late.[55]

For the next several days, Osterhaus's division camped at Osage Springs, five miles from Bentonville. The rebels had decided to move twenty miles farther south into the Boston Mountains, effectively out of reach of the Union force. Curtis's outnumbered command was already more than two hundred miles from Rolla, and food and forage were becoming more of a problem as the days went by. Halleck informed the concerned Federal commander that he could spare him neither troops nor horses. Nonetheless, Curtis decided to stay, blocking the route to Missouri and preparing against the possibility of a strong Confederate attack out of the Boston Mountains. To the north, he posted Davis's division on the bluffs of Pea Ridge overlooking Little Sugar Creek valley and controlling the Telegraph Road, the main route into Missouri. If it came to battle, this would be a good site: his army would be positioned on the bluffs overlooking the river and the road south with the ridge and their communication to Missouri protected at their backs. Curtis, with Carr's division, camped a few miles south of Pea Ridge in McCulloch's old winter camp, also on the Telegraph Road, while Sigel's command at Osage Springs was twelve miles to the west.[56]

In January, Maj. Gen. Earl Van Dorn, a West Pointer from Port Gibson, Mississippi, had been appointed to plan and lead an ambitious Southern spring campaign into Missouri in command of Price's MSG, Brig. Gen. Ben McCulloch's Arkansans, and Brig. Gen. Albert Pike's native regiments from the Indian Territory. Van Dorn did not hear of Price's flight until the Confederates were already in the Boston Mountains, then immediately journeyed to join his command. When Van Dorn learned how widely the elements of the Union force were scattered, he saw a golden opportunity to strike immediately, catch them while they were spread out, and defeat Osterhaus's and Asboth's divisions before they could rejoin Curtis. Then he would take care of the other half of Curtis's army. He had a great numerical advantage: at this point, McCulloch reported his strength at eighty-four hundred; Price had about sixty-eight hundred more, and Pike was ordered to rendezvous at Bentonville with a thousand more, mostly Native Americans whose tribes had signed treaties with the Confederate government.[57]

Figuring that speed was of the essence in order to catch the Federals before they could unite, Van Dorn ordered the troops to travel light. Two mornings after they started out, they ate the last of their rations, a bit of parched corn or a biscuit, and began slogging the final twelve miles to Bentonville to catch Sigel, Osterhaus, and Asboth unaware. Fortunately for the Federals, on the previous afternoon Curtis learned of the Confederate advance and immediately ordered all of his divisions to fall back to Little Sugar Creek. Osterhaus did not get the word until about ten that evening that the whole Confederate army was heading in his direction and that his assignment was rear guard to the supply train, behind Asboth's division. This was a most frustrating exercise, particularly with the enemy nipping at his heels. In the pitch-black night, the snow was blowing sideways, and the road was a hopeless confusion of troops, guns, and wagons. By the time everyone was organized, with the hard-to-handle wagon trains in the road ahead of Osterhaus, the column stretched several miles and took about three hours to pass a given point. Fortunately, the Confederates failed to catch up.[58]

When Osterhaus finally arrived in Bentonville near dawn of March 6, Sigel detached eight companies of his original Twelfth Missouri as well as two cavalry units and five guns as a rear guard, six hundred men in all. Then he sent the rest of his troops and the trains, Osterhaus still guarding the rear, on to Curtis at Sugar Creek. As the tired and cold bluecoats filed through Bentonville past the Eagle Hotel, Sigel made quite a sight, a small man with coal-black hair casually finishing his breakfast in the dining room. Sigel later claimed that he had decided to stay behind to feel out the enemy. He certainly did that. About the time that Sigel finished his breakfast, the last of the main Union column disappeared into the defile leading to the Little Sugar Creek valley and the first of the Confederates, Col. James M. McIntosh's cavalry, appeared south of town on the Elm Springs Road. By the time Sigel finally got his small detail on the road, his detachment was in danger of being surrounded by rebel cavalry. In the early afternoon, just as Osterhaus arrived at Curtis's camp at the Telegraph Road, he received a message that Sigel was under attack. Osterhaus immediately reversed his four regiments that were still on the road and marched them at the double-quick toward Sigel, followed by Asboth's two regiments and a large cavalry force. After only three or four miles they met Sigel and company, who had already battled through the worst of their harassment relatively unscathed. The relieved Osterhaus immediately opened artillery and rifle fire after the withdrawing rebels.[59]

At Sugar Creek, Curtis had already deployed Carr's and Davis's divisions in a defensive line facing south, but Sigel's wing was the missing whole right side of the defense. While he was waiting for the rest of his army to show up, Curtis directed a detail to use boulders and trees to obstruct a dirt track, the Bentonville Detour, leading around the right end of his position toward the rear. All of the Union wagons were safely ensconced with a rear guard in a well-protected field near the log Elkhorn Tavern, a mile or so north of camp. Now, with the deployment of Asboth on the far right facing west and Osterhaus at the junction of the Little Sugar Creek valley road and Telegraph Road, Curtis's long line on the heights was about as ready as it could be to repulse an attack either up Telegraph Road from the south or from the Little Sugar Creek valley road to the west. As the tired men rested on their arms, looking forward to the battle sure to come in the morning, through the thin winter forest Osterhaus could see the enemy campfires down the Sugar Creek valley road to the west.[60]

Coming along the Sugar Creek road, Van Dorn called a halt at Camp Stevens, an old rebel campsite. Had they kept going on that road another mile or two, they would have rejoined the Telegraph Road in front of Osterhaus's position. Instead of resting his weary troops, Van Dorn thought of a way to retrieve the element of surprise. McCulloch had pointed out the Bentonville Detour that ran eight miles to the north around the back side of Pea Ridge past Big Mountain, ultimately rejoining the Telegraph Road three miles behind the Union army. Van Dorn figured that if the Confederates could slip around behind the outnumbered Curtis by daybreak, they would be able to surprise him from the rear and would also be positioned between the Federals and their escape route into Missouri. But Carr's obstructions made slipping around the bluecoats anything but easy. Missing his dawn goal by hours, Van Dorn with Price's big division didn't reach the Telegraph Road until ten o'clock on March 7, while the rear division under McCulloch, including Col. Louis Hébert's infantry, McIntosh's cavalry, and Pike's cavalry, out of contact on the other side of Big Mountain, straggled along three miles behind him and did not get there at all. Trying to salvage surprise, Van Dorn decided to have McCulloch's troops turn back southeast and cut across in front of Big Mountain on a connecting road in order to shorten their march. He would meet them at Elkhorn Tavern around noon.[61]

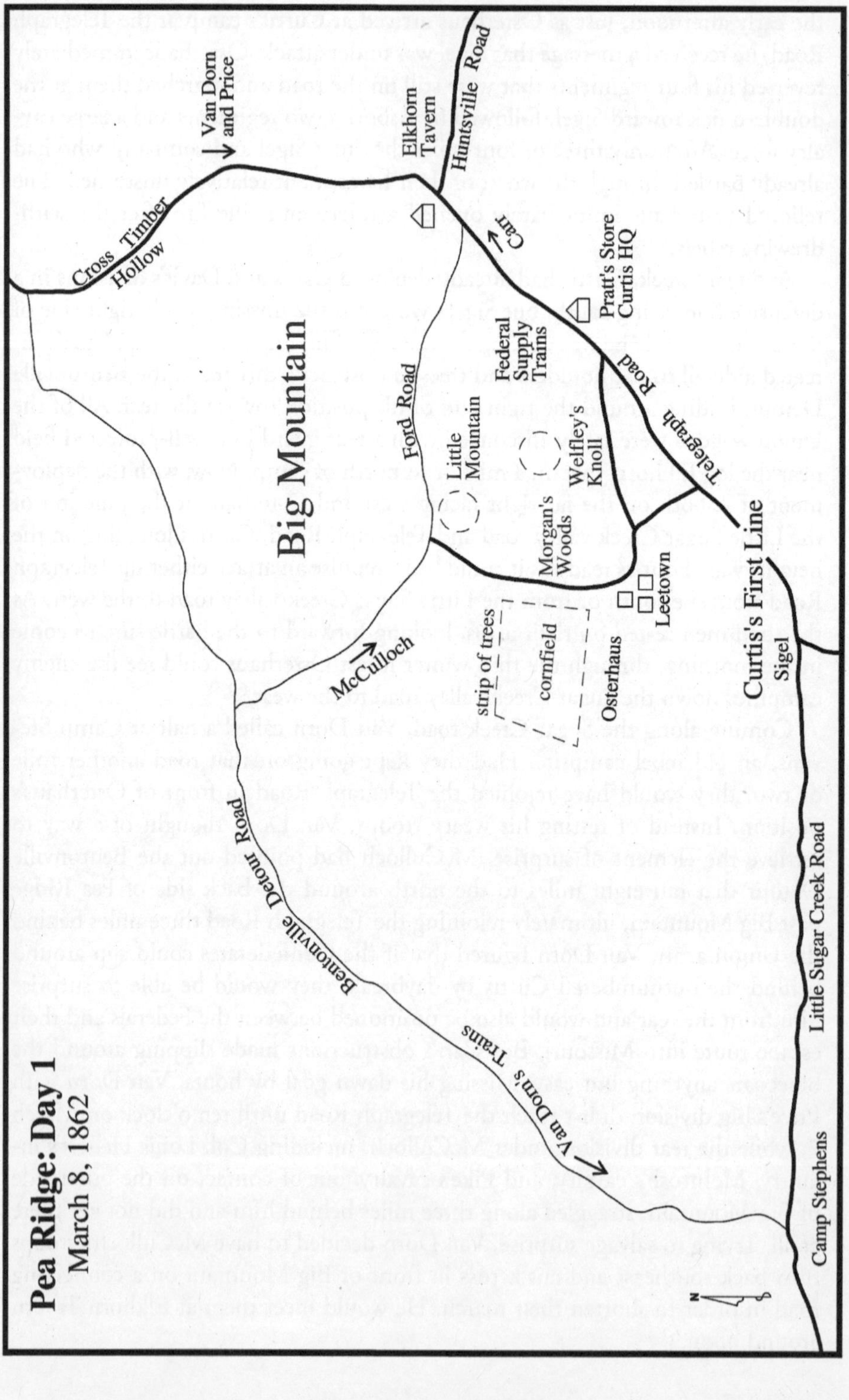
Pea Ridge: Day 1
March 8, 1862
Van Dorn and Price
Elkhorn Tavern
Huntsville Road
Cross Timber Hollow
Curtis
Pratt's Store
Curtis HQ
Big Mountain
Ford Road
Federal Supply Trains
Telegraph Road
Little Mountain
Welfley's Knoll
Morgan's Woods
Leetown
Curtis's First Line
Sigel
strip of trees
cornfield
Osterhaus
McCulloch
Bentonville Detour Road
Van Dorn's Trains
Little Sugar Creek Road
Camp Stephens
N

By nine o'clock the next morning, Curtis was just tumbling to the enormity of the Confederate envelopment and met with his division commanders at General Asboth's tent to get their take on the situation. Davis and Dodge wanted to stand and fight; most of the other officers counseled retreat up the Telegraph Road. Having made the decision to fight, Curtis decided to open with a reconnaissance in force toward the rebel flanking force of unknown strength reported to be on the Bentonville Detour near the hamlet of Leetown, choosing Osterhaus for this key mission. Ninety minutes after Osterhaus left to organize his first-ever large-scale advance into battle, Curtis's decision to stand rather than retreat was vindicated when Price's Missouri State Guard was sighted on the Telegraph Road, a mile north of Curtis's position. The Union commander began to realize that he had the bulk of the Confederate army in his rear, not his front, and immediately began to reverse his front toward the new threat. The coming battle was developing in a direction that he had not anticipated.[62]

As the council of war continued at Asboth's tent, Osterhaus marshaled his cobbled-together detachment and prepared to head north on the Leetown Road toward the Bentonville Detour. Curtis had tried to give Osterhaus sufficient men for the demonstration in force without weakening his Sugar Creek line, which was still facing south toward the expected Confederate main attack. Osterhaus would have part of his old Twelfth Missouri under Maj. Hugo Wangelin with 360 men and the Thirty-sixth Illinois under Col. Nicholas Greusel with 830 more. (Greusel was that rarity, an experienced officer, having served in the Mexican War as a captain.) Curtis also detached Davis's Twenty-second Indiana, 400 strong. Since Osterhaus's First Division had no cavalry of its own, Curtis assigned Col. Cyrus Bussey with 600 riders from various units. Osterhaus's artillery was Capt. Louis Hoffmann's Fourth Ohio, three twelve-pounder howitzers from Capt. Martin Welfley's battery, and half of the First Missouri flying battery with three twelve-pounder James rifles.[63]

Osterhaus's immediate priority was to organize this motley force quickly against an opposition of unknown strength and position. His first action was to send Bussey forward with the mounted troopers and the flying battery to reconnoiter the rebel column, while Greusel got the infantry moving on the Leetown Road. At about eleven thirty Osterhaus himself rode into the small hamlet of Leetown. There were no enemy troops in sight at this point; he assumed they were still to the north on the Bentonville Detour. A large field of dead cornstalks, lying just north of the settlement and west of the road, looked like a good initial battle position; Osterhaus decided to deploy his infantry on the south side of the field behind a rail fence. Beyond the field to the north was a deep strip of forest where the enemy might collect, but they would then have to cross four hundred yards of cornfield to close with his infantry. In this position his brigade could also guard the Leetown Road along their right flank against an enemy strike toward the Union camp on Little Sugar Creek.[64]

Modern view of Leetown battlefield, looking from Osterhaus's position across the cornfield toward the strip of trees. (Author's collection)

Leaving directions for Greusel as to where to place the infantry regiments when they arrived, Osterhaus rode ahead through the sunny, frigid morning to join his cavalry to find out just what he was facing. About noon, as they emerged on the north side of the strip of woods, the six hundred Federal horsemen were shocked to see about ten thousand Confederate cavalry and infantry only a half mile away across a large wheat field. It was McCulloch's three brigades: Hébert's infantry, McIntosh's cavalry, and Pike's Indian brigade. The Southerners were trudging along in column from left to right along Ford Road toward Elkhorn Tavern. Osterhaus immediately realized the fix he was in. If he could not distract this large rebel column, they would reinforce the other Confederate wing that he could hear already hotly engaged against Carr's Fourth Division two miles to the right near the tavern. Of equal importance, Curtis's vital supply trains were only a mile and a half away, highly vulnerable to an attack either ahead along the Ford Road or around by the Leetown Road. Yet if Osterhaus were successful in capturing McCulloch's attention, he would then have the serious problem of holding this far superior force in check until he could be reinforced.[65]

Sending to Curtis for help, Osterhaus now made one of the key command decisions of this battle. Despite the daunting odds, Osterhaus decided he could not hesitate to strike. Calling for the flying battery to set up in the edge of the trees across the open field from the rebels, he ordered the rest of the cavalry into line of battle, except for two companies of the Third Iowa sent off to attack the tail of the rebel column about a half mile to the west. Even before all of his troopers were in position, Osterhaus ordered his battery to open fire at the huge gray column across the field. The sudden explosion of several volleys in quick succession in their flank and rear completely surprised the exhausted Confederate infantry, stopping them in their tracks. While they milled around, Osterhaus ordered Bussey's five hundred remaining troopers to charge across the field to keep them off balance. However, Confederate Brig. Gen. Ben McCulloch recovered quickly from Osterhaus's surprise bombardment and ordered his own cavalry to charge as well. Bugles blaring, McIntosh led his screaming horsemen racing across the field at the Union cavalry like a disturbed nest of hornets before Bussey could get his own charge going. Although Bussey's troopers and the artillerymen tried to hold off the sudden attack of what Osterhaus called a "wild, numerous and irregular throng" of riders, after firing one round the bluecoats gave it up and broke for the rear. In their confused and panicked flight they abandoned all three of the guns of the flying battery when the horses harnessed to the guns were killed or scattered. The shocked Federal survivors, some of whom ran down several men in Welfley's battery in their retreat, came galloping on through Greusel's brigade in the cornfield, just then forming into line, shouting at the infantrymen to run for their lives. Osterhaus himself had galloped back to the cornfield to prepare Greusel for the onslaught, very concerned that the green soldiers would panic, but was relieved to find that Greusel had them standing fast, bucked up by an effective artillery round he ordered that discouraged the hotly pursuing Confederate cavalry.[66]

During the relative lull that followed as McCulloch, still behind the strip of trees, tried to reorganize his excited cavalry and evaluate the extent of the Union threat to his moving column, Osterhaus reviewed his own precarious position. Having stung the Confederates into responding, he had not a man to spare in standing up to the consequences. With Bussey now off in the woods to his rear trying to corral the disorganized cavalry, Osterhaus had to rely on just his three small regiments and his batteries, about sixteen hundred men all told, to take the brunt of an attack by a much larger foe. Both of his flanks were vulnerable, he had no reserves, and he could not expect the reinforcements he had just requested for at least an hour, if at all, given the sounds of Carr's intense battle on his right. To make matters worse, he could see one of Welfley's howitzers that had been abandoned across the field when the tongue of its gun carriage broke during the cavalry rout. This battle was Osterhaus's first experience commanding artillery, but he was well aware that for an officer, losing a gun was tantamount to loss of honor. After his flying battery had been overrun beyond the trees, he was determined not to lose this howitzer as well, so in the lull he sent Welfley's artillerymen and two companies of the Twelfth Missouri scrambling across the broad field through rebel skirmish fire to retrieve it. (He later was also able to retrieve the unspiked guns of the flying battery.) Now he had Greusel deploy a line of skirmishers from the Thirty-sixth Illinois across the field on his left to watch for signs of an enemy advance or flanking movement.[67]

Greusel was a strong leader who kept his head, traits that were a great asset to Osterhaus in this situation. In keeping with Osterhaus's strategy of keeping the Confederates off balance, Greusel now suggested that Hoffmann and Welfley lob some artillery rounds blindly over the strip of trees. Osterhaus agreed that even though they could not see the enemy, the shots just might do some good. Somewhat to their surprise, this ploy was wildly successful, for one thing terrorizing Pike's Native American contingent, who were untrained in the white man's warfare and had never seen artillery before. While they were crowded around with the rebel cavalrymen admiring the captured guns, shells came out of the sky, and the Native Americans skedaddled into the trees, not to be heard from again during the battle.[68]

Some of Osterhaus's blind shots also fell among Hébert's infantry brigade of four thousand, still marching eastward to join Van Dorn at the tavern. Hébert ordered his troops to get off the road and take cover at about the same time that McCulloch became convinced that he was going to have to stop to deal with the Union threat on his flank. The Confederate general ordered Hébert to form his infantry in line of battle while he deployed the rest of his forces in the wheat field just north of the strip of forest. Facing Osterhaus's two and a half regiments, screened by the trees for the moment, were five regiments of dismounted cavalry under McCulloch, with three more cavalry regiments behind them in a second line under McIntosh. Hébert's four large regiments faced Morgan's Woods on the east side of the Leetown Road, seriously threatening Osterhaus's right flank. McCulloch's plan was for Hébert to start forward through the woods on a flanking movement when he heard McCulloch open fire. McCulloch himself rightly expected to make quick work of what looked to be a small Union diversion. Osterhaus was in big trouble.[69]

About half past one McCulloch rode into the strip of forest to reconnoiter the Union position and strength before he signaled the attack. Although he sent rebel skirmishers ahead as protection, Federal skirmishers from the Thirty-sixth Illinois spotted him from their position behind a rail fence on the north side of the field and shot him dead. McIntosh, when informed of McCulloch's death, immediately ordered a general advance toward Osterhaus through the strip of forest. When Osterhaus saw the Confederates coming on through the woods, colors flying, he directed a withering artillery barrage to sweep the tree line. This was answered by rebel artillery, both sides trading fire that was "more demoralizing than destructive." Meanwhile, the Sixteenth Arkansas, advancing on Osterhaus's left through the strip of woods, caught the skirmishers of the Thirty-sixth Illinois making a dash back to their own lines and opened fire. Suddenly, the

Union riflemen found themselves hugging the ground in the middle of the big field looking for better cover than withered cornstalks. Unable to stand by and watch his men being picked off, Greusel ordered the rest of the Thirty-sixth forward to rescue them. His excited regiment delivered a massed volley that drove the Arkansans back and allowed the skirmishers to slip through the line to safety. Just then McIntosh was leading another regiment forward through the woods against the right side of the Union line. Greusel spied them and ordered another volley by the Thirty-sixth, this time killing McIntosh with a bullet to the heart in full view of his own men. This shock was enough to demoralize the Confederates. They withdrew again beyond the strip of forest, where their remaining leaders decided to wait for guidance from Hébert as to their next move. But Hébert, not knowing that he now had a whole wing to command, was himself moving forward through the tangle of Morgan's Woods as per McCulloch's plan. It was two o'clock.[70]

Back at his headquarters at Pratt's store, Curtis struggled with the problem that beset most Civil War commanders operating in wooded terrain: he could not see what was going on and had to trust his division commanders to carry the battle and keep him informed. At twelve thirty, when Carr became seriously pressed by Price's whole division north of the tavern and appealed for more help, Curtis decided to send him most of Davis's Third Division. But just after the courier left to deliver those orders to Davis, the message from Osterhaus arrived, describing the large Confederate force he had encountered at Leetown and urgently requesting reinforcements there. Curtis had to decide which division most needed help, and he ultimately chose Osterhaus because of the nearness of this threat to the main Union camp and the supply trains near Little Sugar Creek. Still not sure of Van Dorn's deployment, he kept Sigel and Asboth in reserve on the original line of battle.[71]

Just after McIntosh's death, Osterhaus spotted the first of Davis's fourteen hundred men arriving at the cornfield. The vastly relieved Osterhaus, who could now see large numbers of rebels infiltrating the brushy Morgan's Woods on his right flank, quickly briefed Davis, who immediately deployed his men (Osterhaus gave Davis back his Twenty-second Indiana) into the woods east of the Leetown Road while Osterhaus advanced into the field to face north against the large rebel force he knew still lurked just beyond the trees. Now began an intense struggle in the dense wooded ravines of Morgan's Woods between Hébert's four regiments and Davis's four, while Osterhaus with a regiment and a half stood ready to repel another attack from across the cornfield. After about forty-five minutes of sustained firing in the smoky confusion of the woods, in which neither side was able to mount a coordinated attack, a determined if disorganized Confederate charge led by Hébert himself suddenly burst from the woods across Leetown Road, drove Davis's Thirty-seventh Illinois back into the cornfield, and captured a part of one of Davis's batteries.[72]

Now all of Osterhaus's incessant drilling of his regiments paid off. With his own right flank threatened by this breakthrough, Osterhaus ordered a right wheel of his remaining regiments and artillery at double-quick time right in the middle of the big field so that they were now facing east toward Morgan's Woods instead of north. To cover his open left flank, Osterhaus sent skirmishers as well as Bussey's now regrouped cavalrymen to the north side of the cornfield. Concerned about the vulnerability of his remaining artillery in this lineup, Osterhaus kept only two howitzers on the field, withdrawing the rest to Leetown. As soon as they were in their new position Osterhaus's line let loose a hail of bullets, shell, and spherical case, while Davis's Eighteenth Indiana and Thirty-seventh Illinois charged toward the captured Federal guns. That volley and charge quickly forced the Confederates to abandon the guns and race back into the partial protection of Morgan's Woods. Thinking that the Union movement they had just witnessed in the big cornfield heralded heavy reinforcements joining the Union line, the Confederates at this point decided to retire. When they were unable to locate Hébert, the remaining Confederate officers led the way back through Morgan's Woods to Ford Road, where they found the majority of McCulloch's command, idle and waiting in vain for orders from Hébert. (Hébert had gotten separated from the bulk of his command in the thick woods and was captured by skirmishers of the Thirty-sixth Illinois after the battle.) Pike, now the ranking officer, decided to continue on the Bentonville Detour, arriving late that night with some of the men; the rest of McCulloch's force trickled in the next morning.[73]

When Curtis at last called him into action around two o'clock, Sigel took ample time making his appearance. When he finally rode past Leetown with his three remaining regiments, it was already four thirty. The bloody cornfield where he congratulated Osterhaus and Davis on their victory was silent now except for the cries of the wounded; all the noise of battle came from the direction of Elkhorn Tavern. Resuming command, Sigel led a small advance force north toward Ford Road and then eastward in the waning light. Once at the edge of the open fields that gave on Elkhorn Tavern, a half mile away, they formed into line opposite the Confederate right, but by then it was too dark to do much to help Carr. As Osterhaus saw to his men, now trying to rest in line in full battle gear in the bitter cold without blankets, food, or fire, he could still see flashes of fire in the distance as Carr battled on into the evening. Carr's forces, fighting for their lives and running out of ammunition for their batteries as well as their rifles, had been driven a half mile south, back from the tavern almost to Union headquarters at Pratt's store. A brief counterattack by Federal reinforcements led by Curtis himself stopped the rebel advance, and fighting stopped for the night as both sides ran low on ammunition. Both Carr and Asboth were wounded in the fighting.[74]

Toward morning Van Dorn was informed that his supply train was still eleven miles away at Camp Stevens and his men, besides starving, were close to being out of bullets and shell. In the Union camp, even without knowing of Van Dorn's dire supply situation, Curtis was still confident of a victory despite the fact that the rebels blocked his communication route to Missouri. The outnumbered Union army was now reunited, and Curtis still had Sigel's fresh divisions that had seen little sustained action thus far. Besides, half of Van Dorn's army was now leaderless, evening the odds somewhat. In contrast to their commander, most of the Federal troops and officers, including Asboth and Carr, who had borne the brunt of the day's fight at the tavern, saw little hope for the Union on the morrow, imagining that the whole army might be captured. Sigel was most concerned about maintaining an escape route. Osterhaus's position is not recorded.[75]

Osterhaus's command spent the night in a bitterly cold, damp cornfield near headquarters, trying to sleep on their arms without blankets until a little food (flour for "homeopathic doses of flapjacks") arrived in the morning. As the sun rose over the still, smoky fields around Elkhorn Tavern on March 8, Osterhaus rode out to reconnoiter placement for Sigel's wing in the coming day's battle. Riding up on a small knoll in the middle of the large open field to the west of the tavern, Osterhaus realized what a perfect site for artillery it was, commanding the entire Confederate position. As he hurried back to inform Sigel of his discovery he could hear Federal artillery already opening up on the right of the line. While Sigel galloped several batteries up to the knoll, Osterhaus hustled the First Division into line regiment by regiment, and by eight o'clock a most awesome sight greeted the Confederates from their own line around the tavern and up on the ridge: across the open fields in front of them, the blue line stretched farther and farther right until it extended for three-quarters of a mile, east to west. Interspersed with the regiments were the batteries, which opened fire as they came on line until all forty guns were roaring continuously.[76]

The battle quickly turned into an artillery duel, Osterhaus on the extreme left personally directing destruction of a particularly troublesome Confederate battery up on Big Mountain. He was convinced that the enemy position on the ridge and in the woods was so strong that softening up by artillery was mandatory before the Union infantry could charge across the broad open field with any hope of success. Sigel's artillery on the left side of Curtis's line soon dominated the outnumbered active Confederate batteries, Welfley's and Hoffman's crews taking them out one after another as Sigel personally directed their sighting and firing from the knoll (later called Welfley's Knoll) that Osterhaus had earlier identified. During the two hours of this literally deafening barrage, Osterhaus ordered the Union infantry to lie flat except when they were advancing. Thus, the harm inflicted by the Confederates was slight. After the first hour or so, the Confederate guns began to fall silent. Osterhaus gradually wheeled his division around from north to east facing, advancing his regiments and batteries one at a time in textbook style while the other regiments provided support. The woods could not effectively protect the Confederate infantry against the barrage from Sigel's guns, creeping ever closer. At the same time, Curtis began advancing the right wing in similar fashion up the Telegraph Road toward the tavern. The Union army now curved in a semicircle around the woods containing the rebels, enabling the bluecoats to fire on the Confederates from two directions.[77]

About ten thirty, as the Confederate artillery firing dwindled, Curtis called for an infantry advance. Osterhaus shouted in his mangled English, "Now boys, strike that the chips may fly!" (thereby earning the new nickname "Chips" Peter), and skirmishers of the First and Second Divisions led the way, cheering across the field and into the woods and up the rocky slopes of Big Mountain while the Third and Fourth charged up the Telegraph Road toward the tavern. For the most part they met little resistance, as Van Dorn had begun a pullout down the Huntsville Road, southeast from the tavern. Soon after, the two Federal wings converged on the abandoned tavern and, suddenly realizing that the day was theirs, began to celebrate deliriously their unexpected victory and "great deliverance" from what many had feared would be a catastrophe. Even the usually dour Sigel was caught with a twinkle in his eye, and "Osterhaus, never more jolly or at home than on the battlefield, was overflowing with encomiums upon 'der prave poys,' and expressions of entire satisfaction with the result." Osterhaus especially praised his Twelfth Missouri, who had recovered the flag and two brass pieces of Capt. John J. Good's Texas battery, offsetting in part his own loss of cannons. In turn, Osterhaus himself was especially commended in Curtis's battle report, noting that he "displayed great skill, energy and gallantry each day of the battle."[78]

North of the tavern, hundreds of suddenly motivated rebels in the neighborhood all managed to scramble into the woods or north up the Telegraph Road in a confused mass, leading Curtis and Sigel to think that this was the main Confederate escape route rather than the Huntsville Road. Directing Sigel to pursue them as far as practicable, Curtis returned to the battlefield. To Curtis's dismay, Sigel now mounted what looked suspiciously like a retreat, ordering Osterhaus to take the entire First Division after the rebel remnant all the way to Keetsville, Missouri, seven miles north of the Bentonville Detour, and even sending word for Curtis to send the trains as well. Curtis was furious when he found half of his army gone in the wrong direction: the next morning he brusquely ordered Sigel to return his command to the battlefield. Meanwhile, Van Dorn's and Price's battered divisions had escaped relatively unmolested down the Huntsville Road.[79]

In American newspapers, any mention of Osterhaus's significant contributions to this underdog Federal victory was greatly overshadowed by the rapturous coverage of Franz Sigel, portrayed as the true architect of the victory and Curtis as ostensibly favoring surrender. Overall, Union losses killed, wounded, and missing were 13.6 percent. The two regiments actively engaged under Osterhaus's command for both days, the Twelfth Missouri and the Thirty-sixth

Illinois, had a casualty rate of 9.1 percent, with proportionately more wounded than killed. This is an indication that their fighting was from a distance rather than close in, as a result of the tactics Osterhaus used in this open terrain. As for Osterhaus's leadership ability, Pea Ridge was the acid test: he commanded ten times the men he had led at Wilson's Creek and directed artillery and cavalry for the first time. Up for the challenge, he clearly demonstrated a grasp of the strategic thinking demanded at the level of general officer. Even had the rebel commanders not been killed at Leetown, Osterhaus's prompt spoiling action there gave the Confederate right wing enough pause to make a vital impact on the final outcome of the battle. Here also Osterhaus first demonstrated his talent for employing batteries effectively, both in creating an element of surprise at Leetown and in the strategic placement of guns for the offensive bombardment of the second day. Osterhaus also must have been especially gratified by the smart response of his well-drilled infantry to his order for a right wheel under fire in the middle of the battle at Leetown, as well as their textbook form during the advance the next day. With his cavalry Osterhaus had less success, although the desperate situation as the Battle of Leetown opened made high cavalry losses somewhat inevitable (Bussey lost 21 percent). All told, Osterhaus fairly earned a promotion to brigadier general in this battle. Whether he would get it was not at all certain.[80]

Pea Ridge marked the high point of Franz Sigel's military career. Finally promoted to major general after the battle, he was soon transferred to the eastern theater and continued a completely undistinguished performance, the low point of which was his loss to the Virginia Military Academy cadets at the Battle of Newmarket in 1864. The other commanders at Pea Ridge all went on to distinguished careers for the remainder of the war, Osterhaus serving later in other campaigns with Carr, Davis, and Dodge. Brig. Gen. Samuel Curtis was promoted as well. Assigned west of the Mississippi, he took part in no other major battles during the war, although he was instrumental in turning back Price's last raid into Missouri in 1864.[81]

After three weeks near the battlefield, Curtis took his command on a difficult march eastward across southern Missouri to counter a move Van Dorn was making in the same direction but farther south. Since Sigel had been promoted and had departed for the eastern theater, it was Osterhaus, now their permanent commander, who led the First Division in the advance of this movement. When they arrived at Batesville, Van Dorn was gone across the Mississippi, and Curtis received new orders to take Little Rock instead. Staying in Batesville by the telegraph, trying to arrange supplies and waiting for the spring floods to abate, Curtis sent Osterhaus forward with three thousand men to the Little Red River to set up a forward base just sixty miles from Little Rock. This Federal troop concentration became a thorn deep in the hide of hostile Arkansas for the next month.[82]

Osterhaus now was in independent command for the first time and had to learn to contend with a whole new range of problems. He faced a small but fierce force of irregulars who did not stand and fight but struck viciously by stealth and then slipped away when he tried to pursue. Staying in one location made the bulky army more vulnerable to Southern depredations, because by necessity the bluecoats had to range ever wider into unsecured country in order to feed themselves and their animals. And despite gathering every scrap of information he could glean from patrols, spies, scouts, and Union sympathizer-informers about Southern military activities, Osterhaus had no clear picture of what he was facing. Communications with Curtis were dicey: couriers failed to arrive, spies disappeared, messages were lost or intercepted, and there was no telegraph between Searcy and Batesville. With Curtis's other two divisions thirty miles away, ready backup was not available should Osterhaus run into a significant Confederate force. Maj. Gen. Thomas C. Hindman, who took over the meager defensive forces in the state at the end of May, conducted an astute campaign of disinformation that disguised the fact that Arkansas was virtually defenseless, with but a few companies of trained Confederate soldiers available to defend it in addition to many enthusiastic individuals and irregular rebel groups.[83]

As the weeks dragged by, the violence in Osterhaus's sector was increasing. Several of his soldiers were killed or captured; one Union soldier was beaten, mutilated, and murdered after he ill-advisedly swam across the river. That news prompted Curtis to issue instructions to Osterhaus that when the perpetrators were captured, "such villains [were] not to be taken as prisoners." On May 19 a bloody encounter between Osterhaus's foragers and the rebels took place on the south side of the Little Red River at Searcy's Landing while the Federal gleaners were unwisely spread out at several farms with their cavalry escort on down the road and no artillery support along. A hundred horsemen of the Confederate Twelfth Texas and about fifty irregulars from the Searcy area suddenly rode down the isolated bluecoats before they could take cover, mutilating and slaughtering many of those who had been wounded, even those who had already surrendered. Curtis was particularly unhappy about the fact that no artillery had been assigned to the expedition, an oversight not lost on Osterhaus in his later expeditions. Searcy's Landing was the deepest penetration the Federals were able to manage toward Little Rock on this campaign. Two weeks later Osterhaus made what he characterized as a retrograde movement back to Batesville when his supply situation became untenable and more news of a Confederate buildup made him and Carr (whose division by then was also at the Little Red) uneasy.[84]

A few days after his return, Osterhaus, to his great satisfaction, finally received the long-delayed commission of brigadier general, U.S. Volunteers, from the U.S. Senate. All spring he had been stewing about why he had been passed over, when Congress had approved the promotions of Carr, Asboth, and Davis in

March. The answer, not appreciated by him at the time, was that his was as much (or more) a political appointment as it was a military one, and in the end was achieved more by political pressure than by his performance. Although Osterhaus considered himself and conducted himself as a nonpolitical professional soldier to be judged on his performance, President Lincoln also had to consider the impact this promotion would have not only on his German American constituency but also on the governors of other states pressing him for appointments. Pressure gradually built in Osterhaus's behalf. Gustave Koerner (lieutenant governor of Illinois and Osterhaus's old friend from Belleville) wrote the president after Osterhaus finally appealed to him to do so. Now that Sigel was out of the picture, Halleck, who had held up the nomination, assured the insistent Koerner that he considered Osterhaus one of "the most intelligent and dashing officers in the service." In a private letter to Abraham Lincoln dated April 23, Forty-Eighter and now brigadier general Carl Schurz also "most earnestly" requested that the president appoint Osterhaus. This, plus an active letter-writing campaign in the St. Louis German American press, may have done some good. Lincoln resubmitted the nomination to the Senate two weeks after he received Schurz's letter, and it was soon approved.[85]

Although in rank and seniority his new grade was roughly two levels below brigadier general rank in the regular army, Osterhaus welcomed the additional income it would mean for his family as well as the recognition it conferred. If his diary of 1864 is an indication, Osterhaus wrote often to his family, so he must have been delighted to pass on the news. During the next two weeks in camp the new general held daily maneuvers, which in the burgeoning summer heat amid the swarms of gnats quickly became just as onerous to the men as patrol had been. They were eager to get on the move again, just to escape drill practice, but Osterhaus felt strongly that drill and discipline were essential.[86]

Stymied by the limits of his land supply line, Curtis's best hope for getting relief was via steamer up the White River from the Arkansas River from an expedition being led by U. S. Grant. On June 25, his men now completely out of food, Curtis made the independent decision to move his army down the White River to meet the rescue flotilla at Clarendon. This began what was the first instance in the war of an army moving through enemy territory entirely unsupported and out of communication with headquarters, presaging Sherman's March to the Sea (which, of these commanders, only Osterhaus would experience) but without the benefit of a bountiful countryside to sustain the army.[87]

On July 10 the blue column finally reached Clarendon. They were by now completely out of food except for whatever beef they could round up in the vicinity; even the army-issue crackers that had been selling briskly for a dollar each were long gone. The only drinking water came from the swamps, covered in enough green scum to "float a hat." But just twenty-four hours before Curtis finally brought his struggling army into Clarendon, the Federal supply boats moved from there downstream to deeper water on Grant's orders. Curtis could not find any information about the whereabouts of the supply boats so decided to turn away from the White and sprint toward the Mississippi River at Helena, sixty miles due east, where he could be sure of resupply. He would mount his attack on Little Rock from there.[88]

This would be a situation in which a division would want to be in the lead, both to escape the worst of the dust and to have first pick of whatever gleanings there were, and Brigadier General Osterhaus finally had the advance. His men were efficient: "A march of twenty-one miles was made with little food, Osterhaus' German troops having swept the country bare," commented an officer following in the Thirty-third Illinois. In his memoirs Osterhaus vividly described this last leg of the march: "This march was a rough piece of work; it led through the dismal Cane brakes and Swamps, thickly set with Cypress trees of the River Cache and other sluggish watercourses; there were no buildings or Roads, and torrent-like rainstorms impeded our progress. No wonder that an outcry of joy, rung up from our Column, where after six weary days the yellow waters of the Mississippi and the snug houses of Helena came in sight."[89]

It was on this last segment of the march through the swamps that Osterhaus began to complain of symptoms of malaria. Once at Helena, Osterhaus began to lose weight, suffering from high fever and dysentery. Although urged by his officers to take a sick leave, Osterhaus continued to gulp quinine and swore that he would rather die than to leave his men just then. However, his once robust health quickly deteriorated to the point that Curtis granted him a twenty-day leave to go to St. Louis for treatment, accompanied by his body servant, Pvt. Adolph Wagner. By this time he was so weak that he could not walk without support.[90]

After a brief stay in St. Louis with his family, whom he had not seen in nearly a year, Osterhaus returned to Helena and resumed his command on August 4. He lasted just three weeks before he was sent home for another month, this time not returning until October 2. A few days later, Curtis ordered Osterhaus's division up the Mississippi on an expedition to Ironton, Missouri. But as soon as the troops were loaded onto steamers, Osterhaus was forced to take to his cabin, deathly ill once more. Back he went to St. Louis, where he spent the rest of the year in bed under the care of his old friend Dr. Adam Hammer, chafing that he had had to leave his command in the midst of a campaign.[91]

Osterhaus would never regain the robust health he had always taken for granted, but nonetheless he was anxious to get back to active duty. He fully expected to resume command of his division at Helena when he had recovered, but his new disappointing orders assigned him to command of just one of three brigades of his old division, now reorganized and enlarged, the whole to be commanded by West Pointer Frederick Steele. Fortunately for Osterhaus, before he was well enough to join it, Steele's division left on December 20 to support Maj. Gen. William T. Sherman's strike against Vicksburg at Chickasaw Bayou. And when Osterhaus finally returned to the war on December 31, it was to a very different assignment: the command of a large nonethnic division in the army of Maj. Gen. U. S. Grant.[92]

Chapter 3
The Vicksburg Campaign

AS BRIG. Gen. Joseph Osterhaus languished in bed at home during the fall of 1862, the Union effort faltered. Toward the end of the year, Osterhaus read with dismay that the Union troops had suffered severe losses in the East, most recently at Fredericksburg, and the war effort had stalled in the West. But he was encouraged to read about the latest Federal effort now getting under way to capture Vicksburg, which controlled river traffic on the Mississippi. The prospects seemed daunting: Vicksburg was nearly impregnable. Confederate batteries along its high bluff covered the Mississippi River for three miles in each direction and prevented an infantry attack from directly across the river. A few miles north of town, the Yazoo River dribbled into the Mississippi from the east in a series of swamps and bayous, with the high ground between the tributary and Vicksburg commanded by Confederates. Beyond that to the north was more wet, low, roadless, impassable country. Similar wet terrain to the south of the town would limit the landing and movement of troops there for many miles as well. The only possible land approach was from the east through rebel-held country, where miles of Confederate trenches protected the city.[1]

In mid-December, Grant launched a two-pronged attack toward Vicksburg in which he would push south overland to draw off Gen. John C. Pemberton's defenders to the east of Vicksburg, while sending Maj. Gen. William T. Sherman to attack the town from the Yazoo River at Chickasaw Bayou. But Grant's half was aborted, and Confederates on the bluffs easily repulsed Sherman's bluecoats as they struggled through the swamps of the Yazoo. As Sherman was pulling back his frustrated and bloodied army to regroup across the Mississippi at Milliken's Bend, ten miles above the mouth of the Yazoo, Maj. Gen. John McClernand arrived on the scene. This much-disliked congressman, a friend of Lincoln who outranked Sherman, was full of ambition to take on overall command of the Vicksburg campaign. Despite having had no military training, he was a quicker study than some and had performed reasonably well in command of a division under Grant at Shiloh. Unfortunately for his ambitions, he blew his own horn to a degree that seriously pained both Grant and Sherman, who were close friends as well as colleagues.[2]

At Milliken's Bend on January 3, McClernand, Sherman, and Rear Adm. David D. Porter met to hear Sherman's latest proposal: he wanted to take his two divisions, supported by the navy's gunboats, about fifty miles up the Arkansas River to knock out a rebel fort at a town called Arkansas Post. This rebel stronghold had the capability to disrupt any operations on Vicksburg by interfering with Union river traffic. To Sherman's disgust, after listening to the plan, McClernand decided to take along all four divisions in his command, thirty thousand bluecoats, and lead the expedition himself. Sherman and Porter both loathed what they saw as McClernand's posturing and ambition, and the friction among the three Union leaders in this battle impacted how history would view Osterhaus's contribution to its outcome.[3]

Only ten days out of bed, the still somewhat wan Osterhaus left St. Louis for the front by steamer on December 31, joining McClernand's expedition on its way upriver on January 6. When he reported for orders he found McClernand to be a tall, wiry man with dark hair and beard who asked a lot of questions once he appreciated Osterhaus's expertise. McClernand had divided his four divisions into two corps under Sherman and Brig. Gen. George W. Morgan. Morgan's corps was composed of the First Division under A. J. Smith and the Second, Morgan's old division, yet unassigned. After talking to Osterhaus, McClernand decided that the German would take this division. Although Osterhaus was flattered, this unit being much larger than any of his previous commands, the appointment caused him no little consternation. For the first time, he would not know a single one of the native-born men or officers whom he would command. Back on the transports after their defeat under awful conditions at Yazoo Bluffs, the badly demoralized Second Division had had no chance even to clean the swamp muck off or to eat a decent meal since then. After all the men had gone through, Osterhaus worried that having an immigrant general assigned as their commander might be the last straw.[4]

Osterhaus had only four days to prepare his ten new regiments for another battle, during which time his command was separated on a dozen different transports steaming toward Arkansas Post. The best he could do was to digest and clearly communicate the battle plan, issued the same day he arrived, to his three brigade commanders, Cols. Lionel A. Sheldon, Daniel W. Lindsey, and John F. DeCourcy. He also made a point of meeting with his new gunners, Capt. W. J. Lanphere of the Seventh Michigan Light Artillery with one thirty-pounder Parrott and two ten-pounder Rodmans, and Capt. J. T. Foster of the First Wisconsin Light, the "La Crosse Artillery," with four twenty-pounder Parrotts. This was the first time that Osterhaus was to use Parrotts, big rifled guns weighing nearly a ton each.[5]

Newly minted Brig. Gen. Osterhaus, December 1862. His ceremonial sword is at the Missouri Historical Society, St. Louis. (Courtesy the Library of Congress)

Late on the afternoon of January 9, the impressive Union flotilla pulled to shore three miles downstream from the fort, named after Maj. Gen. Thomas C. Hindman, Osterhaus's nemesis in the Arkansas campaign the previous summer, and began to disembark Sherman's two divisions. Meanwhile, Morgan immediately split Osterhaus's new command, sending Lindsey's brigade, with a section of ten-pounder Parrott rifles detailed from A. J. Smith's division, to a position across the river and upstream from the fort to block Confederate reinforcements. Before they left, Osterhaus issued Lindsey, a Kentucky lawyer with no battle experience so far, very careful instructions on how they should proceed, given the reports of rebel cavalry in the area, and with crossed fingers sent them off. Osterhaus had learned from sad experience the fate of ill-prepared forays into enemy territory.[6]

The Federal flotilla had been spotted that morning by the Confederates, whose commander, Brig. Gen. Thomas J. Churchill, did not have to know the exact numbers in the blue horde to realize he had a daunting task ahead, in fact was outnumbered six to one with little prospect of relief. In response to vigorous Union naval shelling, he entrenched his two brigades in a line of rifle pits just north of the fort. That evening the Union gunboats began another two-hour barrage, this time of the fort itself, firing from a cramped range of less than four hundred yards because the Confederates had driven pilings into the river to pinch its navigable width opposite the fort. Fort Hindman's cannon responded, but no real damage was done on either side, with one exception: one Federal gunboat took several hits from the rebel guns.[7]

Once ashore late on January 9, Osterhaus lost two of his mighty Parrotts, detached by Morgan and shipped across the river to reinforce Lindsey. Osterhaus had been given a special assignment for the next day: Porter had requested that the army take out the lower casemated cannon that had been so troublesome during the evening barrage. Osterhaus's assigned position on the Union left flank would make his batteries the logical ones to do the work, but now with only two Parrotts, this would be a challenge. Smith's division sent him four six-pounder howitzers in partial compensation, but Osterhaus thought they would be of little use for his assault on the casemates, and he expected to keep them in reserve.[8]

The earthen fort that the Union army faced had been built on a high bluff on the outer curve of a hairpin bend of the Arkansas River. Looming a farther ten to twenty feet high and surrounded by a deep ditch, the fort was shaped like a four-pointed star. On the river side, one point, or bastion, pointed upstream and another downstream. Churchill had three big smoothbores, borrowed from the Confederate navy, all facing the river: a nine-inch Columbiad in each of the two bastions and one eight-incher in the middle of the wall. (An eight-inch gun could throw a sixty-five-pound shot more than two miles.) The northernmost two guns were casemated, protected by roofs of railroad iron and oak plates.

The other, a nine-incher with a special swiveling mount, was situated on a platform atop the wall behind a low parapet so that it could fire over the top instead of through an embrasure like the others. This gave it much more maneuverability of aim than the casemated guns, but also made its crew more vulnerable to enemy fire. In the gun emplacements overlooking the land sides of the fort were eight smaller field pieces. Commanding the brigade and artillery inside the fort was Col. John W. Dunnington, late of the Confederate navy.[9]

On the northwestern (land) side of the fort, the line of Confederate trenches closest to the fort, by dint of all-night digging, now extended from the fort wall seven hundred yards to a shallow bayou and swamp to the west. In front of the trenches was a ditch full of abatis and brush that transitioned into a deep gully at Osterhaus's end of the line, nearest the river and fort. Looking over the ditch, the Confederates had a clear field of fire across a marshy field that afforded little cover for the bluecoats. McClernand's soldiers would have to dash from the woods across the open field and negotiate the ditch, squeezing through the abatis one at a time before they could charge the trenches.[10]

With Lindsey's brigade across the river and DeCourcy's brigade, which had been terribly cut up at Chicasaw Bayou, assigned to the rear to guard the transport boats with Captain Lanphere's three artillery pieces, as the battle began on sunny January 10 Osterhaus commanded just Sheldon's brigade (three regiments) and the two twenty-pounder Parrotts. By ten o'clock Lt. Dan Webster and the First Wisconsin battery had wrestled the pair of Parrotts over the swampy ground and through the trees next to the river, about eight hundred yards northeast of the fort. Osterhaus had him set up his cannons in a concealed position behind a big log, with orders not to unmask the Parrotts until ready to fire in order to minimize the chance of their getting blasted by the much larger guns they were facing. He supported the battery with the 118th Illinois infantry. The 69th Indiana and 120th Ohio were in line in front, connected on the right to A. J. Smith's division. Along the crowded front to the west, Sherman's corps completed the Union deployment beyond Smith to the bayou, ranked several lines deep in the tree line across from the rebel trenches. McClernand's battle plan called for a bombardment by Porter's gunboats beginning at one o'clock, which would be the signal for the Federal field batteries to join in from the edge of the woods. After a half hour, the guns would halt for a Union charge toward the Confederate trenches, beginning at Sherman's end at the bayou and ending with Osterhaus's brigade on the river.[11]

Osterhaus had placed his two rifled Parrotts opposite the tip of the nearest bastion, so that they could enfilade both faces with clear sight lines to the offending casemate. Then he had the sense to get out of the way and watch. As soon as the gunboats fired the signal shot, his gunners immediately began to home in on their assigned targets, only sparing the largest gun above on the parapet for Porter's gunboats to take out, at the admiral's request. With just a few shots the First Wisconsin gunners calibrated the trajectory to hit the gun embrasures, and once on target they continued to pump shot after shot into the apertures until the nearest nine-inch and the eight-inch Columbiads were knocked out, as was a twelve-pounder on the north parapet. Osterhaus galloped up excitedly in the midst of the cannonade to congratulate Webster on his success: "You are doing more good than all the gunboats; I have never seen such shooting!" he roared. This was the first time he had observed the accuracy that rifling added to artillery fire, since in his other battles the field pieces had been mostly twelve-pounder howitzers, smoothbores with a higher and less precise trajectory. It was also the first time he had seen the new ironclad boats in action.[12]

A short time later, the Union ironclad *De Kalb* took a direct hit from the nine-inch Columbiad high on top of the wall, destroying one of the gunboat's big ten-inch guns. The fort's big cannon was apparently too high for the naval gunners to reach at their guns' maximum elevation, crowded as close in to the bank as they were because of the narrow channel. Osterhaus had seen enough: "Silence that gun or it would sink the fleet," he ordered, and it was so done with just three or four shots that fractured the massive barrel and disabled the carriage. Later a rebel gunner who had been working the guns in the lower casemates commented, "That little battery on the field did us more harm than all the fleet, as it would not let us work our guns."[13]

Once the biggest smoothbores were silenced, the Union advance began against the trenches, but the infantry still found it heavy going. The Confederate riflemen held their fire until the Federals were within short range and then let loose a murderous volley that pinned them down, driving them to ground behind any mound or tree stump they could find. When it was Osterhaus's turn to send out his brigade, he waved the 120th Ohio forward, but they ran into the same withering fire from the rifle pits. Ordering the men to stay flat, Osterhaus hustled up the battery of six-pounder howitzers, the excited gunners facing their first battle, and set them to fire at the rifle pits ahead and then down the length of the Confederate trenches, a tactic that did great damage. Then he galloped up to the 120th Ohio and ordered them to jump up and charge at the double-quick, shouting with a cheer that the Southerners were "nearly whipped." To his relief, the men obeyed their new German commander immediately, although they were soon pinned down again in the gully below the wall of the fort. One soldier described the harrowing experience: "The blue beans flew into our ranks, bringing death and destruction. Since it was impossible to get over the barricade, we were all crowded into the trap and our boys fell like flies." There they lay, firing from a prone position, until white flags went up from the Confederate trenches a short time later.[14]

By now some of the Federal gunboats had boldly churned upriver past the silenced guns of the fort and were blasting it from both up- and downriver, as well as blocking the Confederate escape route. Under cover of their fire, Colonel Lindsey across the river moved Osterhaus's other brigade closer to a point opposite the fort. Now Lindsey had a perfect line of fire down the rebel trenches, and he began lobbing in shells as well. Soon it was all over. Wrote Confederate colonel Robert R. Garland, "The enemy's batteries and gunboats had complete command of the position, taking it in front, flank and rear at the same time, literally raking our entire position." At four thirty the Federal forces entered the fort and accepted Churchill's surrender.[15]

In his battle report McClernand praised Osterhaus's performance and had relatively little to say about the work of the gunboats. In his own official report, Porter claimed that the guns were silenced by his three ironclads, although not one of his captains made that assertion directly. (Only Lt. George M. Bache of the *Cincinnati* reported that the fortress gun assigned to him "was silenced," but he carefully did not indicate by whom.) But Porter stated later unequivocally, "I attacked it [the fort] with three ironclads and several smaller vessels, and in three hours disabled all the guns." In the contemporaneous news accounts of the battle as well as in later histories, all credence was given to Porter's claim, and his friend Sherman supported this version of events, although from his position at the far inland end of the line he probably could not see what actually happened. Parroting Porter, the press gave Osterhaus almost no credit for his battery's contribution to the victory, although one obscure early history did credit his rifled guns with silencing the fort cannon and the 120th Ohio with being the first into the fort.[16]

Even though they were given at best dual credit with Porter's gunboats, eyewitnesses such as Osterhaus, Sheldon, and Lindsey, as well as the Union gunnery spotter who visually tracked each shot all the way in, made a convincing case that the artillery work of Osterhaus's division was the key to taking this well-defended Confederate position. Webster of the First Wisconsin battery observed that the Confederate smoothbores were higher than the maximum elevation of the Federal naval guns, causing most of the navy's shots to hit the bank below the fort. Too, his men got the first shots in right after the signal gun was fired, and by the time the ironclads steamed within range the Confederate guns were already silenced. The enfilade fire from Lindsey's position across the river was the coup de grâce that hastened the surrender.[17]

Osterhaus's first experience attacking a fort and well-entrenched rifle pits was an eye-opener. Here were defenders outnumbered six to one who were handily holding their own against a massed frontal assault. The advantage was definitely to entrenched and fortified defenders unless some way could be found to flank them, or, as happened here, to mount an artillery enfilade of their trenches. In Osterhaus's first work with rifled Parrotts he was awed by their power in the hands of a skilled artillery team. "The effect of the combined fire of the Fleet and Army was perceptible, my 20 Pounders proved of extraordinary weight; the embrasures of the bastion were cut and opened into large ouvertures, increasing the destruction made by their shells, within," he wrote. Osterhaus would not be the first officer riveted by the terrible beauty and power of artillery.[18]

After a few days of work to raze the fort, on January 14 in a pouring rain Osterhaus's new division reembarked on their several fetid transport steamers, which had been their homes for the past month and would be for several more days to come. Now Osterhaus had a whole new set of concerns, besides keeping his boats together with his flagship *Tigress* and finding fuel ashore for them. As they slowly made their way back to Milliken's Bend, the joy of victory could not overcome the misery of their truly hellish living conditions, made more excruciating by rain that flooded them out of their bedrolls on the decks followed by an unusual cold snap leaving five inches of snow. On the first mild day, Osterhaus endeared himself to his men when he ordered his boats thoroughly cleaned and the men into the river to bathe, orders that were greeted with cheers. This remedy did not reach all of his boats, but did help some of the men and improved morale. With satisfaction, he noted that he never had a speck of resistance to his "foreign" leadership after that.[19]

The men were finally able to escape their floating misery on January 21, trading it for a camp in four inches of gluey mud and incessant rain at Young's Point, Louisiana, on and behind the Mississippi levee a bit west of Vicksburg. Shortly thereafter, Grant officially superseded McClernand, dropping him to command of the Thirteenth Corps. Osterhaus continued to lead Morgan's old Second Division, now designated the Ninth, under McClernand. With this change, Osterhaus became the only immigrant division commander serving under Grant for the first two years of the war, but it almost did not happen: in mid-March McClernand had to resist Grant's attempt to foist another general on him, saying that he was reluctant to replace either Osterhaus or Smith, both men "having proved their merit and gained the confidence of their men." Most of Osterhaus's units were the same as those he had led at Arkansas Post, although he added the Seventh Kentucky Infantry and Third Illinois Cavalry and lost the Third Kentucky Infantry Regiment. Osterhaus's two now larger brigades were led by Col. Lionel A. Sheldon, an Ohio judge, and the Seventh Kentucky's Brig. Gen. Theophilus T. Garrard, a Kentucky state legislator who had served in the Mexican War but had no combat experience (Garrard regarded Osterhaus as "one of the most unassuming and energetic officers I have met").[20]

Grant had strung his large command for miles up and down the levee on the west side of the Mississippi. Osterhaus described in graphic fashion the miserable Young's Point camp that housed his six thousand men:

> At the time of our landing, the river was very high and rising: extensive sheets of water covered the level lands and left only few dry spots. Indeed the Levees along the river were the sole protection of and the ground itself for our Camps,

> which extended from Milliken's Bend (XIII Army Corps) south beyond Young's Point (15th Army Corps). They, the levees, had not only to furnish the necessary room for the Men and officers, hospital and all appurtenances of an Army but also the burial places of our Dead. And we had to register numbers of Dead; many regiments were decimated and their effective strength had dwindled down to 200–100 and even less. The dire necessity of the active operations since November had subjected the troops to extraordinary hardships, while crowded together in narrow dingy steamboats, or passing the winter nights exposed to all the inclemmencies of the season and the malarial climate. It was most melancholy to see from the Camps on the levee Coffins with departed Comrades, floating by; the swollen stream had torn from the levees a part of the ground reserved for a cemetery, and carried the remains to a watery grave. But such is war.[21]

The camp itself was on marshy land behind the levee, the water level at that time fifteen feet higher than the camp and rising practically as a man watched. There was no way to dry out and no fresh food to be found. Worst of all, there was no clean water, which added to the incidence of disease. Many of the men were ill, and a good number were dying of contagious diseases such as typhoid, dysentery, smallpox, and measles, complicated by homesickness, malnutrition, scurvy, and poor medical care. Osterhaus suffered along with his men: in his case a return of his malaria and dysentery. One regiment, the 114th Ohio, reportedly was burying from two to seven men a day. Morale was abysmal. Osterhaus tried to instill proper sanitation, cleanliness, and nutrition to reduce the sickness, but in these conditions he was fighting a futile battle. He was appalled at the "miserable, careless and unmilitary style" he observed in men performing guard duty; he found one man stripped and picking off lice when he should have been on guard. Many of the officers and physicians spent their time drinking and gambling, neglecting their responsibilities. Commenting on one resignation, the frustrated Osterhaus wrote, "Besides being deficient in military knowledge and spirit it would appear from the style of his resignation that Capt. Clark is utterly illiterate." Osterhaus struggled to replace this sort of duly elected officer when he could, encouraging the good ones with kindness and respect.[22]

Despite the lack of available fresh produce and other foodstuffs, officers had not only to furnish their own food but to fund mess servants; Osterhaus was under an obligation to entertain his officers occasionally at mess. Somewhere in this campaign he acquired a valued mess caterer, Joe Miller, a slave who had run away to join the Northern army. (Miller became a prosperous farmer and carpenter in Kansas after the war.) "Negro Joe" was with Osterhaus for most of the rest of the war and was adept at procuring food, but during these winter days the pickings for a decent meal were very slim.[23]

To top it all off, the Ninth Division's assignment for the next few weeks was to help dig a ditch. This was not just any ditch, but Grant's attempt to bypass

Vicksburg by cutting a navigable canal sixty feet wide across the base of the oxbow bend in the Mississippi. If they were successful, Vicksburg's fortifications could be rendered moot. Toward the end of February the rain eased, and with a full moon the men worked day and night to finish the channel. Unfortunately, in the first week of March, the temporary levee across the north end of the canal dig suddenly broke in a heavy rainstorm, and water poured in, inundating their work, flooding the peninsula, and nearly drowning the men. With their camps now underwater, they hastily scrambled higher onto the levee.[24]

Osterhaus and his men were lucky: there was not room on top of the levee for all the troops, so the Thirteenth Corps was loaded back onto the boats and headed upriver to higher ground at Milliken's Bend. If Young's Point had been purgatory, the higher ground at Milliken's Bend was an Eden to McClernand's muddy and miserable army. There was plenty of room for Osterhaus to set up a dry and orderly camp in the broad fields, and the fresh green shoots of grass popping up were good for combating scurvy. The general lost no time in ordering the men to be washed and combed, cleaned and brushed, tucked in and buttoned, boots polished and blackened, and reinstituted the ever-popular daily drills while leaving time for baseball in the afternoon. More important to their health, he kept a sharp eye on the latrines and disposal of other waste, both at Milliken's Bend and throughout the campaign. The men reveled in a clean camp and clean clothes and gradually regained their "wonted elasticity and vim."[25]

They were thrilled when the paymaster finally caught up with them and they were paid months of back wages. Osterhaus now had the wherewithal to put on a fine German dinner for his officers. It was in this atmosphere that his staff got to know their new ethnic commander a bit and judged him to be "a German officer of admirable qualities, who had distinguished himself at Pea Ridge and other important engagements in the west." Osterhaus was deemed a by-the-books sort of leader, "Dutch as sauerkraut," but one who was approachable. One of his officers wrote of his first impressions of his new commander: "Contrary to my expectations . . . I found a man free from any of those prejudices usual almost with German Officers and besides all this a Gentleman and an Officer who from the very first had treated me with much cordiality and Preferment. . . . General Osterhaus is one of natures Nobleman and the best and most active General as i yet met in America. . . . He is a good man, intelligent and a splendid scholar."[26]

During that wet spring, Grant kept his army busy with other schemes to try to capture Vicksburg, but all failed. Toward the end of March, Washington was getting decidedly testy, and Grant had nothing to show for his efforts except determination. The only way he could see to get the army across the Mississippi onto firm ground to the rear of Vicksburg was to move it to a suitable jumping-off point several miles south of town beyond the batteries. The problem was that his gunboats and transports, as well as his men, were all north of the Vicksburg guns. But as spring advanced and the river began to fall, roads and fields started to emerge from the stagnant floodwaters. A land route south began to look feasible.[27]

In 1863 the Mississippi River meandered southeast at Milliken's Bend, turned generally south at Vicksburg for twenty miles, then back westward to New Carthage, before wending south once more. The rich bottomland west of the Mississippi River was underwater that spring except for the natural levees the river had thrown up over the millennia next to its vestigial courses, now faded into a series of shallow bayous and narrow lakes full of alligators, snakes, and mosquitoes. The narrow, flat levees, only a few feet above the stagnant water, were punctuated every mile or two by wider spots occupied by now mostly deserted plantation houses. The only roads in the area were isolated local segments on the levees, frequently interrupted by water breaks, some natural, some added lately by Confederates. This early in the year, all the levee roads were still a morass of knee-deep bogs and puddles that would swallow a wagon's axles.[28]

Grant's latest plan to approach Vicksburg was to take a land route via mostly unmapped back roads south from Milliken's Bend via Richmond to meet up with the meandering river at New Carthage, well below the Vicksburg batteries. Once back at the Mississippi the army would join Porter's gunboats and transports, assuming they could successfully run the Vicksburg batteries, and then prepare for the big troop crossing. Moving a large army with all its wagons and supplies through that soggy country, running the formidable naval gauntlet, and finding a dry spot big enough to stage a full-scale invasion across the river constituted such a daunting challenge that most of Grant's generals were skeptical, if not downright negative. Only McClernand was enthusiastic and indeed eager for the assignment of leading the way. Over the objections of his other generals, Grant ordered McClernand to kick off the campaign, and McClernand chose Brig. Gen. Joseph Osterhaus's Ninth Division to lead what has been called "the most difficult advance of the war."[29]

Osterhaus was eager to start. Now he really came into his element, his skills in leading the advance through unmapped hostile country having been honed in the swamps of Arkansas the summer before. For the next month the Union army would move down the narrow levees from plantation to plantation like a giant inchworm negotiating a fragile twig, with Osterhaus as its eyes and McClernand running back and forth to Milliken's Bend to keep Grant informed. To kick off the campaign, on March 31 Osterhaus sent off an initial reconnaissance patrol that he figured should be ready for almost any contingency: the Sixty-ninth Indiana Infantry under Col. Thomas Bennett, two cavalry companies, two mountain howitzers, a company of Kentucky engineers under Capt. W. F. Patterson, and a bevy of pontoons and small boats on wagons. Calling themselves "the Argonauts," this excited group of a thousand men, with visions of being the first to

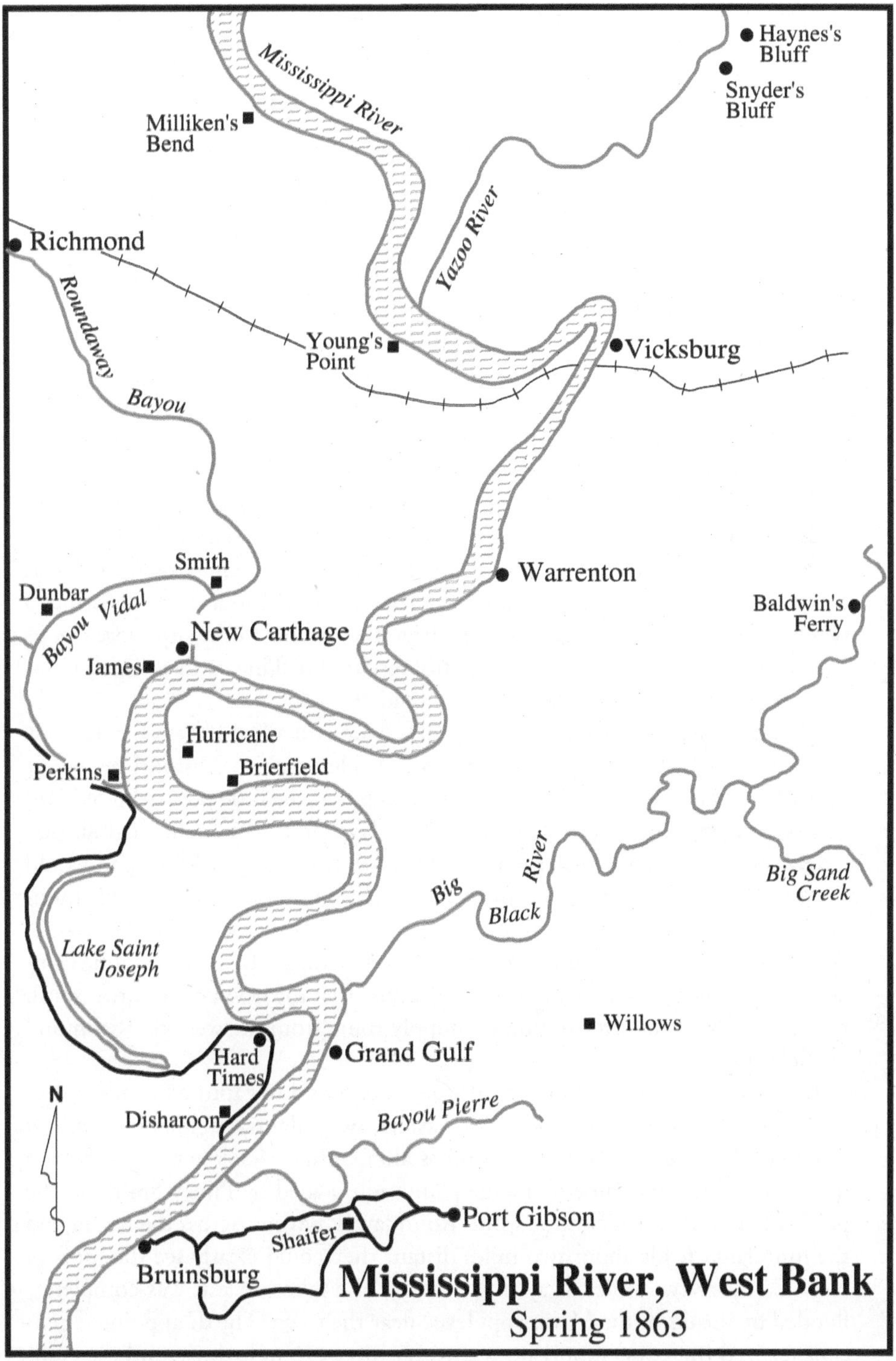
Mississippi River
Milliken's Bend
Haynes's Bluff
Snyder's Bluff
Yazoo River
Richmond
Roundaway Bayou
Young's Point
Vicksburg
Smith
Dunbar
Bayou Vidal
New Carthage
James
Warrenton
Baldwin's Ferry
Hurricane
Perkins
Brierfield
Big Black River
Big Sand Creek
Lake Saint Joseph
Willows
Hard Times
Grand Gulf
N
Disharoon
Bayou Pierre
Port Gibson
Shaifer
Bruinsburg
Mississippi River, West Bank
Spring 1863

sample the bounty of the deserted plantations in the area, stepped out eagerly on a beautiful spring morning, watched by glum comrades left behind.[30]

The only Confederate force keeping an eye out for Federal activity in the area was a single cavalry battalion, the 240 men and six howitzers of the Fifteenth Louisiana Cavalry under Maj. Isaac F. Harrison, with orders to report anything significant to Lt. Gen. Edmund Kirby Smith, commander of the Confederate Trans-Mississippi, at Shreveport, Louisiana. But Harrison knew that any support he needed would have to come from nearby, so he also made courtesy reports to Brig. Gen. John Bowen, across the Mississippi at Grand Gulf (Bowen had been Osterhaus's prisoner in the Camp Jackson affair). Bowen in turn reported to Lt. Gen. John Pemberton, commanding the entire Vicksburg arena east of the river from his headquarters fifty miles east at the state capital, Jackson.[31]

Osterhaus's patrol soon spotted Harrison's pickets at Richmond, across Roundaway Bayou from the road's end. Quickly launching their small boats and using their rifle butts as oars, the dismounted Second Illinois Cavalry paddled eagerly across the swift-flowing bayou, then outflanked and drove the Confederate pickets down the levee road a few miles, while Bennett took possession of the town. Next day, Osterhaus came forward himself, and by the evening of April 2 had moved another brigade into the town and had directed Patterson to construct a two hundred–foot log bridge across the bayou so he could bring up more troops and wagons. Meanwhile, his cavalry patrol reported making contact with a Confederate patrol about ten miles down the road.[32]

Harrison suspected something unusual was up and asked Bowen for support, which Bowen was able to provide on April 4. He sent two Missouri regiments under Col. Francis Cockrell across the Mississippi to the little port town of Hard Times, followed by a third regiment a few days later. (Osterhaus had already faced Cockrell's tough Missourians at Wilson's Creek and Pea Ridge and would see them repeatedly throughout the war.) Cockrell immediately set up his thousand grayclads in a strong position on the Mississippi levee at the burned-out Perkins plantation, a few miles south of New Carthage. Back in Jackson, Pemberton still was not overly concerned; he figured that the new Union thrust south was merely aimed at interrupting the supply route from the west via Richmond to Vicksburg.[33]

Early on April 3 Osterhaus set off from Richmond to capture his first objective, New Carthage, taking about 250 cavalry, two infantry regiments, and four mountain howitzers. About twelve miles along, after McClernand had ridden up to join him, they came to a large plantation owned by Pliney Smith, at the point where Bayou Vidal flowed into Roundaway Bayou. Across the bayou and the inundated fields about two miles distant they could clearly see the roofs of New Carthage two miles away in the midst of a lake, since it was completely flooded by breaks in the Mississippi levee near the town. The disappointed generals realized there was simply no way to get there except by boat, and the Confederates had either destroyed or appropriated for their own use all the boats in the area.[34]

At that point, spotting Harrison's mounted pickets in the distance on his own side of the bayou, Osterhaus and a patrol took off after them down the levee road as it veered to the west from Smith's plantation to another plantation, Dunbar's. By the time the Federals galloped up to the property, the Southern pickets had splashed out of reach east across Bayou Vidal to their encampment on the Perkins plantation over on the Mississippi. His progress stymied until he could get hold of some sizable boats, Osterhaus took his patrol back to Smith's, leaving cheerful pickets at Dunbar's and several other plantations along the route. (Two weeks after they started out Osterhaus reported that there had not been a single instance of wanton destruction, by which he must have simply meant arson since the looting was ubiquitous: one officer wrote his wife, "My boys live in clover; they all eat off of china dishes . . . and have their tents carpeted.")[35]

When they got back to Smith's there was still daylight left, so Osterhaus and McClernand decided to take their skiff and a small flatboat and scout along the fragmented levee that extended along Roundaway Bayou to New Carthage. They wanted to see whether the levee could be repaired or, alternatively, if steamboats would be able to ferry troops via the bayou to the Mississippi levee near the flooded town. Accompanied by one of McClernand's staff and three soldiers, the two generals strolled along the levee, boarding the boats when they had to in order to navigate the several crevasses or breaks that they encountered. On this foray things went poorly for Osterhaus, who, after all, had swum entire rivers to escape the Prussians in his earlier life. At one crevasse, as he stepped into the flatboat it suddenly dipped away, leaving him suspended with both feet in the boat and one hand on shore. After an endless, teetering moment he ignominiously splashed in. The laughter was uproarious, and he probably joined in, even though he must have been terribly embarrassed by the indignity in front of his commander. Standing up with difficulty, he tried to wade across the gap, but the current was too swift. Finally, the men had to haul him into the skiff by the scruff, wet as a water rat.[36]

Farther along the levee, about a half mile from the town, a rebel bullet from pickets in the town suddenly zipped through the little party, forcing them to dive for the back side of the levee. Osterhaus caught McClernand, sure he was about to fall in, and the soldiers whipped around behind him to shore him up. McClernand thought they were hiding behind him and blustered, "Damn you, stand fire, don't you run, stand fire, damn you!" That set the men off in fits of giggles. The odd little patrol ducked down behind the levee and traded fire with the Confederates for a while, finally reboarding their boats and making their way back to the Smith plantation, soggy but in good humor. Despite the excitement, they had accomplished their mission: it seemed feasible for steamers to transfer the troops waiting at Smith's plantation across to New Carthage, that is, if Grant could find a way to get the boats to McClernand through the maze of bayous. That evening McClernand in his dispatch to Grant commended Osterhaus's "activity and zeal," despite the dunking his general had taken. Osterhaus's men gave him high marks as well. John Ritter, doctor for the Forty-ninth Indiana, wrote his wife, "Thus far Gen. Ostehaus is quite a favorite. He is a Dutchman, a verry plain man, quite Socible."[37]

While McClernand was writing his dispatch that evening, five escaped slaves appeared in camp and told Osterhaus that there was a big flatboat hidden several miles downstream on Bayou Vidal, guarded by Confederate pickets. The contrabands offered to guide a Union patrol to go get it, and Osterhaus wasted no time sending them out. This vessel became the centerpiece of the armada that Osterhaus quickly improvised to take New Carthage. The ingenious Patterson and his Kentucky engineers quickly adapted the flatboat as a primitive but useful gunboat, building up the sides as high as a man's head with wood planks in which they cut portholes for oars and for the mountain howitzer that they mounted in the bow. With its rows of seats, the odd craft looked like a "war galley of old." The men aptly christened her the *Opossum*.[38]

On April 6 the little attack force was launched: two infantry companies from the Forty-ninth Indiana and Sixty-ninth Indiana and the mountain howitzer, fifty-four men in all. With commodore Osterhaus as figurehead, the *Opossum* carried twenty-five soldiers and the howitzer. The rest of the men manned flats, skiffs, and canoes. "Spread out like a line of skirmishers," the little fleet picked its way through bayous and across fields, occasionally getting tangled in the undergrowth and limbs of the submerged woods. Tying up near the inundated town, Osterhaus advanced his patrol down the Mississippi levee for about a mile until they came to a plantation defended by about thirty of Cockrell's Confederate pickets. After trading fire for an hour or so, the rebels, impressed by a broadside from the unorthodox Union flagship, headed downriver toward their camp at Perkins's plantation, no doubt wondering if Cockrell would believe their story.[39]

The plantation Osterhaus had come upon sat on about twenty dry acres between the Mississippi and the swamp and was owned by avowed secessionist Joshua James, unlike most of his peers still very much in residence. Osterhaus learned from the antagonistic but icily courteous James that all but a picket of Harrison's battalion (in which James's several sons, including a fifteen-year-old, served) had pulled back to Lake St. Joseph. James allowed that there was a good road along the Mississippi levee from his plantation to the Perkins plantation, three or four miles south on higher ground, although he failed to mention Cockrell's several hundred Missourians there. The road then led west away from the river along narrow Lake St. Joseph, circling back to the Mississippi River at the hamlet of Hard Times, just around the bend above the Confederate Grand

Gulf batteries. In his dispatch to McClernand and Grant, Osterhaus noted that he could see "Hurricane" and "Brierfield," the plantations of Joseph and brother Jefferson Davis across the Mississippi, "a very tempting view." (The general succumbed to that temptation later in the campaign and ordered "Hurricane" burned.)[40]

While Osterhaus interrogated the crusty James, the battalion quickly established a barricade and ditch that blocked the levee to the south in the direction of the Perkins plantation. In short order Osterhaus used his few available boats to move up the rest of the Sixty-ninth Indiana and two more mountain howitzers to hold the James place, while he ordered Garrard's brigade to establish garrisons all the way back to Richmond to protect their route. He maintained his own headquarters across the water at Smith's plantation for the time being. With possession of the James plantation, Osterhaus had given the Federals a base on the Mississippi where Porter could tie up his armada if he successfully ran the gauntlet of the Vicksburg batteries.[41]

As Osterhaus worked to consolidate his forward position over the next few days, his men were constantly harassed by Confederate snipers. Osterhaus, now well aware of Cockrell's substantial rebel base camp at the Perkins plantation as well as Harrison's cavalry patrol still in the area, sent howitzers down to Dunbar's plantation on April 7 to fire across the bayou at Harrison's sharpshooters, the barrage forcing them south toward their Lake St. Joseph camp. As for Cockrell, the Federal garrison at Dunbar's was in perfect position to enfilade any attack the Confederates might mount up the Mississippi levee toward the James plantation.[42]

McClernand's other divisions, led by Brig. Gen. Eugene Carr's Fourteenth Division, were inching down the bayou levee behind Osterhaus, corduroying the muddy road and building bridges as they went. This allowed Osterhaus's garrisons to move forward, and he concentrated most of his regiments near the Smith plantation, while Patterson's men built flatboats to move them across the "lake" to the James plantation. Both McClernand and Osterhaus were concerned about the vulnerability of the Union troops who had a toehold on the exposed Mississippi levee. There was no way for the forward garrison, now reinforced by the Forty-ninth Indiana, to retreat or to be rapidly reinforced if they were attacked. Besides Cockrell's threat, at least two rebel gunboats were thought to be in the area. A rebel armorclad had in fact been spotted, prompting the garrison to hastily build more fortifications facing the river. Osterhaus had ordered them to hold the position at all costs pending arrival of the Union gunboats that were about to attempt the Vicksburg blockade.[43]

But the only major Confederate counterattack to the Federal advance came on April 15, when Bowen ordered Cockrell's Missourians to take both the James and the Smith plantations and push the Federals back up the levee road. Dividing his men, Cockrell sent a regiment wading across the thigh-deep water of

Mill Bayou to attack the Union outpost at Dunbar's. He formed his other two regiments opposite the fortifications at the James plantation, ready to roll over them once his left flank was secure and then move on to Smith's plantation if all went well. Unfortunately for him, Osterhaus quickly reinforced the Union outpost at Dunbar's, and they fended off the attack, causing the whole Confederate plan to fizzle. Osterhaus had known of the impending attack from an escaped slave and was quite prepared. His wry comment after the Union's easy win was that Cockrell must have "thought that I was a very poor general."[44]

Cockrell kept scouting patrols out continuously in small boats, feeding their observations immediately to Bowen at Grand Gulf. Bowen, becoming more and more concerned himself, still could not get Pemberton to take the Union threat south of Vicksburg seriously. For the Union, Osterhaus reported detailed and accurate intelligence of Bowen's defenses at Grand Gulf even as Grant was working feverishly with Rear Adm. David Porter to prepare a convoy to run the Vicksburg batteries so that the second half of his plan could begin.[45]

On the night of April 16, Admiral Porter's flotilla was ready at Milliken's Bend, all vessels protected with cotton and hay bales stacked on their decks. As Grant watched from a small boat nearby, the little armada slipped downstream at about ten o'clock. That night at the James plantation, Osterhaus and McClernand were among the group of officers waiting eagerly on the second-floor gallery of the mansion to spot some sign of a successful run. Excitement was high; the officers sang the new hit "Rally 'Round the Flag" and other patriotic ditties ad nauseum to pass the time. About eleven o'clock there was a sudden boom of cannon, and a great light filled the sky, indicating that the Vicksburg batteries had discovered the fleet. The noise went on until three in the morning, but still no news or sign of the fleet. At daylight masses of burning cotton bales started floating by, along with fragments of the steamer *Henry Clay*, to Joshua James's delight. Soon, three unmanned barges loaded with supplies drifted down, but nothing more was spotted until noon. Tensions were high when finally someone spotted smokestacks above the trees, shortly followed by the majestic appearance of one gunboat after another swinging into view until all were anchored or tied up in front of the mansion. From the time the smoke was sighted, Osterhaus "seamed to be highly delighted," while James was now devastated. Only the *Henry Clay* had been lost.[46]

As soon as Porter's flagship, the *Benton*, tied up, Osterhaus went aboard with McClernand, grinning from ear to ear. "Now," said Osterhaus, "dose dampt fellers, dey'll catch it; give dem gunboat soup!" Porter agreed, and in the midst of the general celebration of Porter's success, Osterhaus boarded the *Tuscumbia* and arranged with Lt. Cdr. James W. Shirk to shell the woods along the river in support of the Forty-ninth Indiana and Sixty-ninth Indiana, who were already on their way to the Perkins plantation to take on Cockrell's garrison. But the Southerners had cleared out when they spotted the arrival of the gunboats, making their way by forced marches back on the levee road around Lake St. Joseph to Hard Times, where Bowen safely evacuated them across the Mississippi the same night. Within three days, all of Osterhaus's division had moved up to the new forward outpost on the Perkins plantation.[47]

On the morning after Porter's armada arrived, Osterhaus, Grant, and Porter left the flagship *Benton* in a cutter to reevaluate the troop-transport possibilities near New Carthage. With the water now dropping rapidly and gluey mud emerging, Grant saw that water transport to New Carthage would no longer be practical for the bulk of the army rapidly moving down the back levees. He desperately needed a means to march his men and wagons across to the Mississippi levee, so he ordered Osterhaus and Brig. Gen. Alvin P. Hovey to check the feasibility of completing the road along the Bayou Vidal levee (dubbed "Bayou be damned") from the Smith plantation past Dunbar's all the way back around to Perkins's plantation, a distance of twelve miles. The two, reconnoitering the route from each end, met in the middle, pronounced the enterprise "entirely practicable," and got their divisions to work repairing the road, the bulk done by Hovey's Twelfth Division. The enthusiastic soldiers did a yeoman's job despite the ubiquitous bugs and alligators. Hovey had the loan of Patterson and his energetic Kentucky engineers. They contributed a 780-foot bridge completed in eighteen hours, and another one 280 feet long, completed the same day. More than 2,000 feet of bridges were built in just four days, creating a land route from Smith's plantation to the Mississippi levee, bypassing New Carthage and emerging at Perkins's plantation.[48]

After the momentous and critical achievement of running the batteries, Grant's plan for crossing the Father of Waters proceeded rapidly, making that next few days perhaps the busiest in Osterhaus's entire career. Porter immediately began scoping out the defenses at Grand Gulf, a few miles to the south and the closest possible landing point on the other side of the river. To his alarm, he found that Bowen's Confederates were busy perfecting what was already a formidable position for their batteries on the bluff above the river. The admiral urgently requested McClernand to get a division ready to support a hastily conceived naval attack, which he wanted to launch on the morning of April 23 before the Southerners had time to finish their fortifications. McClernand picked Osterhaus for this dubious honor. While his detail was finishing their portion of the Bayou Vidal Road, Osterhaus spent that frantic morning boarding his eight remaining regiments and two batteries on any boat that would float, ready to support Porter and establish a bridgehead as soon as the navy reduced the defenses. Despite the nearly impossible logistical problems, by eleven o'clock Osterhaus had his division ready to go.[49]

But at noon Porter returned from downriver and called off the attack, convinced that the defenses were already so formidable that it would take a whole corps to secure Grand Gulf. McClernand, unhappy about Porter's change of mind, decided to see for himself and took Osterhaus downriver aboard the ram *General Price*, Osterhaus's temporary headquarters, to take a look. Both of them, after all that work, wanted to proceed, and were not too impressed by the rebel entrenchments they spotted. But they could not convince Porter, so the attack was scrubbed and Osterhaus debarked his troops. The next day Porter took Grant himself down to see the fortifications. Grant agreed with McClernand and Osterhaus that the thing was possible but with Porter that it was possible only if more men could be landed.[50]

There was room for only two divisions at Perkins's plantation, now occupied by Osterhaus's and Carr's, and Grant wanted to have a much larger concentration of forces before he attempted a bridgehead in Mississippi. He also needed detailed information about the road south of Hard Times and potential landing sites on the other side of the river. So at Grant's specific request, the next morning McClernand ordered Osterhaus to reconnoiter in person the levee road over which Cockrell had escaped all the way to Hard Times, a location that not only was closer to Grand Gulf but also had a much larger space for staging and supplying the army. But as Grant's attack plans evolved, he needed Osterhaus nearby, not off on patrol. So instead of going himself, on April 25 Osterhaus assigned the mission to a patrol led by Col. James Keigwin, consisting of two regiments, a detachment of cavalry, and a section of Rodman guns from the Seventh Michigan Battery. Lt. Francis Tunica of the Corps of Engineers led the bridge-building efforts. Harrison's cavalry battalion, once again the only Confederate force in the area after Cockrell's withdrawal, resisted this enterprise tenaciously all the way, burning all the existing bridges and setting ambushes at nearly every one. Brilliantly inventive, Tunica rebuilt four bridges in three days while the infantry kept Harrison at bay. Even before it was completed, A. J. Smith was hustling a brigade down Keigwin's new road, marching on April 27.[51]

The day after Keigwin rode out, Grant intended a major assault at Grand Gulf and ordered McClernand to get the troops on board immediately. But McClernand delayed a day while he was rounding up the scattered vessels. That afternoon, April 26, aboard the *Benton*, while the impatient Grant was castigating McClernand for not being ready to go, Adj. Gen. Lorenzo Thomas was making a pitch to Joseph Osterhaus and A. J. Smith about President Lincoln's new plan to form black regiments. Despite being distracted by the war plans afoot, Osterhaus was intrigued by the advancement opportunities that commanding such regiments offered, particularly to immigrant officers, and shortly began to encourage members of his officer cadre to apply. Over the next months he was recognized as one of the few generals who gave active support to this enterprise. At the moment, though, black recruitment was definitely not one of Osterhaus's immediate priorities.[52]

While Keigwin was pushing through a viable road to Hard Times for Grant's rapidly converging army, on a rainy and muddy April 27 Grant again ordered the assault of Grand Gulf, jumping off at Hard Times and using McClernand's divisions that were now available at or near Perkins' plantation: Carr's, Hovey's, and Osterhaus's plus Smith's brigade. Hovey and Osterhaus were each assigned several indifferently seaworthy boats and barges and instructed to have their men board immediately. This they did, despite grave misgivings on Osterhaus's part regarding the safety of some of his boats: the ram *Empire City* not only had to carry three full regiments and the artillery horses but also towed both a barge carrying the battery's guns and men as well as the disabled steamer *Anglo Saxon* with another regiment and more horses. The two floating divisions carefully made their way down to Hard Times, where Hovey debarked his men so the transports could return for Carr's. While he was waiting aboard the *Anglo Saxon* at Hard Times, Osterhaus sent a message to Keigwin: "Hurry up—I want you in the fight! . . . [A]nxiously awaiting your news." When it came, the news was great: in only three days Keigwin's crew had opened the road all the way from Perkins's plantation. Osterhaus immediately sent a cavalry patrol south and found the road open fourteen miles on downriver to a point opposite Bruinsburg on the Mississippi side of the river, fulfilling Grant's last request on this assignment.[53]

Prior to boarding the boats and barges at the Perkins plantation on April 27, Osterhaus issued a general order full of practical instructions that reinforced all the drilling in camp:

> Soldiers:
>
> We are about to attack the enemy and we must conquer him. You are brave—be cool. Perhaps we may have a hard struggle. Be careful in firing. Don't waste your ammunition. Take good aim and see that your balls hit. Whether in dispersed order or in line of battle keep your proper places and never straggle away, but always remain within the hearing of your commanders and obey all orders promptly.
>
> When advancing, be lively, when falling back, retire slowly and never cease firing except ordered to do so.[54]

By nightfall the last barges and steamers were moored at Hard Times, crammed with soldiers and their gear. The men stood on the boats for the next eighteen hours, some of them in seven inches of stinking water despite pumps going continuously, waiting for Porter to silence the Grand Gulf batteries so they could establish their beachhead. At least the waiting bluecoats were entertained by a ringside view of the "grand exhibition of pluck and endurance" put on by Porter's gunboats on April 28 against the batteries of Grand Gulf, the most intense naval battle ever to take place on the river. But when the far-outnumbered Confederate batteries refused to cave in to Porter's attack after nearly six hours of bombardment, the attempt was broken off.[55]

Grant's backup plan called for a massed landing at Rodney, about nine miles farther downriver. So, after the Union navy withdrew from the bombardment, Osterhaus finally was able to debark his soggy men at Hard Times, Grant not wanting to risk them against the still-lethal batteries. With the rest of the Thirteenth Corps, Osterhaus marched his men three miles across the peninsula and beyond the batteries, bedding down with them on the damp ground that night under the stars a short distance below at Disharoon's plantation. Meanwhile, Porter's empty boats slipped silently by the Grand Gulf defenses to meet them.[56]

As Osterhaus settled for the night at Disharoon's plantation, he thought back on the labors of the last month. The accomplishments of this army, his division in particular, thus far were truly spectacular, in no small part due to his steady and inventive leadership. As one observer put it, "With troops less capable and commanders less resolute and resourceful, we might well have been beaten before getting within reach of the enemy. . . . When it is remembered that those bridges were built by green volunteers, who had never seen a bridge train nor had an hour's drill or instruction in bridge-building, some conception may be had of the quality of the men and officers who carried through that remarkable work."[57]

Before dawn on April 30 Osterhaus began cramming his men aboard steamers and gunboats for the final time. The men of the Ninth were across into Mississippi in the first wave, landing somewhat anticlimactically with Grant at the burned-out little town of Bruinsburg before noon with no opposition in sight. It took until late afternoon before the seventeen thousand men were issued three days' rations, the last they were to receive for two weeks, and were ready to move out. Carr's division led, followed by Osterhaus. Bruinsburg was across Bayou Pierre from Grand Gulf, Grant's objective, and the army headed inland to find a bridge leading there, without benefit of cavalry scouts but with accurate intelligence from locals.[58]

John Bowen at Grand Gulf had repeatedly warned Pemberton that the heavy Federal troop concentration foretold a landing in his sector. However, Pemberton, who had just fifty-four thousand troops to defend a line about 150 miles long and was still expecting the main Union attack at Vicksburg, saw fit to send him only five thousand troops. Now, with news of a massive Federal landing at Bruinsburg, Bowen rapidly gathered what defenses he had available and moved them to meet this overwhelming threat, hoping to delay the Union juggernaut until Pemberton could send him adequate forces to throw them back and trap them against the river.[59]

Grant discovered that the nearest Bayou Pierre bridge was located near the town of Port Gibson, a few miles inland. As the Federals headed away from the river through the twilight they encountered a line of low bluffs that marked the edge of a swath several miles deep of loess hills, a honeycomb of flat ridgetops cut by deep ravines, the marshy bottoms covered by impenetrable canebrake, the perpendicular walls choked by trees, dense brush, and poison ivy. Since the ravines were virtually impassable, the narrow dirt roads in the area kept to the cleared ridgetops, converging and diverging to avoid dipping into the downhill thickets wherever they could. "This country is the most broken and difficult to operate in I ever saw," grumbled Grant, and certainly Osterhaus agreed. Grant had two route options between the landing site and Port Gibson: the Bruinsburg Road alongside Bayou Pierre and the slightly better Rodney Road, running along a parallel ridge about a mile south. He chose the latter. Because the ridges had been cleared of trees, the ridge roads were often easily visible to each other although separated by the impenetrable ravines.[60]

Gen. John Bowen meant to prevent Grant from taking his bridge and chose the site to defend accordingly, four miles west of Port Gibson. There a farm lane connected the two ridge roads and the farms on each: A. K. Shaifer's farm on the Rodney Road and William Andrews's spread on the Bruinsburg Road. Bowen and Brig. Gen. Martin E. Green decided to set roadblocks on both ridge roads just east of the farm lane. Except for failing to capitalize on the farm lane's importance in communicating between his separated units, Bowen's choice of ground was admirable: the steep ravines provided cover for his sharpshooters and hampered movement, or, better yet, confined the Federals to the cleared ridges and roads where they were sitting ducks. These terrain advantages were worth hundreds, if not thousands, of men, one man undercover estimated to be worth at least three in the open. Because the defenders rarely revealed themselves, during the battle the Northern commanders, including Osterhaus, were certain they were facing a much larger enemy. The bluecoats were convinced that there were several thousand rebels shooting at them from the bushes.[61]

The beleaguered Bowen needed this advantage: he was forced to try to hold the Grand Gulf fortifications and at the same time stem the Federal onslaught with all told sixty-eight hundred grayclads, many of whom had to make grueling marches to get to the battlefield by even halfway through the battle. With all the Southern troops that could be scraped together locally, as the battle began Bowen had on hand fewer than twenty-six hundred determined Confederate soldiers to hold the enemy's first four divisions (about sixteen thousand men) until the hoped-for Southern reinforcements could get there.[62]

First contact between the armies occurred around two in the morning when Carr's advance stumbled upon Green's brigade of Arkansas and Mississippi regiments and traded shots for a couple of hours. Back down the Rodney Road behind Carr, Osterhaus's exhausted men had just bedded down on the chilly ground without blankets. While the men tried to sleep, their commander listened to the firefight ahead and reflected on the morning to come, when he would be taking an entire division into battle for the first time. Of some concern was the fact that he would have to rely on two brigade commanders who had

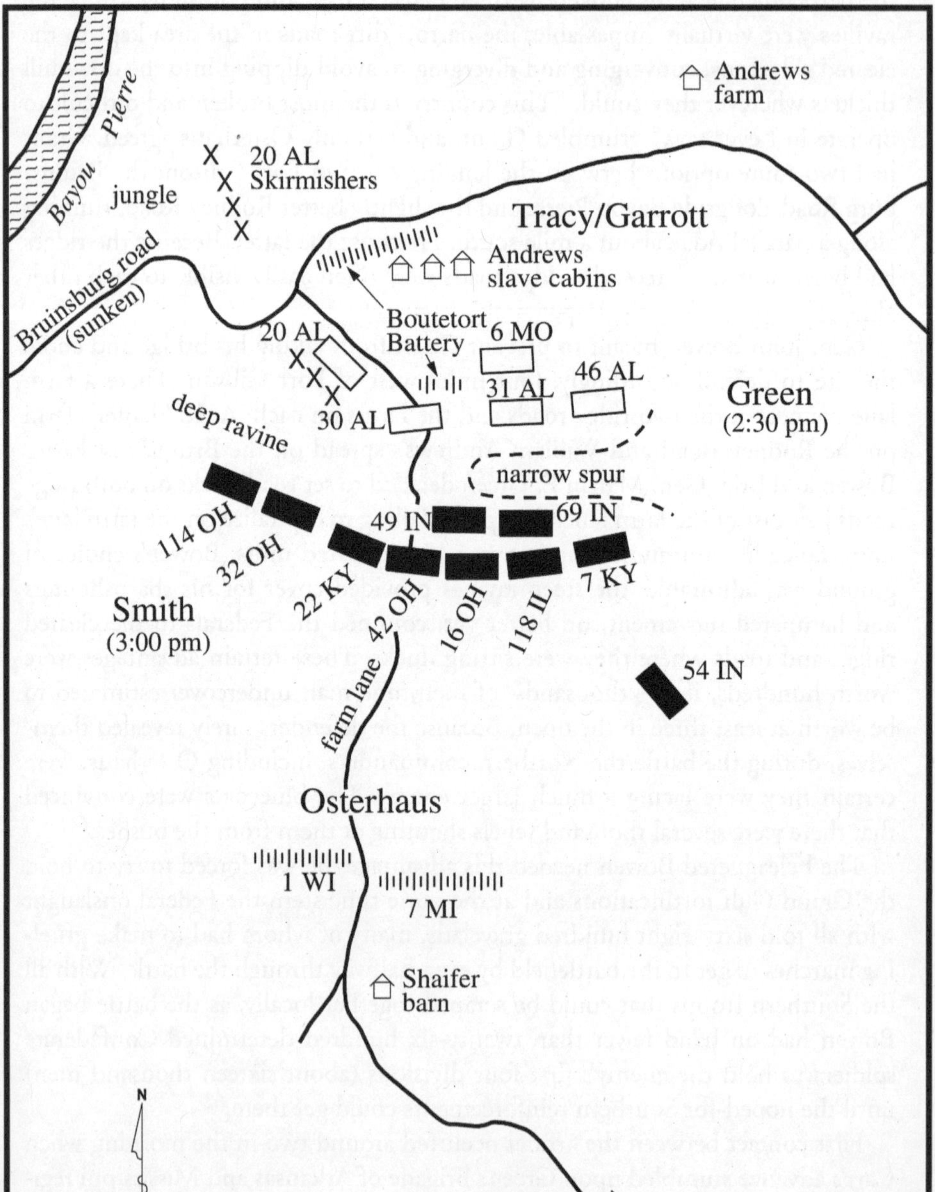

Port Gibson
May 1, 1863

had no formal military training. Although Col. Lionel A. Sheldon, a judge from Ohio, had been at Arkansas Post and Chickasaw Bayou, his other brigade commander, Col. Theophilus Garrard, had seen no battle worthy of the name.[63]

The first day of May dawned clear and warm. McClernand, now up with Carr at the Shaifer farm, discovered not one but two Confederate positions of unknown strength: besides Green's roadblock on the Rodney Road, a probe turned up more rebels over on the ridge that bore the Bruinsburg Road. Unless someone drove them off, this second unit could use the Shaifer farm lane to attack the Union rear as they moved forward on the Rodney Road against Green's position. McClernand, uncertain of what he was facing, decided that the main Confederate force must be Green's on the Union right, and deployed three of his four divisions, about thirteen thousand strong, to deal with what initially was just four regiments and four guns, about eleven hundred men. He sent Osterhaus's division, effective strength thirty-two hundred men and officers, up the farm lane to divert what McClernand saw as the comparatively weak end of the Confederate line. This turned out to be Brig. Gen. Edward Tracy's Alabama Brigade with just four regiments and a six-gun battery from Botetourt, Virginia.[64]

Even though he had twice as many men as his foe, Osterhaus's assignment turned out to be much harder than he first appreciated, and it would take all day to accomplish. He quickly positioned his lead artillery section, two ten-pounder rifled Rodman guns of Lanphere's Seventh Michigan Battery, on an elevation in a plum orchard behind the Shaifer barn to take on the Confederate Napoleons. Then he ordered a skirmish line of the Seventh Kentucky pushed forward across a cornfield and into the ravine to the right of the lane. Osterhaus himself followed behind his skirmishers to inspect the ground and the enemy position. These were his observations:

> After passing the yards and outhouses of Shaifer's, the road winds over a pretty large field, not of a regular form but variously intersected by gullies and ravines more or less densely covered with undergrowth, cane, etc. The surface of the field is undulating and bordered on the north by a ridge running east and west. At the point where the Port Gibson [Bruinsburg] Road reaches the crest of this ridge, there are several houses [Andrew's slave cabins] commanding all the land around. At the foot of the elevation the [farm] road runs over a very narrow strip of land with deep ravines on both sides forming only a backbone of from thirty to eighty feet wide, thus affording an excellent defile for defense, being the only approach to a military position on the hill.[65]

As Osterhaus described it, the Confederate defensive position resembled nothing so much as a castle rampart with ravines where a deep moat would be and a "backbone" of land instead of a drawbridge. There were actually two ravines discernible through the tangle on the Union right slanting away from the lane, with a narrow spur dividing them. The Thirty-first Alabama, forming the left of Tracy's line, had set up just behind the crest of the narrow spur. Tracy had positioned twelve-pounder Napoleons in a rather exposed position at the foot of the ridge pointing down the lane toward the Federals, and another two at the top of the ridge near the Andrews farm's slave cabins. These structures also provided cover for the center of Tracy's line, the Thirtieth Alabama.[66]

On Tracy's right was a very deep ravine in front of the Bruinsburg Road; beyond that road there was more impenetrable jungle for eight hundred yards to the edge of Bayou Pierre. A man down there would have been lucky to see three feet in any direction. To cover this entire right flank, Tracy had only the Twentieth Alabama. Two of its companies he sent into the jungle near the bayou to try to prevent that flank's being turned, and two more went into the deep ravine in front of the Bruinsburg Road as skirmishers, while the remaining companies connected to the Thirtieth. At about eight o'clock 160 men of the Forty-sixth Alabama trotted up, breathless after marching all day and night to get there, and formed on the left of the Thirty-first Alabama. Tracy now had every man he could find on the line.[67]

By seven o'clock the other four guns of Osterhaus's Seventh Michigan Battery had come up to complete the battery behind the Shaifer barn. Sheldon's Second Brigade and the First Wisconsin Battery were still down the road, marching in column toward the cornfield. Meanwhile, the pesky Virginia Napoleons quickly found the range of the Michigan battery and began to take a toll among its crew. Lanphere's battery was able to knock out both rebel cannons at the base of the slope; however, the two at the top continued to wreak havoc. About eight o'clock Tracy himself was killed by sniper fire as he stood near his battery, and command fell to Col. Isham W. Garrott of the Twentieth Alabama just as Osterhaus decided to move the battery forward into a dip that provided a bit more cover and ordered a general infantry advance in support. As his right flank plunged into the first ravine, the intense Confederate response made Osterhaus convinced that "all the ravines and gullies in front of them were full of the enemy's infantry." Despite the heavy fire, by about ten o'clock the right side of the Federal line had driven the Confederate skirmishers back across the second ravine to the slopes and the cover of the slave cabins. On the left, the advance struggled on but did not get far, as the ravine "forbids all passage of troops with any kind of order."[68]

While the Union infantry advanced in no semblance of a coordinated line through the claustrophobic ravines, doing battle as much with the vegetation as the enemy, Lanphere's gunnery teams were still getting hammered by the Virginians: he ultimately lost three killed and three wounded. Osterhaus, most anxious to put into action those big twenty-pounder Parrotts of the First Wisconsin that had been so impressive at Arkansas Post, galloped back down the congested Rodney Road on his somewhere-appropriated mount to hustle the artillerymen up, and found them brewing a quick pot of coffee while they waited for the road to clear in front of them. "I can wait no longer, boys; come mit me!" he shouted and off they tore, trying to keep from sloshing the boiling coffee in their canteens, Osterhaus meanwhile telling them what a superior location he had found for them.[69]

They were not too impressed when they saw the position, but quickly unlimbered. At that point the Botetourt battery's last two guns were hurling canister into the ravines on the right, now full of Union soldiers, but the Federal Parrotts quickly put a stop to that. Wrote a gunner, "In seven or eight minutes we dismounted both guns, killed every horse, the Chief of Artillery, Lieutenant commanding the battery and several men. . . . It was not in any sense a battle. . . . It was a giant crushing a pigmy." Bowen had sent two more Napoleons from the Rodney Road to support the Botetourt guns; now these were withdrawn to save them from the same destruction, and the rebel guns went silent.[70]

Meanwhile, three of Garrard's regiments crept forward deep in the ravines on the right side of the lane, with another on the right flank, and worked their way to within sixty yards or so of the Confederate units opposite. Only the 120th Ohio remained in the big ravine to the left of the lane. With his right now pushed far forward into the second ravine, Osterhaus was concerned that he was leaving his right flank unprotected and a large gap between his line and McClernand's left flank back on the Rodney Road. Sheldon's Second Brigade had come up just before the Virginia guns were silenced, so he quickly ordered Sheldon to deploy three regiments to the right to try to fill the gap (and also get out of the artillery fire). However, when Osterhaus and Sheldon both looked more closely, they realized that the jungle was so dense down in the ravines that there was little immediate danger of the enemy getting through there.[71]

Osterhaus began to comprehend that this battle was really two completely independent fights, so he canceled the order and instead arrayed the Second Brigade in his front. He sent one regiment into the left ravine and had Sheldon's other three regiments form a single assault line arrayed across the center of the cornfield. Misreading the number he was facing, he concluded that he could not afford to keep a reserve: "The large number of Rebel infantry occupying every inch of ground in my front made . . . deployment of my whole infantry force necessary." However, he still thought that he could drive the enemy out of his position, and turned down McClernand's offer of reinforcements at that time.[72]

With the Confederate guns silenced, Osterhaus now ordered a frontal assault. After a heavy Union artillery barrage, his skirmishers led off, followed by a charge of the three center regiments across the field toward the narrow "backbone." Two of the three regiments plunged into the ravine and continued forward on the left, but Lt. Col. Don Pardee's Forty-second Ohio ran into a problem. Rapidly advancing to the edge of the ravine near the "backbone," they loosed a heavy volley, only to discover to their horror their own Sixty-ninth Indiana ahead of them in the ravine. At the same time they were met by a wall of bullets from the waiting hidden rebels and had to dive for cover. Osterhaus concluded that "it would have demanded too great a sacrifice of life to have persisted in this attack." The Forty-second Ohio, about three hundred men, took the brunt of the damage, losing twelve killed and forty-seven wounded for the day, including several line officers (two of the three highest regimental numbers of deaths for the day were in Osterhaus's regiments, the other high toll in his command being in Bennett's Sixty-ninth Indiana).[73]

Besides the near impossibility of keeping his line coordinated and closed up, Osterhaus now saw that friendly fire was a major hazard in trying to maneuver ten regiments in this constricted, irregular, and obscured field of battle. Although a few bluecoats were wounded by Lanphere's shrapnel, most of the danger was from Union rifles. The slope of the ravines had drawn one brigade inexorably in front of the other, but the vegetation was so dense that Second Brigade commander Lindsey was not aware of some of the locations of the First Brigade. The lack of horses for his couriers made Osterhaus's communication with his units extremely difficult.[74]

It was now eleven o'clock. The assault had stalled. Osterhaus concluded that the only way to pry the Confederates loose from their position was to divert them with a strong flanking movement to the far left near the bayou, while slipping a striking force across the "backbone" and onto the foot of the main ridge for a general charge at the sniper-filled cabins. Since all of his men were already deployed, he asked Lt. Col. James H. Wilson, Grant's assistant inspector general, for reinforcements. As McPherson's corps began to trickle in via the constricted Rodney Road, Grant directed Brig. Gen. John E. Smith's brigade from Maj. Gen. John "Black Jack" Logan's division to reinforce Osterhaus, but it took more than three hours for Smith's men to reach him. While they were waiting, Osterhaus's men kept up the pressure on the Confederates, although he ordered no further frontal charges, nor did his outnumbered opponent, not surprisingly. Meanwhile, Osterhaus's four lead regiments wormed their way to within ten to fifty yards of the enemy in some places, keeping up the firefight in the ravines. He consulted with Grant around noon when the Federal commander came over to check on progress, but for several hours the battle took on a strange, static quality with no sustained fighting while Osterhaus awaited his reinforcements. The batteries were also quiet, not close enough or in the clear enough for effective canister and having no opposing batteries to bombard.[75]

Garrott's small Confederate command had held on through a nerve-wracking morning. Garrott had not been informed of the battle plan, but he figured that "the enemy was in our front, and I knew of no order to retire." Bowen eventually confirmed that he was to hold the position "at all hazards." That Garrott did, despite the fact that he had no practical artillery support and was also running low on ammunition. But Osterhaus's pressure late in the morning caused the Southerner to rob his weak right to shore up the center, so the Southern right flank was dangerously vulnerable as the afternoon began. When two brigades of grayclad reinforcements finally arrived over on the Rodney Road, Bowen was able to pull Green's disorganized and shot-up brigade back from McClernand's front and send it around to his right to help Garrott against Osterhaus. About two thirty, near the time that corps commander Maj. Gen. James McPherson finally arrived on the field in person with Smith's brigade to reinforce Osterhaus, Green's brigade also arrived to reinforce Garrott. The exhausted new Southern arrivals extended the Confederate left, but were not a factor in the battle. Where Garrott desperately needed more reinforcements was on his far right, over by the bayou. Fortunately, the Sixth Missouri, part of Cockrell's brigade, arrived at about the same time and was used to shore up Garrott's center so that he could move other companies back to his scantily held far right.[76]

As Smith's five regiments of bluecoats were gathering in the orchard, so were the Union commanders. Osterhaus had the advice of Grant, McClernand, McPherson, and later Logan as to the best way to proceed. According to both Osterhaus's and McClernand's reports, McPherson, who had never commanded a major unit in battle, wanted to try an assault over the "backbone" before plunging into the jungle on the proposed flanking maneuver, even though Osterhaus told him that a frontal attack flat would not work. "The men advanced gallantly, but of course had to give way as soon as they came within range of the enemy's missiles," reported Osterhaus, "thus attesting the correctness of General Osterhaus's admonition upon that point," chimed in McClernand. Neither Logan's nor McPherson's report corroborate this assault, but a man from Smith's brigade described a repulse of the Forty-fifth Illinois, easy targets for devastating fire as they crammed onto the narrow "backbone."[77]

Finally at about three o'clock, two of Smith's regiments slipped into the cane on the Union far left to begin the flanking movement that even Grant had recognized was necessary to win the battle. It took another hour to deploy them in the jungle near the bayou; to reach their position, the men had to let themselves down into the ravine by clinging to branches and vines, and then they crawled on hands and knees through the dense cane, hoping they would not run into a canebrake rattler or any number of other nasty surprises. Garrott frantically reinforced his right flank as best he could when he spied a mass of Federals oozing in that direction. He also decided to recall the two guns he had retired earlier, greatly surprising the Federals by opening fire into the woods from a knoll behind the rebel line. The Southern battery was disabled in a fierce firefight, but not before they had scattered the gaggle of Union generals gathered around Webster's battery.[78]

As the Federals inexorably built up strength on the Confederate right, Col. Eugene Erwin of Cockrell's Sixth Missouri in the center ordered a diverting charge that took his regiment to the brow of the narrow spur between the two ravines on the Union right, pushing the Federals opposite him back about a quarter of a mile into the first ravine. McClernand later claimed that Osterhaus had ordered this withdrawal as a feint to lure the Confederates forward so he could push past them up the hill. Grant obviously did not share this view, because when he saw the bluecoats retreating he sent for Brig. Gen. William P. Benton's brigade from the Rodney Road to come over and help out. As it turned out, that help became unnecessary as Osterhaus finally made his move.[79]

Around four o'clock, Smith's regiments, now deep in the jungle over by the bayou, began to press Garrott's thin right flank. Osterhaus immediately ordered an assault with the 114th Ohio over the "backbone" and the Forty-ninth Indiana to its right in the ravines. At this point, Grant was on the field and saw the charge; possibly, he ordered it. Under supporting fire these two regiments quickly gained the base of the ridge and spread out. With his usual infectious enthusiasm, Osterhaus immediately shouted for a charge up the slope, bayonets out, himself in the lead, the other regiments following, and quickly took the ridge and cabins. Modestly calling it the most gallant charge he ever saw, Osterhaus afterward practically lifted Keigwin of the Forty-ninth Indiana off his feet in his excitement. Later, as his men cheered him, the relieved German pronounced, "Vell, boys, I dells you vat it is: you do as vell tomorrow as you does today and we whip dem repels undil they can't eat sauerkraut!" His official report reflected this enthusiasm, although a bit toned down: "The charge was a complete success," wrote Osterhaus, with no little satisfaction.[80]

But the gallant charge was an empty gesture, because by then the Confederates had finally had enough, after hours of holding off an enemy at least twice as large as they. By about five o'clock they had slipped away, leaving the Union army in command of the field. Despite Grant's objective to capture the bridge intact, none of the tired Union divisions pursued the Confederates to secure it. Bowen was able to burn the bridge and two more near Port Gibson. However, the spans were soon repaired, and, out of options, Bowen evacuated Grand Gulf. Grant's bridgehead in Mississippi was secured.[81]

In their reports of the Port Gibson battle, both McClernand and McPherson complimented Osterhaus's division on its "gallant" and "brilliant" charge. Grant merely noted that Osterhaus had been unable to move the Confederates from their position until reinforced and a better position obtained (the flank buildup) that enabled the combined force to drive the enemy from the field. Osterhaus could not agree with him more. In his memoirs he stated the situation succinctly: "I succeeded only, when a demonstration executed by fresh troops brought forward against the rebel right begun to be felt." Osterhaus enjoyed national attention for his contributions in newspaper accounts that described how "he ordered a charge, and, leading it in person, fell in such fury on the rebel line, that it was shattered into fragments and fell disorderly back."[82]

However, recent historians have suggested that Osterhaus was excessively cautious. (It may be instructive to note that none of these historians had the benefit of Osterhaus's own report of the battle, which was not published with the others in the *Official Records*.) The crux of the matter seems to be whether Osterhaus's choice of a flanking attack versus repeated frontal assaults was reasonable or indicated a loss of nerve. Use of a flank attack assumed an experienced general with accurate knowledge of the enemy's flanks and enough control of his forces to launch a coordinated attack. Since Smith's brigade was now on the field, it was logical that Grant would coordinate a combined attack, and he probably did.[83]

Once Osterhaus settled on a flanking maneuver, clearly he saw no reason to waste lives unnecessarily while he waited for the reinforcements required. He had no means of mounting a coordinated general assault through the barrier of tangled vegetation; even his artillery offered no advantage on this field, and they were relatively idle. His opponent, Garrott, was content just to hang on, so until the final push there was no sustained general fighting in front of Osterhaus, although a number of uncoordinated firefights rumbled in the ravines. In this battle, Osterhaus by no stretch could be considered impetuous, but his tactics accomplished the mission with probably less loss of life than had he continued to hammer up the middle of this treacherous battlefield. McClernand was also later accused of overcaution at Port Gibson, so perhaps Osterhaus suffered by association. However, in the next big battle the charge of excess caution would be renewed against both men, perhaps with more merit.[84]

With the Union victory at Port Gibson, the port of Grand Gulf fell to Grant as Bowen, irretrievably flanked, moved his division north across the Big Black River. Sherman's entire corps as well as tons of supplies were landed at the port over the next two weeks, having made the tortuous trek from Milliken's Bend to Hard Times via the roads that Osterhaus's division had opened the month before.[85]

For the next three weeks, Grant's army lived off the land as it struck toward the heart of Mississippi, the plantations along the way bearing the brunt of the blue horde. One landowner particularly incensed by repeated waves of foragers was Elizabeth Mary Meade Ingraham, the Southern married sister of the North's Maj. Gen. George Meade. Her plantation at Willow Springs was used as a bivouac by Osterhaus's division on May 4, Osterhaus's men taking all her molasses and sugar. That night she reluctantly housed General McClernand, traveling with Osterhaus's division, and apparently Osterhaus too, since she recorded angrily in her diary, "Osterhaus' division, scum of St. Louis, camped in the big field. All the corn ruined in the field, and nearly all consumed in the granaries." No other St. Louis scum was on her land at the time except Osterhaus himself.[86]

Osterhaus's actions did little to mollify the woman. Earlier that day the men of the First Wisconsin Battery had cheered their general as he told them, "'Here you camps; there is water; I send you a load of corn.' He pointed to a rail fence and said, 'You must look around and get you some chickens and some pigs, and make yourselves comfortable.' We did," commented a gunner laconically. As long as the subject was food, Osterhaus's men came first. A few weeks later, one of his surgeons recalled that Osterhaus had no sympathy for a complaining farmer, telling his men, "You always brings me de livers and den I never knows notin about the killin of de animales." Osterhaus was not alone in incurring Mary Ingraham's wrath; she complained about McPherson's corps, her first Federal visitors, who "must open every door, pillage every place," and Sherman's corps coming along later, declaring them "mean and low . . . the quintessence of rascality." Because the soldiers had been issued only two days' cooked rations, which for some consisted of one meal of beans, foraging was intense. Those in front got the lion's share, adding to Mrs. Ingraham's and other planters' woes, and those who followed went hungry a good part of the time. Osterhaus's efficient foragers caused a gunner from the First Wisconsin to comment, "I pity the chickens and pigs on the road." However, there is no evidence that Osterhaus condoned plundering of nonnecessary items, even though that clearly happened under his command. In fact, later that month he was instrumental in returning stolen household silver to a Southern woman and punishing the thief.[87]

Following the old Natchez Trace on the high ground east of the Big Black River, the Union army marched in a northeasterly direction toward the little town of Raymond, the main hub between Grand Gulf and Jackson. Osterhaus, leading McClernand's advance, once again became the eyes and ears for the Thirteenth Corps and, on occasion, Grant's whole army. Not content to wait for reports, he frequently went on reconnaissance himself. For example, on May 4 he went out with a patrol, found and interrogated a deserter, and was thus able to give Grant critical information about rebel movements toward the Big Black. The next day Osterhaus's division led the entire Union advance. Along the route, his cavalry skirmished briskly with a Confederate patrol at the Big Sand Creek crossing, and Osterhaus ordered a charge with drawn sabers by the Second Ohio Cavalry, a unit that had been detached to him. That picturesque moment delighted Osterhaus, who enthused in his report that the minor skirmish was "without doubt one of the most brilliant cavalry engagements of the war."[88]

Over the next few days, as he waited for the rest of the Union army to catch up with him, Osterhaus took time to propose several of his officers for promotion into the colored regiments then forming. He also continued his thorough surveillance efforts, covering all the roads leading toward the enemy. "Last night I was on a recognoitering expedition with General Osterhaus and we had a lively time with the Rebs," wrote Col. Marcus Spiegel of the Forty-second Ohio to his wife on May 9. Osterhaus soon was able to notify Grant through McClernand that Pemberton's army had crossed the Big Black and was headed east for nearby Edwards Station (about midway between Vicksburg and Jackson).[89]

On May 11 Osterhaus had a chance to greet the men of his old Missouri command, who cheered him wildly as they passed by with Sherman's corps on its way to take the center spot in Grant's lineup. Now that Grant had all his corps in a row, he ordered a general advance northward toward the railroad the next day. McClernand's corps still held the Union left, facing Pemberton's main force now converging at Edwards Station, just two miles away. But now Grant had intelligence reports of a bigger-than-expected buildup of Confederate troops in Jackson, thirty miles to the east, with Maj. Gen. Joseph E. Johnston, who outranked Pemberton, expected to arrive to lead them all. Grant decided to hold Pemberton briefly at arm's length at Edwards Station while he used two of his three corps to quickly take care of the growing threat in Jackson.[90]

Early the next morning Grant sent Sherman's and McPherson's corps east toward Jackson. McClernand's role that day was to make Pemberton think he was preparing to attack Edwards Station, and then to slip his thirteen thousand men quietly off stage right past Pemberton's entire army and head for Raymond. Grant later commented with some satisfaction that McClernand had executed this difficult maneuver "with much skill and without loss." One casualty that Grant probably did not know about: Maj. Gen. William Loring notified Pemberton that evening that General Osterhaus's "negro, horse and dinner" had been captured. The mess steward (probably Joe Miller) tried to contribute misinformation by telling his captors that Osterhaus had ordered him to cook his dinner and bring it to him in Edwards Station. However, it was clear from Loring's dispatches that the Confederate general had correctly detected McClernand's move on Raymond.[91]

As Osterhaus led his bedraggled division through the pouring rain into Raymond at midnight, Joe Johnston pulled into Jackson by train to take command over the Confederate forces in Mississippi. His first order was to pull up stakes that same night and slip north to Canton, twenty-five miles away, leaving Sherman's and McPherson's corps, now converging on Jackson, to face only a rear guard. McClernand had sent two of his divisions along as backup, keeping Osterhaus's division to garrison Raymond and keep an eye out for Pemberton. Later the evening of May 14 in the captured capital, Grant intercepted a copy of a message Johnston had sent to Pemberton ordering him to attack the Federal rear. Grant immediately ordered McClernand's corps reversed and concentrated at the railroad at Bolton to face Pemberton. Osterhaus's division, with the shortest distance to go, got to the town first at eight o'clock on May 15, capturing the village with no resistance, seizing stores and burning road and railroad bridges. From captured prisoners and reconnaissance patrols that he sent toward Edwards Station, Osterhaus unearthed consistently ominous reports that the

Confederates were moving with a force of twenty-five thousand eastward from Edwards Station toward Bolton.[92]

In preparation for possible battle, McClernand ordered his four divisions to cover all three of the roads leading west toward Edwards Station and Pemberton's position. He sent Osterhaus, followed by Carr, three miles back down the Bolton Road and then onto the Middle Road leading toward Edwards Station. Osterhaus's men, just getting started on some prime foraging as the first unit into Bolton, grumbled that their leaders were clueless. They could not understand why they had to retrace their steps almost immediately, but off they marched. A few miles onto the Middle Road they bivouacked for the night after some active skirmishing with Confederate mounted patrols. Hovey's division was now a mile north of Osterhaus as the crow flies, closely followed by McPherson's two divisions. South of Osterhaus, Frank Blair's and A. J. Smith's divisions were ordered to bivouac on the Raymond Road, about four miles from Osterhaus's camp.[93]

Just as Osterhaus had entered Bolton that morning, Pemberton himself had gotten his army on the road but not eastward toward Bolton. Instead, he headed south from Edwards Station toward Raymond, with the intent of capturing Grant's supply train. Improbably, that whole day about forty thousand men were in motion on little country roads within just a few miles of each other without either side's being fully aware of the other's movements. As Confederate campfires were lit that night, rebel scouts rode in, telling Pemberton of sighting a large body of Union troops near Bolton, to add to the earlier reports of skirmish contact with Osterhaus's division. But refusing to be alarmed, Pemberton decided to stay put until morning and reassess the Federal threat then. He still believed his outdated intelligence that the bulk of the Union army was heading away from him toward Jackson and that he had an opportunity to catch the supply trains before the Federal divisions guarding them could be reinforced. He was not expecting an imminent battle.[94]

Next morning, May 16, Grant ordered McClernand to cautiously feel the Confederate position, but not to bring on a fight until "we are entirely prepared." Meanwhile, just as Pemberton was finally beginning to grasp the fact that he was now facing the entire Federal army, a courier galloped in with Johnston's urgent message to join him at Clinton. Not wanting a fight just then, Pemberton made a snap decision to obey Johnston's order and to countermarch his command back along the road to Edwards. But he was too late. A. J. Smith's howitzers on the Raymond Road were already firing on the head, now tail, of the Confederate column as it reversed direction. And so, despite Pemberton's wishes and without adequate preparations, the Confederates were forced to stand and fight the decisive battle of the Vicksburg campaign at Champion Hill.[95]

Smith's opening salvo caught Pemberton's three large divisions strung out for three miles in column on a secondary road, the Ratliff Road, that ran between the Raymond Road and the Middle Road. That meant that their line of battle in this encounter was, by necessity, their marching order. But the ground they were caught on was not so bad. By quickly deploying into line of battle on the heights facing east, they could use the road behind them to move from one end of their line to the other. By contrast, the Federal couriers and troops had to pick their way over crowded roads back several miles to the Bolton Road to communicate from one part of their line to another, which seriously hampered their coordination.[96]

The south end of the rapidly forming gray line sat at the junction of the Ratliff Road and the Raymond Road, where Maj. Gen. William Loring's big Confederate division faced A. J. Smith, with Frank Blair's division on the road behind him. Strung along the Ratliff Road, Bowen formed the center portion of the Confederate line with two of the South's best brigades: Green's Alabamans and Cockrell's Missourians, who had fought so hard at Port Gibson. For now, there were no Union units directly facing them, because of the huge gap between Osterhaus on the Middle Road and A. J. Smith on the Raymond Road to his left. Farther on up the Ratliff Road, the Confederates needed to control the crossroads at the Middle Road to make good their retrograde movement. Maj. Gen. Carter Stevenson's division of four brigades would protect the vital junction, expecting the main Federal attack to come from Osterhaus and Carr on the Middle Road and Smith on the Raymond Road. At the north end of the Confederate line, beyond the crossroads, the Ratliff Road became the Jackson Road and crested a small hill known as Thompson's Hill, or Champion Hill, after the farm on which it sat. What Pemberton had not counted on was another large Federal force moving toward Stevenson's left flank on that road. This was Hovey, backed by Maj. Gen. John "Black Jack" Logan's division, with Sherman's entire corps coming up behind.[97]

McClernand set his command post with Osterhaus on the Middle Road. Given the difficulty in communicating with the rest of his spread-out divisions, McClernand wanted to be absolutely sure that Grant was ready before he ordered an attack. Hovey, a mile to Osterhaus's right, had sighted Stevenson's Southerners and had sent a message to McClernand asking if he should attack. McClernand deferred him to Grant and in turn sent Grant a message of his own, requesting permission to attack on the other two roads. Grant did not receive McClernand's message until noon. In the interim, Grant ordered Hovey to attack about ten thirty.[98]

Osterhaus had already had his division on the march for ninety minutes when he heard the sound of Smith's opening guns to the south at about seven thirty. He continued to press forward on the very tortuous Middle Road, through the "most difficult terrain for the passage of troops that can be imagined," urging his troops on in order to coordinate his attack with Smith. The terrain between him and Smith was rough but fairly open, but toward Hovey's position on his right it was almost a jungle, reminiscent of the Port Gibson battlefield. Visibility there was generally limited to less than one hundred yards. Osterhaus judged the right side of the road totally impractical for anything but skirmishers, and the whole field of battle difficult to impossible for artillery and cavalry.[99]

Shortly after he heard Smith's guns, Osterhaus's advance cavalry encountered a Southern regiment concealed in the woods. Pursuit through the tangle on horseback was impossible, so the general withdrew the cavalry to allow Garrard's infantry brigade to take up the chase. Garrard's brigade was able to push the Southerners about a mile through the woods and up and down the hills in heavy skirmishing. As Osterhaus rode up, he found the Union line stopped by a Confederate roadblock located on the other side of a cornfield, beyond which the Ratliff Road junction was visible. The Confederate position was manned in skirmish order by two regiments of Brig. Gen. Alfred Cumming's Georgia Brigade backed by Waddell's Battery. Cumming had taken the rest of his brigade a few hundred yards farther north on the Jackson Road to join with Stevenson's other two brigades in facing Hovey's new and unexpected threat there.[100]

In addition to hearing sounds of battle from Hovey's position to his right, Osterhaus could now see heavy Confederate columns advancing along the Ratliff Road from his left. He prudently strengthened his line by adding a couple of regiments from Lindsey's brigade to Garrard's, in line athwart the Middle Road, while the rest of Lindsey's command supported a battery on high ground to the left rear. However, the mass of grayclads kept going past, toward Hovey. After about ninety minutes of heavy skirmish fire at the roadblock, Osterhaus reconnoitered farther to his left and spotted a large force on a ridge (probably Bowen's division) that he assumed was opposing Smith and threatening his own open left flank. (At this point, Blair was still at least a mile away.) To help fill the gap, Osterhaus sent Lindsey's last two regiments to his left and asked McClernand for reinforcements from Carr's division in the rear. At eleven o'clock Grant had ordered Blair to swing to his right up next to A. J. Smith to close the gaping hole, but this continued to be a major concern for McClernand until midafternoon; by then he had already pulled one of Carr's brigades over to partly fill the gap from the other side.[101]

Meanwhile, Stevenson's three brigades had maneuvered at right angles to the Jackson Road to meet the new Union threat coming up Champion Hill from the north. This change made the Confederate line resemble the figure 7 with the long leg along the Ratliff Road. The short leg of the 7 across the Jackson Road saw the brunt of the battle. Hovey's Federals soon spotted a three hundred–yard gap yawning in the gray line between Cumming's right flank and the two regiments he had left on the Middle Road facing Osterhaus. The bluecoats seized the opportunity, flanking Cumming and routing his brigade. Seeing this, the two Georgia regiments blockading the Middle Road ignored the threat from Osterhaus and wheeled ninety degrees to face the Union onslaught on their left

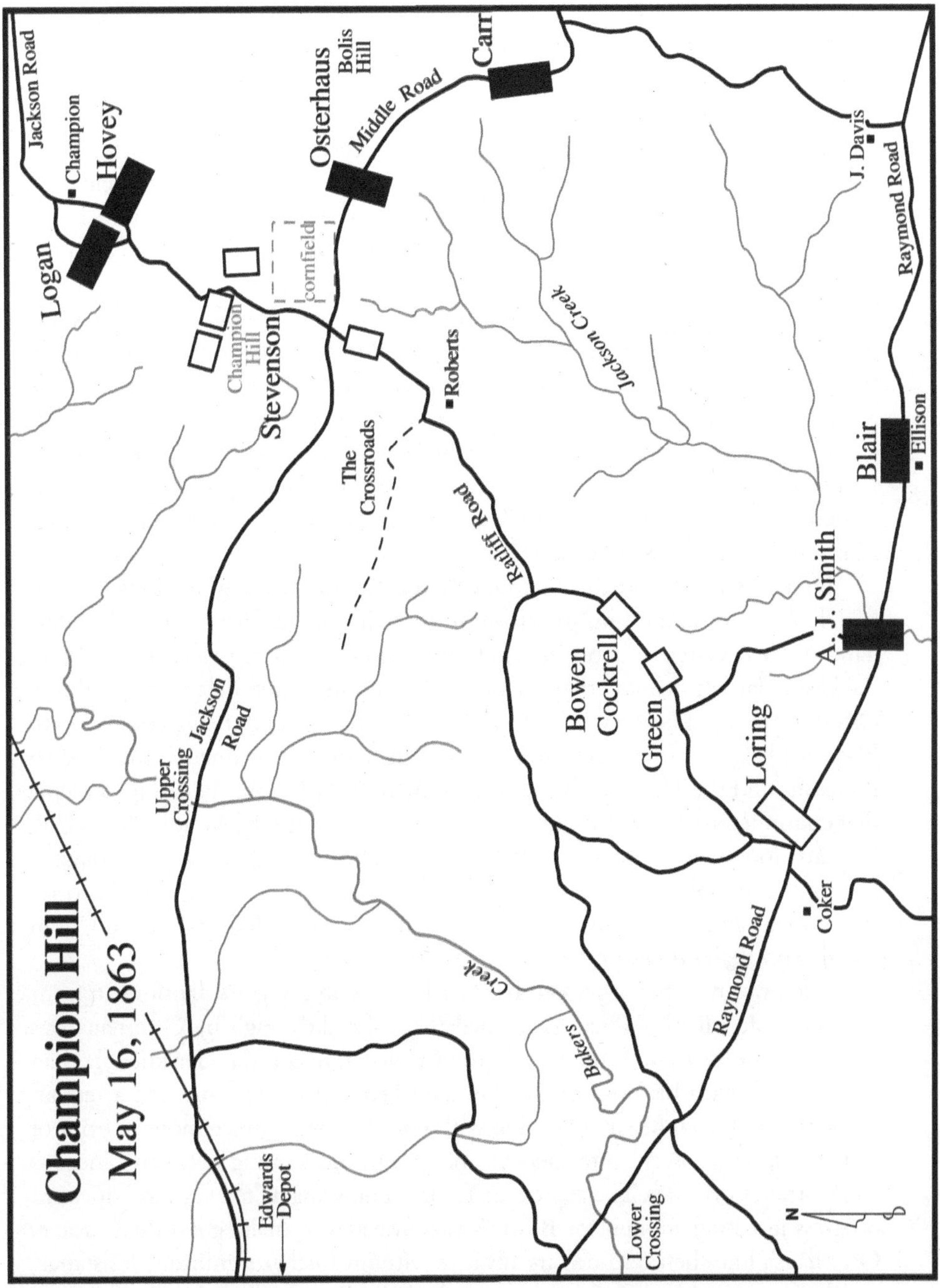
Champion Hill
May 16, 1863
Jackson Road
Champion
Hovey
Logan
Osterhaus
Bolis Hill
Middle Road
Carr
cornfield
Champion Hill
Stevenson
Roberts
The Crossroads
Ratliff Road
Jackson Creek
J. Davis
Raymond Road
Blair
Ellison
A. J. Smith
Bowen
Cockrell
Green
Loring
Upper Crossing
Jackson Road
Coker
Raymond Road
Bakers Creek
Edwards Depot
Lower Crossing
N

flank, accompanied by Waddell's guns. But they, too, were soon swept back and out of the fight and their guns captured, as Hovey's division gained control of the crossroads at about one thirty. Now only Cumming's orphaned skirmishers stood between Osterhaus's division on the Middle Road and the Union-held crossroads. Although all of this action unfolded within range of McClernand's binoculars, he still had not received permission from Grant to attack and so did not. Osterhaus watched the fierce battle from a ringside seat, as did his men, who could not understand why they "were standing idle and waiting close by while this fierce conflict was being fought by a single division. For four hours we stood there listening, waiting and wondering why we were not put into the fight."[102]

Bowen, his flank not being particularly threatened by Osterhaus, now ordered Green's and Cockrell's brigades up the Ratliff Road from left to right in front of Osterhaus's position to counterattack Hovey's division. Green's brigade actually swept right across the cornfield in full view, within a few hundred yards of Osterhaus's skirmishers. In fierce fighting, Bowen quickly pushed the bluecoats back from the crossroads nearly a mile, leaving the junction again in Confederate hands and now seriously threatening the Union supply train, parked near the Champion farmhouse.[103]

About this time, two thirty, Grant's return message finally made it back to McClernand, ordering him to "attack in force if opportunity occurs." McClernand ordered Osterhaus forward and sent a similar message to A. J. Smith on the Union far left, who, perhaps because of communication delays, did nothing. Osterhaus ordered his own brigades forward, despite still not being connected to Blair. With Osterhaus's new threat, two fresh Southern regiments, the Twelfth Louisiana and the Thirty-fifth Alabama, were peeled off from the reinforcements that continued to stream by and were ordered to shore up the Middle Road. Col. Edward Goodwin's Thirty-fifth Alabama now handled Lindsey's brigade roughly. His units scrambling back across the field in confusion, Lindsey worked to regroup them and waited for reinforcements to extend the left end of the Union line toward Blair's division.[104]

Bowen was now being pressed hard by Hovey's and Logan's divisions in front and on his left flank. When he learned that a breakthrough by Osterhaus was imminent on his right flank as well, the Confederate commander knew he had no way to sustain his position and notified Pemberton, who ordered a retreat. Cockrell and Green began a fighting withdrawal, crossing once more in front of Osterhaus, with Green's stragglers at one point even coming between Lindsey's and Garrard's brigades. The aggressive Twelfth Louisiana halted Garrard's forward progress just long enough for Bowen's two brigades to make good their escape. Osterhaus's line then resumed its advance without further significant resistance, and by the time his skirmishers approached the Ratliff Road the Confederates were in full retreat. Just as Grant rode up to the crossroads to view the new situation at four thirty, Osterhaus's skirmishers broke onto the Ratliff Road, with Carr already there, farther to the left. Grant ordered Carr's column to pursue Pemberton's army, followed by Osterhaus, since both of those divisions had seen little sustained action, while Hovey and Logan had suffered severe losses.[105]

Osterhaus's only real contribution to this battle was that his advance in force near the crossroads late in the day finally convinced Bowen to retreat. Of McClernand's four divisions, only Hovey's division was heavily engaged, losing fully a third of his men: neither Carr nor A.J. Smith had a fatality, although seventeen soldiers under Osterhaus died in this battle. Osterhaus has been criticized by historians for hesitance at Champion Hill, for unwillingness to proceed without reinforcements. On the other hand, at least one regimental account had McClernand holding Osterhaus back during the day. How much of Osterhaus's inactivity was in deference to McClernand's orders remains unclear. Nor is the extent to which Osterhaus's own concerns about his open left flank may have influenced McClernand's decisions, although the impact could have been considerable. Osterhaus had formal military training and was willing to share it, in contrast to the Regular Army officers who disdained political appointees in general and McClernand in particular. McClernand, a reasonably capable amateur, was astute enough to glean any wisdom his subordinate had to offer.[106]

Regardless of his field position, McClernand definitely believed his hands were tied without an attack order from Grant. Once that came, the slow advance (from two thirty when they received the attack order until four thirty when they reached the Ratliff Road) is hard to explain from this distance in time, due to uncertainty about the exact timing and sequence of events throughout the day. Despite Grant's ultimate overwhelming victory, for a time the battle was a near thing with the outcome very much in the balance. Had Federal communications been more effective, an aggressive attack by Osterhaus and A. J. Smith earlier in the day very probably could have trapped the Confederates before they could escape to Vicksburg.[107]

In the waning day, the bulk of the battered Confederate army retreated via Edwards Station toward the Big Black River, a distance of about ten miles. There, the exhausted Southern rear guard bedded down in trenches on the east side near the railroad bridge. Their Union pursuers stopped at Edwards Station, delighted to be able to rescue rancid hams and extra ammunition from boxcars that the Confederates had set afire before escaping.[108]

The pursuit resumed before dawn. Just as light was breaking, Carr's lead units spotted the manned fortifications stretching more than a mile along the east side of the Big Black River, guarding the railroad bridge leading to Vicksburg. Carr quickly deployed his men to the right behind a big cornfield, while Osterhaus held the center, just to the left of the railroad track that ran straight at the works; later A. J. Smith brought his division up to extend the left flank of the Union line. The rebel artillery began immediately to play upon the Federal position. The "alert and vigilant" Osterhaus took one look at the situation and called for his favorite Parrott rifles from Captain J. T. Foster's First Wisconsin Battery to soften up the rebel trenches before a charge was attempted across the broad open field. "Always a genial gentleman, his battle enthusiasm was unbounded, and he seemed to think we were his trump card," recalled a gunner. "Osterhaus, as usual, flattered the boys with promise of an elegant position. 'I shows you where you gets a good chance at 'em,'" he promised, directing them to a position at the top of an incline near the tracks. The movement of the Parrotts toward the new position attracted the attention of several Confederate gunners, and they immediately cut loose. Just as a Union gunner threw up the lid of his limber box to reach for a shell, a Confederate shell made a direct hit on the box, fatally burning the gunner. Several other men were hurt in the explosion, including Foster, with a shoulder wound, and Osterhaus, who sustained a good-size flesh wound on his left inner thigh from either a piece of flying shell or a wood splinter from the chest.[109]

McClernand sent his aide, Brig. Gen. Albert Lee, to relieve Osterhaus As the reluctant German went to the rear for treatment, the Seventy-seventh Illinois heard him shout to his men, "Git em out mit de bayonet—I'm mit you." Osterhaus limped to the division's field hospital, some distance behind the lines, searching for Dr. Joel Pomerene to take a look at his wound. (Pomerene, the division's chief surgeon, had already been treating Osterhaus's malaria for a month.) By the time Pomerene checked him and dressed the wound, the day was won for the Federals in grand style by a lightning charge by Brig. Gen. Mike Lawler's brigade from the Union right against the weak Confederate center. More than fifteen hundred Southerners were captured; the rest hightailed it for Vicksburg. Osterhaus was pleased that his division had captured seventeen artillery pieces.[110]

Pemberton was well tucked into his Vicksburg fortifications by the time the Federals headed out the next morning, Osterhaus traveling by carriage in deference to the throbbing and probably infected leg wound that made it hard to sit a horse. By evening the Union army had reached the outskirts of Vicksburg, twelve miles west of the Big Black River bridge, and had made camp in the open fields about two miles outside the defensive works. Sherman's Fifteenth Corps was on the north, near Chickasaw Bluffs, McPherson and the Seventeenth Corps held the center, and McClernand's Thirteenth Corps with Osterhaus was on the Union left.[111]

The next day, May 19, Grant scheduled an attack for two o'clock to capture the city before Pemberton could get his defenses organized. As the day began, Osterhaus's Ninth Division was still two miles away from the fortifications over rough ground. Osterhaus, even though he was "hardly able to move about on horseback" because of his fresh leg wound, resumed command and rode forward with McClernand's staff on a reconnaissance of the terrain. What he saw was not encouraging. Between their camp and the Southern fortifications outside Vicksburg ran three roughly parallel ridges. The intervening ravines were so steep that the only way Osterhaus's men could move a gun weighing hundreds of pounds would be to haul it by hand up and down the cliffs. Beyond the last ridge the reconnaissance party could see the Confederate fortifications on the heights closest to the town, flags waving. In McClernand's sector those defenses consisted of an irregular line of shallow rifle trenches interspersed at intervals with artillery emplacements set to pour cross fire into the side ravines that provided the only offensive access to the trenches. McClernand decided to array his divisions with Osterhaus on the left, forming the left flank of the entire army, Smith on Osterhaus's right and Carr in reserve. Most of Hovey's battered division was still at the Big Black. Manning the rebel fortifications in this sector were the same Alabamans Osterhaus had faced at Port Gibson, now under the command of Brig. Gen. Stephen D. Lee.[112]

Just opposite Osterhaus's assigned position loomed the Square Fort. Dominated by three field pieces, it was constructed of fourteen foot–thick loose-dirt walls and ringed halfway up by a defensive ditch fourteen feet wide and seven feet deep, filled with spikes. Farther down at the foot of the hill a strong line of abatis bristled. Beginning roughly a thousand yards north of Osterhaus's position, two similar earthen forts guarded the Southern Railroad cut into the city, both assigned to McClernand's corps. The nearest to the Square Fort was called the Railroad Redoubt. To the north beyond them, along the eight-mile Confederate line of rifle pits, McPherson and Sherman faced five other fortifications commanding the other road cuts into Vicksburg.[113]

At about noon Osterhaus ordered his division forward. They drove the Confederate pickets through the first two ravines without a problem, stopping just behind the crest of the last ridge to wait for the signal to attack. Meanwhile, Osterhaus had Capt. W. J. Lanphere's battery manhandled forward. As his skirmishers deployed ahead, Osterhaus and his staff came up on foot to reconnoiter the eight hundred yards remaining between the last ridge and the rebel line. What they discovered was not pretty: his men would still have to cross tumbled bumps, ravines, and gullies in their approach, with no chance to scout the ground first. Osterhaus saw for the first time the impenetrable abatis squatting at the foot of the slopes leading to the fortifications. Most worrisome, once past the abatis, the hard climb to the Confederate rifle pits and fort was up bare, steep slopes that provided the grayclads a clear field of fire from both sides of each ravine.[114]

At the appointed time, three volleys by all of the Union batteries signaled the jump-off. That morning Osterhaus had assigned Albert Lee to command his First Brigade after Garrard had been transferred at the last minute, and now Lee led his new brigade past the barren ridge crest and into the ravines before the enemy works. Osterhaus's division had no support against the line of Confederate rifle pits farther south of the Square Fort, so the brigade got hammered from two directions. Soon the tangled terrain forced the men to their left, where all five regiments bunched up in some confusion in a ravine offering a bit of protection. As Lee struggled to straighten his line under the rain of bullets and canister, he sustained a serious facial wound. Meanwhile, Osterhaus ordered Lindsey's brigade forward to the right to close the gap that had developed between Lee's bunched position and A. J. Smith's division to the right.[115]

On this exposed ground the men endured a daunting fusillade from the enemy's rifle pits and batteries. Col. Marcus Spiegel of the 120th Ohio wrote his wife that the charge was "perfectly terrific awful; I never saw shot, shell, crape and Bullets fly thicker in my life." After Lee was wounded, the Union attack stalled in the ravine. All but Keigwin's Forty-ninth Indiana stopped where they were or moved back behind the crest of the ridge. Osterhaus shouted for a section of the First Wisconsin Battery to be hauled forward to give his infantry some protection, and this was set up atop a steep hill about eight hundred yards from the fortifications. From this position Lanphere could reach the Confederate artillery emplacements, but the damage his guns did was only temporary, quickly repaired by the defenders later that night. A man from the Forty-second Ohio wrote bleakly, "We retired to the Gorge to rest, supperless and tired, our faces black with Powder, and no water to Wash. Our supplies non-present, and many of our comrades non-respondent." Elsewhere, the rest of Grant's attack ground to a halt as well, the other corps meeting similar obstacles and the same murderous enemy fire. At the end of the day, the most that could be said was that Grant's line was now within striking range of the fortifications, but that seemed enough to content the Federal commander.[116]

Now came two days of preparations for a better-organized Union assault, which Grant set for ten o'clock on the morning of May 22. Osterhaus spent the interim setting up a formidable line of artillery, to be directed the next day by Hovey, whose division had been so decimated at Champion Hill. Some of Osterhaus's officers decided not to tell their men about the new attack plans, but word inevitably got out. Having seen the "monster Work looming up" just over the ridge, the men were more nervous than usual, many writing hurried letters home and trying to set their affairs in order as best they could. They were right to be worried: from the vantage point of a volunteer in the Forty-second Ohio, the assault of May 22 "will ever be remembered by the Soldiers of Grant's Army as one of the Bloodiest of the campaign. In ordering the Charge on the entrenched Position of the Enemy, May 22nd., General Grant Sealed the fate of Hundreds of his best Soldiers. It was not a charge; it was not a Battle, nor an assault; But a Slaughter of Human Beings in cold Blood. We done our best; we struggled manfully; we fought desperately; all would not do, we were repulsed and with fearful loss." Yet a man from this same unit wrote, "I believe that the 42nd regiment as a general thing had the greatest respect for General Osterhaus." Clearly, they saw him as obeying onerous orders from above. Grant, although he did not have high hopes for success, went ahead with the attack that day at least in part because he thought that the troops would not have been as patient during the siege if they had not been able to try it.[117]

Before the battle, all division commanders had been ordered to establish their own points of attack, so Osterhaus met with brigade commanders Cols. James Keigwin, now commanding the First Brigade, and Daniel Lindsey, getting their reading of the difficult ground they faced. He ultimately chose a ravine in front of Lanphere's battery in which the two brigades could form up under cover. The grade to the fort was steep here, but the slope itself was cut by two ravines that, he reasoned, would provide at least some cover and handholds during the climb. Lindsey's two columns were to charge into the two ravines center and right, and Keigwin's third column was to go over the bare ridgetop on the left that led to the deep ditch and abatis below the fort. McClernand ordered Col. W. T. Spicely's brigade from Hovey's division to support Osterhaus on the left, standing by in reserve. Most of Osterhaus's massed batteries, twenty-two guns in all, were aimed at the two formidable strongholds that flanked the railroad cut into the city. Facing Osterhaus's division, Lee's brigade of Alabamans was set up in ranks two deep in order to be able to pour a continuous fire down the slope. Lee instructed his men to hold fire until the bluecoats approached the ditch in front of them, where they could not maneuver easily because of the abatis.[118]

Beginning at dawn, a heavy Union bombardment announced to the world that an attack was afoot. Shells from Hovey's batteries knocked a hole in the Railroad Redoubt, but had no such luck with the Square Fort, which was not visibly damaged by the bombardment. At precisely ten o'clock by everyone's synchronized watches, the shelling suddenly stopped, and with a roar the entire blue line charged at quick time. For a moment everything was eerily still except for the yells of the attackers, the Confederates holding their fire and the Northerners brandishing fixed bayonets with orders not to fire until they were into the works. Then, before Lindsey's columns could hit the ditch,

> The Rebels' parapet became a fringe of gray and steel, from which streamed a livid sheet of fire. Twenty thousand foes, a double rank along the whole front of the Federal army, rose up behind that parapet, and at from ten to sixty yards poured a withering volley into the advancing columns. Field guns, double-shotted, were run out over the parapet and fired, and heavy ordnance swept the ridges with canister. . . . The skirmish line was swept away in a moment. The head of the regiment appeared over the crest of the hill, but was literally blown back. The whole surface of the ridge up to the ditch was raked and plowed with a concentric fire of musketry and cannister at pistol range. . . . [T]he head of the ravine was the focus of a converging fire from three points, armed by heavy batteries. . . . Every part of it was enfiladed from the hostile parapet, which was too high to be climbed without bridges or scaling ladders.[119]

Lindsey's columns were in serious trouble from the outset. They somehow got past the abatis on the right, but Lindsey found it "utterly impossible" to reach the enemy's works at the point Osterhaus had ordered. The attack point Osterhaus had picked turned out to be a bad choice in a situation in which there were no good choices, so he ordered Lindsey to hold his position. Any further advance was out of the question. The men were pinned down, showers of bullets and canister "throwing up sprays of dirt not unlike a furious hailstorm on a dusty road" and pelting the unfortunate soldiers who were most exposed.[120]

Osterhaus, frustrated, ordered a twelve-pounder howitzer brought forward and shouted to the Southerners, "'You shoost stay there and I give you hell smell.' He sighted the gun and hit it [a rebel gun], turning it bottom side up, and excitedly said: 'Didn't I told you I make you hell smell?'" That earned the general a dubious new nickname, "Old Hell Smell," that his veterans still remembered fifty years later. He also sent orders to Keigwin to have his sharpshooters take out the Southern gunners or at least force them to keep their heads down. His courier in this case was M. M. Lacey, one of the officers of the Forty-ninth Indiana, drafted because Osterhaus was short of staff officers just then. Although Lacey had to make two hazardous trips across open ground carrying messages, he recalled, "I could not refuse, and he thanked me in his grand old courteous way, which made one ready to do anything."[121]

On the left, Keigwin was faring little better than Lindsey. The Seventh Kentucky led the charge over the ridge and was immediately blasted back. The 118th Illinois, coming behind, "saw so many of the 7th Ky. fall that they, I suppose went upon the principle that good men were scarce, and they just went back under cover," recalled Keigwin years later. The regiments that did maintain forward momentum ran into the "almost impassible" abatis that only the Forty-ninth Indiana succeeded in negotiating, only to be pinned down immediately in the ditch by fire from three directions. Osterhaus did not bother to call in Spicely's brigade because there had been no breakthrough to exploit with his reserves.[122]

Osterhaus was not alone in his failure to take his objective. The entire Union attack had bogged down within thirty minutes, with the exception of a few brave souls from Lawler's brigade who had quickly made it through the hole into the Railroad Redoubt to precariously hold that position for a time. In the early afternoon, McClernand repeatedly asked Grant for support for Lawler's toehold on the fortifications. McClernand himself had peremptorily ordered Osterhaus either to use Spicely's brigade to make a diversion or release him to Carr, but neither happened, for reasons unclear. Although not convinced of the miraculous breakthrough, Grant reluctantly ordered both other corps commanders to make fresh diversions and sent Brig. Gen. Isaac F. Quinby's division from McPherson to McClernand for assignment.[123]

Unfortunately, Quinby's reinforcements, two miles away, did not reach McClernand until four o'clock, and the Thirteenth Corps commander was unable to use them to good effect. By the time the reinforcements were in position to be deployed, the blazing sun was low in the west, blinding the attackers. McClernand had sent Col. Samuel A. Holmes's brigade to Osterhaus, who ordered them to form in line but then canceled the attack due to the late hour. Osterhaus wrote that "with a good deal of talk" he persuaded McClernand to delay a further advance that evening, which would "keep us in possession of the general line and save the men." As the second assault finally petered out at dark, again the only thing Grant had gained was a more forward position from which to conduct the siege, this time at the cost of a great many lives. Osterhaus lost the fewest of any engaged division, perhaps because his ground was so hopeless he was not encouraged enough by the possibility of success to send more men to their deaths.[124]

Even so, that evening Osterhaus wrote McClernand that his troops were "very much exhausted," calculating that he could turn out only about a thousand men, and those "in a broken down condition." He requested relief by fresher troops so that his soldiers could have one day's rest, if such could be arranged without compromising plans for the next day. Instead, the Union high command had other plans for Osterhaus.[125]

The next morning, as Osterhaus began issuing the Ninth Division's orders for the siege of Vicksburg, Grant ordered him instead to take a brigade and two sections of a battery and head east twelve miles to guard the Big Black River railroad-bridge crossing. Osterhaus's men were initially disgusted with their new assignment, coming so soon after the two assaults on Vicksburg on May 19 and 22. "After five days of the most laborious, hazardous and terrible hardship and privations, when we expected relieve, we received an Order to get ready to march in an hour," griped one. But, philosophically, they figured Osterhaus received this assignment because he was "a splendid man, officer, fighter and commander." One wrote his wife that Osterhaus was "a careful, brave and discreed General who is always sent with his fighting Division to the most difficult places." Another said that by sending Osterhaus to the Big Black, "General Grant showed his estimate of him as General of an independent command."[126]

Choosing Osterhaus did make a lot of sense for Grant. His only ethnic lieutenant was generally recognized for his careful intelligence reports and his experience in handling the myriad problems of independent command. Charles Dana, observing Grant's Vicksburg campaign for Lincoln, described Osterhaus as "a pleasant, genial fellow, brave and quick, [who] makes a first-rate report of reconnaissance. There is not another general in this army who keeps the commander in chief so well informed concerning whatever happens at his outposts." Osterhaus did not disappoint Grant in this assignment. His orders were to observe Gen. Joseph E. Johnston's movements to the east and determine his troop strength, with the implication that Osterhaus's five regiments would be the first line of defense in a Confederate attempt to break Pemberton out of Vicksburg. But that was not the general's entire assignment. Besides conducting intensive surveillance on a line at least twenty-five miles long, Osterhaus was also to penetrate deep into rebel territory east of the bridge, destroying all bridges and railroads and confiscating or ruining any conveyances, food, or livestock that might aid Johnston in mounting a rescue effort. Other than a brief brigade-strength foray by Blair, for the first month of the siege Osterhaus's brigade was the only Union presence outside the siege lines.[127]

The brigade was off for its new post the morning of May 24. Col. James Keigwin, a bricklayer in private life, had shown great energy and resourcefulness during the move down the west side of the Mississippi as well as in battle, so his First Brigade was Osterhaus's natural choice to accompany him. When Osterhaus arrived at the bridge, there were only about fifty troopers of Carr's Sixth Missouri Cavalry under Col. Clark Wright waiting for him, and the colonel himself was not then, or later, inclined to take orders from Osterhaus. Not happy, Osterhaus immediately appealed to McClernand for more artillery and a full complement of cavalry. Although Grant had precious little cavalry to spare, he turned Wright's whole outfit over to Osterhaus, and by May 27 the general had all of Wright's two hundred troopers off on patrol or manning vedettes. A pattern soon emerged: while Osterhaus sent intelligence directly to Grant, he went through McClernand for needed resources.[128]

In a very few days Osterhaus accomplished an enormous amount with his thousand men. His extensive patrols brought in a steady stream of information that he forwarded to Grant with his own interpretation. His work parties, protected by cavalry, were highly effective, although the area was frequently patrolled by Southern cavalry camped within ten miles of the Big Black. Ranging far to the north and south of the railroad, the Federals destroyed all railroad bridges for twenty miles east and burned any railroad cars and stores they found, including ten thousand bushels of corn and hundreds of bales of cotton. They brought in livestock, horses, and mules by the hundreds, all of which Osterhaus forwarded to the appropriate authorities. This destruction of civilian property he found distasteful: "I am doing a terrible work (I feel rather bad about it)," he wrote McClernand.[129]

To augment his own men for his work parties, Osterhaus actively recruited willing African Americans in the area. His crews began to restore the Confederate fortifications on the bluff west of the Big Black for Union use and to repair the railroad from the river west to Vicksburg. Even though he had ordered the destruction of all the Confederate rolling stock east of the river, Osterhaus resourcefully salvaged enough materials to construct a flatcar, drawn by four mules instead of a locomotive, to help move his hauls westward on his repaired railroad segment. After a week of this nonstop activity, the countryside was pretty well picked clean, and Osterhaus's men and horses were exhausted. But no relief was in sight: Osterhaus asked McClernand for Lindsey's brigade on June 6, but except for two regiments they were not released to him until two weeks later.[130]

By the first week in June, Johnston had accumulated about twenty-three thousand effectives east of the Big Black, including Maj. Gen. John C. Breckinridge's division at Jackson. Osterhaus's surveillance had turned up a cavalry force more than twice his own strength actively patrolling the countryside opposite: about twenty-five hundred troopers. Despite feeling weak and exhausted from a flare-up of his recurrent malarial fever and dysentery, Osterhaus continued to personally inspect the Big Black crossings for miles northward to ascertain the risk of each one as the water level dropped and the Southern cavalry raids increased across the river. He also felt the need to fortify his bluff defenses at the bridge. He had his engineer, Lt. Francis Tunica, draw up plans, but this time he had problems getting local black labor to augment his work parties. By now Union recruiters were urging the contrabands to join the army, so Osterhaus was competing with his own recruiters for manpower. Osterhaus asked McClernand to borrow a hundred of the new black recruits for his work teams. Just three weeks later the recruiters were asking McClernand to return Osterhaus's workers (now swelled to three hundred) to help fill their regiments, but in the meantime they got the work done. The fortifications guarding the crossing, now extending three-quarters of a mile and "making the position a strong one and easily defended against a large force," became another stumbling block to Johnston's plans.[131]

His own active patrol presence to the contrary, Johnston had already concluded that he did not have enough men to challenge Grant for Vicksburg. Osterhaus's and Blair's destructive activity that first week was enough to discourage him even further. Johnston reported to Richmond that the surrounding countryside was "well nigh exhausted. . . . Horses for artillery, mules and wagons had to be purchased or impressed and brought from a considerable distance. It was not till late in June that these wants were met and then but partially." The Federals' stripping of the countryside forced Johnston to haul all of his supplies and fodder with him, and he complained bitterly to Richmond that he lacked the wagons and teams to go on the offensive. Although devastating to the local economy, this was exactly what Grant had hoped for.[132]

After the initial flurry of manual labor, the work in Osterhaus's camp settled into a routine of long patrols and frequent picket duty, with inspection and dress parade on Sundays. The canton on the bluff was in a pleasant, shady area, much more comfortable than the lines behind Vicksburg. There were no tents yet, but the men made do with shelters of willow branches to keep off the sun in sultry weather that reached 110 degrees. The constant bombardment at Vicksburg could be heard clearly; in fact, it was audible as far away as Jackson, where Breckinridge's Confederate troops also waited and listened. Osterhaus had patrols out day and night, frequently meeting and chasing hit-and-run Southern cavalry patrols. Grant occasionally had specific requests for information, and Osterhaus kept both him and McClernand apprised of his discoveries. Displaying his "delight in the game of intelligence gathering," his dispatches during this period gave a very detailed account of the best information he could glean, and he tried to corroborate one source with another whenever he could in order to make it more reliable.[133]

About mid-June, Osterhaus began asking McClernand for a telegraph line and operator to hasten the frequent message traffic back and forth with both superiors. Grant agreed, and line was strung and an operator assigned. But just as Osterhaus was about to send his first message, Sherman's pioneers came along and cut down the line to use the wire to tie fascines, even though local citizens told them the wire had been strung less than twenty-four hours before by Federal troops. Osterhaus notified McClernand that he was repairing the line himself, but McClernand went further, writing to Grant in his usual imperious style, "Please have it restored and further interference stopped." Sherman denied knowing anything about the damage, saying that it was too late to mend it in any case. It was indeed too late; Osterhaus had already taken care of it.[134]

Getting Osterhaus his telegraph line was about the last thing McClernand did for him: Grant relieved McClernand on June 17 on a technicality, the culmination of Grant's animosity toward the Thirteenth Corps commander that had been building for months for a variety of reasons. Fortunately, Osterhaus was far enough away to stay out of the controversy; he had been in this situation before, first with the removal from command of John Frémont and later when Franz Sigel was passed over for promotion. As was his pattern, Osterhaus declined to get involved with the politics surrounding these political generals, and usually managed not to burn his bridges. Instead, he methodically reported to his new commander, Maj. Gen. Edward O. C. Ord, and kept going. Ord, an old West Pointer who had served with Sherman in the Mexican War, kept himself firmly in the center of the information flow: most of Osterhaus's communications from this point were through Ord to Grant rather than to Grant directly.[135]

Osterhaus had established his headquarters in a private home a mile or two from the Big Black, and, for the first time, this "most approachable of men" had direct dealings with the subjugated citizens on a broad variety of concerns. Besides questioning local individuals about military information they were suspected to have, here he daily met delegations asking for protection, permission to pass through the lines, food rations, or reparations for possessions stolen by Federal soldiers. The general seemed to enjoy these visits, mostly from mistresses of local plantations, during which he argued politics and occasionally teased the ladies. A frequent visitor was Ellen Bachelor, whose sons were serving in the Confederate army and whose runaway slave, Mary, Osterhaus had taken on as a cook. At one visit Mrs. Bachelor asked him for a guard for her property, which he granted but then told her that if she did not behave herself he would be obliged to send her to Ship Island. That chance remark led to his being characterized shortly after the war, in a memoir written by a woman who spent the war years far away in Richmond, Virginia, as that "Dutch General Osterhaus" who exerted a "tyrannical despotism . . . quite equal in its rigor to that exercised by Butler in New Orleans." (Maj. Gen. Benjamin F. "Beast" Butler had sent a rebel woman to prison on Ship Island for laughing at the funeral of a Union soldier.) On the contrary, Osterhaus seemed reasonably mellow in the face of the thinly veiled contempt of these die-hard Southerners. Another Union officer who regularly visited in the Bachelor home was incensed that "here we are giving regular rations to such people as these, who openly denounce and abuse us, who laugh at our charity at the same time they *demand* it, and whose male kindred are all in the armies in our front."[136]

On June 22 the biggest skirmish so far on the Big Black line had Grant fully expecting an attack by Johnston in that northern sector. A month after he had sent Osterhaus to cover his second front, he committed fully five divisions under Sherman to do a more thorough job of patrolling the entire area from Osterhaus's position north to the Yazoo. Osterhaus, finally reinforced with his other brigade, now reported temporarily to Sherman, although he continued to report intelligence to Grant directly or through Ord. The eastern front remained quiet; however, in the first week of July all that changed. Consistent new intelligence emerged that Johnston was finally on the move to rescue Pemberton. It was true: on June 29 Johnston had set off with five divisions toward the Big Black, camping about ten miles east of the river on July 1. His plan was to make a diversion so Pemberton could "cut his way out." (Of course, Pemberton did not know this. The message that Johnston was coming did not reach the besieged commander until July 10.) For the next two days Johnston made a leisurely reconnaissance of the crossings, finally deciding that Osterhaus's fortifications at the bridge and Sherman's Union troop strength north of the railroad would force him to cross south of the railroad.[137]

On July 3 Osterhaus captured one of Breckinridge's men, who told him that Breckinridge had moved seven thousand men and a large train west from Jackson to Bolton, and that Johnston was to meet him at the river somewhere in front of Osterhaus's twenty-five hundred troops at the railroad bridge. Breckinridge indeed had moved out on July 1, and late in the afternoon of July 5 had marched as far as the Champion Hill battleground, ten miles from the bridge. Johnston's plan was to mount an attack on Grant's rear on July 7, right through Osterhaus's position. Fortunately for Osterhaus, the evening of July 5 Johnston received word that Vicksburg had fallen the day before, so instead, the next morning, he ordered his dejected command to hustle back to the state capital. Port Hudson capitulated two days later, and the Mississippi River was again open to Union shipping over its whole length.[138]

Osterhaus did not have much time to celebrate the fall of fortress Vicksburg; the campaign was not yet over. Sherman sent him orders that same day to report back to Ord and prepare to move out. Sherman signed his chatty orders with an informal, "Truly, your friend," rather than the usual formal closing, and assured Osterhaus that he would put in a word for him with Ord, to whom Osterhaus was a comparative stranger. Perhaps his tone was to make amends for the earlier telegraph incident. But Osterhaus did not need an introduction. Ord was soon to discover that the general was a skilled artillery commander who coordinated infantry and artillery actions much better than most of his peers.[139]

Osterhaus again took point as the Thirteenth Corps chased Breckinridge back to the state capital, while, under the overall command of Sherman, the Fifteenth Corps and part of the Ninth Corps pursued Johnston's other divisions on parallel roads to the north. Osterhaus by now had both of his brigades plus about fifteen companies of cavalry under Maj. Hugh Fullerton, who brought along their own mountain howitzers. Six twenty-pounder Parrotts of the First Wisconsin Battery and six ten-pounder Rodmans of the Seventh Michigan Battery also made the trek in support. Osterhaus nipped Breckinridge's heels all the way to Jackson over the next four days in spite of the grueling heat and the lack of potable water en route. Brisk skirmishing with Breckinridge's rear guard began only a mile into the march and continued on a daily basis as the Confederates yielded ground slowly. These skirmishes were mostly running fights between cavalry units, but occasionally the Southerners would stop to make a stand, as Breckinridge did in a favorable defensive position near Bolton on July 7. At that moment, Osterhaus's infantry column was some distance back, following along in the heat as fast as they could under the brutal conditions, so the general dismounted some of his troopers to skirmish through the woods, meanwhile threatening Breckinridge's flank with the rest of his cavalry. The tactics quickly worked. "No man could move a skirmish line faster than General Osterhaus," a gunner recalled. And he was usually in the thick of it: "He never says 'go, boys,' but, 'follow me.' Brave to a fault."[140]

In his somewhat unorthodox style Osterhaus kept up the pressure on the grayclads, using his mountain howitzers or "jackass batteries" to relieve sticking points, followed by the heavier guns if things warmed up. "We always knew when 'P. Jos.' Osterhaus had the advance, because he advanced a battery with his skirmishers and shelled everything in sight, believing the government could buy ammunition cheaper than it could soldiers," recalled a veteran. When Osterhaus called up Lanphere's First Wisconsin, "the intervening troops would oblique out of the road to right or left, and we go forward to our own, ownest comrades on the battlefield," recalled a gunner. This battery loved to come to the rescue, racing "over dry ditches where a farmer would not drive a wagon, through clumps of bushes, over logs a foot thick, every horse on the gallop, every rider lashing his team and yelling. . . . The guns jump two feet high as the heavy wheels strike rock or log, but not a horse slackens his pace, not a cannoneer loses his seat." Holding onto her hat, Mrs. Lanphere rode to the front with her husband, usually staying until the firing became quite lively.[141]

A heavier-than-usual cavalry skirmish on July 9 near Clinton led to another stand by Breckinridge. As Osterhaus's cavalry thundered through the woods after the grayclad troopers, they came upon a superior number of infantry drawn up in line of battle, supported by twelve-pounders that had the range on Osterhaus's smaller mountain howitzers. It was time again for his big guns. This time Osterhaus called for the Seventh Michigan Battery. Waiting until he had his infantry in line of battle, Osterhaus opened his Rodmans on the Confederate position, meanwhile advancing his sharpshooters as skirmishers in front and making a massed cavalry charge to threaten the Southern left flank. "The effect was complete," wrote a satisfied Osterhaus, and the Southerners soon retired. The next afternoon Osterhaus and the Ninth Division advanced to a position only two miles from the capital, where they found a considerable Confederate force turned out to contest their approach to the town. Using the same tactics he had the day before, Osterhaus drove them back into their fortifications.[142]

While on their approach to Jackson, Osterhaus was dismayed to learn of the circumstances of the death of one of his young German American staffers from the Third Kansas Cavalry, who had been captured by a Third Texas Cavalry patrol. Before dying, the man told the Union troopers who found him that he had been shot down by a sergeant of the Texas regiment because he was carrying papers that commissioned him to raise a colored company, very likely as a result of encouragement from Osterhaus.[143]

The bulk of Johnston's Confederate army made it back to the burned-out capital on July 7. When Sherman's expeditionary force closed in two days later, he found the Southerners ensconced behind their fortifications complete with siege guns, their backs to the Pearl River on the east. Both Grant, still in Vicksburg, and Sherman were content to wait Johnston out with another siege, hoping he would skedaddle across the Pearl and out of the state. At this point the exhausted Union troops were in no condition to pursue. The next day Osterhaus, in the center of the Union line, had breastworks constructed for his guns and set his men to entrenching. Artillery firing was constant, and Osterhaus, as always, kept an eye on his batteries. Once during that day Osterhaus saved his First Wisconsin Battery from annihilation when he noticed that Keigwin was not paying attention to placement and had put them in an untenably exposed position in range of the big rebel siege guns. Even so, several men and horses were killed or injured before they could be extricated. The only other action that day was a Confederate sortie against his right, which was repelled without problem. When things had quieted down, Osterhaus went to the trenches to check on his men. "Sitting down in the trenches facing the rebel works, he remarked, 'I takes a front seat.' Just then a shell came howling overhead and exploded behind the general. Quick as thought, he whirled around and taking a seat on the other side of the trench, he said, 'I takes a pack seat.' The men hailed the movement and the remark with cheers and roars of laughter."[144]

On July 16 Osterhaus's weary division was relieved and took a position in reserve. That same night, as Johnston had his best band serenade the Federals from the fortifications, the rebels silently slipped across the Pearl River and out of the state. The blueclads enjoyed the music but did not seriously pursue the Confederates. Five days later Osterhaus's exhausted and sick men began another grueling three-day march in the oppressive heat back to the Big Black. They had suffered badly on this trek: one company that had left the Big Black with forty-one men returned with only eight, the rest felled by "remittant and congestive fevers" and sunstroke rather than by gunfire. The guns were silent at last; the campaign to open the Mississippi was finally over. As the column neared the river, Osterhaus spotted Lt. Daniel Webster of the First Wisconsin Battery and called him over. "Vebster, come here; I want you mit the Battery. Foster [injured with Osterhaus at the Big Black] has been gone too long. You come and we'll put bayonets on the guns and make charges with them. It is the best Battery I ever saw. Twice they gets into the fight ahead of my skirmishers." Although joking as usual, this was high praise for his beloved Wisconsin gunners, whom he would never command again.[145]

General-in-Chief Henry Halleck wasted no time breaking up the huge army Grant had accumulated for the Vicksburg campaign. On August 7 he peeled off Ord's Thirteenth Corps and sent it on to Maj. Gen. N. P. Banks, commanding the Department of the Gulf. Osterhaus's Ninth Division was dismantled and its units reassigned. Only Grant's remaining two corps, the Fifteenth under Sherman and the Seventeenth under McPherson, remained in the Vicksburg sector. Osterhaus was relieved of command of the decommissioned Ninth Division, next assignment to be determined. When his men learned that he would not be accompanying them to the Gulf, they were upset. "He was very popular with his troops . . . and we were very much worried when he was taken from the command of that division," recalled John Entrekin of the 114th Ohio. Osterhaus felt the same way about his first nonethnic command: "There are very few Germans in it; but that is no matter. I assure you they have fought for the good cause as bravely as ever Germans could have done," he told a German American audience in St. Louis after the campaign. "The 9th Division . . . through the campaigns I shared with it, had become dear to me. Officers and men deserve high encomiums for their steadiness, reliability and good discipline," he recalled later.[146]

A day after the German was relieved, he was on his way home for a twenty-day furlough. Pale and weak, taking quinine and constantly having to watch his diet because of his chronic diarrhea, Osterhaus at long last could rest and try to recover. Although he was delighted to see his growing family after so many months in the field, he was concerned to find his wife in poor health. After the national press had reported his injury at the Big Black, he had written to reassure her that he was not badly hurt. But rumors were rampant that he had been killed at Jackson, and these had no doubt reached her as well. Even though his own men scoffed at this ("They did not get our old 'dutchman' if they did shoot close," wrote one), Matilda must have had a turn when the rumor reached her. A similar scare later in the year would possibly contribute to her untimely death at age thirty-eight.[147]

Chapter 4
The Chattanooga Campaign

WHEN Osterhaus returned from leave on August 21, Grant sent him to the Big Black River to report to Fifteenth Corps commander William T. Sherman. However, the general's next assignment was by no means assured: Sherman at that point had more generals than he had divisions, and two other generals outranked Osterhaus. Despite this, when Osterhaus asked for the command of his old Missouri compatriots, who had fought with distinction at Vicksburg in Frederick Steele's First Division, his request was granted (Steele recently having been transferred). Sherman's decision was an indication of his esteem for Osterhaus as well as the fact that the German had been recommended for promotion by both McClernand and Ord. Osterhaus would continue to command the First Division throughout both the Chattanooga and the Atlanta campaigns, but at present he had just a few weeks to whip his new division into his idea of shape before the next assignment materialized.[1]

His large First Brigade, under Brig. Gen. Charles A. Woods, included the three mostly German American regiments that Osterhaus had led in the Arkansas campaign: the Third Missouri, his own original Twelfth Missouri from St. Louis and Belleville, and the Seventeenth Missouri from St. Louis. The other regiments were new to Osterhaus: the Twenty-seventh, Twenty-ninth, Thirtieth, Thirty-first, and Thirty-second Missouri as well as the Thirteenth Illinois and the Seventy-sixth Ohio. The laconic Woods was new to him as well, an Iowan and West Point graduate with a good reputation. Woods turned out to be extremely capable, inheriting the division after Osterhaus moved on in 1864. The Iowan was a favorite of Sherman's as well as of his own men, who admired his informality ("more common than a Potomac Lieut. in both dress and deportment") and coolness under fire.[2]

Osterhaus's much smaller Second Brigade, under Col. James A. Williamson, were Iowans to a man: the Fourth, Ninth, Twenty-fifth, Twenty-sixth, Thirtieth, and the Thirty-first Iowa; the Fourth and Ninth Iowa were veterans of Pea Ridge. Williamson, before the war a lawyer from Kentucky, had served with bravery as Grenville Dodge's adjutant at Pea Ridge and was much later awarded the Congressional Medal of Honor for his performance at Chickasaw Bayou. But, although unquestionably courageous, he was somewhat of a complainer. Williamson and Osterhaus were destined to butt heads as time went on. By contrast, Osterhaus was delighted with his artillery, more of a known quantity: the First Battery of the Iowa Light under Lt. James Williams, Battery F of the Second Missouri Light under the redoubtable "Flying Dutchman," Capt. Clemens Landgraeber (a former Prussian artillery officer with quite a fighting reputation whom Osterhaus had met at Pea Ridge), and the Fourth Battery of the Ohio Light under Capt. George Froehlich, all commanded by Capt. Henry Griffiths. Osterhaus had commanded the Fourth Ohio battery at Pea Ridge.[3]

Osterhaus spent the next month at the Big Black camp, running the usual patrols and destroying Mississippi infrastructure in addition to drilling his troops daily. In late August, he heard that Grant had been severely injured in a fall from a horse and confined to bed for several weeks. When Grant's wife and son hurried to his side in Vicksburg, Osterhaus kindly agreed to help occupy young Frederick Dent Grant, thirteen, allowing him to tag along on his black horse whenever possible as the general made rounds and went for short trips outside the lines. Osterhaus was happy to help Grant, whom he greatly admired and respected, much later calling him "one of the strongest military figures of the nineteenth century, a man who would have been great in any of the European wars of the last hundred years."[4]

On September 22 Grant was still flat on his back when he received a dispatch from General-in-Chief Henry Halleck. After a disastrous defeat at nearby Chickamauga, Maj. Gen. William S. Rosecrans's Army of the Cumberland was trapped in Chattanooga by Gen. Braxton Bragg's Army of Tennessee, "closely beleaguered with no communications and the scantiest sustenance," as Osterhaus put it. Grant tapped Osterhaus, and again his most ethnic of generals did not disappoint his commander. Grant was able to report to Halleck that Osterhaus was on the road that same day to relieve Rosecrans. Sherman's other divisions would follow. As Osterhaus recounted: "On September 22nd 1863, General Grant called me to the telegraph and asked when the 1st Division could be ready to move to Vicksburg and from there to Memphis. The Division was ready and could leave as soon as the Tents were struck. On the evening of the same day it left," the first of Sherman's four divisions to get under way. "Wherever the Red One (Osterhaus) can go, we can go too. . . . The assurance that General Osterhaus will lead us wherever we are going satisfies me," wrote Henry Kircher of the Twelfth Missouri.[5]

The Fifteenth Corps's assignment included opening the railroad across northern Mississippi and Alabama to provide a vital supply line for Chattanooga, so Sherman expected progress to be slow. For the next month Osterhaus's First Division had the advance as the corps crept through a fifty-mile stretch between

Corinth, Mississippi, and Tuscumbia, Alabama, repairing and building the railroad and fending off the daily harassment of both guerrillas and Confederate cavalry under Stephen D. Lee, Osterhaus's opponent from the Vicksburg campaign. Osterhaus's division fought several major skirmishes at Cane Creek and Cherokee Station as they went. On October 21, Lt. Col. William M. Torrence of the Thirtieth Iowa was killed in one of these almost daily actions.[6]

At the end of October, Grant ordered Sherman to abandon the railroad and make haste to Chattanooga. In response, Sherman sent Osterhaus forward to Tuscumbia to occupy Lee's pesky cavalry while he moved his other divisions up and prepared to cross the Tennessee River. In a major skirmish at Tuscumbia, Osterhaus drove Lee back several miles beyond the town and then returned to protect the rear of Sherman's column as he headed for the river. Because the Union pioneers had to corduroy miles of soupy roads, what should have been a short march took two days. While waiting, the First Division had to spend a miserable snowy and wet night in the woods without blankets or tents. By now Osterhaus, like his men, was tired and stressed, but he had not lost his biting humor. On stopping at a house during a steady downpour to wait out yet another interminable delay, he and his officers took shelter on the covered porch. The woman of the house bustled out and complained to Osterhaus, "'I wish you would have these soldiers get off my porch, they are getting it very muddy.' The General said, 'All right, Madam, I will make them get off.' He went to the house door and said, 'Boys, come right in the house, don't stand there, you are getting the porch muddy.'" The soldiers enjoyed this story about their general: "Everyone in the division loved the General and would cheer when he rode by, and he was a fighter to the finish," wrote Calvin Ainsworth in his diary.[7]

Osterhaus kept Lee at arm's length as Sherman got the rest of his divisions across the Tennessee River. The First Division would not complete its own crossing until November 4. Two days before, while the men awaited their turn to board the boats, a rider galloped up to Osterhaus with an urgent telegram. Rather than the usual dispatch from Sherman, this time it was shocking news from his wife Matilda's physician in St. Louis. Matilda was dying, and if he wanted to see her once more he had to leave immediately. Whether Osterhaus had known just how ill she was that fall is uncertain, since no diary or letters have been found of this period. Now Osterhaus had an excruciating decision to make: rush home to his wife, dying in a strange country with no family except her young children around her, or stay long enough to see his division over the river and out of Lee's path.[8]

As he had in Mannheim and later in St. Louis, the general put his country ahead of his family: his duty was to shepherd his division across the Tennessee. The wait for his men to cross the river must have been agonizing for him. Not until the evening of November 3, when all but his last two regiments were across, did Osterhaus head for home on a twenty-day emergency leave.

Osterhaus started toward Memphis on the railroad that he had helped reopen to Iuka, then proceeded by steamer three hundred miles to St. Louis. When he finally arrived home he found that he was too late: Matilda, just thirty-eight years old, had died on November 5, 1863, of disease of the liver and spleen. According to a much later newspaper account, she had collapsed after reading a report of her husband's death in battle in her local newspaper; perhaps this was Torrence's death, misreported. Even if Osterhaus had been able to leave the campaign the moment he received the dispatch, he probably would not have been in time to see her again, but that was of little consolation.[9]

Osterhaus arrived in time to see his beloved wife buried properly in Bellefontaine Cemetery in St. Louis on November 10, but could not stay longer to comfort his stunned family. With the help of friends, he made hurried arrangements for the care of his essentially parentless children: Anna, fourteen, was in a convent school; twelve year-old Hugo and the three younger children, Alexander, Emma, and four-year-old Karl, were probably placed with friends. Since the Osterhauses had no relatives in the United States, he sent an urgent message to Matilda's family in Kreuznach, Germany, begging for Matilda's unmarried sister, Amalie, to come to take care of the children. And then he headed back to the front, leaving behind a bereaved young family without a parent's comfort.[10]

During Osterhaus's sad journey home to St. Louis, his division, led by Woods, had marched two hundred tough miles in two weeks, but they still had a difficult trek ahead on roads that were "not only bad but rascally." Stuck behind a long wagon train, they became exhausted prying artillery and wagons, hauled by now worn-out teams, out of "impassible, cut up and seemingly bottomless" muck. On November 22 Woods started the division again at eight o'clock, but they made barely a mile and a half in three hours. Then around noon Osterhaus finally caught up with his struggling command. As he rode through his regiments, his men, who all knew about his wife's death and wanted to show their support, greeted his return with "thundering cheers. . . . [W]e again feel like Uncle Sam's boys ought to[,] sure of victory." "He enjoyed [the cheers] as an expression of confidence, and the men were glad to see him," recalled the men of the Thirteenth Illinois. And Osterhaus probably welcomed the distraction that the upcoming battle would offer. Just as he arrived and relieved Woods, an urgent dispatch came from Grant: "You must get up with your force tomorrow without fail. Pass the wagon train and leave it to follow with rear guard. If you cannot get up with your artillery, come without it, leaving it to follow. I will expect the head of your column at Brown's Ferry by 10 a.m. tomorrow (23d) without fail." Here was something Osterhaus could do. They made eight more miles before dark.[11]

The Union position at Chattanooga was besieged on three sides by Bragg's lines with the surging Tennessee River on the fourth, north, side. East of town Bragg's forces were arrayed on a low series of hills called Missionary Ridge, and continued across the valley south of the town to a higher prominence on the west, Lookout Mountain. Despite Bragg's superior position, Grant worried that the Confederate commander had good reason to withdraw instead of fight: the Federal army, soon to be eighty thousand bluecoats with Sherman's corps, would have a two-to-one advantage over him, since Bragg had sent James Longstreet toward East Tennessee with two divisions. Grant believed that the need to engage Bragg was urgent before he could reunite with Longstreet. The Union battle plan called for Sherman's corps to cross the meandering Tennessee at Brown's Ferry west of town, slip around Chattanooga unseen, and attack Bragg's right flank on Missionary Ridge. Meanwhile, Maj. Gen. George H. Thomas's Army of the Cumberland would demonstrate against the center of the ridge, and Maj. Gen. Joseph Hooker, with a division under Brig. Gen. John Geary, would also demonstrate against Lookout Mountain from the west to hold the Confederates there so they could not help Bragg on the ridge.[12]

On November 23 Osterhaus had his men up and on the road at midnight, determined to meet Grant's deadline. Though the head of his division missed the ten o'clock rendezvous at Brown's Ferry by fifty-five minutes, the bulk of Osterhaus's troops had arrived at the river by two o'clock, and there they waited, because Sherman's other three divisions did not finish crossing over the fragile pontoon bridge from below until midafternoon. By the time it was the First Division's turn to cross late in the day, the bridge had begun to break apart. The engineers worked furiously for hours to repair it, but Hooker finally had to telegraph Grant that Osterhaus would not be able to cross for at least twelve more hours. About midnight Grant replied that he could not wait any longer. He needed Sherman and his available divisions to move into position immediately, so Osterhaus would instead have to stay west of Lookout Mountain and support Hooker, who at that point commanded only Geary's division from the Army of the Potomac and a detail of two additional brigades of Brig. Gen. Charles Cruft's division from the Army of the Cumberland. With Osterhaus's division now available as well, Grant issued new orders for Hooker to take Lookout Mountain with this patchwork army if it seemed feasible: "If Woods [Osterhaus] can't cross, you can take the point of Lookout, if your demonstration develops its practicability." Osterhaus recalled that, as tired as he was after his long trip and having been on the march since midnight the night before, "I directed my Men into Camp and rode off to find General Hooker's Headquarters, where I passed the greatest part of the night, in discussing the operations of next morning and the participation allotted therein to my Command. It was midnight when General Hooker was ordered by General Grant, to abandon the scheme of a feint, which was intended at first and with the assistance of my Division to attack and dislodge the Rebels from their Lookout positions." "Fighting Joe" Hooker, having been relieved as commander of the Army of the Potomac after his indecisive handling of the Federal disaster at Chancellorsville, knew that Grant did not trust him and intended for him to take a minor role in the upcoming battle. According to Osterhaus's recollection of that night, Hooker implied to him that the new dispatch from Grant simply ordered him to take the mountain, no "if practicable" caveat mentioned. Hooker seemed determined to restore his name by a spectacular victory.[13]

Intriguingly, Osterhaus seems to have been the only general officer present to help Hooker hatch his new attack scheme. Hooker may have needed considerable help. Even Salmon P. Chase, secretary of the treasury and a great friend of Hooker's, on first meeting him had judged Hooker to be "of somewhat less breadth of intellect than I would have expected." Besides his failings at Chancellorsville, more recently one of Hooker's divisions had been embarrassed by Lt. Gen. James Longstreet in Lookout Valley. So perhaps that night Osterhaus contributed more than a little to the new plan that Hooker issued to his commanders after Grant gave up on the bridge repair. (Hooker was quite impressed with Osterhaus; he praised him later to Chase as "a glorious soldier . . . the best representative of the European service it has been my fortune to become acquainted with.") After his session with Hooker, Osterhaus finally went back to his own camp near dawn to snatch a couple of hours of much needed rest before the battle began. About the time he blew out his lantern, both Geary and Cruft were awakened to receive their new orders from Hooker.[14]

While the Confederate rank and file were convinced that Lookout Mountain was impregnable, their commanders knew better: unless they commanded a much greater force than Bragg wanted to commit, their mountain fortress was in fact highly vulnerable. A two thousand foot–high, miles-long ridge, its northern end is shaped like the toe of a boot, with its tip nudging the Tennessee River west of Chattanooga. Lookout Creek empties into the Tennessee just west of the tip. Halfway up the steep ridge and wrapping around its north end is an uneven bench where Robert Cravens had built a house overlooking the Chattanooga Valley. At the west edge of the bench, grayclads had cobbled together a crude and discontinuous breastworks, and beyond the house to the east was a secondary line of rifle pits. Brig. Gen. Edward C. Walthall's five Mississippi regiments and the Alabamans of Brig. Gen. John C. Moore's three regiments had been hunkered in bivouac near the Cravens house for days, trying to stay out of the line of fire of the Union batteries at Moccasin Point just across the river, which covered every inch of their position.[15]

From the bench, the last fifty feet to the top of the ridge is a vertical rock palisade crowned by a generally level, flat top. At the northern tip of the mesa, Confederate artillery bristled from rocky Point Lookout. But despite their lofty location, the Confederate guns were too small to do any good. Their effective range was only a mile, so they could reach neither the big Union batteries across the Tennessee River nor the masses of bluecoats and their field batteries gathering to the west across Lookout Creek. Not only that, but shortly after Union troops crossed that creek they would be in a shadow below the angle that the pieces could be depressed, making the artillery completely useless for defense against frontal attack from the west. Thus, Federal artillery superiority alone made the whole Confederate position on the mountain indefensible. And Maj. Gen. Carter L. Stevenson had a total of six brigades with which he was expected to defend both the length of Lookout Mountain and half of the five-mile-wide Chattanooga Valley against Joe Hooker's nearly three Federal divisions.[16]

Hooker's new plan called for a simple flanking maneuver: Geary's division would cross Lookout Creek well beyond the end of the Confederate picket line and then sweep northward along the steep slope toward the Cravens bench, rolling up the Confederate flank and rear. During Geary's movement, Osterhaus was to feign an attack from the Union left to attract Southern attention away from Geary. As Geary's advance reached the Confederate left flank and began to pivot around the end of the ridge below the palisade, his line would connect to Osterhaus's division, now charging up on the Union left. Supported by artillery, together they would sweep around the toe of the mountain like a crack-the-whip and drive everything in their path. Cruft's division was split into two assignments: Brig. Gen. Walter C. Whitaker's brigade was to support Geary, and Col. William Grose's brigade was to repair the turnpike road bridge across Lookout Creek for use in the upcoming assault and support Osterhaus.[17]

There were two hitches to the plan. First, the bluecoats were on the wrong side of raging Lookout Creek, which was too deep to ford. The only bridges near its mouth, both partially destroyed, were well guarded by Confederate pickets. Second, the flanking movement Hooker envisioned would take place under the rifles of the sharpshooters up on the ridgetop, with the leafless trees offering little cover to Geary's men below. Osterhaus had assured Hooker he could take care of the creek problem. Creating some bridges would be simple for his pioneers, and he would keep the Confederate pickets down by the creek so occupied that they would not notice either the bridge building or Geary's approach from the south against their flank and rear. As it turned out, Hooker had some help from a higher authority for the problem of the cliff-top sharpshooters. That morning a dense fog rose off the river and fields, blanketing the sides of the mountain up onto the plateau so thickly that it would mask Geary's movements from the men on top of the palisades. In addition, at times during the day low clouds covered the top of the crest as well, further hampering visibility there.[18]

After a couple of hours of sleep, Osterhaus was up well before the dawn of November 24 in the cold, misty rain, out on his bobtail bay examining the ground. By the time the sky grew pale he had positioned his artillery with Hooker's on and between several little knolls that lined the west side of Lookout Creek. He also found a perfect location for his pet Parrotts. Because Lookout Creek twisted to the east just before it emptied, his battery there was actually behind the Confederate picket line along the creek and was angled to enfilade both the pickets and the rifle pits from the creek up to the Confederate earthworks on the plateau. (This placement subsequently caused particular mischief, according to Walthall.) Counting the guns on Moccasin Point, nearly a quarter of Grant's artillery was now trained on Lookout Mountain.[19]

Assigning three regiments from Williamson's Second Brigade to support the batteries, Osterhaus ordered Woods to take his First Brigade and a section of artillery eight hundred yards up the stream from the railroad bridge to provide covering fire for the pioneers as they quickly threw more footbridges across the deep-running creek, cutting down large trees and augmenting them with fence rails and brush. The gunners on top of the ridge heard axes in the valley, but because of the fog could not see what the bluecoats were up to. Since Grose's men were stymied by hot picket fire when they tried to repair the damaged bridge, Hooker directed him upstream to use Woods's new bridges to cross when the signal came.[20]

Geary got his men in position and began moving forward on the mountain flank on schedule. Meanwhile, after Osterhaus's bridges had been thrown over the creek, the general, in plain sight of the rebel pickets, ordered his command to line up for brigade and division drill and proceeded calmly to review his thirty-five hundred troops. After all, he had been away from his command for some time while they had been on an arduous march, and he wanted to see how the men were doing. Reassured after watching maneuvers, he pronounced them "as fresh and vigorous as ever." Riding back and forth on his bay horse, the wind blowing his greatcoat cape back over his shoulders to reveal flashes of the scarlet lining, the tall Osterhaus made a tantalizing target for the rebel pickets across the creek. One Southerner called across to ask if that was old U. S. Grant himself up on that horse, and the answer was, "Sure thing." That was not as rash as it sounded. Fortunately for Osterhaus, the Southerners had been on picket duty for at least a month; talking and trading rations had been common with Union pickets across the creek. There were informal ground rules in place: "Neither side thought of shooting without first giving notice," recalled one picketer. It seemed only fair. So the Southerners may have gawked at Osterhaus, but they did not shoot. All this activity served to distract the rebel pickets' attention from Geary's movements upstream, even though Walthall's scouts had detected a Federal movement in that direction.[21]

About eleven o'clock, Osterhaus began to hear firing from across the creek as the Southerners in the rebel works facing him suddenly realized that the shooting was coming from above and behind them, as well as to their left. Osterhaus immediately had his artillery open a crashing fire, and first Woods's and then Grose's brigades charged across the rough bridges to connect to the left of Geary's onrushing line. Meanwhile, Osterhaus pushed skirmishers from Williamson's brigade forward to the creek bank to keep the Confederate pickets occupied there. His First Division infantry, who had been innocently preoccupied with their first drill in some time, were shocked to be suddenly thrown into battle. "We were ordered double-quick over the creek, then, to our amazement, in line-of-battle on a double-quick up Lookout Mountain. The surprise was complete to both the rebels and ourselves," recalled a soldier from the Seventeenth Missouri. The Southern pickets directly across the creek were so surprised that they lay down their guns without firing a shot, surrendering in groups of fifty or more. Those who could get away fled up the slope to their entrenchments, harried all the way by the Union artillery in the valley that covered every foot of their journey.[22]

The enfilading artillery fire and Woods's rapid charge on the Union left cut off two hundred or so Confederate pickets at the extreme right end of the gray line. The men who survived now found it impossible to scramble up the steep north face of the mountain under the pounding of the Moccasin Point and Osterhaus's guns. They had nowhere to go but into captivity. Soon there were mobs of prisoners: "We . . . met them coming back in squads of from five to forty, disarmed, hurrahing for Yankee Doodle and shaking hands with us," noted a man from the Fifty-ninth Illinois in his journal. There were so many captives, more than a thousand all told, that Osterhaus had to detail an entire regiment to guard them.[23]

On the Union far-left flank, Woods had to move his brigade much faster than Geary to keep up with the pivoting Federal line. He finally resorted to taking two regiments at the double-quick along the turnpike across the toe of the mountain, winding up on the eastern slope facing south, his right stretched up the mountain toward the bench. Meanwhile, Geary's division had quickly driven the Southerners from their breastworks on the bench, and his men now ducked behind a stone fence near the Cravens house. Walthall's Mississippians scrambled back in disorder until they could reach Moore's three regiments still on the eastern slope.[24]

Down at the foot of Lookout Mountain, Williamson was frustrated that three of his regiments had been detailed to protect the batteries, another assigned to oversee prisoners, and Hooker had snatched still another for his own purposes elsewhere. Osterhaus's Second Brigade commander had just one regiment, the Thirty-first Iowa, to take up the mountain into battle. While Hooker stayed in the valley moving regiments here and there, Osterhaus now took Williamson's last regiment away, personally taking the lead about noon as they crossed the creek and clambered on foot up the mountain, over logs, across gullies, and around rocks sometimes the size of houses, arriving on the bench in the midst of thick fog. Geary himself had yet to arrive, and some of his men behind the stone fence were nearly out of ammunition. Osterhaus ordered the Thirty-first Iowa and Woods's Third Missouri and Twenty-seventh Missouri into line in time to repulse a counterattack by Moore, who quickly retired to his entrenchments on the east side of the house.[25]

Moore, Walthall's fragment having passed through his line in its flight, was desperate for reinforcements, seeing Yankees everywhere he looked. But no help was immediately forthcoming. When Stevenson, still up on the palisade, spotted Woods's two regiments on the turnpike rounding the toe of the mountain on the double-quick, he had visions of a breakthrough into the valley of the Chattanooga, where he had few defenders to prevent his whole wing from being trapped on the mountain. The best he could do was send a few regiments down from the palisade to shore up the pressed brigades now taking the brunt of the Union attack on the bench.[26]

The men from both of the huge armies spread out in the Chattanooga Valley had been listening for hours to the incessant crack of rifle fire and the artillery booming from the other side of Lookout Mountain, imagining the battle that was going on and rooting for their side. But briefly the fog and mists on the mountain cleared off, and everyone from General Grant on down now had a ringside seat as Geary's bluecoats chased Moore's and Walthall's gray, flags flying, across the suddenly visible bench. (The spectacle was so striking that the battle was soon dubbed "the battle above the clouds" in the media.) At the sight, a huge cheer of relief went up from the valley, many Federals having greatly feared that Hooker was being chewed to pieces on the mountain. As for the Confederates, the realization that supposedly impregnable Lookout Mountain was being lost plunged them into understandable gloom.[27]

Up on the mountain Confederate brigade commander Moore was in luck. The bluecoats stopped their pursuit: the suddenly cautious Hooker ordered his brigades to halt when they got to the bench. After relieving Geary's exhausted mountain climbers, Osterhaus connected the rest of his line with Woods's brigade on the east slope. There they faced the first organized Confederate resistance of the day. Moore had kept some semblance of order in his Alabamans, now reinforced by three regiments and resituated behind a defensible ridgeline that ran eastward into the Chattanooga Valley from the bench. But neither side moved as the daylight waned, making the smoky murk gloomier than ever. Stevenson sent frequent messages to Bragg for reinforcements; Hooker petitioned Grant for ammunition and more men as well.[28]

By now it was pitch-dark and frigid, a stiff wind blowing the fog away. The action was reduced to skirmish fire back and forth. Time seemed to crawl for the cold, hungry, and tired men on both sides, hunkered behind logs or rocks in the night chill, returning fire by sighting on muzzle flashes. The show was spectacular for the watchers below in the valley, who in the clear night air could plainly see the muzzle flashes twinkling like fireflies up on the mountain, soon joined by two strings of fires running parallel down the mountain as Moore's and Osterhaus's men huddled up, trying to get warm. Then, in the middle of the night, leaving their fires burning as a ruse, Stevenson's brigades finally made a silent withdrawal down the mountain and across the valley. Without a pause, they were immediately marched up onto Missionary Ridge to augment the rebel defense.[29]

Sherman failed to take his objective that day, but because of Hooker's aggressive assault on Lookout Mountain, both the mountain itself and the Chattanooga Valley were now clear of Confederates for the first time in two months. An apocryphal story that may have at least a grain of truth tells of Grant commenting to his staff that the success on Lookout Mountain should not be attributed to "Fighting Joe" Hooker but to "Peter Joe" Osterhaus.[30]

The next morning, November 25, Thomas amended Grant's earlier plan and ordered Hooker to hustle his command across Chattanooga Valley to Rossville Gap at the south end of Bragg's line on Missionary Ridge. Once Hooker was there, he was to notify Thomas, and they would begin a combined movement against Bragg's center and left flank while Sherman again tried his right. As Osterhaus's division led the way off Lookout Mountain that morning, he saw Missionary Ridge for the first time, a low "chain of narrow heights, running south and west; the sides are very steep and rough." Tree cover on Missionary Ridge was scanty, and through his glasses Osterhaus could easily see Bragg's two corps bunched toward the north end. Bragg's headquarters was about midway along the ridge, with Maj. Gen. John C. Breckinridge's in another home about a half mile farther south. Against Sherman at the north end of the ridge, Maj. Gen. Patrick Cleburne's division had the honors, backed by two more large divisions. The south four miles of the Confederate line, under Breckinridge's command, were much more thinly held, with just three divisions to cover the whole distance. In the space between the two headquarters and extending a bit farther south was Maj. Gen. A. P. Stewart's lean division: one brigade and five other regiments at the crest deployed in a thin line a mile long, with three more regiments in the rifle pits at the base of the ridge. From there south, Brig. Gen. Henry Clayton's Brigade, temporarily under the command of Col. J. T. Holtzclaw, was the only Confederate force available to cover the entire last two miles of the ridge to Rossville Gap except for Col. R. J. Henderson's two regiments of Georgians, who were already down in the gap itself.[31]

That seemed adequate to Bragg: "The position was one which ought to have been held by a line of skirmishers against any assaulting column," he insisted, even after the battle proved otherwise. He had spent little energy on the earthworks on top, which were badly placed, too far back to be able to sight down the hillside. The gun placements along the top of the ridge were even less thought through, the grayclad gunners unable to depress the guns to a range any closer than the rifle pits on the plain below without firing into their own men. However, the Southerners on the ridge, in a tenuous single line with the men spaced up to eight feet apart, remained confident of their superior defensive position even though awed by the spectacle of Thomas's four divisions now stretched out shoulder to shoulder along the valley floor below.[32]

As Osterhaus crossed the valley toward Chattanooga Creek, the pall of smoke he saw hanging over the line of trees ahead left him with no illusions that he would find the bridge intact. This burned span turned out to be a major obstacle to Thomas's plans for a combined attack. Knowing the stakes, Osterhaus immediately set his pioneers to cobble together a new crossing, but it would take them three hours to construct a structure sturdy enough to support artillery. Osterhaus could not afford to wait. At about eleven o'clock, as soon as a couple of driftwood logs could be thrown over the creek, he pushed the Twenty-seventh Missouri across as skirmishers to test the Rossville Gap's defenses. Trotting behind them toward the gap, Osterhaus soon spied Henderson's two regiments arrayed in line of battle in front of the notch in the hills. After setting his skirmishers to keeping the Southerners busy for the next hour or two, Osterhaus galloped back to the creek and worked furiously to push the rest of his division across the footbridge, by necessity leaving his artillery behind for the time being.[33]

As soon as they spied Osterhaus's long blue column now jogging toward them on the double-quick, Henderson's battery opened fire. Without slowing down, the bluecoat brigades split to the right and left past the big guns and sprinted up the slopes on either side of Henderson's position to flank him. When Henderson saw what was about to happen, he quickly ordered a retreat and pulled his brigade up to the top of the ridgeline to the north. The rebels were already long gone when Williamson's brigade reached the top, in their haste abandoning a six-inch gun in the gap along with a big wagon train with their medical supplies.[34]

By midafternoon Hooker had the last of his other two divisions and artillery across Osterhaus's new bridge. Up on the ridge, when Breckinridge spotted the massive new blue column now moving rapidly toward the gap, he became rightly concerned about the security of his left flank and rear. At around three o'clock he collected his staff, including his son Cabell, and robbed Stewart's already thin division of Holtzclaw's (Clayton's) Brigade for a reconnaissance of his left flank. Stewart, fervently hoping that Breckinridge would be able to handle the large force of Federals threatening his left flank, concentrated on the masses in his front.[35]

Meanwhile, after quickly driving Henderson's two regiments from the gap, Osterhaus paused at a fork in the road just beyond the gap. The general had discovered a glaring chink in the Confederate defenses: the left fork ran north along the back of Missionary Ridge on the next low ridgetop and looked like it would lead right up into the rear of the Confederate position. Osterhaus sent a message back to Hooker proposing to slip his division behind the enemy while Cruft's two brigades swept straight up to the top from the gap and

Geary's division, in column behind them, paralleled along the front (west) base of the ridge. Osterhaus was sure that they could roll up the Southern flank before the Confederates knew what hit them. While Osterhaus was waiting for Hooker's reply, young Col. Cabell Breckinridge, CSA, "a sharp looking fellow" riding a fine horse, mistakenly rode right into a cluster of Union soldiers taking their ease, without realizing who the men were. He nearly bluffed his way out, but was finally corralled by some Ninth Iowa skirmishers up on the ridge. Cabell was soon on his way to a Northern prison, and Osterhaus had himself a beautiful new horse to replace the bobtail bay, much to the amusement of his men.[36]

Hooker immediately saw the beauty of Osterhaus's proposal and without delay issued orders to put it into effect. Meanwhile, trotting toward them but still out of sight along the ridge crest was Breckinridge's reconnaissance in force, now absent Cabell. Unaware that Henderson's brigade had already been chased out of the gap, Breckinridge's plan was to back Henderson up with Holtzclaw's brigade from the top of the ridge. At that moment, Osterhaus had his column hustling up the back road on the double-quick while he rode ahead on his new horse to scout the ground. Suddenly spotting the enemy column trotting in the opposite direction along the ridge crest above him, he immediately sent a heads-up back to Cruft and Hooker and began angling his line to his left toward the back slope of the ridge. Just then, Holtzclaw's skirmishers reached the last knoll of the ridge and peered down into the gap. To their shock, instead of locating Henderson's brigade, the grayclad sharpshooters discovered the head of Cruft's brigades in the gap, with Osterhaus's full division already past it and a third yet to get there. The timing was perfect: just as the Confederate skirmishers spotted the Federal column and fired into it, the bluecoats faced left and started up the ridge on a dead run to press them. As Cruft began to drive Holtzclaw's skirmishers back, Osterhaus urged his division up the back slope of the ridge, slanting toward the top at the rear of the Confederates, "our men running, yelling, shooting with furious impetuosity. The most restless charge I ever witnessed," wrote a man of the Thirty-second Missouri.[37]

Holtzclaw, frantically trying to form a line of battle against Cruft, did not spot Osterhaus's division immediately. As Osterhaus's skirmishers neared the crest, they were in position to enfilade Holtzclaw's line from a distance of only fifty yards. Now Geary, moving along the western base of the ridge, had his batteries fire into the other end of the confused Confederate line. "We've got 'em in a pen!" shouted Osterhaus, pushing his advance beyond the enemy flank and into their rear. Before Holtzclaw could successfully get his column into line of battle, he discovered both of his flanks enveloped. One of Cruft's soldiers marveled, "It is wonderful how quick the movement was made and how soon we were all at work on the top of that ridge while Osterhaus's Division marched north along the eastern base. Old Gen. Hooker rode along with his horse's nose just behind our file closers, as serene as if nothing of moment was going on."[38]

In the words of a dismayed Confederate who fought there, the encounter was "a free fight . . . without the slightest warning from any of our superior officers of what we were to expect, or to brace ourselves for--a pitched battle, in fact, between the short line of one brigade and three of the largest and best divisions of the Federal Army." The pressure soon forced Holtzclaw to withdraw his brigade northward along the ridge, but many were caught in Osterhaus's pen. Osterhaus narrowly missed capturing Breckinridge père as well as fils. Amid the confused melee, the elder Breckinridge galloped up to Col. L. T. Woodruff of the Thirty-sixth Alabama, the ranking officer still on the line, shouting that the enemy had broken through on the ridge to the north and ordering him to retreat with all survivors by any means possible. Those who could not squeeze through the tightening noose were soon "a swirling, struggling mass of panic-stricken men, signaling frantically to make us understand they surrendered," recalled a man from the Seventy-sixth Ohio, but Breckinridge was not one of them. Osterhaus did capture a gaggle himself, however: "The Rebels already alarmed about the issue of the battle became restive when the Volleys of my Infantry apprised them of the Attack on their Right and Rear. When their Fire appeared to slacken, I rode up to them and demanded to lay down their Arms. They did so." In the growing dusk, as his opponents evaporated or were captured, Osterhaus quickly re-formed his division into column and raced up the ridge crest toward Breckinridge's headquarters, followed by Cruft's brigades.[39]

The breakthrough to the north that Breckinridge had spied was the Army of the Cumberland cresting the ridge. All day Thomas had been champing at the bit for Hooker to get into position at the gap so that the Cumberlanders could move against the center of the Confederate line. As the hours ticked by and adequate daylight for battle was about to fade, Grant continued to prod Thomas to move, but the perhaps too serene Hooker neglected to inform Thomas that he was already up on the ridge. Thomas must have figured it out from the noise, because he finally sent his Army of the Cumberland surging forward with a roar toward the rifle pits at about three forty-five. The minute the Confederates retreated from the rifle pits the revenge-filled Cumberlanders started chasing them up the steep and treacherous slopes, shouting, "Chickamauga!" Just as Stewart was trying to rally his men to face this new threat, he looked behind him and saw Osterhaus's division racing toward him through the dusk, flags flying. And to the west, Geary's division had begun to climb the slope, reaching the top at the same time as Brig. Gen. Richard W. Johnson's division on Thomas's right flank, now just to Geary's left.[40]

Surrounded on three sides by bluecoats in a space of only four hundred yards, Stewart's Southerners knew the day was lost. Wrote a man in Johnson's division, "Soon after the enemy gave way, Osterhaus opportunely came up from Rossville, and obliquely approaching our right, joined us, thus forming an acute angle within the area of which the enemy was huddled together in great masses." By means of much undignified scrambling, some Southerners managed to escape down the rear of the ridge to the east, but many others were captured by Osterhaus and Johnson. As a soldier from the Thirteenth Illinois put it, "The troops on the other side of the ridge had shaken the tree and we were holding the bag to get the fruit."[41]

Confederate accounts indicate that Thomas's army reached the top and broke through to the north of Breckinridge's headquarters just before Hooker's command got there. The sudden appearance of Osterhaus on their left flank and rear demoralized the Southerners in the vicinity who were trying to rally to meet Thomas's new threat on their right. Capt. Winfrey Bond Scott, Nineteenth Louisiana Infantry, added, "No one seemed to dream of being driven from this position. . . . When we felt that all was safe they had broken our lines on our left and ere we knew it we were flanked and fired upon from our rear." The entire Confederate line gradually crumbled; Patrick Cleburne's division, having stymied Sherman, covered their retreat eastward. Watching from Grant's headquarters, Maj. Gen. William F. "Baldy" Smith was convinced at the time that the appearance by Osterhaus and Geary in Hooker's advance won the battle: "Hooker's forces were so near the place at which Johnson, with the right division of Thomas, ascended the ridge, that the enemy in the centre, who must have heard the firing on the ridge, lost their morale, and, fearing the flank attack did not resist as they could have done the charge of the four divisions of the Army of the Cumberland, and thus allowed the attack to succeed."[42]

With Hooker's command now linked with Johnson's division from the valley and masses of Confederates laying down their arms, the bluecoats realized they had won the battle, and "one thundering harrah after the other burst forth." Amid the shouts and cheers, Osterhaus rode through the ranks, waving his kepi and exulting, "Two more hours daylight and we'll destroy this army!" In the excitement of rounding up prisoners, Osterhaus was nearly captured by the Union army as he rode forward on his fine new horse. Col. A. G. McCook of the Second Ohio took the "old fellow [he was forty] on horseback with a fur collar" for a rebel officer, and demanded his sword. Beaming, Osterhaus laughed, "Ah, colonel, this is glorious!" Hooker wrote later that "the troops were wrought up to an intense degree of excitement, and I believe that there is no one of them, from the highest to the lowest, who will not say that those four days were not only the most eventful, but the happiest of their lives. We started out with two days' rations, but that was enough. We lived on the excitement."[43]

Osterhaus had every reason to beam. He and his division had made a solid, if less than showy, contribution to the Union success at Chattanooga, incidentally making Hooker look good. He had helped Hooker plan the last-minute Lookout Mountain assault and then had made a successful diversion before supporting the advance. That victory had put Hooker's command in position to play a key part at Missionary Ridge. There, while vigorously spearheading Hooker's flanking movement, Osterhaus had identified a critical opportunity to roll up Bragg's flank that worked beautifully, precipitating the Confederates' collapse. In both Chattanooga fights his men had experienced little more than a brisk run and skirmishing as they moved up the slopes, at very small cost to the division. That cold night his hungry command, finding that excitement did not really replace victuals, bedded down in the vicinity of Bragg's headquarters amid the moans of the wounded scattered all around. Osterhaus could not know that all of his early success was about to change.[44]

Bragg took his ragged army east across the valley of Chickamauga Creek, heading for Ringgold Gap and on into Georgia. The Union pursuit was not vigorous: Hooker finally got his patchwork corps on the road east toward the little railroad town of Ringgold on the afternoon of November 26, Osterhaus's division bringing up the rear. After six miles, the head of the column was forced to halt at a burned-out bridge over the creek. While the infantry picked their way over a makeshift bridge and pushed on across the valley until well after dark, all the batteries remained stuck behind the creek until a new bridge could be built. Near midnight, as Osterhaus finally ordered his troops into bivouac about five miles from Ringgold, he learned that the following day Hooker wanted him back in the lead as they drew closer to the enemy. That order no doubt delighted Osterhaus. Geary and Cruft had had the honors of the previous two fights; maybe now he and the First Division could show their mettle.[45]

By the time Osterhaus finally turned in on that bitterly cold night, Bragg had managed to push the head of his Confederate column through Ringgold Gap, stopping just beyond. Behind him, the long trains carrying his vital remaining stores and ammunition, and, most important, his remaining batteries (forty fewer guns than he had had three days before), were still in the gap, delayed by bad roads and the multiple creek crossings just east of the gap. Only Patrick Cleburne's division, acting as rear guard, was left in the Chickamauga Valley. General Cleburne fully expected a running fight while he pulled off his escape; instead, to his dismay, about midnight Bragg sent him orders to make a stand in the gap and hold it against the whole Union army until the vital trains were well away.[46]

At four in the morning of November 27, Cleburne rode through the quiet town to look at the gap and plan his defense. What he saw was encouraging. Taylor's Ridge runs north and south just east of the town, split near the settlement by a gap very similar to the Rossville Gap. An embanked railroad track runs along the base of the ridge, passing by a long one-story stone depot just before it curves eastward into the gap. The ridge on the north side of the gap (known locally as White Oak Mountain) is rocky and creased with ravines, with little timber cover at the top but a lot of undulations that Cleburne could use to advantage. The space between the railroad track and that ridge was at the time cleared farmland, ending with a strip of young timber hugging the base of the slope. In the gap north of the track there is a narrow, flat strip in which Cleburne could array his army. A deep-running creek paralleling the track along the base of the very steep south slope of the gap could be used to protect his left flank.[47]

Cleburne decided that the terrain lent itself to an ambush and quickly proceeded to deploy his more than four thousand men in the brief time he had before the Federals closed in. Cleburne planted a regiment on top of White Oak Mountain near the gap to keep an eye on his right flank and sharpshooters up on the steep slope south of the gap. He concealed the rest of Col. H. B. Granbury's Texas brigade of dismounted cavalry on White Oak Mountain's lower slopes in the young timber near the mouth of the gap. In the narrow passage in the gorge he hid Col. D. C. Govan's Arkansas Brigade. For artillery he was practically defenseless: he had only two twelve-pounder Napoleons. (He would have worried less had he known that all of Osterhaus's batteries were trapped behind the creek.) Where Cleburne sited them near the mouth of the gap, the Napoleons commanded open fields with only the few stone and log buildings on the nearby Jobes farm to protect the approaching Federals. Even the town itself was within their range. To create his ambush, Cleburne ordered the artillery masked with brush so that they would be invisible to an advancing army until they were too close to escape. and gave strict orders to hold fire until he gave the word.[48]

Cleburne kept his other two brigades under Brig. Gens. Lucius E. Polk and Mark P. Lowrey in reserve back in the gap behind the Arkansans, ready to climb up to whatever threat developed. Ahead in the town he had left a small cavalry detail and one regiment to guard the bridge and ford leading to the town. When these decoys saw the Federals they were to fire the bridge and skedaddle back to the gap after just a volley or two as if they were joining the rebel exodus. The wagon trains still visible far into the gap were a further enticement to draw the bluecoats into his trap.[49]

Osterhaus was in the saddle by half past five on what promised to be another beautiful, clear morning, eagerly heading toward the ford with his guard of a dozen troopers to see what lay ahead. Sure enough, at the ford the guard flushed the Confederate cavalry, who duly scrambled back into town. Then Osterhaus, riding close behind his skirmishers, spotted the railroad depot ahead and decided to use it for his base during the operation to follow, it being admirably situated to overlook the entire field. When Osterhaus stood on the platform and checked out the gap with his field glasses, all he could see was the tail of the wagon train, including four field pieces, and a "feeble line of skirmishers." The thousands of rifles pointing toward him were well hidden. To Osterhaus, this looked like another case of the Confederate army caving and running, just as it had in the past two clashes. It was between eight and nine o'clock by now,

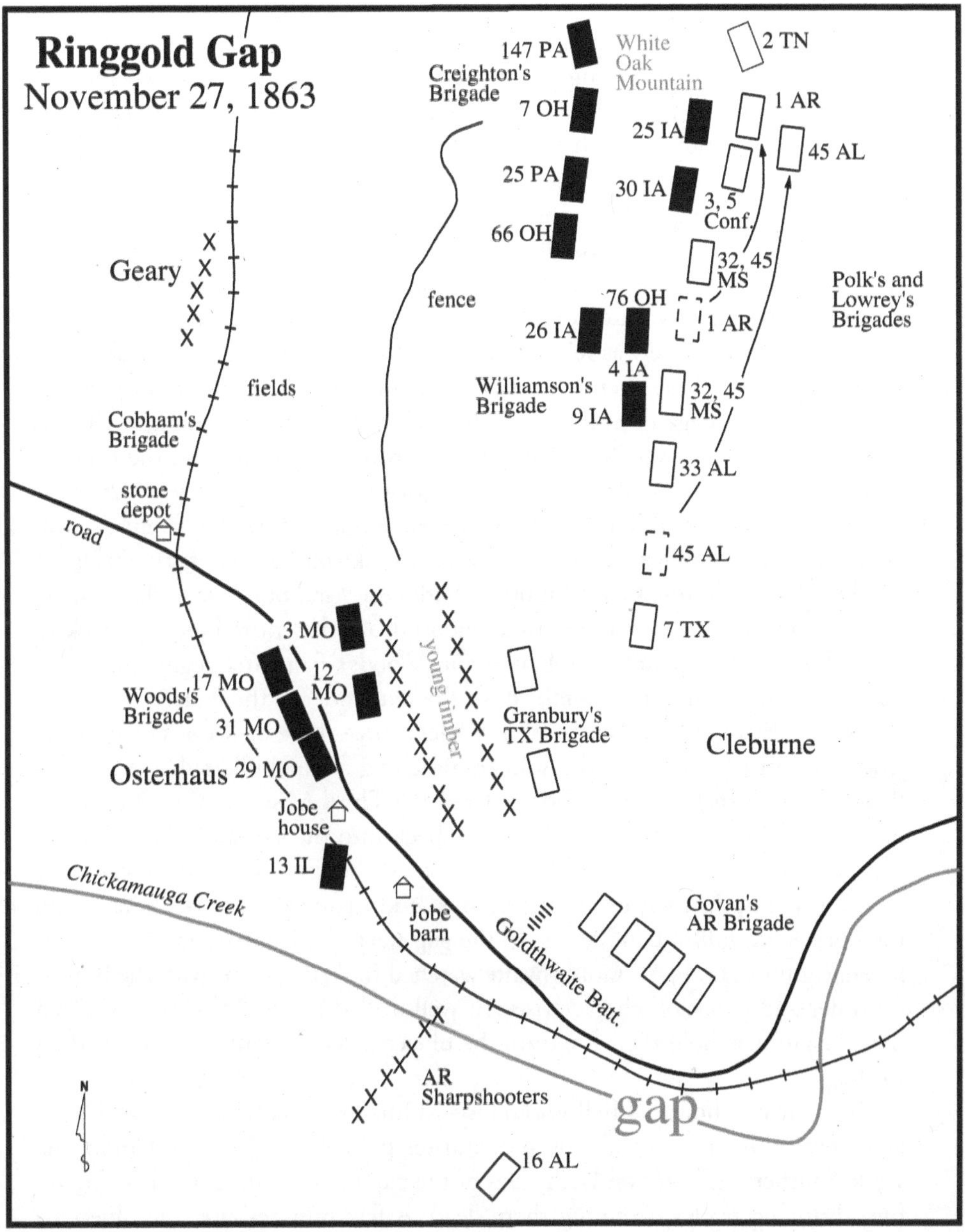
Ringgold Gap
November 27, 1863
147 PA
Creighton's Brigade
7 OH
25 PA
66 OH
White Oak Mountain
2 TN
1 AR
45 AL
25 IA
30 IA
3, 5 Conf.
32, 45 MS
76 OH
1 AR
Polk's and Lowrey's Brigades
26 IA
4 IA
Williamson's Brigade
9 IA
32, 45 MS
33 AL
45 AL
7 TX
Geary
fence
fields
Cobham's Brigade
stone depot
road
3 MO
12 MO
17 MO
Woods's Brigade
31 MO
29 MO
Osterhaus
young timber
Granbury's TX Brigade
Cleburne
Jobe house
13 IL
Jobe barn
Chickamauga Creek
Goldthwaite Batt.
Govan's AR Brigade
AR Sharpshooters
gap
16 AL
N

and Hooker arrived at the depot, reporting that townspeople had told him that the Confederates were scrambling away in disarray. Osterhaus replied that he thought he could capture that artillery in the gap with a small force of cavalry. Hooker desperately wanted Bragg's train for the personal glory and professional vindication of completely routing the Confederates, so he ordered Osterhaus to attack immediately, promising him that, if needed, his frontal attack would be matched by a flanking move to the north as Hooker's other divisions arrived in the town. Never mind the still-absent artillery: if Osterhaus could blow through the inconsequential rear guard, the rich prize lay just beyond.[50]

The looks of the ground on cursory inspection must have encouraged Osterhaus, similar as it was to Rossville Gap, where his troops had easily rolled over Henderson's weak opposition. Otherwise, he would normally have had qualms about sending his men into combat without both better scouting and artillery support. But even if he was reluctant, he had to respond to a direct order from Hooker to feel out the enemy position. Abandoning his usual careful preparations, Osterhaus began feeding his regiments into the gap as soon as each unit arrived in town, the men still panting after trotting two miles on the double-quick. Woods's brigade arrived first. Sent forward into the gap were the Seventeenth Missouri and Thirty-first Missouri, supported by the Twenty-ninth, whose skirmishers quickly drove the few enemy skirmishers across the fields toward the base of White Oak Mountain. Suddenly, Granbury's Texans tore from their cover in the timber and with a whoop drove the entire blue line back in disarray behind the railroad embankment. Woods's first three regiments, thoroughly shocked, could not be rallied for the remainder of the fight.[51]

As the Missourians were scrambling back, three more of Woods's regiments trotted into town, some of the soldiers flinching at the bullets that were now flying through the streets. Woods ordered the Third Missouri and Osterhaus's old Twelfth Missouri to drive the Texans back into the gap and sent the Thirteenth Illinois out on the right flank to extend the line toward the creek. The men formed up in their usual snappy style and marched jauntily forward into the open field, full of confidence. In the gap next to Cleburne, admiring Confederate gunner Lt. R. W. Goldthwaite watched them come on "with the beautiful order and precision characteristic of well-drilled troops." Cleburne insisted that the gunners hold their fire until the bluecoats got to within three hundred yards.[52]

Then, at his shout, all hell broke loose. Quickly unmasked, the two Napoleons fired three rounds of shot and canister point-blank into the Union line while Southern infantry on both sides of the gap opened enfilading rifle fire on the advancing troops, stopping them dead. A few minutes later the bluecoats got to their feet and mounted another gutsy charge toward the guns that ended the same way. A man of the Seventy-sixth Ohio who watched the charge was appalled: "It seemed like the senseless exposure of brave men. They were in unobstructed and easy range of the batteries . . . and were mowed down in swathes by the grape and cannister that swept the field. It was simply murderous, and horrifying to look at."[53]

A few dozen sharpshooters of the Thirteenth Illinois now sprinted toward the stone farmhouse and outbuildings of the Jobes farm and set up sniper fire from windows and doorways. But the Confederate gunners took shelter in a ravine just behind their pieces, and few were hurt. A short time later, the 270 men of the Thirteenth Illinois made another desperate attempt to charge the guns, this time getting to within fifty yards under heavy rifle fire before the guns belched another load of canister and shell. From that point, all three Union regiments remained pinned down in a plunging enfilade fire from the Texans and the Arkansas regiments in the gap, taking devastating losses. The Federals could not do more without artillery support.[54]

To relieve his helplessly exposed troops, Osterhaus started Woods's final regiment, the Seventy-sixth Ohio, up White Oak Mountain on his left flank with orders to swing over and fire into the gap once they arrived at the crest. Now, as he watched the regiment cross the fields and begin to climb the steep slope, he saw that Cleburne had detected the movement and was rapidly countering with a heavy column made up of his last two brigades that had been waiting in the gap behind the Arkansans. There was clearly more to this rear guard than anyone in the depot had anticipated.[55]

Williamson's Iowa brigade had by now arrived near the depot in column and was waiting in the street for orders, the men ducking bullets and stray artillery fire that killed at least one man. Realizing that the Seventy-sixth Ohio would be quickly annihilated without support, Osterhaus ordered Williamson forward on his left flank. Williamson immediately sent the Fourth Iowa to join the Seventy-sixth Ohio up near the crest of White Oak Mountain, with the Thirty-first Iowa detailed as sharpshooters behind the railroad embankment to provide covering fire. There was little resistance as the two regiments picked their way up through the loose stones and shale up a grade "steep as the roof of a house" to a point near the crest, but then they met with heavy flanking fire on both sides by the First Arkansas that soon made their situation untenable. There was very little protection there, just a few large rocks, scattered trees, and downed logs. In the fifteen-minute battle the Seventy-sixth Ohio lost heavily: eighteen men killed and forty-four wounded, including four officers. Eight flag bearers fell before their banner, but not their flag, was captured as well. The Fourth Iowa lost thirty-three men and their flag. Retiring about fifty yards to a more sheltered location, the two battered units held their position for the rest of the battle.[56]

By then Williamson himself, without waiting for his entire brigade to form up, had taken the Ninth and Twenty-sixty Iowa up the mountain to link to the left of the Fourth Iowa. They took cover near the crest in the "constant and severe fire," trying to pick off Southerners who stuck their heads over the crest.

Williamson then waved his final two regiments, the Twenty-fifth Iowa and Thirtieth Iowa, up the mountain even farther to the left to the vicinity of the crest to try to outflank the enemy. Confederate generals Polk and Lowrey, responding promptly to each developing threat, kept shifting their own arriving reinforcements to their right, often in the nick of time to meet each new challenge. The Federals climbing the ravines were sitting ducks for Confederate regiments, who were able to enfilade the bluecoats from both sides as they advanced. The excellent Southern marksmen had a field day with Union officers, wounding seven of the twenty-six officers of the Twenty-fifth Iowa. Despite the withering crossfire, the last two Iowa regiments reached within a hundred yards of the crest, their skirmishers within seventy-five feet of the top. This put them, in places, only twenty to thirty feet from the Confederate line. There they crouched.[57]

Osterhaus was stymied. So much for forcing his way quickly through the gap to capture the trains. It was now after ten o'clock. His frontal assault was pinned down, his flanking maneuver had slowed to a halt, severe casualties were streaming back into town, and nothing had been accomplished. If Hooker had wanted him to feel out the enemy, that he had certainly done, pulling back a bloody stump. This was the first battle Osterhaus had fought without solid artillery support, and he could see no way to break the impasse without more flanking support until the artillery could come up to tip the balance. His dismay is evident in his note: "A simultaneous movement, which was to be made in conjunction with us on our left did not come in time; we had the fight all to ourselves," a desolate observation given that the town by then was filling with milling bluecoats as Sherman's and Thomas's units trickled in.[58]

The flanking movement Osterhaus hoped for would finally come from Geary. Cleburne had set Hooker up cleverly, and now the Union commander had to make a decision about whether the prize was worth the pain. Perhaps it was time to call the whole thing off and let Bragg get away with his train. But Hooker still was not convinced. Turning to Geary, whose division was now formed in column in the shelter of the railroad depot and behind the railroad embankment, Hooker told him to get up the mountain and turn the enemy's right flank. Geary assigned Col. William R. Creighton's First Brigade to the task.[59]

Like Osterhaus, Creighton also sent in his entire brigade piecemeal. First up, the Seventh Ohio sprinted over the fields under heavy rifle fire and marched up the mountain in line of battle, upright, elbow to elbow with fixed bayonets. This tactic was not quite the thing for a tortuous climb under fire, but the buckeyes wanted to show these western troops hunkered down behind rocks how it should be done. Unfortunately, the stubborn Ohioans, now panting with effort, marched right over part of Williamson's line rather than extending it. Col. George A. Stone of the Twenty-fifth Iowa tried to convince them to move off to the left so as not to obstruct the Iowans, but they refused. Their path put the still proudly upright Seventh Ohio twenty or thirty paces in front of the Iowans, between them and the enemy.[60]

Polk and Lowrey, quickly shifting rebel units to meet this latest threat, ordered their men to hold fire until the bluecoats were close and then blasted them with a devastating volley that tore through the Seventh Ohio and sent the buckeyes running back down the hill "like a whirlwind," right through the Twenty-fifth Iowa. Stone of the Twenty-fifth had predicted what would happen if the Seventh Ohio continued forward, and had shouted at his own men to hold fast and not run. But the panic was contagious, the buckeyes screaming as they raced by that they had been flanked and the enemy was upon them. That was too much for the men of the Twenty-fifth Iowa, who turned tail and ran right with them, not to be rallied until they had reached a fence at the base of the slope. "I never ran, or tried to run so hard in my life," wrote Calvin Ainsworth of the Twenty-fifth Iowa in his diary that night. At the fence the Seventh Ohio milled, essentially leaderless, having lost twelve of its thirteen officers, including its colonel, as well as sixty-one soldiers killed and wounded. Only thirty-three men and a lieutenant were left. Then Creighton himself was killed while trying to rally them at the fence. The Twenty-fifth Iowa fared little better: besides its seven wounded officers, it had twenty-two wounded men.[61]

Still working their way up the ridge were four more of Geary's regiments, but they retired to the base one at a time after their flanks were threatened. That left on the mountain just Woods's battered Seventy-sixth Ohio and Williamson with the Fourth, Ninth, and Twenty-sixth Iowa. In the gap the Third and Twelfth Missouri and the Thirteenth Illinois were still pinned down and running out of ammunition. Now Hooker was convinced. Obviously, nothing further could be gained until the artillery showed up, so he sent orders for all units to hold their positions and hold their fire to conserve ammunition.[62]

The uncoordinated flanking movement on White Oak Mountain by Geary's brigade, even though it failed, had stretched Cleburne's resources to their limit. All of Polk's and Lowrey's regiments were committed, and they were almost out of ammunition. If Hooker were to send in any of the additional bluecoats that Cleburne could see milling in the Ringgold streets, chasing chickens and pigs while they waited to be called to the line, Cleburne would have had no resources with which to respond. Fortunately, a message from Bragg arrived about noon, giving Cleburne permission to retire at his discretion now that the wagons were through the gap and out of danger. After successfully retrieving his two Napoleons, the relieved Cleburne was setting his rear guard of skirmishers and moving his brigades out when the first Union artillery finally tore into town and sounded off.[63]

Five miles back, at Chickamauga Creek, Capt. Clemens Landgraeber, "the Flying Dutchman" of Vicksburg fame, had not been able to start his Second Missouri Light Battery F over the new trestle bridge until eight o'clock. Frantic

Looking toward the railroad station and White Oak Mountain, Ringgold Gap on the right. (Courtesy the Library of Congress)

to get to the front, as soon as he secured the right-of-way he and his mounted battery "fairly flew along that stony road, bidding it to be cleared for his men," recalled a sharpshooter in the Thirteenth Illinois. Landgraeber's battery, along with a Sixteenth Corps battery, finally clattered into Ringgold around noon and immediately set up to start pounding the gap and the ridge, to the cheers of the beleaguered troops. Williamson now could advance his remaining regiments to the crest of White Oak Mountain, where instead of facing the enemy they caught sight of the backs of Cleburne's soldiers, who were streaming down the slope and through the gap. The Confederate trains were now beyond the gap on the far side of the two bridges over East Chickamauga Creek. About that time, Grant arrived at the depot and gave orders not to continue the pursuit.[64]

As the battle wound down, more and more stretchers came streaming into town carrying men, "injured in a more terrible manner" than at least one battle-experienced surgeon had yet seen in the war. Many men, trapped in the incessant cross fire, had multiple wounds; one man had four fingers shot off one hand and three off the other. Hooker's two active divisions had sustained 509 killed and wounded in just four hours, a horrific butcher's bill for an ultimately pointless fight. Osterhaus's share of that loss was 304. Cleburne reported losses less than half of the Union total. A civilian friend of Grant's who saw Osterhaus on the streets that day wrote that he "was in a very bad humor at his troops being pushed in ahead, to certain destruction," but it is doubtful whether Osterhaus would have shared any of those feelings with a stranger. More likely, he was showing his shock at the severity of his losses. That evening the general, as was his habit, visited his wounded and learned that his Twelfth Missouri had lost six officers and twenty-one men killed and wounded, including many sons of men he had known in Belleville. Among them were Col. Hugo Wangelin, who lost an arm, and Capt. Henry Kircher, who was hit three times and lost an arm and a leg. These casualties must have hit Osterhaus particularly hard, since he knew the men and their families personally. But although he bitterly regretted his losses, blaming them on the lack of artillery and the delay in flank support, Osterhaus still believed that the strategic decision to risk battle was legitimate. And he did not change his mind over time. Passing through the area the next summer he recorded in his diary, "What a success it would have been if we had forced the Gap in time on Nov. 27. The ridges would have commanded the plain ground beyond and played havoc with the enemy Rear."[65]

His officers and men, on the other hand, were vocal about the defeat. In a later speech Williamson mourned, "My tried, brave veteran officers and soldiers fell about me like leaves in the autumn, and yet all this for some cause [that] is lost to history. Many valuable lives were lost--and for what?" A captain of the Twenty-fifth Iowa wrote his wife that "the attack was made very precipitately and without any attempt to flank their position. . . . [A]s fast as the regiments arrived they were ordered to charge up the hill without waiting even to form the brigades." But Osterhaus was not the object of this discontent; Hooker was. A man from the Thirtieth Iowa wrote his brother that "our division was in with old Hooker we dont like him he run us in at Ringgold without artillery but you can bet high on old Osterhaus he is a man that is always around . . . among his men in a fight." And from a soldier of the Thirty-first Iowa with clear priorities: "Through the bad generalship of Old Fighting Joe, our division lost very heavy . . . while Hooker's Potomacs were in town at a safe distance, plundering what by right belonged to us."[66]

Grant was also unhappy with Hooker for attacking, commenting that "this attack was unfortunate and cost us some men unnecessarily." After Charles Dana sent a scathing report of the battle to Washington, calling it "the first fault in this admirable campaign," the national press jumped on the bandwagon in castigating Hooker. Hooker defended his decision to fight, saying that if he had been supported by speedier bridge-building for his artillery, "the greater part of Bragg's army, and certainly all of its materiel, would now have been ours." At least one modern-day historian agrees with Hooker and Osterhaus, that strategically the prize of the battle was worth the risks. If Hooker had taken the time to set up an attack with Osterhaus's usual rigor, waiting for his batteries, the trains would have been out of reach beyond the gap. Swaying the decision to move in rapidly was Cleburne's ruse of a thinly protected rear, and Hooker and Osterhaus swallowed the bait.[67]

Ringgold Gap was the watershed battle for Osterhaus during the war, facing Cleburne, one of the best generals the Confederacy had to offer. Arguably, the only way an attacking force could have beaten the determined gap defenders in their superior position would have been to overrun their flanks with a vigorous and coordinated attack. Fooled by Cleburne into thinking the Southern opposition was scanty, Osterhaus made his situation worse by throwing his units in piecemeal. By the time Cleburne pounced and Osterhaus and Hooker realized the strength of Cleburne's forces, Osterhaus's division was already pinned down, and any opportunity for coordination with Geary was lost. Ultimately, the heavy Union casualties outweighed Hooker's thirst for the prize.

That evening, while Osterhaus was importuning Grant for special permission to set up a hospital in Chattanooga for his many wounded officers, the First Division's hungry and cold survivors huddled around fires on the frozen ground, still without tents or rations. They were relieved when, three days later, Osterhaus received orders to move out to Chattanooga. On December 21 they took up their final march toward a permanent winter camp. No concession was made for Christmas Day; it was just another sixteen-mile trek over rotten roads in abysmal weather. As usual, Osterhaus optimistically ordered no looting on the road or at camp: "We intend to subsist on the country but not rob it." On December 29 the First Division camped a mile from Woodville, Alabama, calling their new quarters Camp Proclamation. The weary men spent the first few days creating snug shebangs, in this case log cabins with chimneys, which afforded them the luxury of solid protection from the elements that they had not enjoyed for more than a year. Some also immediately began applying for leave, including their commander, who had just received an important letter.[68]

Chapter 5
The Atlanta Campaign and the March to the Sea

AS SOON as Brig. Gen. Peter Joseph Osterhaus had ordered a salute fired to the new year of 1864, he left Camp Proclamation on a well-deserved month's leave. He was headed not to St. Louis to see his motherless and scattered five children, at least not right away, but to New York City and Washington, D.C. On December 28 he had received word from Germany that his plea for help had been heard: his late wife Matilda's younger sister, Emma Amalia Born, had agreed to come immediately to run his household for him while he was away at war. Amalie was three years younger than her late sister but as yet unmarried, so she was able to leave Kreuznach on a moment's notice. Osterhaus had no time to lose if he was to meet her steamer, due to arrive in New York on January 8.[1]

Osterhaus had had a warm sendoff from Maj. Gen. Joseph Hooker, who planned to write his friend in Washington, Secretary of the Treasury Salmon P. Chase, commending Osterhaus as "a glorious soldier" and urging his appointment to major general of volunteers. This was the third time that Osterhaus had been proposed for this appointment; the previous two came after the Vicksburg campaign. With Hooker's additional endorsement, perhaps Osterhaus could finally pry the second star loose from Washington. If so, he would be in rarefied company. There were only eleven major generals in the Regular Army and just over a hundred in the Volunteers. Up to this point, of the two hundred thousand Germans fighting in the war only two German-born adult immigrants had achieved the grade of major general: Osterhaus's fellow exiles Franz Sigel and Carl Schurz, both appointed to the Union high command for political reasons despite their lackluster performances in the field. Since Schurz's appointment in March 1863, no other German American had achieved that rank. Osterhaus decided to take advantage of his brief trip to New York to swing by Washington on his way home to see if he could further his cause.[2]

Carl Schurz was in New York at the time, so Osterhaus naturally turned to his old acquaintance for practical advice. After emigrating to the United States in 1852, Schurz had risen rapidly through midwestern politics to become President Lincoln's valued spokesman for the German vote. He had already petitioned Lincoln in 1862 to appoint Osterhaus brigadier general; now two years further into the war this most political of generals would surely know which contacts would be most fruitful for Osterhaus to pursue in Washington. Osterhaus got in touch with Schurz and made arrangements to meet for dinner.[3]

What he learned was not encouraging: finding meaningful Washington patronage was going to be more difficult than he had hoped. Since the beginning of this war, both West Point–trained candidates and political aspirants had relied to a large extent on influential voices in the capital to help convince Lincoln to nominate them to generalships, although in the end Lincoln made the final decision. In this critical election year, Lincoln continued to weigh each hopeful's influence on potential votes as well as his performance in the field, but the president had lately been more inclined to defer to his military leaders' preferences now that he finally had what looked like a winning commander in Grant.[4]

Making the situation more complex was the growing polarization between the "professional" officers of West Point and the political appointees with no military training. The Regular Army men, led by Halleck, Grant, and Sherman, strongly preferred not to see politicians or other amateurs promoted to the highest echelons of command. Lincoln had to balance keeping his top West Pointers happy, on the one hand, with being able to capitalize on the unique nonmilitary contributions of his political generals, on the other. Osterhaus, of course, was not strictly in either category: he had little direct political influence other than his ethnicity, and his professional military training had not been at West Point, thus making him an outsider to academy graduates. All he really had in his favor were a few influential friends and his excellent performance in the field.[5]

Armed with advice from Schurz, on January 16 Osterhaus left Amalie in Philadelphia in the care of old friends while he made a brief trip to the capital. Once there he hurried directly to the Willard Hotel, across from the White House, where much of Washington's governmental business was informally conducted. In his diary that night he recorded his impressions of that historic place: "Quite a large number of guests—Representatives, Senators & lobby. Patriots of course, but non-combatants. Mr. Blow very kind, saw the President, Gratz Brown, *promises.*" Among the crowd, Osterhaus was lucky to find Missouri congressmen to buttonhole, but this might not have done him much good. Senator Brown later that year was a key player in the splinter Republican group that nominated his cousin, John Frémont, to oppose Lincoln in the upcoming election. Republican representative Henry Blow, an abolitionist from St. Louis, also sided with the Frémont faction. Thus, their "promises" were only that.[6]

Osterhaus also saw the president, but it is doubtful whether the president saw him. Fifty years later Osterhaus recounted to a reporter that, indeed, after U. S. Grant had presented him to the president and walked away, he and Lincoln had had a chat about Illinois. The newspaper article claims that this conversation occurred sometime before Osterhaus's appointment to major general. However, if Grant indeed presented him, it would have to have been a year later when Osterhaus was again in Washington, because on January 17, 1864, Grant was in Nashville and thus unavailable to do the honors. (The 1865 date would explain why, according to the same article, when the president asked [by then] Major General Osterhaus what he could do for him, Osterhaus replied that he was perfectly content, thus becoming, according to Lincoln, the first general he had discovered who had no favors to ask.) Before his train left Washington Osterhaus did see Secretary of War Edwin M. Stanton and General-in-Chief Henry Halleck, as well as Second Assistant Secretary of War Charles Dana, and was heartened that all three received him cordially. He did not meet with Secretary Chase after all. Perhaps Schurz had warned him that that meeting would not have done any good, because Hooker was out of favor in the capital and Chase for some time had been at odds with Lincoln's war policies and was actively considering a run for the presidency himself.[7]

Osterhaus's overnight stay in Washington was the extent of his campaign for promotion. His actions in the field would have to speak for themselves. After all, hadn't Sherman in his official report of the Chattanooga campaign called Osterhaus's division "one of my best . . . that has reflected glory on the Fifteenth Army Corps and the Army of the Tennessee"? This was perhaps the greatest praise Osterhaus received during the war, even though a cynic might suspect that Sherman had mentioned Osterhaus's division at least in part because its loss to him before Chattanooga might help to explain why Sherman had not accomplished his military objectives there.[8]

In any case, Osterhaus had done what he could. Collecting the charming Amalie in Philadelphia, he was off to St. Louis. Soon after they arrived, Maj. Gen. U. S. Grant also slipped into town because one of his children lay ill there. Osterhaus learned that Maj. Gen. William S. Rosecrans was expected also. He reckoned that their arrival would be the cause of an "official eating and drinking opportunity, but my radical friends do not seem to be in good humor; they have Frémont on the brain," an early indication of the German American disaffection with Abraham Lincoln. The "official eating and drinking opportunity" turned out to be a formal dinner for two hundred hosted by the city fathers honoring Grant. Besides the honoree, prominent Missourians serving in the war were recognized, including Osterhaus, seated at the head table with Grant, Maj. Gen. John Schofield (who had sworn Osterhaus into the army a lifetime ago), Rosecrans, and Grant's father-in-law, Frederick Dent, whom Osterhaus no doubt regaled with stories about his grandson and namesake, young Fred Grant.[9]

The day before the banquet, Osterhaus had chatted with the now sidelined Maj. Gen. John McClernand and his aide, Lt. Col. Adolf Schwartz, on a visit to Springfield. He described both as still very bitter against Grant for his abrupt ousting of McClernand at Vicksburg. Needless to say, they did not attend Grant's dinner. The day after the city fete, Osterhaus attended another "quite interesting" private dinner, with fellow guests Grant, Schofield, Rosecrans, and other officers. The gregarious Osterhaus seemed to be moving easily between the "outs" and the "ins" in the army, but that ease with the top brass must have come partly because he was in his hometown.[10]

Now it was the end of January; his leave was up on February 3. Osterhaus had already made up his mind to ask Amalie's father for her hand, but not without much agonizing, knowing that he was flouting the European tradition that imposed a year of mourning. Yet the exigencies of the family's situation drove his decision, besides which he was very attracted to Amalie. It was too soon to tell whether she felt the same. After a two-week extension of his leave for illness, giving him more time to plead his case with her, off he went to war again on February 16. On the way to winter camp he stopped in Nashville to report to General Grant. Seeking reassurance regarding his prospects for promotion, he asked Grant's right-hand man, Brig. Gen. John Rawlins, what he thought. "Gen. Rawlins assures me of the most friendly opinion Gen'l Grant has of me," he was happy to report in his diary.[11]

The Fifteenth Corps of the Army of the Tennessee spent the long and tedious winter months in the northeast corner of Alabama patrolling the railroad and the Tennessee River between Decatur and Stevenson. Osterhaus's new commander was yet another political general, Maj. Gen. John A. "Black Jack" Logan, whom he had last seen at Port Gibson. The two had a good bit in common, both men hailing from southern Illinois. Like Osterhaus but unlike many other political generals, including Carl Schurz, Logan had learned his military trade early in the war, initially as a colonel who recruited his own regiment, the Thirty-first Illinois. Although he had also advanced rapidly, Logan labored under the same "political" label as Osterhaus, which would ultimately cost him command of the Army of the Tennessee. Aside from his visits with Logan, Osterhaus chafed at the monotony of winter camp, "just as little and insignificant as a German garrison, without any of its attractions." His thoughts were often taken up with Amalie. She was something of a martinet with the children, not even sparing the general in her scolding, but he eagerly looked forward to her letters and forgave her anything. During the long days he also fretted about "whether we are doomed to remain quietly here or will be permitted to take our hand in the fight" in the upcoming campaign. He was not disappointed.[12]

In April Osterhaus cheered up as he reorganized the division for the campaign ahead. He was glad to have his old friend Col. Hugo Wangelin back, recovered after losing an arm at Ringgold Gap. Wangelin took command of the new Third Brigade, composed solely of Missouri regiments: the Third, Twelfth, Seventeenth, Thirty-first, and Thirty-second. This would be the only German brigade in Sherman's army, and Osterhaus had great confidence in it except for the Thirty-second Missouri, "beyond doubt the meanest Reg. Mo. turned out," in his opinion. Charles Woods still had the downsized First Brigade, now a mix of the Twenty-sixth and Thirtieth Iowa, the Twenty-seventh Missouri, and the Seventy-sixth Ohio. James Williamson continued with his Iowans of the Second Brigade: the Fourth, Ninth, Twenty-fifth, and Thirty-first. Osterhaus's long arm would be the Second Missouri Light Artillery under Capt. Louis Voelkner and the "splendid" Fourth Ohio Light under Capt. George Froehlich, all overseen by Maj. Clemens Landgraeber, the "Flying Dutchman." Osterhaus's overall strength at the beginning of the new campaign was forty-four hundred men. On April 29 he received his marching orders at long last, and the new campaign was finally under way. Over the next week one hundred thousand men of the Union army gathered at staging points around Chattanooga. On May 6 Osterhaus's division arrived and bivouacked near the Chickamauga battlefield, anticipating their march into Georgia the next day with almost giddy excitement.[13]

With Lieutenant General Grant now commanding the entire war effort, Sherman had taken on command of the new Atlanta campaign. His assignment was simple: to neutralize Johnston's army so that it could not reinforce Gen. Robert E. Lee's command, whose defeat was Grant's own assignment. Sherman's strategy was to send Maj. Gen. George Thomas's large Army of the Cumberland directly at the Confederate Army of Tennessee, now commanded by Gen. Joe Johnston. This would pin them in place while Sherman's two more mobile wings, the Army of the Ohio under Maj. Gen. John Schofield and the Army of the Tennessee under Maj. Gen. James McPherson, ran both flanks and threatened the railroad behind Johnston, forcing him to pull back from his works. The railroad supply line would be central to both sides. On May 7 McPherson's army began their march southward toward the little railroad town of Resaca on the deep Oostanaula River, the first major river barrier protecting Atlanta. If McPherson could cut and hold the railroad there while the other two corps held Johnston at his winter quarters in Dalton, the Confederates would be deprived of their escape route over the river.[14]

The Federals were in luck: when they emerged from Snake Creek Gap just west of Resaca they discovered that the village and the railroad were seemingly held by just a few Confederates, albeit behind solid defensive works. This was just the situation McPherson and Sherman had been hoping for: in fact, only four Southern regiments were on hand to face two Union corps. With dark coming on, the Union army went into bivouac near the mouth of the gap, fully expecting battle in the morning. As Osterhaus's orderly, Adolph Wagner, set up his commander's sleeping arrangements, he noted that Osterhaus was beginning to look ill; with execrable timing, another bout of malaria had started its ravages. Would the commander be able to fight in the morning?[15]

He need not have worried. By morning Johnston had quickly reinforced the garrison, and the Federal attack was canceled. That was just as well: by now Osterhaus was so ill with fever and diarrhea that he had to ride in an ambulance. Over the next few days both Sherman and Johnston moved the bulk of their forces to the vicinity of Resaca. By May 12 Osterhaus was feeling better, Sherman and most of the Union elements had arrived, and final preparations were under way for an attack. As the sun set on May 13 more than 150,000 soldiers, mostly veterans spoiling for their first fight of the year, faced each other across a narrow valley just outside Resaca, more combatants than were present at Shiloh, more than at Chickamauga, Spottsylvania, Antietam, or Second Manassas. Another bloodbath seemed likely; extensive hospital preparations were well under way in Snake Creek Gap, a fact not missed by the more nervous of the Union soldiers bivouacked nearby. The sight of the swarming opposition eliminated any reluctance a soldier might have had to start wielding his shovel, pick, or ax and digging himself some protection.[16]

The substantial Oostanaula River curls westward along Resaca's southern edge before turning south. A small stream, Camp Creek, comes in from the north and empties into the Oostanaula about a half mile west of the town. This tributary, site of much of the battle, runs through marshy ground between two low, hilly ridges. In 1864 the disputed railroad ran north-south behind the eastern ridge, straight through the town and on across the Oostanaula, with a second trestle bridge nearby for wagons. The Confederate fortifications protecting Resaca and the railroad occupied the ridge on the east side of Camp Creek. Although Johnston had the deep river at his back, he had the advantage of interior lines and an escape route across the Oostanaula should he need one.[17]

As the Federals poured through Snake Creek Gap, Sherman deployed them in a line west of Camp Creek. Logan's Fifteenth Corps held the Union right flank, with Brig. Gen. Morgan Smith's Second Division on the extreme right and Osterhaus's First just left of him. By midday of May 13 they were about six hundred yards from a Confederate forward outpost in the hills just west of the creek. Late in the afternoon Osterhaus, recovered enough from his bout of malaria to again sit his horse, deployed his brigades and skirmishers and, in line with Smith, began the Federal attack. With the aid of vigorous artillery work, they quickly drove the Confederate skirmishers and their supporting artillery down from the heights and across the Camp Creek bridge. Galloping up to their newly won vantage point, Osterhaus scanned the horizon eastward with his glasses. In plain view on the opposite ridge ran an impressive line of rebel entrenchments, bristling with men and guns and continuing north as far as he could see. The Confederate corps directly opposite was commanded by Maj. Gen. Leonidas Polk. Across the creek but forward of Polk's main line were some lower humps that were also manned by entrenched troops. Beyond the rebel line Osterhaus could see the little town full of scurrying citizens and troops, and he noticed frequent trains headed south across the Oostanaula River bridge, now in reach of his guns.[18]

The next afternoon, May 14, Sherman ordered a general advance. Sherman expected Johnston to merely fight a holding action and evacuate at nightfall, because Logan's artillery was a threat to the river crossings Johnston was relying on. Sherman wanted to keep the pressure on Johnston while he sent two divisions of bluecoats downriver a few miles to make a crossing and flank him. But Johnston watched with satisfaction as the Union attack on his center and right flank was quickly and bloodily repulsed by the entrenched Southerners. Late in the day he ordered an aggressive counterattack by Lt. Gen. John Bell Hood that nearly turned the Union left flank. At that point McPherson directed Osterhaus to make a diversion on the Union right. The general promptly ordered his first and second brigades forward, who succeeded in driving the Confederates away from the creek, gaining a bridgehead on the east side.[19]

As Hood continued to put pressure on the Union left flank, Sherman called for a stronger diversion on his right. Logan responded by ordering two brigades from the Fifteenth Corps to take Polk's forward position on the low humps in front of his main works. Osterhaus detailed Woods and his four regiments for this sortie, accompanied by three regiments of the Second Division under Brig. Gen. Giles Smith. Woods commanded the sortie. Urged on by raucous Federal cheers, the bluecoats succeeded in swarming the Confederate position on the humps, and with just their bayonets quickly drove the two Southern regiments back to their main line four hundred yards beyond. Past the Southern trenches, Woods could see that the vital river bridges were now within a half mile of Union artillery. Osterhaus's advance under Woods offered Sherman the strong possibility of trapping Johnston's army north of the river.[20]

Polk quickly realized that losing his forward position was a serious mistake and determined to take it back, in short order directing a massively heavy artillery bombardment and three separate assaults on the humps, the last coming well after dark. But Woods's and Smith's brigades, supported by Capt. Louis Voelkner's artillery and heavy reinforcements, would not budge, the fighting lasting about ninety minutes. That lodgment was the only successful Union advance for the day: at nightfall the Oostanaula River beachhead downstream was still not secured, and the bloody assault by the Union left had garnered nothing but heavy Union casualties.[21]

After breakfast next morning, May 15, Sherman and McPherson rode forward under overcast skies to inspect Osterhaus's forward breastworks on the humps, where his troops had been exchanging heavy skirmish fire with the Southerners since dawn. Anticipating that the Confederate commander would order Polk to retake that strategic position, Sherman ordered McPherson to concentrate his entire army to defend it, but he declined to order an attack against Polk's main line, vulnerable though it was because of troops being pulled away to help Hood on the rebel right. Despite Osterhaus's favorable position, Sherman chose to attack from the opposite end of his line, again without success. During that assault, the Army of the Tennessee merely traded desultory fire with Polk's command, and neither side made a serious move toward the other. The river bridges remained unmolested. But, several miles to the south, the Union expedition finally succeeded in establishing a beachhead across the Oostanaula, putting two Union divisions now in Johnston's rear.[22]

Johnston soon heard of both Osterhaus's advance and the news that the Federals were now across the river. These new developments forced him to abandon plans to counterattack and instead to focus on extricating his army while he could. But Sherman neglected to close the trap. Johnston was able to keep the Federals at bay all day and that night easily slipped his command south across the bridges under the not-so-watchful eyes of the bluecoats on the hills, who could have stopped the movement with a few well-placed artillery shells. Ironically, Johnston afterward destroyed the railroad bridge himself. Although a huge number of men had gathered in the valley prepared to fight the decisive battle of the campaign, the outcome was not what either commander had hoped; there would be no quick resolution in Georgia. For a confrontation of this size, the battle for Resaca was comparatively bloodless: less than a fifth as many casualties, seven thousand, were sustained as were in the other battles of similar magnitude. The great majority fell at the northern end of the battle; Osterhaus's losses in the entire engagement were 232 killed and wounded.[23]

For the next week, the two armies, now about equal size as Sherman's lengthening supply line bled off garrison troops, skirmished their way due south down the railroad, fighting every day but never coming to formal blows. Osterhaus was delighted when his old mess caterer, Joe Miller, returned at about this time, not that he could help much in finding provender suited to Osterhaus's impaired digestion. Although conditions of the march were tough, Union morale was good: after all, the weather was fair, and the Southerners were retreating. A staff officer in the Army of the Cumberland opined that the prospect of actual battle did not faze these veterans as it had the year before; they had come to realize that of the hundreds of thousands of bullets fired, very few hit anybody.[24]

Johnston continued south to take a strong position in the Allatoona hills, athwart the railroad some eleven miles southeast of the Etowah River. On May 20 Sherman decided to break loose from his railroad supply line at Kingston and try to go around Johnston's fortified position by swinging twenty miles due south to the little town of Dallas, then east toward Marietta, a few miles behind

Johnston on the railroad and not far from Atlanta. To counter Sherman's flanking movement, Johnston sent Lt. Gen. William J. Hardee's and Polk's corps south to Dallas while Hood stayed in the vicinity of the crossroads near New Hope church, four miles to the north. By the time the Federals showed up, the Southerners were ready.[25]

On May 25 the Fifteenth Corps had drawn within three miles of Dallas when Osterhaus heard heavy firing behind him to the north. Hooker's Twentieth Corps, in advance of the Army of the Cumberland, had made first contact with the Southerners at the New Hope crossroads. Hooker's three divisions were easily repulsed by Alexander Stewart's entrenched division, suffering sixteen hundred casualties in that bloody fight. Next morning the Federal line continued to form up, McPherson's army separated from its neighbor by about a mile. Logan's Fifteenth Corps was on the right flank just east of Dallas, Osterhaus first, Smith in the center, and Brig. Gen. William Harrow's Fourth Division at the far-right end. Opposite the Fifteenth at a relatively short distance was Hardee's corps, four divisions entrenched in a semicircle so that they could enfilade the Federal line or perhaps turn the right end. Harrow, anticipating this threat, had bent his line back at an angle to the rest. Entrenching went on the rest of the daylight hours and into the night, as McPherson's other corps gradually moved into position to Logan's left.[26]

Before nightfall Osterhaus ordered Williamson's command to press forward to a high thickly wooded ridge picketed by Confederates. The Iowans of the Second Brigade worked their way up to near the crest of the ridge, where they quickly established a line of rifle pits with their skirmishers thrown forward, at this point within a hundred yards of the Confederate works. After dark Williamson's skirmishers began to report that they had sighted heavy enemy troop concentrations in front of them. While his skirmishers repelled frequent Southern skirmish attacks during that long night, Williamson asked Osterhaus more than once for reinforcements, but the general, expecting Dodge's division to move up momentarily to connect with his left flank, refused. It turned out that Dodge was delayed getting into position on Osterhaus's left, and at daylight Williamson's Second Brigade found itself nearly a half mile in advance of Dodge, creating a gaping hole that the Confederates were at pains to exploit.[27]

Through the thick predawn fog, Williamson saw that his fears were justified: a heavy Confederate force was moving to turn his exposed left flank. He once more appealed to Osterhaus for support and was again denied. Osterhaus's assurance to Williamson that there was no enemy nearby was delivered just as the Confederate attack began in earnest, driving Williamson's scrambling skirmishers in confusion back into his mess tents and camp. Osterhaus, now having seen with his own eyes the Confederate line approaching at right angles to Williamson, directed Wangelin's Third Brigade to Williamson's aid. Osterhaus reported that he ordered his old Twelfth Missouri to lead the Federal counterattack, successfully regaining ground that had been lost by Williamson's skirmishers. By contrast, in his report Williamson claimed he had no help in repulsing the flank attack, an opinion corroborated by his men. Whatever actually happened, Williamson's bitterness was easy to read between his lines, the rancor continuing as he described the actions of the following day.[28]

Sherman now decided to change tactics. The massive Union flanking maneuver had failed against strong entrenchments. His army was strung out; McPherson's army on the right was vulnerable on both flanks. The troops and animals were already hungry after only a week, making Sherman anxious to get back to the railroad and his supply line before he was cut off. Better to drive between Johnston and the railroad than to continue the long way around. Johnston correctly suspected Sherman's intent to move back to the railroad and ordered Hardee to make a reconnaissance of the Union right to see if they were still strongly entrenched around Dallas. Hardee suspected that the bluecoats had already moved out, leaving only a thin rear guard. Because of troop shifts, Hardee's force at this point was reduced to one division available to test that theory, that of Maj. Gen. William B. Bate. Testing Bate could do, but he was clearly in no position to stand toe-to-toe if McPherson's whole army were still there to take him up on the offer. And they were: McPherson's army had not yet begun their pullout, and Bate faced five divisions.[29]

Thinking that he was probably just facing a rearguard skirmish line, Bate's plan was to have a dismounted cavalry brigade charge first at the Federal angled extreme right. If they met little resistance, they were to signal with howitzers, and then Bate's three infantry brigades would attack straight forward toward the rest of the Union "rear guard." The attack began in the sleepy afternoon "with a yell the devil ought to copyright," as the Southerners burst from the dense brush and quickly overran three guns of the First Iowa Battery posted out in front of Harrow's line, plunging through a gap and right into the Federal entrenchments. Meantime, other grayclads began manhandling the Union's forward guns around so they could aim them point-blank at the Federal trenches.[30]

When Logan learned of the ferocious attempt to turn Harrow's right flank, he sent urgently to Osterhaus for reinforcements. Osterhaus personally took Williamson's Second Brigade on the double-quick about a mile to reinforce Harrow's right. "How well, and in what time the movement was executed, I respectfully ask the general commanding to state for me," grumped Williamson, who sounded like he was not invited. Osterhaus arrived to join Logan in the thick of the battle. "When the musketry was playing the hottest, Logan came dashing up along our line, waved his hat and told the boys to give them hell, boys. You should have heard them cheer him," wrote a man in Harrow's beleaguered division. Osterhaus's style was a bit different. Years later a veteran told this probably embellished story: Giving his horse to an orderly, Osterhaus "dropped all dignity for the time being" and darted behind a tree. He was surprised to find that the tree was already occupied by a large German named William Kenny of the Fourth Iowa.

> As Kenny himself was almost too large for the tree, the general said: "Get away, man, get away from here." Kenny turned and in his cool, deliberate way asked: "Must I to the rear go?" Osterhaus said: "No, no, my good man. Stick right here; we cannot spare you just at this time. This tree is big enough for two." "Then," replied Kenny, "togedder we stick." Osterhaus remained behind the tree, directing operations until he was satisfied that the fight was going the right way, and whenever the boys of the Fourth Iowa saw him after that they said among themselves "Togedder we stick."[31]

This story from a non-German regiment gives a flavor of the tension between the ethnics and native-born troops that never entirely disappeared, regardless of a man's regard for a particular individual. Dialect stories with mangled grammar were favorites, in Osterhaus's case often not accurate, as is evident from his grammatically correct written English. Colloquialisms were another matter. This anecdote, part of an article admiring of Osterhaus, is not pejorative. Maj. Robert Finley of the Seventy-fourth Ohio wrote a few weeks later, "At the outset of the war, . . . the officer who would have stood behind a tree on the skirmish line . . . and not have exposed his person by standing upright and in exposed positions, would have been stigmatized as a coward. But now, of the officer or soldier who won't take these precautions, if killed or wounded, the expressions of the soldiers are 'I don't pity him, he had no business exposing himself unnecessarily.'"[32]

With the help of Osterhaus's reinforcements, the Sixth Iowa quickly rallied and repulsed the surprise attack and recaptured their three guns. Bate now had the answer to his question: the Yankees were present in force and ready to fight. He immediately countermanded his previous order for a frontal attack. Unfortunately, the sound of artillery had already set his three infantry brigades off on their charge. Only Brig. Gen. Robert Tyler's Tennessee Brigade got the cancel order; the other two brigades made an uncoordinated charge at Osterhaus's remaining two brigades. The bluecoats, waiting patiently in their double row of log and dirt rifle pits, drove them back by a point-blank salvo and enfilading canister fire. Woods, in charge of these two brigades of the First Division, estimated the attack lasted only a half hour or so, Osterhaus returning as it ended.[33]

By June 7 Sherman had his whole command back on the railroad, but now twenty-five miles farther south. In a month of campaigning the Federals had penetrated ninety miles into Georgia, but now they were stalled for the next several weeks by formidable Southern defenses and extremely wet weather. Johnston had withdrawn to another strong defensive line in the hills two miles north of Kennesaw Mountain, the last significant elevation before Atlanta. Before probing Johnston's position, Sherman took a few days to resupply his depleted army.

During the wait, Osterhaus saw a lot of Sherman, who spent much of his time with the Fifteenth Corps when not otherwise occupied. Osterhaus liked his commander but did not accord him quite the same respect he did Grant, appreciating him "more for his wit and conversational abilities than for anything else. A good fighter, a fine leader, but not a military genius of the very first magnitude," was how he characterized him much later. Sherman had not demonstrated himself to be the great battlefield general that Osterhaus admired; furthermore, Sherman's philosophy of war was much different from that of his peers: he preferred to achieve his results without battle whenever he could.[34]

Pressing forward again, Sherman had his army entrench within sight of Johnston's newest fortifications at the base of Kennesaw Mountain. No further advance was possible because of the terrible weather, but the armies continued to exchange almost constant skirmish and artillery fire for the next several days. On scattered parts of the line, the fighting frequently escalated to hand-to-hand combat. Typical was the action on June 15: Logan ordered a feint, and Osterhaus ordered a charge of his skirmish line four hundred yards across an open field, "a grand sight," taking a line of rifle pits and prisoners and repelling three separate Confederate assaults with minor losses. During this soggy period, the soldiers on both sides hunkered miserably in water-filled rifle pits ducking bullets, watching their clothes rot on their bodies, picking lice, and trading cracks and coffee for tobacco with the foe while they waited for the weather to clear and the roads to dry out enough to move the heavy wagons. Osterhaus was sympathetic to their situation: "Our poor men suffer terribly in the trenches. . . . [I]t was the most horrible time for campaigning I ever saw!" Osterhaus's headquarters, although not in a trench, was not all that safe, either. At one point a solid rebel shot from the mountain pierced one of his tents, apparently without doing injury.[35]

Kennesaw Mountain, only seventeen miles from Atlanta, is really a north-to-south ridge with two prominences, Big and Little Kennesaw, and a lower spur known as Pigeon Hill coming off to the south. During the night of June 18, Johnston moved out of the rifle pits to concentrate his army in a strong line of fortifications on the heights that overlooked the entire Union line and protected the railroad running along the northern base. The next day Osterhaus's division made themselves at home in the recently abandoned Confederate rifle pits at the north end of the ten-mile-long Union line. From his new position Osterhaus could easily see the formidable parapets and batteries bristling on the partially denuded crest above.[36]

On June 24, a rare clear day, Logan decided to test whether Johnston held the crest with more than just skirmishers. Osterhaus pushed his skirmishers up the mountain with the rest of the Fifteenth Corps, who drove to within two hundred yards of the top before they were stopped by a solid line of Hardee's skirmishers. With no orders to attack, Logan withdrew, satisfied that he had uncovered the major Southern position. However, he had not communicated clearly with his generals. Osterhaus, blood up, was unhappy with stopping and blamed McPherson. That night he wrote in his diary, "Advance the line of Skirmishers; they went up more than half the hill, driving the enemy back; the 16th & 17th AC did not keep step and therefore we had to fall back before night. It is shameful. The general arrangements of Army of Tenn very poor." He was clearly less than confident in McPherson's capabilities by then, at least privately, but also was not aware that the skirmish advance had apparently been Logan's idea and the other two corps were not involved. Other officers did not know it, either; one officer in Harrow's division wrote his wife, "The 17th AC which was to the left of the XV C had not advanced any, therefore . . . I received such a heavy cross and flank fire that my left broke. . . . [H]ad I been supported on the left my own skirmisher line would have taken it."[37]

The next morning Osterhaus suffered another onset of malaria, which possibly saved the lives of many of his men in the coming battle. It seems that while the skirmishers of the Fifteenth Corps had been scrambling alone up Kennesaw Mountain, Sherman had finally decided on a general attack to commence three days later. At that point McPherson's army held a line north of the main Kennesaw peaks and circling around to a position opposite Pigeon Hill. Opposite McPherson was Maj. Gen. William Loring, commanding Leonidas Polk's corps, since that worthy had been killed by artillery fire the week before. South of McPherson in Sherman's center was Thomas, followed by Schofield's Army of the Ohio on the Union far right.[38]

Sherman's plan for June 27 was to have a portion of both McPherson's and Thomas's armies attack simultaneously, the Army of the Tennessee to assault the cleft between Little Kennesaw and Pigeon Hill. McPherson decided to use Logan's Fifteenth Corps for his main assault, so during the night Osterhaus silently shifted his division south with the rest of the corps to their new position opposite Pigeon Hill. Initially, Osterhaus's First Division was to be on the right and center of the assault, Harrow on the left, with Morgan Smith's Second Division in reserve. But perhaps because Osterhaus was ill, at the last minute McPherson ordered Logan to replace Osterhaus's division with Smith's. So, although they drew three days' rations and sixty rounds like the others, Osterhaus's men remained in rifle pits in reserve except for about a hundred skirmishers who would go in with the first wave.[39]

Osterhaus, still feeling terrible, must have been secretly relieved at his change of assignment. His take on the situation was that "the enemy's fortifications were on their whole extent very strong and coherent so that an assault could only be undertaken at the risk of great losses." Facing them behind the stout fortifications was Maj. Gen. Samuel French's division, featuring those redoubtable Missourians of Brig. Gen. Francis Cockrell, whom Osterhaus had met in battle twice before. Logan's three attacking brigades charged in dense columns and with great struggle reached to within a few yards of the Confederate battlements, where Smith's scattered column was caught in an enfilading battery fire that "poured death and destruction" on them. They clung to their position for about an hour before finally retreating to the captured rifle pits below. Farther south, Thomas's charge had an even bloodier result. In the three-hour battle, Logan's losses were more than six hundred, twenty-six of whom were Osterhaus's skirmishers; Thomas's losses topped fifteen hundred. To the men who fought there, the day was a waste, an "unfruitful and badly conducted charge" without any particular gain. Osterhaus viewed the decision to assault Kennesaw as a strategic necessity: "The further advance of our Armies depended on the dislodgement of Johnston." But he, too, privately had major problems about its execution: "My skirmishers precede and take the first (Picket) line of the Rebs—some prisoners. The charge a failure—loss heavy. The whole thing utterly unprepared!" he wrote that night.[40]

But Sherman's assault had not been a complete failure: flanked once more, Johnston retreated on July 2 beyond Marietta to fortifications on the banks of the Chattahoochee, the last river barrier before Atlanta. The next day Logan ordered Osterhaus to sweep his division around north of Big Kennesaw to clear the town of Marietta. Then on July 4 the First Division made a grueling march in the heat to take the extreme right of the Union position behind Nickajack Creek near the Chattahoochee. Only a third of the men made it into camp that day; Osterhaus was one of those struck down by the heat, suffering another severe relapse of malaria. The next day he was so ill that he put Charles Woods in charge of the division and took to his tent in misery: "I feel very bad indeed; I wish the campaign was over," he wrote in his diary. A week later, his division received orders to march fifty miles through the relentless heat back through Marietta and on to the east, crossing to the Atlanta side of the Chattahoochee at Roswell on July 14. Osterhaus brought up the rear in an ambulance, still too ill to mount a horse but nonetheless sticking out the horribly hot weather and a deadly lightning storm until he saw his command into a good defensive position on the east bank of the Chattahoochee.[41]

In his official report of the campaign Osterhaus noted that his health had been impaired for several weeks, but he was reluctant to leave the campaign until it was over and won. Now, on the recommendation of his doctors, he decided he had better go. The timing looked good: he thought the plan was to rest the troops for a few days. "General McPherson also considered the present moment sufficiently calm to admit of my taking a few days rest." On July 15 Osterhaus left for the railhead in Marietta to begin a twenty-day sick leave. Meanwhile, contrary to what he had been told, the division was ordered to march again the next day toward Decatur, east of Atlanta, and within ten days would be involved in two major battles without him.[42]

An ailing and war-weary Osterhaus wrote the worried Amalie to expect him in St. Louis on July 21, and a week after he arrived home he quietly married her. It was an auspicious week indeed for Osterhaus, for two days later he was notified by Secretary of War Stanton that he had finally been appointed major general of Volunteers. His delight was tempered by his frustration at being away from his command when he read the momentous war news from Atlanta: President Jefferson Davis had replaced the careful Johnston with the impetuous Hood, who lost no time in going on the attack on July 20 at Peachtree Creek. The day after Osterhaus reached St. Louis his First Division under Charles R. Woods distinguished itself in the Battle of Atlanta, in which McPherson was killed. Then followed the Battle of Ezra Church on Osterhaus's wedding day, "and I could not be with it," he mourned.[43]

The death of Sherman's personal friend James McPherson, only weeks before his wedding day, was a grievous blow to the Union army commander, but he had little time to dwell on it. In the midst of facing Hood in three major battles that week, Sherman also had to deal with dissension among his officers over the fact that he decided against promoting John Logan, senior corps commander of the Army of the Tennessee, to succeed McPherson. Instead, he awarded the command to Maj. Gen. Oliver O. Howard, a steady but uncharismatic West Pointer. "Both [Logan and Blair] were men of great courage and talent, but were politicians by nature and experience, and it may be that for this reason they were mistrusted by regular officers like Generals Schofield, Thomas and myself," recalled Sherman in his memoirs, neatly encapsulating the West Point–political general schism. Sherman then had to deal with the very upset Logan and the angry Joseph Hooker, who also thought he deserved the assignment. In the middle of that tense and at times chaotic week, Sherman and his officers learned about Osterhaus's promotion. It may have been the last straw.[44]

While the oblivious Osterhaus was in Matthew Brady's studio sitting for his portrait in his new two-star uniform, his face clearly showing the physical and mental toll the war had taken on him in the past three years, back in Atlanta all hell was breaking loose over his promotion. Rumors flew. Both officers and soldiers thought they knew where Osterhaus went when he left the front, and both groups were wrong. Scuttlebutt among the men was that Osterhaus had resigned and headed for Mexico to fight. The Union officers outside Osterhaus's division, from Sherman on down, thought that he had headed to Washington to plead his case for promotion. (That notion was still being repeated in print as late as 1875.) This rumor angered many officers, who had been told all along by Sherman not to expect promotion until after the campaign was over. Sherman had reinforced this point in a request to Halleck on July 24 that no promotion be awarded to any officer on leave due to sickness or for reasons other than battle wounds. But he was too late by a day.[45]

Still raw with grief just two days after McPherson's death, Sherman learned the news about Osterhaus's appointment by way of a dispatch from Inspector General Col. James A. Hardie notifying him that both Osterhaus and Brig.

Osterhaus upon promotion to major general, July 1864. (Courtesy the Frederick Meserve Collection, Abraham Lincoln Library, Springfield, Illinois)

Gen. Alvin Hovey, a political general from Indiana who had performed well at Champion Hill the year before, had been appointed major generals on July 23 (in Hovey's case a brevet promotion). Now Sherman had an officer morale problem over and above the Logan controversy. He immediately fired off a tart reply to Hardie on July 25: "I do not object to his [Osterhaus's] appointment, but I wish to put on record this my emphatic opinion, that it is an act of injustice to officers who stand by their posts in the day of danger to neglect them and advance such as Hovey and Osterhaus, who left us in the midst of bullets to go to the rear in search of personal advancement."[46]

Sherman chose not to take into account Osterhaus's sick leave, tarring him with Hovey's brush of ambition even though Hovey's situation was very different. After Vicksburg, Hovey had left the front and spent several months in Indiana recruiting five regiments of cavalry and five of infantry. When he returned to the Atlanta campaign, despite a poor performance at Resaca, he expected Sherman to award him a division with all ten of his raised regiments. Instead, Sherman gave him only the five of infantry, assigning the troopers elsewhere. Hovey, hurt and insulted, left for Washington to plead his case with Lincoln. Understandably, Sherman was upset when he heard of Hovey's appointment and assumed that Osterhaus had left the front to pursue the same ends. He was even more chagrined when he learned that his irate response to Hardie had been shown to the president, discovering this only when he received a surprise message from Lincoln himself the next day:

> I have just seen yours complaining of the appointment of Hovey and Osterhaus. The point you make is unquestionably a good one, and yet please hear a word from us. My recollection is that both General Grant and yourself recommended both H[ovey] and O[sterhaus] for promotion, and these, with other strong recommendations, drew committals from us which we could neither honorably or safely disregard. . . . As to O[sterhaus], we did not know of his leaving at the time we made the appointment, and do not now know the terms on which he left. Not to have appointed him, as the case appeared to us at the time, would have been almost, if not quite, a violation of our word. The word was given on what we thought was high merit and somewhat on his nationality.

Clearly, Lincoln had not seen Osterhaus in Washington recently. When Grant was notified of the promotions, he weighed in on the side of his friend in a dispatch to Secretary of War Stanton on July 26: "Osterhaus has proved himself a good soldier, but if he is not in the field I regret his promotion." Grant obviously did not know Osterhaus was on sick leave, either.[47]

On July 27 Sherman tried to retrieve his dignity as he responded to Lincoln. However, his position had not changed:

> Hovey and Osterhaus are both worthy men, and had they been promoted on the eve of the Vicksburg campaign, it would have been natural and well accepted; but I do think you will admit that their promotion, coming to us when they had gone to the rear, the one offended because I could not unite in the same division five infantry and five cavalry regiments, and the other for temporary sickness . . . I assure you that every general of my army has spoken of it and referred to it as evidence that promotion results from importunity and not from actual service. I have refrained from recommending any thus far in the campaign, as I think we should reach some stage in the game before stopping to balance accounts or writing history.[48]

From this exchange of messages it would seem that Osterhaus's performance and merits were not the issue but simply the timing of his appointment relative to his leave. One month earlier in the campaign another non–West Point brigadier in Sherman's army, Grenville Dodge, had been appointed major general to fill a position being vacated by a resignation, but he was in the field at the time that the outgoing general, Richard Oglesby, personally used his influence with the president to secure his vacated spot for Dodge. In the matter of major generals Lincoln's problem was compounded by the dearth of available commands after the big Federal buildup of 1862 was complete. Thus far in 1864, only five Union major general appointments had been confirmed, Dodge the only one with Sherman at Atlanta. Each position had been lusted after by many, senators as well trying to bring the honor home to their states.[49]

Sherman's concern about timing and morale, seconded by Grant, pointed up the fact that a new process had evolved in these appointments. Up until now the president had exercised full discretion on both candidate choice and the timing of his selection. Those Lincoln selected for nomination would be notified of their appointments by Stanton. The actual nomination and confirmation by the Senate followed later, depending on the timing of Senate sessions. (In Osterhaus's case, he was appointed in July 1864, formally nominated by Lincoln in December, and not confirmed by the Senate until February 14, 1865. His new rank dated from his appointment date, July 23, 1864.) Starting with the promotion of Howard over the more politically attractive Logan, Lincoln now demonstrated that he would generally accede to the wishes of his senior commanders rather than act independently as he had earlier in the war. With Grant at a standstill in front of Lee's fortifications at Petersburg after a very bloody campaign, so far this year neither he nor Sherman had given Lincoln a decisive victory to use as political ammunition in this critical election year. Lincoln wanted to do nothing to discourage his top generals until they had results for him. And those commanders were increasingly of the opinion that West Pointers should be in control of the army.[50]

Lincoln had other political concerns as well: his voter support among the important German American segment was fading because of what they felt was his foot-dragging on emancipation. Instead, as Osterhaus had noted in his diary, the midwestern German Americans began to actively back the presidential candidacy of John Frémont, who campaigned all summer and did not withdraw from the campaign until after Atlanta fell. Since spring, German-language newspapers had also been voicing complaints about what they considered to be Lincoln's shabby treatment of Frémont, Sigel, Osterhaus, and Schurz, calling for better commands for their heroes. Thus, Lincoln's hint to Sherman that Osterhaus's nationality was a factor in his appointment was probably understated. Since that February, Lincoln had been promising that the next appointment (or "the first Dutchman" appointed, depending on which version one cites) would be Osterhaus. Now, in the uncertain summer of 1864, Lincoln had decided to play that card. Whether or not he anticipated that this move would anger his commanders, in his response to Sherman, Lincoln sought a delicate balance between political and military considerations that would mollify them. Sherman duly circulated Lincoln's dispatch among his officers in the hope of settling them down.[51]

Major General Osterhaus returned to the front on August 15, "somewhat rested but not what he used to be," according to his orderly, Adolph Wagner. Atlanta was still under Federal siege. If Osterhaus expected warm congratulations from his peers on his appointment, he was sorely disappointed, dismayed rather than gratified by the chill atmosphere in the high command. Even three weeks after the storm broke and the Lincoln dispatch had been circulated, there was still general unrest in headquarters over all the drama with appointments, not just Osterhaus's. A staff officer in the Army of the Cumberland wrote his wife, "I feel quite certain that if our Generals hadn't fallen to quarreling among themselves, Atlanta would have been ours now. I'm glad I'm not a General to be quarreling with my companions about questions of rank, like a bunch of children quarreling over their painted toys." Wide circulation of the Lincoln dispatch admitting that Osterhaus was a political choice must have been especially galling to the German. A week after he got back, Osterhaus wrote Amalie that he was "disgusted with the service," a telling comment from the war enthusiast of yore.[52]

Sherman was busy moving assignments around in this period. In Osterhaus's division he promoted Brig. Gen. Charles R. Woods to command the Third Division of the Seventeenth Corps. Elsewhere in Logan's Fifteenth Corps, Morgan Smith's Second Division was taken over by West Pointer Brig. Gen. W. B. Hazen, late of the Army of the Cumberland. Hazen now found himself ranking next senior in command to Osterhaus, with Harrow just behind him. The Army of the Tennessee, of course, was now under Howard, with one of its corps also under new management. The wounded Grenville Dodge was temporarily replaced by Brig. Gen. Thomas E. Ransom.[53]

As for finally taking Atlanta, Sherman was not about to risk another Kennesaw. Hood's fortifications completely encircled the city, with a leg southward protecting the nearest few miles of the Macon and Western Railroad, the only supply route left open. After weeks of siege, Sherman decided in late August to send his army on a clandestine five-day movement to disrupt this last supply link, hoping to force Hood to abandon the city by drawing the defenders out from behind their works. On August 26 Osterhaus's division, in the advance of Howard's army, moved south from Ezra Chapel to Fairburn on the Atlantic and Western Railroad. After a day and night of destroying that branch line, the

Army of the Tennessee moved eastward in two columns to Jonesboro, a depot on the main Macon and Western railroad line about twenty-five miles south of Atlanta. Sherman's other two armies, moving more slowly, arrayed themselves along the railroad to the north of Howard.[54]

At dusk on August 30, Logan's Fifteenth Corps, in the advance, neared the Jonesboro depot. Driving grayclad skirmishers across the Flint River, the Federals crested a line of low hills and spotted the line of Southern trenches just west of the depot, about a mile from the river. Howard ordered the corps to entrench and wait for morning. At the moment Howard's army faced only twenty-five hundred Confederate infantry, but he did not know that. While the Fifteenth Corps was digging in at Jonesboro through that night, the Confederates were hastily bolstering their forces from Atlanta via the railroad and long marches, so that by noon the next day the sides were about equal in strength. Now facing Howard were Hardee's Corps, commanded by Patrick Cleburne, and Stephen D. Lee's Corps, both of whom Osterhaus had faced before. Hardee had overall command of this force.[55]

By dint of bayonet and shovel, the Fifteenth Corps was fairly well protected by dawn, in a strong, elevated position with a good line of fire for the artillery. The right end of the Federal line was angled back toward the river and overlooked a creek in a swampy ravine. Osterhaus's division was located near the angle there with Brig. Gen. John M. Corse's division on his right. That morning, August 31, when Logan rode up, Osterhaus assured him that after he finished his coffee he would "make 'em hell schmell," and proceeded to set his batteries to make that happen. He placed two Fourth Ohio twelve-pounders on a hill to the right in front of his line only a thousand yards from the depot, providing good coverage of both the track and the Confederate works. He supported them with one hundred men fronted by skirmishers. This forward position, though risky, was particularly devilish for the Confederates trying to debark Hardee's arriving troops. Osterhaus's forward battery began shelling the Confederate position and depot at noon, demonstrating how vulnerable the railroad was to Union attack. (Howard credited these guns with forcing the enemy to take the offensive rather than the Federals, thus saving many Union lives.) Osterhaus placed another section of twelve-pounders overlooking the salient angle and covering the path to the river, which was lightly held by Judson Kilpatrick's cavalry. Before they were ready, the Confederate attack began.[56]

The Confederate defenses were hastily thrown together, but that did not matter too much because from Atlanta came Hood's message to Hardee to attack with bayonets and drive the Federals back across the Flint River. At three o'clock, after their own fifteen-minute artillery barrage, the gray line started forward. The attack was to begin on the Southern left with Cleburne's old division and progress *en echelon* to Lee, but Lee jumped the gun and mounted a disorganized assault on the Union left before Cleburne's division started. Lee's grayclads approached to within thirty yards of the Federal works at some points, but "the most terrible and destructive fire" Logan had ever seen soon drove them back. Meanwhile, Cleburne's division finally began moving toward the Union right flank and Osterhaus. But instead of wheeling to face the angled blue line as planned, the entire division kept going straight until it had chased Kilpatrick's cavalry clear across the river, in the process becoming disconnected from John C. Brown's division on their right as they scrambled back into the creek ravine in disorder.[57]

During the charge, Osterhaus almost lost his forward guns and barely avoided being surrounded himself. In their headlong rush to the river, Cleburne's men had double-quicked right past Osterhaus's skirmishers, threatening his most exposed two guns. The "rebel avalanche" nipping at his heels, Osterhaus personally directed the rescue of these guns, bringing them back behind solid breastworks while his detachment covered the movement. One of Logan's bodyguards happened to see Osterhaus at about this time:

> Diverging to the right we came in behind the position of Gen. Osterhaus and the 1st Division. Here we halted for a few moments, protected by the works of a six-gun battery. I shall never forget that scene. Osterhaus was walking back and forth in his shirt sleeves, suspenders down like a wood-chopper at work, giving directions first here, then there; now to a gunner, now to a rifleman, admonishing the men to lower the muzzles of their rifles and not shoot in the air, for most of the men were loath to get their heads very far above the works as there was a hail of bullets sweeping the line.
>
> The rebels were making their first charge from the protection of the nearby woods, but our fire soon drove them back. How those cannoneers worked their guns! One who never was in action cannot believe that men could load and fire so fast. Sweating and black with powder, they looked like coal heavers on a river steamboat. But there was no shrinking.[58]

When Brown's division charged obliquely across the swampy ground at Corse and Osterhaus, they were easily repulsed with heavy loss. The Confederate commanders managed to get two or three more charges out of their dispirited men, but even the Federals noticed that their hearts were simply not in it. Frontal assault on well-protected defenders who could shoot at will took a terrible toll, as they all had learned repeatedly. On this day the Confederates suffered casualties on the order of several times those of Logan. As Hardee reported officially, "The attack could scarcely have been called a vigorous one, nor is it surprising that troops who had for two months been hurled against breast-works only to be repulsed or to gain dear-bought and fruitless victories, should now have moved against the enemy's works with reluctance and distrust."[59]

The next day Sherman was in no mood for an all-out assault on Hardee's trenches and the ensuing bloodshed that that guaranteed. Instead, in the afternoon he ordered just Jeff Davis's division to attack the salient at the north end of the defensive line, halting him due to darkness after he was modestly successful. Osterhaus had little to do but hold Hardee's attention with artillery during the day. Meanwhile, Sherman tried to hustle his other forces around Jonesboro to surround the Confederate position. But Hardee successfully extracted his command that night, moving them six miles southeast to Lovejoy Station. Although Union troops followed Hardee, by the time they were close Hardee was behind solid entrenchments. After a halfhearted effort on September 2, Sherman called off the late-afternoon Union attack when he learned that Hood had abandoned Atlanta. The Union commander decided to end the campaign with the capture of that highly symbolic city, handing Lincoln the first great Union victory of the year just in time for the election. It had taken Sherman two months to drive to Atlanta and another two months to take it. He would worry about Hood's army a little later. After burying all the dead of both armies and moving the wounded, the Fifteenth Corps and the rest of the Federal army moved to the vicinity of Atlanta to rest, recover, and reorganize.[60]

The battle at Jonesboro marked the last time Osterhaus would lead his division in action, the last time many of the men would face a charge by a full division of screaming Confederates. However, none of them knew this in early September 1864, as they busily set up a proper camp a few miles south of Atlanta. Here the battle-weary soldiers of the First Division could finally scrub the lice from their bodies and ragged uniforms and, for the first time in three months, sleep without worrying about sniper fire or the odd cannonball. But all was not perfect. Pay was eight months overdue; after a month in camp, rations were still short; and that stickler Osterhaus insisted on proper uniform for officers, company drill twice a day, and battalion drill four times a week. "In fact we are put through the hardest I ever knew. The men are tired of camp already—they would rather be in the field," groused one. Osterhaus had sound reasons for this rigor: "Our men become more or less rusty during the long campaign and a thorough overhauling is urgently needed to recover that alacrity and promptness without which a Battalion degenerates into an armed mob," he wrote in General Order No. 72.[61]

Osterhaus, again ailing, soon said good-bye to his friend Hugo Wangelin and most of Wangelin's Third Brigade of Missourians. Some companies with earlier enlistment dates had dribbled away earlier in the summer, but now a big contingent was boarding trains for home, breaking up the only mostly German American brigade serving in Sherman's army. The decision of whether to reenlist was not too difficult this time around, now that the Union effort was finally going well. In a remarkable understatement, a man in the Third Missouri said that after thinking it over he and his comrades had decided that "we had enough of this sort of thing for the time being." Osterhaus soon had to leave his old division behind as well. President Lincoln had asked two of Sherman's political-general corps commanders, "Black Jack" Logan and Frank Blair, to leave the field to stump in Illinois and Indiana, where Lincoln was not doing well in his reelection campaign. On September 22 Osterhaus, as senior division commander, assumed temporary command of Logan's Fifteenth Corps, while thirty-year-old Brig. Gen. Thomas Ransom, another non–West Pointer up through the ranks, took on the two divisions of Blair's Seventeenth Corps, making both of Howard's corps commanders substitutes for the coming campaign.[62]

Osterhaus had mixed feelings about leaving his old command. He had no illusions that his new temporary assignment was a step up for him, observing that he was appointed not on merit but simply because he happened to be senior. He was not terribly pleased with the thankless job of being a conduit of orders from above rather than an executor of those orders, much preferring to be where the action was. Worse, now he would be moving in the politicized atmosphere of army headquarters, a proximity that he had studiously avoided so far and especially so since the hostile reaction to his promotion that summer. Of Sherman's other five direct subordinates remaining after he sent Thomas's corps to Nashville in September, the two wing commanders, Howard and Maj. Gen. Henry Slocum, were West Pointers, and the only two other corps commanders Osterhaus knew at all were Frank Blair, who had returned after the election, and Jeff Davis, with whom the German had served at Pea Ridge. But both these men were tight with Sherman. Davis, like Sherman, was a veteran of the Mexican War, and Blair was not only highly regarded by Sherman but also currently on the outs with the St. Louis German Americans over their support for Frémont in the presidential campaign. (The fourth corps commander, Brig. Gen. Alpheus Williams, was a political general whose career had been mostly in the eastern theater.) As the only foreign-born commander, every time Osterhaus spoke, his peers were reminded of his outsider status. With his German friends now departed, Osterhaus must have been lonely.[63]

Moreover, Osterhaus knew that the soldiers of the Fifteenth Corps were sorry to lose the charismatic Logan. As Logan left his cheering men, he commended the Fifteenth to Osterhaus, telling them that they could feel safe under their new commander; Osterhaus had a good reputation as a fighting general. But leadership habits that soldiers were able to overlook in their own division commanders irritated them at higher levels, particularly arbitrary or harsh disciplinary actions and lack of respect. New commanders were put to the test, one way or another, to see what the men might expect of them. Even though he had been an approachable division commander, Osterhaus was to be no exception to this testing, especially at the hands of his old division.[64]

After Atlanta fell, Sherman's first order of business was reorganization. In the shuffle, Osterhaus's Fifteenth Corps picked up Corse's Second Division, which now became the Fifteenth's Fourth Division. Charles Woods was back to command his old First Division, and Osterhaus's other divisions were Hazen's Second and John E. Smith's Third. To replace Wangelin's departed Third Brigade, the First Division was bolstered by Brig. Gen. Charles C. Walcutt's brigade, late of Harrow's Fourth Division. At the end of September the total strength of the Fifteenth Corps was 23,479 officers and men present for duty. Sherman promptly detached Osterhaus's Third and Fourth Divisions (Smith to guard the railroad supply line and Corse to garrison the Allatoona pass and Rome), leaving Osterhaus with just Woods's and Hazen's divisions starting into the fall campaign. That must have been agreeable: Osterhaus was comfortable working with Woods, and Hazen had only praise for his new commander, "both as a soldier and a man."[65]

Meanwhile, Osterhaus tried to figure out how to work with his new commander, Oliver O. Howard. The German had little common ground with this man, unlike the relationship he had enjoyed with the fiery Logan. Osterhaus knew that Sherman thought highly of Howard, a former West Point mathematics instructor who had lost an arm at the Battle of Fair Oaks in 1862, considering him both a Christian gentleman and a zealous fighter. Howard was kind to ladies, hated swearing, believed fervently in abolition, and preferred not to fight on the Sabbath. He was also a teetotaler; the thought of German beer gardens must have appalled him. Despite Sherman's admiration for Howard, even he found his wing commander a bit much at times. Osterhaus was fond of relating the following story, captured years later in an interview:

> Sherman came to Osterhaus' tent early one morning and asked him for a drink, a request which astonished Osterhaus, for Sherman was known as an infrequent drinker. Osterhaus summoned his adjutant, an Irishman [Capt. William E. Gordon], who was entrusted with the care of such matters, and in a short time the chief commander was supplied. Then Sherman went on to explain. "You see," he told Osterhaus, "I have just spent the night with Howard."
>
> Howard was an abolitionist, an iron willed man of great piety and with the strongest temperance views. [Said Sherman,] "We worked all night over plans and maps and I was getting exhausted. I asked Howard if he had anything to drink. He told me solemnly that he had nothing. Then he thought a moment, and added, as seriously, that he did believe he had some Epsom salts. I fled."[66]

On September 29 Hood's army broke camp and headed toward the Western and Atlantic railroad in the vicinity of Kingston, Georgia. His fall assignment was to destroy Sherman's supply line to Chattanooga, forcing the bluecoats to either retrace their steps or remain stranded without supplies deep in Southern territory. Shortly, Sherman started after him. Delighted finally to be excused from monotonous drills, Osterhaus's men were glad to be on the march again, laughing and joking as they marched. Osterhaus's new status was soon put to the test by his old division. A few weeks earlier in camp, Hazen had witnessed Osterhaus's First Division calling out "Hard-tack!" and "Sowbelly!" as the new Fifteenth Corps commander rode by. As usual, Osterhaus ignored them. However, when a soldier in the Twenty-ninth Missouri yelled "Sowbelly!" again early in October, he angrily put the whole regiment on picket duty for a full twenty-four hours. This was not the Osterhaus they remembered. Then it happened again a few days later. Osterhaus probably would have ignored the usual shouts of "Hard-tack!" and "Sowbelly!" but this time something a little uglier was added. Charles Wills of the 103rd Illinois, newly arrived in the division as part of Walcutt's brigade, wrote in his diary on October 11:

> While we were resting to-day, Osterhaus (at present commanding our corps) rode by our regiment and a few scamps hollowed "sowbelly, sowbelly." You know the men have been living on army beef for a month, and it is not desirable fare; still they were only in fun, and I noticed the general smile, but some puppy finally cried out "kraut," and another echoed it with "kraut by the barrel." The general wheeled his horse and rode up to us, his face white with passion. "Vat regiment ish dis?" No one answered. He rode up near me and again asked, "Vat regiment ish dis?" I told him. "Vy don't you kit up?" I arose and again answered him respectfully, "The 103rd Illinois, sir." "Vare ish your colonel?" "At the right of the regiment, sir." He rode up to Wright and gave him the devil. I have not been so mortified for a long time. We all think a great deal of Osterhaus, and just coming into his division were all desirous that his first impressions of our regiment should be favorable. As it is, two or three insulting puppies have given us a name with him that I have no doubt will cause us trouble for a long time. Yelping "sauer kraut" at a German is a poor way to gain his favor.

This incident points up the frustrations of Osterhaus's new assignment. As approachable as he could be in his own division, at his now more removed level with more than seven hundred officers between him and the men, there were not the opportunities for camaraderie to offset the necessary discipline that he had to enforce. Soldiers who had not served under him therefore saw him as somewhat of a martinet, and even his old First Division veterans were happy to see the ebullient Logan return in early January.[67]

On through October, Sherman's army would follow the more nimble Hood toward Chattanooga. The only real battle to occur was on October 4 at the

Union supply depot at Allatoona, where Corse's outnumbered Fourth Division, with some difficulty, repulsed a determined attack by French's Division of Southerners. By October 13 Hood was back where the campaign had started, within twenty-five miles of Chattanooga at Dalton; Sherman's army was two days behind at Resaca. Hood decided to leave the railroad at Dalton, slipping southwest into Alabama. On October 16 Osterhaus's old First Division finally caught up with the Confederate rear guard in Ship's Gap, west of Villanow, Georgia. It took about an hour for the First Brigade to dislodge the Twenty-fourth South Carolina Regiment from the gap, capturing most of the garrison and all of the officers. "Quite a nice affair," wrote Osterhaus.[68]

That was as close as Sherman came to catching Hood, but then the Union commander was not in a hurry. "We followed his [Hood's] track in easy marches, profiting of the good things, this rich country had kept in store for the army (probably not for ours) and reached Gaylesville by the 21st October," recalled Osterhaus. During this period, Osterhaus's main concern aside from managing the logistics of the march was to control plundering. The local farms had just harvested, so foraging was plentiful; however, Osterhaus noted that there was also a "great deal of pilfering on the march." He issued orders that the men could take anything to eat, but they were forbidden to enter homes or take anything from them on penalty of death. A single guard was posted at each door they passed, but many houses were plundered anyway.[69]

Sherman decided to stop at Gaylesville, just inside the Alabama border, ordering Osterhaus's corps on forward as far as Gadsden on a reconnaissance in force. Osterhaus headed out on this assignment with both of his divisions on October 23. After long marches and a bit of skirmishing, he was back at Gaylesville three days later, confirming Sherman's suspicions that Hood was long gone. Osterhaus had fallen ill with diarrhea the night before he left Gaylesville on his reconnaissance, and he was still miserable five days later as the army started its return march to Atlanta. Howard's other corps commander, Ransom, had also been ill for several days, but in his case it proved to be typhoid fever and he died on the march. Sherman noted with admiration that Ransom had "insisted on going along with his command," even when so ill he could not sit a horse. This was not unlike Osterhaus's experience before Atlanta earlier in the summer, but in his case Sherman had been more irritated than admiring.[70]

Osterhaus bivouacked his corps near the Chattahoochee River to refit and cull his command for the upcoming campaign eastward. They were still there when the presidential election was held. If Lincoln was worried about the army's support, the soldiers were not. Osterhaus, a solid Lincoln supporter right along, predicted that "Old Abe will have a glorious vote," and he was right. Although the sickly Osterhaus privately pined to go home to his bride, sometime in the next few days he learned that Logan would not be returning for this campaign.

Logan became ill after the election and spent the fall at his home recuperating while Osterhaus continued to command the Fifteenth Corps.[71]

When Logan begged off, Howard sent a private communiqué to Grant speculating on Osterhaus's suitability for permanent command of the Fifteenth. "Osterhaus . . . does quite well. He is brave and energetic, and I am reluctant to disgust him by putting him back, and more reluctant to send the efficient and excellent commander, General Woods, (Charles R.), back to a brigade, he has commanded a division so long. But I am always free to say that, other things being equal, I prefer an American corps commander to a German." Howard perhaps formed his opinion of German American corps commanders in good measure at Chancellorsville, where he had taken command of the Eleventh Corps after Franz Sigel left. Howard recalled then, "There was much complaint in the German language at the removal of Sigel . . . and that I was not at first getting the earnest and loyal support of the entire command." Although Osterhaus could never be accused of dogging it and actually commanded few German Americans, Howard obviously still had reservations about someone he considered to be a foreigner, not an American.[72]

On November 9, when the bluecoat veterans finally received their orders regarding the upcoming march, most of them were in complete agreement with Sherman's strategy to help bring the war to an end, particularly liking the injunction to "forage liberally on the country." From highest to lowest ranks, everybody was excited at the prospect. "The Army [was] in wonderful spirit and animated by the conviction that success was before it," wrote Osterhaus later. Despite his earlier homesickness, Osterhaus himself was no exception: "We are off! For Savannah ho!" he wrote in his diary on November 15. Osterhaus's strictly trimmed-down, "strong and nimble" Fifteenth Corps, with four divisions and more than fifteen thousand combatants, still was the largest Federal corps on the march by more than two thousand men. By contrast, Frank Blair, who commanded the Seventeenth Corps' three divisions, had the smallest with eleven thousand. The northern, left, wing was composed of the six divisions of the Fourteenth and Twentieth Corps. In support were Maj. Gen. Judson Kilpatrick's five thousand cavalrymen.[73]

The right wing's first eighty miles led southeastward toward Macon and the Ocmulgee River, the first of three river hurdles between the Federals and Savannah. Osterhaus found the countryside they were traversing during the early days "rich, fertile and beautiful. . . . [S]igns of the war, which divided the nation were hardly perceptible. . . . The Boys . . . treated the usual *piece de resistance* of the Army ration, 'sow belly' and 'beef dried on the hoof,' as they styled them, with periodical contempt, as long as turkeys, chickens, pigs, even young bears together with roasted yams, peanuts and other good things, too many to mention, invited the rough warriors to sit down at the table dressed *a la fortune du pot.*" The only real Southern opposition near the right wing, aside from a few civilians gamely trying to defend their towns, was the Georgia Militia, with about four thousand infantry stationed in Macon. Joe Wheeler's twenty-five hundred mounted troopers harassed the column occasionally, even corps commander Osterhaus not being exempt from their forays. On the morning of November 20, as the Fifteenth trudged through the town of Clinton in a dense fog, Wheeler's Confederate cavalry unexpectedly almost bumped into the blue column. According to the rebel cavalryman's account, six of his troopers dashed into town and nabbed Osterhaus's personal orderly, standing within twenty feet of his headquarters, before being chased away. Osterhaus merely noted in his diary the next day, "Rebel cavalry rather bold."[74]

Osterhaus, usually routing his command on parallel roads, made sure that every day the advance was rotated between and within divisions, giving each unit an equal shot at foraging. His biggest problem was keeping his vital wagon train, 850 wagons and 150 ambulances, up with the column. Sometimes they stretched back more than thirty miles, causing Howard to fret that the roving Southern cavalry would pick them off. He specifically admonished Osterhaus about this on the first day of the march, but later on seemed to trust the general's judgment more. Osterhaus's euphoria continued: "Good roads. Fine weather. Splendid horses, superb mules and an abundance of grub. The soldiers feel glorious." But soon the terrain and worsening weather began to cause more trouble. The first big river of the march was the Ocmulgee, requiring pontoon bridges to be laid for the wagons. Once over the river, a prolonged spate of rain and uncharacteristically cold weather made the roads nearly impassable. Not all the mules turned out to be splendid after all; in fact, those that pulled the pontoon train were emaciated and simply could not haul the waterlogged floats once they were pulled from the river. The trains began to lag far behind the column.[75]

The right wing now wheeled to a more eastwardly direction, crossing the state north of the industrial center at Macon, which lay twenty miles to the southeast. By a week into the march, Osterhaus's command was more than a hundred miles from Atlanta, making slow progress spread out on four muddy roads in the pine woods and hampered now by rain mixed with snow. Confederate harassment increased the farther they went, and Osterhaus became more uneasy, particularly about his wagon trains and herds, now lagging far to the rear, shepherded by Corse's full division. The grand wheel to the east had exposed his right flank and rear to attack by Confederate forces, which he had learned through prisoners and other sources were concentrating to defend Macon.[76]

On Sherman's orders, Kilpatrick's cavalry made a halfhearted feint toward Macon on November 21. (Osterhaus was disgusted with Kilpatrick's effort, complaining in his diary, "*Kilpatrick did not take Macon!*") Sherman ordered Osterhaus's whole corps to feint toward Macon the next day and break up the railroad. Meanwhile, Hardee, in charge of the Georgia defenses, had concluded that because of the weakness of Kilpatrick's feint, Sherman must be headed for Augusta instead to take out the munitions factory. He ordered the four thousand–man garrison at Macon to head for Augusta that same day to respond to the Yankee threat there. As Osterhaus accompanied Woods's First Division heading toward the railroad station at Griswoldville, four miles north of Macon, Judson Kilpatrick and his cavalry came galloping up to inform Osterhaus that they had uncovered a strong Southern party of dismounted cavalry behind a nearby creek. Osterhaus sent Walcutt's Second Brigade off on reconnaissance in that direction, and they handily drove Wheeler's troopers back to their horses and off toward Griswoldville. Respecting Wheeler's capabilities, Osterhaus did not want Walcutt's brigade haring off after them without backup. Instead, the general pulled him back and ordered him to set up a defensive position athwart the road with his back to the woods, the swampy Sandy Creek at his feet, and a broad field beyond, across which any attack would have to come. Some of Walcutt's men were armed with the new Spencer repeating rifles, and they were supported by a section of the First Michigan Battery, with Kilpatrick's cavalry guarding the flanks. Osterhaus sent orders for his other three divisions to continue on their way, destroying track as they went, then rode off to Gordon, eight miles distant, to brief Howard.[77]

Walcutt's veterans figured all this preparation was overkill, because all they expected to see out there were scattered elements of the cavalry who probably were not interested in a head-on confrontation. The bluecoats quickly threw together a light breastwork of rails, then began cooking their dinner and settling in. By now, unbeknownst to Walcutt, the Confederate troops from Macon were moving along the railroad track heading for Augusta, a route that would take them right past Walcutt's position. Their commander, Maj. Gen. Gustavus Smith, was still in Macon; leading his advance column was Brig. Gen. Pleasant J. Philips. When Smith learned that there was a large body of Federals in the vicinity, he sent an urgent recall message to Philips, but Philips received it too late. Believing the Federal force that he spotted across the field to be a small one, Philips ordered a general attack, and Walcutt's brigade was startled from their midday meal to suddenly find a bona fide line of infantry advancing toward them across the broad field. Now at Gordon, Osterhaus heard cannon fire and immediately galloped back to Griswoldville to find that Walcutt had repulsed several determined but futile attacks by the Southerners. To the dismay of the bluecoats, the large number of rebel casualties were mostly teenagers and gray-haired old men. In contrast, Walcutt lost fewer than one hundred veterans killed and wounded. The action at Griswoldville, called "unnecessary, unexpected, and utterly unproductive" by one Southern historian, was the only real fight of the campaign until the blue tide reached the coast.[78]

While Osterhaus was dealing with Griswoldville, Howard, ahead at Gordon, discovered that the sodden pontoon train had ground to a halt miles to the rear. With the next river hurdle, the Oconee, coming up about twenty miles ahead, Howard needed fresh mules immediately to get those bridge units up and in place for the crossing. He sent an order to Osterhaus to cull fifty-five teams of six mules each from his headquarters wagons and send them to rescue the train. When the irritated Osterhaus read the message, he "braced himself up majestically to his full hight [*sic*] and exclaimed, 'Vell, I pe tam. Do Cheneral Howart dink I poot my hand in my bocket and pull out mules?'" But he dutifully relayed the order, and the mules were produced.[79]

At the Ball's Ferry ford, the rebels had set up a strong position across the river on a bluff, with a mile-wide stretch of swamps on the near side preventing the bluecoats from getting close without being picked off. Blair's and Osterhaus's corps both reached the river at about the same time; Osterhaus sent out skirmishers and set up artillery, while Blair went upriver to find an unguarded spot to boat across a flanking force. Upon his success, the rebels abandoned their position during the night, and the crossing, now that the pontoons had finally arrived, was accomplished the next day. According to Osterhaus's diary, "Rebels oppose our crossing. Some skirmishing, before night artillery in action (17 AC arrives at the same place and ferry 2 regiments across 2 miles above the ferry). Rebs skedaddle in the night." Blair's report confirms Osterhaus. Although his official report at the time agreed, Howard later wrote a different version: "Osterhaus, coming back, told me before he dismounted that he could get no farther, as the enemy was too strong on the other side. I told him that that was no way to talk, but to keep deploying his skirmishers up and down the river until he got no return fire, and report. He soon returned and assured me that he found no enemy a few hundred yards up the river. I then instructed him to send in a brigade with the canvas boats." Since Osterhaus had never been one to lack resourcefulness in moving through rebel territory, one wonders if this otherwise inaccurate recall from fifty years later indicated an underlying lack of respect by Howard toward Osterhaus or just confusion in Howard's memory as to whom he was addressing. One does sense little love lost between the two.[80]

For the rest of the trek, Osterhaus shepherded his command along multiple narrow and faint roads, mainly absorbed in the logistics required to get his wagons through the increasingly swampy territory. As on the chase after Hood, Osterhaus tried to control his corps' foraging activities, threatening to fine looters a month's pay in addition to having his officers reread General Order No. 26 ad nauseum, warning that looters would be shot. None of the efforts caused even a pause in the proceedings. Despite guards stationed at every house, each new unit that came by had a go at the same plantations, driving their owners into the swamps to hide their belongings. In at least one case the soldiers even used Osterhaus's name to intimidate the inhabitants. Unfortunately for home owners, Union soldiers were competing for forage with Joe Wheeler's large Confederate cavalry force, also living completely off the land, in addition to other opportunistic or desperate Southern civilians, both black and white, and Southern infantry. Although plundering was pervasive, few documented cases of rape or murder could be attributed to the Union army. Osterhaus himself claimed not to hear of much egregious behavior ("acts of brutality occurred very seldom, and only few complaints came to the cognizance of headquarters"), although there was at least one court-martial for looting in his corps, outcome unknown.[81]

By December 1 sandy pine barrens had given way to very swampy country, requiring corduroying of the roads. Houses were few; forage was becoming harder to find. Osterhaus ordered half rations of crackers and sugar, but meat was still plentiful. As the blue columns advanced toward Savannah, Southern resistance gradually increased at the fords. The third river crossing was approaching: the Ogeechee, running in a southeast direction right past Savannah and emptying into the Atlantic a few miles south. Once they reached the river at a point about thirty miles northwest of Savannah, Osterhaus's Fifteenth Corps began to move downstream through the swamps. A week later they camped only fifteen miles west of Savannah, on the Ogeechee at Jenk's and Wright's bridges. Confederate skirmishers, supported by artillery, contested the river crossings and had burned both bridges. But with a little work, Osterhaus's divisions flanked the grayclads out of position and made the crossings the next day. Meanwhile, he personally took Hazen's and two brigades of Woods's divisions south a few miles to Bryant Courthouse to capture a well-defended bridge over an important tributary, the Cannouchee. This time a local black man told him where to find an old ferry landing, and Osterhaus sent men across there, flanking the defenders. Osterhaus certainly demonstrated no lack of vigor or expertise in these actions, and later Howard was officially complimentary of his "great activity and energy displayed throughout the entire campaign."[82]

As they neared the coast, the western soldiers were struck by the strangeness of the terrain, huge watery rice fields interspersed with coastal swamps teeming with snakes and alligators that "bellowed like bulls at night." By December 10 Osterhaus's advance reached the Ogeechee canal running northeast toward the city, and he began to move his divisions into position along the canal towpath and the Savannah Road. Ahead Osterhaus could see an impressive line of Confederate defensive works across "a complete sea" of flooded swamps and fields blocking the Savannah Road. There were also scattered Confederate batteries in the swamps to the east. Hardee had concentrated his ten thousand men at the most vulnerable points of his defenses, the five elevated causeways carrying roads and railroads into Savannah. He knew that a Federal charge at his line would have to come over these narrow roads, well covered with Southern artillery, or straight through the deeply flooded swamps. On the positive side, the Confederate commander did have plenty of food and ammunition, and he was pretty sure that Sherman's hordes would at this point be eating a lot of rice and not much else.[83]

Osterhaus's Fifteenth Corps now held the extreme right of the Union line. There the Confederate artillery fire was pretty hectic, even shelling Osterhaus out of his headquarters on December 12. Nevertheless, Sherman made his headquarters near those of Howard and Osterhaus on the Anderson plantation. Sherman would not frontally attack Hardee's naturally strong position, but rather was content to settle into siege mode beginning on December 10. As the Federal officers probed a way to crack the defenses, the soldiers were more interested in cracking rice to get enough to eat for themselves and their animals. For a week, all they had for provisions were the copious sheaves of rice that had just been harvested, but nobody knew how to husk the grain to make it edible. Some finally tried putting a handful in a blanket, beating it with bayonets or rifle butts, then tossing the blanket up to blow away the chaff. It took hours to make a meal, and then all some of them had to season it with was mustard. However, the men were not too worried, knowing that the U.S. Naval fleet was nearby and they could expect an early end to their misery.[84]

With his army rapidly running out of food, Sherman's ability to maintain a siege was limited. It was vital for him to make contact with the fleet awaiting his arrival at the entrance to the Ogeechee River. The problem was Fort McAllister, an earthen fort crouched on the southern bank of the Ogeechee River, which prevented Union boats from moving upstream to meet Sherman's army. The anxious Federal commander knew that Fort McAllister had to fall. His first plan was to have Kilpatrick's cavalry take the fort, because Sherman knew the works were lightly manned by an isolated garrison, and he felt that speed was of the essence. The fort had formidable cannon that would keep any flotilla at bay, but its land side on the south was much more vulnerable. However, on Howard's urging, Sherman decided he would use infantry instead, and began the planning with Howard. At this point, Osterhaus was still in the dark about the new plan, even though one of his divisions would get the assignment.[85]

On December 12 Howard ordered Osterhaus to send the Twenty-ninth Missouri and a battery to a rice mill located on the left bank of the Ogeechee River across from the fort. Osterhaus thought this move was to support Kilpatrick's attack, which he privately predicted would fail. Later that day Howard surprised Osterhaus by ordering him to send Hazen's division to take the fort the next day. Hazen himself received his orders in person from Sherman and Howard; even though Osterhaus was nearby, he was not present. Howard chose Hazen's Second Division for the task at least in part because it was camped closest to the river, and, coincidentally, was Sherman's old command. Osterhaus and Blair of the Seventeenth apparently uttered "warm words" because the Second Division had been given the honor of the definitive assault of the campaign. Given his choice, Osterhaus would most assuredly have assigned Woods and his old First Division.[86]

The next morning, December 13, Sherman and Howard rode down to the rice mill to watch the action across the river. Osterhaus remained behind to make a demonstration with the rest of his command against the main Confederate line. It took Hazen most of the day to move his division to within attack range of the fort, scout the terrain, and plan his approach, but the assault near sundown was over in about twenty minutes. At almost the same moment that Hazen attacked, Sherman spotted the navy steamer USS *Dandelion* coming upriver to finally establish contact with the army.[87]

Osterhaus, still at Anderson's plantation, spent the next few days in preparation for a major assault on the Confederate works planned for December 21. But that night Hardee and his command escaped across the Savannah River into South Carolina before burning their pontoon bridge, and Savannah fell uncontested into Federal hands. On December 21 Sherman's army entered the city, and Osterhaus found it very much as it still is today: "a beautiful city, nicely laid out with squares, rich with flowers and shrubs, and with lovely surroundings. A feeling of pride and satisfaction pervaded the army, officers and men. After long marches and hard work during so many weeks the price of victory was won: Savannah. From the high ground, veranda like, the eye embraced the rich level lands of South Carolina, and the soldier's heart beat with hope: Home and Peace."[88]

Suddenly, the campaign was over, but there was still much to do. The Federal troops were still hungry and ragged, not getting full rations for the first time until around Christmas Day. But that did not stop Sherman from ordering a triumphal dress parade through downtown Savannah for December 24. Osterhaus's was the only corps selected to parade; the others had their turns a few days later. Despite the condition of his troops, Osterhaus expected the Fifteenth Corps to appear "as clean and neat as possible, officers with saber and sash, the men in light marching order." Even the regimental bands were to be in place. Although they grumbled, the men came through. Osterhaus, with some pride, noted that it was, with "drums beating, colors unfurled a grand and impressive spectacle."[89]

Although Osterhaus took a leading part in the well-chronicled "March to the Sea," commanding more than a fourth of the army, he was never given recognition for this effort. Recent historians have failed to even mention his name in books devoted entirely to this campaign, or have merely mentioned that he was a substitute for Logan and have left it at that. Perhaps this is because of the nature of his assignment: all the key decisions were made by Sherman, forwarded by Howard through Osterhaus, and carried out by the divisions. For whatever reason, although Osterhaus delivered his usual competent performance, his contributions were ignored at the time and still are. His men did not forget, though. At the close of the campaign, a captain in the Seventy-sixth Ohio wrote a popular song called "General Logan and the Fifteenth Army Corps," with the following verse:

> Our Generals are all good at fighting,
> Brave Smith and Walcott too;
> And when they see General Osterhaus coming,
> The Rebs look mighty blue.
> The two General Woods and General Hazen,
> And gallant General Corse;
> Better fighting men never went into battle,
> Or whipped the Rebels worse.[90]

Chapter 6
Mobile Bay and Reconstruction

SOON after the Federals marched into Savannah, Joseph Osterhaus learned of "Black Jack" Logan's imminent return to the Fifteenth Corps and spoke with Army of the Tennessee commander Oliver O. Howard about his own next assignment. Osterhaus was an excellent division commander, but he was well aware that going back to his old First Division was problematic. At this point, Charles Woods had commanded the division for several months, both during the fiercest of the fighting around Atlanta and on the fall campaigns ending in Savannah. No one, including Osterhaus, wanted to return Woods to brigade command after such a fine performance. Assuming command of another corps was not an option, either. There were no corps commands available in Howard's army, and, although Osterhaus outranked three of Sherman's other corps commanders, he did not care for that level of command enough to pursue the issue. Osterhaus was somewhat philosophical about his unsettled situation:

> I had in the course of the war been promoted to the highest rank I could aspire to; being in the political as well as public life an utterly unknown person—*homo novus*—it was almost a necessity that my military career should come to its close soon. Considering the situation of my friends and comrades and being aware, that disputes about rank had been raised, I concluded it the best means to avoid all difficult personal questions, to apply for a change in my employment. In a discussion about the matter with General O. O. Howard, in whose sincerity and uprightness I always had the greatest confidence, I thought to understand him to be of my opinion, and I acted accordingly.[1]

Osterhaus's comment about being "an utterly unknown person," or outsider without connections, reflected the feelings of alienation he had experienced in Sherman's high command. Clearly weary with army politics, he was reluctant to stir the resentment that had surrounded his promotion to major general the previous summer by asking to replace a division commander less senior. Instead, he asked for reassignment. Secretary of War Stanton was in Savannah at the time;

no doubt, Howard took the opportunity to confer with him about Osterhaus. Perhaps to formalize these discussions, the same day that Logan returned to duty Howard wrote a most complimentary letter to Stanton on behalf of Osterhaus: "I wish to commend to you again Major-General Osterhaus for a brave, energetic, and faithful soldier. He has been of essential service to me during the last two campaigns, where he added new luster to a reputation already national. If you could assign him to a field of labor suited to his taste and talents, I feel sure that he would honor the Government and perform his trust with assiduity."[2]

Logan relieved Osterhaus of command on January 8, 1865, and shortly afterward the general was on his way back home to St. Louis and his bride for a welcome month's leave while his reassignment was being considered in Washington. His new orders, arriving on February 16, came as a pleasant surprise: Stanton had assigned him to be chief of staff to Maj. Gen. Edmund R. S. Canby, headquartered at New Orleans. For the first time Osterhaus would not be in field command, but this new role might be interesting. Taking leave of his family, the general passed through Washington, D.C., before he reported to Canby, chatting with both Grant and President Lincoln while he was there. Given the nature of the assignment, Grant may have had specific instructions for Osterhaus regarding his new posting.[3]

Once again Osterhaus was to serve a commander who was under a cloud, an assignment that in this case made a lot of sense for the War Department. Canby was an integral part of Grant's grand plan for winning the war, but so far had not performed as Grant had expected. Perhaps Osterhaus could lend some practical expertise that would get him moving. Canby, a good friend of Sherman's, had been a mediocre West Pointer (ranking dead last in his class in artillery). In 1862 his small command had managed to convince the Confederates to abandon their designs on New Mexico Territory, even though Canby did not win a battle. The next eighteen months he spent behind a desk in the Adjutant General's Office in Washington and in command of the City of New York during the draft riots of 1863. He received his second star three months before Osterhaus did, in May 1864, having never led so much as a division in a full-scale battle. Despite his inexperience, that same month Grant sent Canby to New Orleans to replace the disgraced Nathaniel Banks as head of the Military Division of the West Mississippi after Banks's Red River expedition ended in fiasco. Canby's brief was administrative: to coordinate various Federal troop dispersals throughout the region in order to keep the Confederates in the Trans-Mississippi under control and the river itself closed to Confederate shipping. His performance was questionable: later that fall, Howard confidentially complained to Grant that Canby had no sense of priorities in troop placement and tended to believe and react to all the rumors brought to him. Howard's input may have colored Grant's opinion of Canby as 1865 began.[4]

As Grant contemplated the spring campaign that could wrap up the war, he recognized that Sherman's trek northward from Savannah through the Carolina swamps would be much more arduous than Georgia had been: not only was the terrain more difficult, but Joe Johnston had twenty-seven thousand grayclads waiting for him somewhere in the area. To protect Sherman's western flank, Grant ordered George Thomas from Tennessee and Canby from Mobile to strike at the heart of Alabama, their targets the arsenal and foundries at Selma and the state capital, Montgomery. These operations should serve to tie up the remnants of Hood's army, now under the command of Lt. Gen. Richard Taylor at Meridian, Mississippi, while keeping Bedford Forrest's cavalry busy as well. The head count of these Confederate forces was changing rapidly as men deserted, but probably numbered fewer than twenty thousand under Taylor plus Kirby Smith's remote and scattered forty thousand or so across the Mississippi River.[5]

Sherman left Savannah on his march through the Carolinas on the first of February. To be of any protection to him, the Alabama operations had to begin immediately. Grant sent Canby orders on January 17 that urged him to quickly take Mobile and then get on with the foray into the interior of the state. Canby was to have the services of A. J. Smith's Sixteenth Corps, plus the Thirteenth Corps, under Gordon Granger, and about two divisions under Frederick Steele, for a total of about forty-five thousand men, plus the support of the U.S. naval fleet in the Mobile area. This assignment would be a huge challenge: Canby had never organized a military operation of this, or really of any, scope. Six weeks after Grant sent Canby his orders, much to the Federal commander's dismay, Canby was still in New Orleans, about 150 crow miles west of Mobile Bay. Canby explained that the unusually wicked weather had delayed his start: just gathering his command took weeks. Grant, impatient with what he saw as dithering, ordered Canby to get started and insisted that he lead the effort in person. This was the situation when Canby's new chief of staff, Joseph Osterhaus, reached New Orleans the first week of March.[6]

The chief-of-staff role was new to both Osterhaus and Canby, but at least Osterhaus had some ideas about how the post should work. Besides watching Grant's chief of staff, John A. Rawlins, in action, Osterhaus had a concept of the role from his Prussian military training. Since the Napoleonic era, senior staff officers had been integrated in the Prussian command structure to offer guidance to senior commanders, ideally forming flexible partnerships that capitalized on the strengths of each member. In the American Civil War, the role instead devolved into more of a central coordinator of the commanding general's headquarters staff, including the military staff (artillery chief, cavalry inspector, chief engineer, provost marshal general, and chief signal officer) and administrative staff (medical director, chief quartermaster, paymaster, commissary, and ordnance officer). The idea was for the chief of staff to handle administrative details efficiently so that the commanding general could concentrate on strategy and tactical issues. In this case, however, Canby's experience was in the administrative and logistical and Osterhaus's the tactical and strategic aspects of organizing masses of soldiers. Fortunately for them, in the Union army the role of chief of staff was not implemented consistently or completely, leaving a commander some practical leeway on how the duties could be interpreted. No doubt, Canby and his new chief of staff gradually felt their way into some hybrid arrangement. Given the scope of the current campaign, Canby clearly needed help, or at least moral support. He took to Osterhaus immediately; on March 5 he wrote Grant, "Osterhaus has just reported and has impressed me favorably, but I do not yet know him well except by reputation."[7]

On the other hand, Osterhaus knew nearly all of the veteran commanders now gathering under Canby, like himself battered but still active after four years of war. Several went all the way back to that first summer of the war at Wilson's Creek, the first major battle in the western theater. He was pleased to see Brig. Gen. (militia) James Totten, the crusty Missourian whose battery Osterhaus had defended at Wilson's Creek and who now commanded Canby's siege train of heavy guns. Canby's Thirteenth Corps was led by Maj. Gen. Gordon Granger, who at Wilson's Creek was a staff officer to Nathaniel Lyon and had worked alongside Osterhaus to rally the outnumbered Union forces late in the day. Later Granger had led a corps at Chattanooga but had incurred the wrath of Grant, who thought him incompetent at corps command. Osterhaus also knew two of Granger's three division commanders: Brig. Gens. James Veach from Atlanta and William P. Benton from Vicksburg. Col. William T. Spicely, a brigade commander here, had been Osterhaus's reserve at the second assault on the Vicksburg fortifications. Osterhaus was also pleased to see that three units of his old Ninth Division from the Vicksburg campaign were still in the field at Mobile Bay: the 114th Ohio, 120th Ohio, and four companies of the 69th Ohio.[8]

Canby's Sixteenth Corps was commanded by Maj. Gen. A. J. Smith, whose division had fought next to Osterhaus at Champion Hill in the Vicksburg campaign. Smith had never led a corps before. Of Smith's three division commanders, Osterhaus had fought beside two: Brig. Gen. Kenner Garrard at Resaca, and the recently breveted Maj. Gen. Eugene Carr at Wilson's Creek, Pea Ridge, and Vicksburg. In fact, Osterhaus, Carr, and Smith had constituted three of the four division commanders under John McClernand in the original Thirteenth Corps at Vicksburg. Canby's other column, gathering at Pensacola, Florida, was commanded by Maj. Gen. Frederick Steele. Steele and Osterhaus had commanded battalions that fought elbow to elbow at Wilson's Creek, and both had commanded divisions at Arkansas Post and Vicksburg. It was Steele's division that Osterhaus had taken over after Vicksburg when Steele was moved west to the Arkansas region to command the Little Rock sector. The next year Steele led about seven thousand men on the ill-fated Red River campaign, finally retreating back to base with high losses. This was his only corps-level battle experience.[9]

Osterhaus knew these men and how they performed from firsthand experience, very valuable input to give Canby, who himself knew only Granger. Osterhaus also had experience with corps command, which all but Granger and, arguably, Steele lacked. It would turn out that Osterhaus knew of three of the Confederate commanders as well: in the trenches of Spanish Fort, one of the two Union objectives, were Brig. Gens. James T. Holtzclaw, whose brigade Osterhaus had chased across Missionary Ridge, and Randall Gibson, who had also commanded a regiment there. Missourian Brig. Gen. Francis M. Cockrell, whom Osterhaus had faced through four years of war in every campaign except for Chattanooga, held the fort at Blakely, the other objective, in command of French's division. Despite being shot four times at the Battle of Franklin, Tennessee, the previous November, Cockrell was back in the fray with the remnants of his brigade, now just a third of what it had been before that disastrous day for the South.[10]

Two days after Osterhaus arrived, Grant was relieved to note that Canby had finally arrived at the mouth of Mobile Bay, the staging point for the new campaign. Osterhaus quickly familiarized himself with the lay of the land. Mobile Bay is a wide expanse that runs north to south for more than twenty miles; at that time the channel to the open sea was bracketed by Union-held Forts Gaines and Morgan. A few miles up the bay on the east side is Fish River, navigable for several miles. At the top of the bay, a complex river system from the north empties into the bay in a jumble of islands, waterways, and small bays. Canby's supply line into the interior of Alabama would require him to use these waterways, but the navigable channels in the bay and rivers were protected by two Confederate-held earthen forts on the upper-east side of the bay, Spanish Fort and Blakely, as well as two much smaller gun emplacements on nearby islands in the marshes, Forts Huger and Tracy. Mobile itself was located in the upper-west corner of the bay, several miles across the water from Spanish Fort, protected by its own extensive fortifications.[11]

The Confederate forces in the entire upper Mobile Bay area, under the command of Maj. Gen. Dabney H. Maury, amounted to only about twelve thousand men, ranging from battle-hardened veterans like Cockrell's command to teenagers in the Alabama reserves who had never seen a battle. About half were in the Mobile City defenses; the rest, under Brig. Gen. St. John R. Liddell, manned the forts on the eastern side of the bay. The fortifications themselves, elevated on bluffs, were as strong as long war experience could make them, all approaches well protected by abatis and other obstructions and extensively mined. A Confederate flotilla under Cdre. Ebenezer Farrand still operated in the bay, even though its egress was sealed off, and the upper bay and the river channels were also heavily mined against U.S. Navy incursions.[12]

By mid-March the Union forces were finally concentrated: Steele's column of thirteen thousand at Pensacola forty miles east, and Gordon's and Smith's corps camped near Forts Gaines and Morgan. One of Canby's first assignments for Osterhaus was to inspect the troops at Fort Morgan to determine their readiness for the upcoming campaign. The two Federal forts guarding the bay were on flat, sandy ground, making for difficult camping conditions, but as was his habit, Osterhaus insisted on decent hygiene anyway. During one inspection "Gen Oysterhouse" found a soldier in the Ninety-third Indiana so filthy that he ordered him scrubbed with a root brush while he personally supervised. The happy scrubber wrote (with some satisfaction), "I did it well for this same fellow Had been an Ie Sore to the company for ovr 2 years."[13]

Canby's plan called for his two corps to advance up the eastern side of the bay toward the forts, while Steele's column at Pensacola cut off Mobile's rail communications before circling around to join them. To Canby's relief, the weather, though still soggy, was finally moderating a bit. Osterhaus coordinated both Smith's movement by means of naval transport upriver and Granger's as his command struggled overland through waterlogged country. The two columns were to converge six miles up Fish River and proceed overland the twenty miles to the forts. But because of yet another tropical storm miring them down en route to the meeting place, the two columns were not able to able to leave the rendezvous for the forts until March 25.[14]

By that date, although they did not realize it, the whole expedition was moot. Sherman, already in North Carolina, had already defeated Johnston at Bentonville and occupied Goldsboro on March 22. The reason for the Federal thrusts into Alabama had just become significantly less important to Grant. Nevertheless, they went forward. On March 22 Maj. Gen. George Thomas finally started Brig. Gen. James H. Wilson on his way from Tennessee toward Selma with ten thousand cavalry, while Canby pointed toward Mobile. In hindsight, Grant opined that "much valuable property was destroyed and many lives lost at a time when we would have liked to spare them," but he did not choose to abort the missions. He later acknowledged, "They were all eminently successful, but without any good."[15]

Canby's column finally arrived at Spanish Fort ten days after they started out, and Steele's column arrived to invest Fort Blakely on April 1. The Federal commander, impressed by the strength of the fortifications they faced and not knowing how many men opposed them, opted for prudence and ordered a siege mounted. During the next days Osterhaus had his hands full coordinating troop movements and then supporting them logistically until a supply depot could be established five miles down the bay. While they were waiting for ammunition, the experienced trenchers of the Union army began digging in, creeping ever closer to both forts as Osterhaus worked with the corps commanders to get the gun emplacements set up.[16]

In the frequent telegraph messages flying back and forth, one can see evidence of the vigorous role Osterhaus took in the siege activities. It is hard to tell just when the general was speaking for himself and when for Canby, since Osterhaus's orders to corps commanders frequently did not acknowledge Canby's oversight. On occasion both Osterhaus and Canby sent similar messages the same day to the same man. This suggests that Osterhaus felt free to give some independent orders to line officers, an impression strengthened by some hands-on involvement he had on the front lines at Blakely a bit later.[17]

While the Union siege lines crept deliberately toward Spanish Fort and Blakely, elsewhere in the war momentous events would not wait: on April 2 Gen. Robert E. Lee finally abandoned his Petersburg, Virginia, fortifications and headed west, pursued closely by Grant. Two days later, Lincoln himself visited the abandoned Confederate capital, Richmond. In the western arena, Wilson's cavalry handily defeated Bedford Forrest and captured Selma, Alabama, on April 2, with no help from Canby. The fall of both Selma and Richmond elated Canby's bluecoats when they heard the momentous news on April 6. Surely, the end must come soon. With Forrest defeated at Selma, the beleaguered Confederates manning the Mobile Bay forts now knew that they could expect no relief.[18]

Finally, on April 8, the thirteenth day of the siege at Spanish Fort, Confederate commanders Gibson and Holtzclaw agreed that they had to evacuate the garrison as soon as possible. They either had read their foe well or had accurate intelligence: that same day Canby made the decision to assault the fort next morning after an evening bombardment. By then Osterhaus had ninety cannon, both Totten's siege guns and field pieces, trained on the fort and another six pointed at Forts Huger and Tracy, and at half past five a massive Union bombardment began that lasted two hours, the last monster artillery display of the war. Under cover of the big guns, the Eighth Iowa of Carr's division charged and quickly overran one end of the Confederate entrenchments. The bluecoats immediately began enfilading down the line of rifle pits, capturing two hundred Confederates and two hundred yards of their line in the process. With this lodgment, Gibson had seen enough and ordered Spanish Fort evacuated immediately. About a thousand Southerners made good their escape through the swamps, so that when the rest of the disappointed Union forces entered the fort at midnight, they found it mostly deserted.[19]

The next day, April 9, with sixteen thousand Federal troops now converging at Blakely, every Union soldier from commander Steele on down wanted to begin the assault immediately before this garrison could slip away as well. They knew that with the fall of Richmond, this was going to be one of the last battles of the war, and they were determined to be part of it. During the morning, Osterhaus stopped by his old unit, the 114th Ohio, to check out the Confederate fortifications. One of his old veterans recalled, "After a close observation through his glass, he remarked to the officers and men standing around, 'Poys, we will eat our saur kraut and sow-belly over there to-morrow morning,' pointing to the rebel works."[20]

By that time the Union trenches had been pushed forward unevenly, but there was still a long way to charge over open broken ground that was heavily mined and replete with man-made barriers. On the Union right, the skirmishers in Brig. Gen. J. P. Hawkins's U.S. Colored Troops (USCT) division had moved closer than any other part of the Union line, and now his First Brigade commander, Brig. Gen. W. H. Pile, decided to take the rebel rifle pits three hundred yards ahead. About midafternoon, Pile and Osterhaus rode up to the forming line. Unable to resist helping, Osterhaus dismounted and went over the ground with Pile, moving his men to what he considered better positions. When the assault began, a detachment of determined soldiers of the Seventy-third and Eighty-sixth USCT handily took the first and, with more difficulty, the second line of Confederate rifle pits, now defended by some of Cockrell's brigade. This was the first time Osterhaus had seen African American troops in action, and he was impressed. "General Osterhaus declared that they fought as well as the best of troops," reported C. C. Andrews of Granger's Second Division.[21]

After capturing the second row of rifle pits, Lt. Col. Henry C. Merriam of the Seventy-third, a white officer, asked Osterhaus directly if his regiment could charge the works (stepping far out of his chain of command in doing so). Osterhaus ordered him to wait. "I will go and order the white troops up," Merriam quoted Osterhaus as saying. Upset, Merriam interpreted this to mean that Osterhaus wanted the white troops to have the honor of being first into the fort, so he immediately turned to his own brigade commander for permission. Pile told him to wait until the division on his left went forward, and then he could charge. A recent account of the initial capture of the rifle pits echoes Merriam's interpretation: "So successful were they [the USCT] in attacking the Rebels' outposts that when Merriam requested to attack the main works General Osterhaus refused, saying 'I will go and order the White troops up.'"[22]

In fact, saving the glory for white troops was almost certainly not Osterhaus's intent. In spite of the success of the U.S. Colored Troops' advance, Steele had determined that the whole Federal line would charge at once, a far sounder plan than one suicidal regiment at a time, as Osterhaus had learned from sad experience at Ringgold Gap. Although communications down the long Union line were far from perfect, at five thirty the Federals advanced, somewhat in echelon so that they would all hit the spread-out works at roughly the same time. The forward movement began on the left and ended with Hawkins's division on the right, whose brigades simply charged when they saw the division to their left advance. Whether Merriam in fact waited per Piles's order is unclear from his own account; Merriam later won a Congressional Medal of Honor for this charge "in advance of orders."[23]

With Canby, Osterhaus witnessed this last Union charge of the Civil War from his vantage point near Hawkins's headquarters, a satisfyingly "picturesque and grand" spectacle. In the fort were only about thirty-five hundred defenders braced for the blue onslaught; the right end of the Confederate line of redoubts was held by green youngsters and old men, who fought bravely but not well against the horde advancing against them. Since one of Cockrell's veteran regiments had earlier been pulled to help contain Merriam's feisty regiment, there was a big hole in the thin Confederate line that the Federals were able to exploit. Within minutes they had overrun the youngsters and were firing down the trenches toward the Missourians. Many of Cockrell's veterans fought fiercely, not yielding an inch until they were completely surrounded and were forced to lay down their arms. Others made a break toward the water behind the fort and tried to swim their way to safety. After twenty minutes the last battle was over. No one there at that moment knew that Robert E. Lee had already surrendered at Appomattox a few hours before.[24]

Confederate commander Liddell later called Canby's assault "one of the most magnificently timed and executed assaults in the Civil War," rather generous words from the loser. If so, credit should go to the commanders leading the assaults as well as to Osterhaus, whose hand can be detected in the success of the assault by the otherwise never-tried Canby and inexperienced corps commander Steele. Osterhaus himself downplayed his contribution, saying simply, "I accompanied General Canby's expedition against Mobile, Ala, and assisted at the siege of Spanish Fort, Mobile Bay, taken by storm on April 8, and the following day at the assault and capture of Blakely."[25]

Two days later Maury led his forty-five hundred remaining Confederate troops out of Mobile to join Taylor at Meridian. While the Federals were moving into Mobile on April 12, James Wilson and his cavalry were accepting the City of Montgomery's surrender. But that did not halt Canby; now that he had succeeded in capturing the forts, he went forward with the rest of Grant's orders anyway, even though Wilson had already taken both objectives in the interior. Most of Canby's forces were to leave two days later. Smith's corps would march into upstate Alabama, with Steele to follow on boats, all to be orchestrated by Osterhaus. Then on April 25 Osterhaus received another assignment as well: orders came from Grant to immediately prepare a seaborne expedition to Galveston "with all the force you can spare." (This was later canceled.)[26]

In the midst of all of Osterhaus's frantic activity, the stunning bulletins from the North kept coming in. Word of Lee's surrender on April 9 was closely followed by the shocking death of President Abraham Lincoln on April 15, news of which rocketed its way around the country by telegraph within twenty-four hours. On May 1 Osterhaus telegraphed all the commanders not only to be on the lookout for Confederate president Jefferson Davis, still in flight, but now to allow Pinkerton detectives access to the area in their search for Lincoln's assassin (Osterhaus had not learned that John Wilkes Booth had been captured and killed on April 26).[27]

By now Osterhaus had no doubt also received the welcome news of the safe birth of his wife Amalie's first child, Teresa, on April 20, but he had little time to dwell on it. The next bulletin from the North reported that Joe Johnston had surrendered to Sherman on April 26. On hearing this, Confederate commander Richard Taylor in Meridian felt that with Richmond gone and Lee's army surrendered, any further resistance would be a tragic waste of more lives. He requested a meeting with Canby to discuss options. On April 29 Canby, Osterhaus, and a large Federal entourage met with Taylor and a couple of aides ten miles north of Mobile, where Canby and Taylor, who were old army friends, agreed to an immediate cease-fire pending more specific instructions from their respective commanders. Then followed a surreally cordial lunch and serenade by the Union musicians. But, according to Taylor's memoirs:

> There was, as ever, a skeleton at the feast, in the person of a general officer who had recently left Germany to become a citizen and soldier of the United States. This person, with the strong accent and idioms of the Fatherland, comforted me by assurances that we of the South would speedily recognize our ignorance and errors, especially about slavery and the rights of States, and rejoice in the results of the war. In vain Canby and Palmer tried to suppress him. On a celebrated occasion an Emperor of Germany proclaimed himself above grammar, and this earnest philosopher was not to be restrained by cannons of taste. . . . [N]either tyranny nor taste can repress the Teutonic intellect in search of truth and exposure of error.[28]

Clearly, the sincere but unsubtle Osterhaus simply saw Taylor as a vanquished foe who needed to realize the error of his ways, rather than as the once and future peer his old West Point friends considered him. (Had Osterhaus known that Taylor would condone the murder of African Americans after the war, he might have been even less worried about insulting Taylor's Southern sensibilities.) The German's disregard for the nuances of rapprochement in a country no longer to be divided was to serve him ill in his next assignment, and he certainly made no friend of Taylor that day.[29]

The next day Canby received word that Grant had rejected the surrender agreement Sherman had forged with Johnston and had ordered hostilities renewed. The war was not yet over. When Canby notified Taylor that firing would begin again, Taylor immediately chose to surrender his army rather than to resume the fight. On May 4 at Citronelle, thirty miles up the railroad from Mobile, Osterhaus witnessed Canby accept Taylor's surrender on the same terms as Lee's the previous month, while Commodore Farrand surrendered his Confederate fleet to Cdre. Henry K. Thatcher. With that, the Confederate army east of the Mississippi ceased to exist. "The time of great battles was over; the rebels themselves saw the hopelessness of further resistance and yielded before us," recalled Osterhaus.[30]

The only Confederate commander still in the field and yet to be heard from was Edmund Kirby Smith, commander of the Trans-Mississippi, headquartered in Shreveport, Louisiana. While he still wanted to fight, his own officers were split on the issue. Those who wanted to surrender journeyed under flag of truce to New Orleans to see Richard Taylor, requesting that Taylor broker a meeting with Canby to explore surrender of the Trans-Mississippi Confederates. Among the petitioners were Osterhaus's early foe, Sterling Price, and Kirby Smith's chief of staff, Simon Bolivar Buckner, who claimed that they were able to act, subject to Kirby Smith's approval. At that point, Canby was still in Mobile, leaving Osterhaus in command of his headquarters in New Orleans. Osterhaus forwarded the Confederate feeler to Canby on May 21.[31]

By then Kirby Smith himself was in a stagecoach, rattling his way toward Houston. He had decided to shift his headquarters there (with the expectation that his army would follow) to await the arrival of Jefferson Davis, not aware that the ex-Confederate president had already been captured. Meanwhile, Kirby Smith's subordinates met with the Union representatives at Citronelle, Alabama, on May 26 to formalize the surrender agreement for Confederate forces west of the Mississippi. Since Kirby Smith was not present, P. Joseph Osterhaus signed the final document with Simon B. Buckner. Canby ratified the agreement for the Union and sent it off by ship to Galveston for Kirby Smith's signature. When the Confederate commander of the Trans-Mississippi Department arrived in Galveston, he discovered that his army had evaporated, his erstwhile disgruntled Confederate soldiers looting Galveston in lieu of unpaid wages on their way home. By the time the Federal ship bearing the surrender documents arrived in the harbor, Kirby Smith, in his own words "a commander without an army," had no choice but to go aboard on June 2, 1865, to ratify the document that Buckner and Osterhaus had signed. This was the final surrender of regular Confederate forces in the war, and Osterhaus was proud to have been a part of it. He recalled, "With these capitulations the great war came to its conclusion. To me it will always be a highly valued recollection, that it was my good fortune to set my name under these final agreements."[32]

But Osterhaus's military service did not end there. The day after he and Simon Bolivar Buckner signed the peace agreement, E. R. C. Canby appointed Osterhaus military commander of the District of Mississippi, effective as soon as he could wrap up in New Orleans and get himself upriver. Busy with the myriad details of the final peace agreements and troop deployments, Osterhaus had not kept track of what was going on in the state of Mississippi as the war whimpered to its ill-defined end and the postwar problems intensified. He certainly expected to find Mississippi troubled by civil disruptions, some war-related destitution, and a damaged economy, since he had seen these already during the war at the Big Black River, but when he arrived at Vicksburg he must have been surprised at the magnitude of the state's problems.[33]

Due, ironically, in no small part to the devastation Osterhaus's own troops had so efficiently caused during the Vicksburg campaign, the farm economy that was the backbone of the state was in an appalling shambles. The spring crops, planted while the war was still on, had been meager at best, given the little seed available and the scarcity of laborers or animals to plow the fields. Money was extremely scarce. Much of the cotton hoarded during the war to pay debts had by now been stolen, confiscated by the Federal government, or destroyed. Few people had cash to pay creditors or workers, and lines of credit were unavailable to most business owners or farmers to buy seed and stock, repair or purchase needed machinery, fence their fields, or patch their levees. What little industry the state had was at a halt, with very few industrial plants still in operation.[34]

Before the war Mississippi had held the second-highest percentage of slaves of any state. In fact, the majority of the population of the state was black, in some planter districts as high as 90 percent. Although a good portion of the state's four hundred thousand newly freed, now destitute African Americans stayed on the plantations, many others congregated around Vicksburg and other towns or military posts, where they lived in shanties or caves and depended entirely on the Federal army for food. Smallpox and cholera were rampant; many were dying. Even so, few freed people were willing to continue to work the fields except as renters or owners of their own parcels, both of which options the landowners absolutely opposed. If they did work under contract with the planters, field hands frequently did not receive the pay they were promised for one reason or another, or they walked away because the discipline was still too harsh. These absent field workers could not easily be replaced. Then, moving the harvested crops to market required wagons and mules that were in scant supply. Segments of railroad lines and many bridges had been damaged or destroyed, most of the rolling stock had been diverted for military use or destroyed, and the railroad companies had no money for repairs.[35]

Public safety was a thing of the past. Despite a few courts and law enforcement officers that continued to function, if weakly, during the war, lawlessness was rampant, especially the theft of valuable cotton and farm animals. As the war ended, armed bands of white deserters and other brigands continued to roam the roads preying on freedmen, suspected Unionists, or anyone else likely to yield valuables. "Cutting and shooting," vigilante justice, was the order of the day, and few were safe outside of the towns or army posts. After years of distress, the citizens were most anxious for a return of law and order.[36]

Now, in the midst of continuing economic turmoil and civil unrest, the people of Mississippi were also forced by their loss of the war to make immediate and profound changes in the basic structure of their society. This shift threatened the long-entrenched entitlement beliefs of the whites and demanded of the African Americans a skill for independent living that they had not had a chance to learn. Blacks and whites had diametrically opposed notions of what the new order should look like. Osterhaus saw the problem clearly: whites wanted above all to be able to control absolutely their labor force by whatever legal means they could contrive, and blacks were equally determined to finally assume complete command of every aspect of their own lives.[37]

For the next six months, Osterhaus would struggle firsthand with the difficulties of beginning to restore this defeated land to the Union. Osterhaus, long the champion of the brave and noble cause of nationalism and a man who saw things in moral absolutes, was convinced that with decisive defeat the misguided Southerners needed only to realize the error of their ways in order to begin their recovery. But the problem was not to prove that simplistic. The general would have to deal daily with ambiguity and political guile in a people who stubbornly refused to admit they were wrong and who demonstrated almost no loyalty to the United States, which they still considered the oppressor. Worse, Osterhaus experienced the unfamiliar sensation of receiving conflicting direction by his own superiors, of even having his orders questioned, if not countermanded by his commander in chief.

As the war ended, the mission of the Federal army in the Southern states was ill-defined, since Federal occupation of domestic lands in peacetime had never occurred before. Division of responsibilities between the military arm and other government agencies, including the Treasury Department, was not clearly spelled out, allowing for wide individual interpretation by various district commanders. Theoretically, the military had several goals: to keep the peace during the transition to civilian government, repair railroads, feed the hungry, administer Federal loyalty oaths to former Confederates, and oversee the election and justice systems until the postslavery civilian apparatus was running satisfactorily. The military was complemented by a separate temporary agency established by Congress in the War Department, known popularly as the Freedmen's Bureau, charged with the protection and welfare of freed people until they could become independent. Overseen by Federal army officers and headed nationally by Maj. Gen. O. O. Howard, this bureau was involved with helping former slaves negotiate work contracts with planters, establishing schools, and seeing that blacks had representation in legal situations in civilian courts. In Mississippi the bureau was run by Samuel Thomas, a Tennessean appointed at about the same time as Osterhaus.[38]

In the weeks before Thomas had his bureau up and running, Osterhaus's military was the only source of protection for African Americans in Mississippi. The German essentially had sole control of the state from May 22, when Confederate governor Charles Clarke was arrested and martial law commenced, to June 13, when provisional governor William L. Sharkey was appointed by President

Johnson. Martial law continued thereafter, but governance grew murky as the civil government gradually tried to wrest more control over its functions from the military. Not surprisingly, over the next few months, white Southerners' attitudes changed from welcoming the return of law and order to wishing fervently that all Federals would leave the state so that they could go back to handling their own affairs.[39]

By two weeks after Osterhaus arrived, he had done a quick assessment and now made his first report to Canby. His early concern was to feed his own eight thousand men at their various posts, for which he needed to import food since there was too little available locally even to feed the citizens. Because of the urgent need to restore railroads to transport food, he had already requested of Grant that the army do some of the repairs rather than to leave it to the railroad owners, permission granted. Besides food for the citizenry (early on, he contributed $150 of his own money to feed the eleven children in the state institute for the blind), Osterhaus also asked for more cavalry to stop the widespread marauding in outlying areas. He described the people as intensely quiet and "only anxious for the restoration of authority, of whatever description," but showing no evidence of patriotism or loyalty to the United States. Even high-level Union officers like himself, if not physically attacked when vulnerable, were at least snubbed and ostracized in a Southern society that considered them usurpers and tyrants. In Osterhaus's case, another source of irritation for the populace was his ethnicity. Little wonder he did not consider sending for his family to join him in Jackson, the partially destroyed state capital.[40]

Like the military commanders of other Southern states, Osterhaus decided that restoration of the agrarian economy was his most important early priority. In addition to urging repair of the railroads, he requested that extra army livestock be returned to the farmers. As for finding farmworkers, his solution, like that of other Federal commanders, was to try to get more freedmen to stay on the plantations to work so that the already meager harvest would not be lost. In doing this, he was torn between supporting the rights of the freedmen and bowing to economic necessity. He came down in favor of the economy, issuing an edict that former slaves should stay on their old plantations "unless they were abused or mistreated." He explained his rationale later: "The wealth and social conditions of the Southern people, once based on a labor system which the results of the war had radically overthrown, had in many instances become most uncertain. While productive labor was for some time at a still stand [*sic*], the former laborers were idling away their time, indolent witnesses of the general calamity."[41]

This comment reveals the paternalistic attitude Osterhaus held toward newly freed blacks, a view common to many whites of the period, including U. S. Grant, who commented that in some cases the freedmen expected the right to be able to live without care or any planning for their own futures. Even fifty years later, Osterhaus still agreed with former Southern slaveholders regarding the "dependent qualities of the Negro and his tendency to laziness." This prejudice persisted despite his own observation of the competence of the African Americans as soldiers during the war. Yet his natural sympathy for the Southern landowners' economic dilemma and to some extent for their paternalism toward blacks did not extend to the abrogation of freed people's rights, rights Osterhaus was determined to protect. An example of his instructions to his subdistrict commanders illustrates the tightrope he was walking, hoping for the best of all possible worlds:

> Give all assistance to citizens who are willing to resume their own pursuits; and questions between blacks and whites must be settled with a view to induce the former to remain at their own homes whenever their former masters recognize their freedom and pay them for their labor. At the same time the negro must be protected against any outrages on the part of their old masters. The latter must accept the changed condition of their laborers and prepare to work their plantations hereafter on a basis of mutual agreement with their laborers. Vagrancy among the negroes must not be suffered. All must work.[42]

Osterhaus's idealistic assessment of and hopes for the South, so radically at odds with those of white Southerners, were summed up in his report to Carl Schurz, who was in Mississippi on a fact-finding mission for President Johnson:

> The elevating feeling of true patriotism will return with the smile of prosperity, and it should be the duty of all men to co-operate together in securing that end. This can only be done by securing for the black race also a state of prosperity. This race, which at present furnishes the only labor in the State, must be prevented from becoming a wandering and restless people, and they must be taught to become steady citizens. This will best be accomplished by guaranteeing them the right to acquire property and to become freeholders, with protection in the undisturbed possession of their property. This and a general system of education will work a quicker and more satisfactory change than the most stringent police regulations could ever achieve.

Osterhaus was convinced that it would take a year or so of both blacks and whites being forced to stay within the law by a neutral force, that is, Federal troops, to cement in place their new relative positions in Southern society. No doubt, he was not shy in sharing his views with any Southerners who cared to listen.[43]

In spite of, or perhaps because of, his good intentions, Osterhaus found himself immediately clashing with the civil government now reemerging in the state, particularly as regards who had authority for the legal system and the basic rights of African Americans. Before he was arrested, Confederate governor Charles

Clarke had sent a delegation to Washington to reassure President Andrew Johnson of Mississippi's eagerness to reenter the Union and to find out what his terms would be. Leading the delegation was planter, ex-slaveholder, and former state supreme court judge William L. Sharkey, who had been born in Tennessee, as had Johnson. Sharkey had been a staunch Unionist who sat out the war, so Clarke figured that he would be a most appealing supplicant. At the time, the president was in the process of appointing provisional governors in seven Southern states, charged with convening constitutional conventions as soon as possible. In Mississippi, Sharkey got the nod in mid-June. Since Sharkey was adamantly opposed to any military intervention in state affairs, he and Osterhaus soon were at odds.[44]

President Johnson's declaration of May 29 set out his requirements that a seceded state must meet in order to return to the Union as a full member (subject, of course, to the approval of Congress). The period of time from this point to the end of the year has been called Presidential Reconstruction, during which Johnson himself set the bar for the states. All he required was the formation of a new state constitution and government that outlawed slavery, with all voters to be required to take an oath of allegiance to the United States. He made no requirements addressing freedmen's right to vote or any of their other legal rights, such as the right to testify in court, or that officeholders must have also taken the oath of allegiance. To relieved Southern whites, Johnson's requirements seemed almost too easy once they passed the oath hurdle; they had earlier feared a much more draconian punishment for their insurrection. In Mississippi, as civilians became more confident and active in the uncertain atmosphere before the constitutional convention could be convened, problems of conflicting authority began to crop up. As early as June 18, Osterhaus had to squelch, as illegal under martial law, an election that had been previously authorized by Confederate ex-governor Clarke.[45]

A short time later, a more serious test of the jurisdiction of civilian versus military courts arose in the case of a white man on trial in a civilian courtroom for murdering a black man. Osterhaus ordered the man removed from the magistrate's custody and remanded to a military tribunal, on the basis that blacks were not allowed to testify in civilian courts in the state. When a civilian judge issued a writ ordering the man's release from military custody, the military arrested the judge as well. Sharkey immediately protested to Secretary of State William H. Seward, who backed Osterhaus and directed that the man be tried by military courts. In this he was upheld by President Johnson, in contrast to his later decisions. However, the action had aroused the competitive spirit of the editor of the *Jackson Daily News*, who objected to the "repeated and outrageous assumption of Osterhaus" in the matter.[46]

By now it was mid-July, and yet another reorganization swept the Federal army as it demobilized the volunteers, reconfiguring the command assignments in all the occupied states. As the political officers rapidly returned to civilian pursuits, all but one district were taken over by West Point graduates, in Mississippi's case Henry W. Slocum, who had commanded the left wing of Sherman's army on the March to the Sea. He in turn assigned Osterhaus, still in Jackson, to the northern third of the state with its thirty-six counties of heavy cotton and corn production. Slocum, now reporting to Phil Sheridan, lasted only two months, after which Osterhaus resumed command of the state district for another month until Thomas Wood, another West Pointer, arrived in mid-November. This rapid turnover, which also occurred in the Mississippi Freedmen's Bureau and in the military commands of other Southern states, was extremely unsettling: every commander had his own understanding of the mission, causing inconsistent interpretation of the new rules and resulting in confusion. For example, in contrast to Osterhaus's hands-on style was that of his old subordinate, Charles R. Woods, now commander of the District of Alabama, who proudly declared that even though the state suffered from general and severe lawlessness, "he did not interfere with civil affairs at all" unless asked, and he rarely was.[47]

Sharkey spent the summer repopulating hundreds of state offices and local positions, drawing mainly on those who had opposed secession but supported the Confederacy once Mississippi seceded. In some cases his appointees had been active Confederates. Meanwhile, among their other duties the Federal troops, who were mostly blacks, were charged with administering loyalty oaths to as many whites as possible, including seeking out returned Confederate soldiers in order to qualify them to vote in the upcoming election to seat members of the constitutional convention, due to begin August 14. Predictably, voter turnout for the election was extremely light, with the Whigs, the minority party in the state before the war, winning the great majority of the seats.[48]

As the first of the Southern states' constitutional conventions began in a somber mood in Mississippi, a resolution was nonetheless passed extending to Osterhaus an invitation to a seat on the floor. Osterhaus, in his gracious response, noted that he was the "first officer of the National forces, to receive such a friendly invitation from our returned brethren." He was still trying to be agreeable. The proposal's sponsor, William T. Martin, late a Confederate major general, commented wryly as he introduced the resolution that he "felt more pacifically disposed than formerly." Over their ten days of deliberations, closely followed in the Northern press, the convention delegates accomplished the bare minimum required by Johnson: they created an amendment to the previous state constitution declaring that slavery should no longer be allowed in the state.[49]

While the convention was in progress, another controversy exploded between Sharkey and Osterhaus, this one ultimately resulting in the resignation of state district commander Slocum. Back in early July, Sharkey had issued a proclamation encouraging citizens to organize their own patrols to police the remote areas that the Federal soldiers could not reach. (In fact, such patrols were suspected of doing much of the marauding themselves, particularly against blacks, while the reverse was not true.) On August 19 Sharkey reiterated his call for formation of white militias in every county, citing lawlessness that was out of the control of the military. Claiming that he had Johnson's permission, he especially appealed to former Confederate soldiers to join these bands.[50]

When Osterhaus read notices in the local papers announcing a call to form militias in his own jurisdiction, he expressly forbade it under military law, but deferred to Slocum to make a ruling for the state in general. Carl Schurz wired Washington in support of Osterhaus's stand. President Johnson responded by a telegram to Sharkey on August 21 asking him to desist in forming militias for the present time. Although Slocum actually had earlier agreed with Sharkey that the governor had the power to form militias, on August 24 he issued an order supporting Osterhaus and prohibiting Sharkey from forming militias anywhere in the state.[51]

In the meantime, President Johnson, now waffling, had wired Schurz that he hoped that Slocum would issue no such orders without checking with the government first, and that, by the way, it was reasonable for Sharkey to form militias if he felt the need. Sharkey now drove the wedge deeper, complaining to Johnson about Slocum's edict and for the first time expressing fears of a black uprising. On August 30 Johnson reversed his previous decision and ordered Slocum to rescind his order, causing both the district commander and Osterhaus humiliation and ridicule in the local press. Slocum resigned two weeks later to pursue elective office, and once more Osterhaus had to take the reins for the state until he could be replaced.[52]

With their new constitution and elected officials, many of whom were unsworn and avowed Confederate sympathizers and officers (their new governor was ex-Confederate brigadier general Benjamin G. Humphreys), Mississippi whites set about creating state and local laws, the onerous "black laws," to keep the freed people in their places, which was to say in the fields and out of the towns. They simply refused to accept the legal equality of African Americans. Among other restrictions, the new laws denied blacks the right to an education or to own arms. The only nod by the state to federal objections was to permit blacks to testify in court, a move that allowed state courts to take back jurisdiction over cases involving blacks, retaining for military tribunal only those cases involving U.S. soldiers. Even though many federal agents and military in the field were convinced that blacks' testimony was being ignored and that blacks' legal rights continued to be trampled, their hands were now tied by edicts from both Howard and Slocum remanding cases to civilian courts as long as blacks could testify.[53]

A week after Osterhaus took over from Slocum for the interim, he locked horns with the new governor, Humphreys. This time it was over the civilian arrest of a Freedmen's Bureau officer on the charge of inflating the fees he was charging. According to Slocum's previous edict, conflicts involving U.S. officers were still to be handled by military courts. When Osterhaus heard of the arrest, he therefore demanded the bureau man's release; when the sheriff refused, Osterhaus sent a detail of troops to physically remove the officer from county custody. The officer of the detail secured the prisoner but went even further and also arrested the sheriff, arousing the wrath of Humphreys. The governor immediately complained to Johnson, and the president again backed him up, informing Osterhaus that he would brook "no further military interference of this type," and ordered the detail officer to be relieved of command. Osterhaus clearly could not win by trying to follow the rules. When Kentucky-born Thomas Wood took over for him in mid-November, the new district commander promptly turned all cases over to civilian courts except in extraordinary circumstances, which settled the whites down but effectively abandoned the blacks and, in good measure, the military to the vagaries of local justice.[54]

Violence against African Americans remained out of control. A militia group in one county actually complained in the local paper that "certain persons not belonging to any regularly organized militia company were shooting negroes on 'private account.'" Richard Taylor, late a high-level Confederate commander, condoned the murders of blacks: "When ignorant negroes, instigated by pestilent emissaries, went beyond endurance, the whites killed them; and this was to be expected." Maintaining order in the state was a key charge of Osterhaus's military, and one they failed in many cases. They simply could not control every remote area with the troops at hand. Even in cases where they did try to intervene, civilians were not willing to give them any information for fear of reprisals later from the local militias or vigilantes.[55]

Compounding the problem was that nearly all of the troops stationed in Mississippi were black. Relations between rural whites and their occupying black troops went from bad to worse, with the whites complaining that black troops were demoralizing the freed people who were hanging around their posts and using abusive language to whites. The whites specifically hated being ordered around by blacks. Osterhaus had made clear his expectations of his officers to model "flawless conduct" for their men and demonstrate to Southern whites how to treat the black free person, and thought, perhaps naively, that they were doing pretty well. But later, incoming district commander Thomas Wood judged that the decentralized military posts lacked proper discipline, including allowing soldiers to participate in cotton swindles and confiscations. Several minor clashes occurred between the white militias and black troops, and vigilante and militia violence against isolated soldiers and military couriers was not uncommon.[56]

By August, as more Federal troops were mustered out, murders of freed people increased even more. Osterhaus, struggling to maintain order with a much reduced force, was convinced that worse would happen if troops were withdrawn completely. But Sharkey and later Governor Humphreys continued to agitate for removal of black troops, citing the potential threat of black insurrection, supposedly to be abetted or even led by black troops. Johnson bought into this fear, assuring the Mississippians and other Southerners that he would get the black troops out as soon as possible. In the fall Grant began a general muster out of black troops in the South that went on well into the next year, at the same time transferring other black units to the West. Wood himself mustered out seven black regiments in Mississippi soon after the first of the year. Yet Osterhaus and others never found any indication that the threat of insurrection had any substance. The rumors provided a pretext for writing the severe black codes, but Osterhaus was right: there was to be no uprising.[57]

On this uneasy note, Osterhaus's final military stint for his adopted country came to an end. New district commander Thomas Wood's style was to mollify the whites wherever he could and intrude the least amount possible into their affairs, regardless of consequences to blacks. Clearly, Osterhaus had not shown himself to be of that mind when trying to interpret his federal responsibilities in light of the machinations of Mississippi politics. Wood arrived on November 15; Osterhaus was mustered out of the army on January 15 and left Vicksburg the same day. One would hope that in the interim he was able, finally, to go home on leave and see his family for the holidays after such a bruising experience, but no record of such a visit has been found.[58]

As for the fate of Mississippi after Osterhaus left, the state was not readmitted to the Union until 1870, and then only after its new legislature had reluctantly ratified the Thirteenth Amendment, prohibiting slavery; the Fourteenth, providing equal rights for all citizens and barring former participants in the rebellion from office; and the Fifteenth, giving the vote to all men of age. Federal troops were not completely withdrawn from the South until 1877, but although African Americans in Mississippi received the vote in 1870, they continued to suffer severe discrimination throughout the next century. Through the years, although the memories of his own frustrations no doubt faded, Osterhaus remained profoundly disappointed in the failure of his adopted country to provide social and political equality to all its citizens. "Gen. Osterhaus cannot understand how or why the north has neglected to care for the Negro which it set free," reported an interviewer in 1914.[59]

Cut loose abruptly by the army, for the first time in nearly five years Osterhaus now had to pick up the threads of his civilian life. He had started the war as a clerk in a hardware-supply business in St. Louis and ended it a major general accustomed to commanding thousands of men and conversing with presidents and governors. Where should he turn from here? During the fall he had been offered a regular army commission but turned it down due to continuing ill health; in fact, all that spring after he arrived at home he was again treated for malaria and dysentery. On his way home from Mississippi he detoured to Washington, no doubt looking for a new, less taxing assignment. While there, on February 9 he was given the honor of being introduced in the House of Representatives.[60]

He received another honor later that spring: Congress appointed him to the twelve-man board of managers for the new National Soldiers' Home being established for disabled volunteer veterans. (The act establishing this home was one of the last that Lincoln signed before his assassination.) Members of the board included President Johnson, Chief Justice Salmon P. Chase, and Secretary of War Stanton, all ex officio, and Generals Richard J. Ogelsby, Benjamin F. Butler, P. Joseph Osterhaus, New Hampshire governor Fredrick Smyth, Ohio state senator Lewis Gunckel, financier Jay Cooke, Rev. Horatio B. Stebbins, and George H. Walker, former mayor of Milwaukee. At their first meeting in Washington in May, this distinguished group elected Ben Butler president and Osterhaus first vice president of the board. The several veterans' homes they envisioned were to be quite elaborate, more planned villages than hospitals, with one of the amenities a beer hall, perhaps due to Osterhaus's influence. But the first home was not opened until 1867, and by then Osterhaus had had to resign his appointment because he had taken a consular assignment in Europe.[61]

Osterhaus had received several feelers from the government regarding foreign assignments. The thought of going back to Europe must have been very appealing to him after the disappointments of the past few months. Besides, he had not seen his German family since 1849, his father was ailing, and his wife, Amalie, now pregnant with what would turn out to be twin boys, yearned to be near her own family. Johnson had appointed to diplomatic posts many officers who had served with distinction during the war, and Osterhaus was no exception. In May Johnson offered him the post of U.S. consul to Amsterdam, perhaps in part because Osterhaus was fluent in Dutch. But the general declined because he did not believe he had the independent means to support the family adequately (he wrote later that he was indigent when he reached Europe). Then, apparently at Grant's suggestion, Johnson offered Osterhaus the post of U.S. consul to Lyon, France, which the German accepted and Congress approved on June 16. The post paid two thousand dollars a year, not princely but enough to support his large family if they were careful.[62]

Lyon was a good choice; it was not terribly far from his beloved Rhine River valley and the cool Alps, and Osterhaus spoke French fluently. The only difficulty would be moving his large American family there in Amalie's advanced stage of pregnancy. His oldest son, Hugo, although only fourteen, would be staying behind. The previous September he had been appointed to the U.S. Naval Academy, and would remain in the United States his entire life. Somehow Osterhaus had his wife and the five other children and their American household all packed up and aboard ship for Europe before the end of summer. This marked the end of Osterhaus's residence in America; Joseph and Amalie were to spend the next several years in Lyon and the remainder of their lives in Germany. But during the last fifty years of his life, Osterhaus never lost his close ties with his adopted country.[63]

Epilogue
The Later Years

IN THE late summer of 1866, Joseph Osterhaus left Amalie and the children at her parents' home in Kreuznach, Germany, until the twin boys' birth in September. By the time his wife and now eight children had joined him in Lyon later that fall, Joseph had found them a spacious apartment. Now began the process of introducing their five very American children to the differences of European life. They must have been content with their new environment: four of the five remained in Europe for the rest of their lives. Only Alexander returned to the United States after the turn of the century, living in Redondo Beach, California, where he worked for the municipal transit company. Growing up, the three youngest children, the twin boys and Mathilde, born in 1868, never knew any other life but Europe. Even so, one of the twins, Ludwig (Louis), also decided later in life to live in the United States. After studying law in Europe, he became a prominent lawyer and justice of the peace in Belleville, Illinois, his father's American hometown. There, much to his father's delight, he married the daughter of Casimir Andel, his Civil War aide-de-camp and Belleville crony. The other twin, Josef, died as a young man in South Africa in 1897.[1]

Osterhaus served as U.S. consul to Lyon for eleven years, reappointed in 1868 by incoming president U. S. Grant and resigning after Rutherford B. Hayes was inaugurated in 1877. Osterhaus was one of nine U.S. consuls posted to economic centers throughout France. Giving them direction from Paris was Chief Consul John Meredith Read Jr. The consulates dealt primarily with trade and business concerns, in contrast to the U.S. minister to France in Paris, Elihu B. Washburne, whose role was much more involved with analysis, policy, and negotiations and who took an active role in Paris during the Franco-Prussian War of 1870–1871.[2]

In Lyon, one of France's largest cities and the center of its silk industry, the duties of the consul were not terribly onerous. Osterhaus's deputy and clerical staff handled the passport and visa traffic and assisted American travelers and the expatriate colony as needed. As head of the consulate, Osterhaus's most important functions were to encourage trade between the two nations and to use public diplomacy to represent the United States in a favorable light to the citizens of France. As part of his duties he gathered data on labor and living conditions in Lyon and filed detailed quarterly reports to Secretary of State Hamilton Fish on commercial shipments from Lyon to the United States. During his sojourn in France Osterhaus shunned publicity, only reluctantly attending local official functions and the occasional ball given in Paris by the emperor. He much preferred discussing politics and world events with friends at his home, and his continuing poor health made this simple life imperative.[3]

Then, after four peaceful years, for the third time in his life Osterhaus found himself living in a country at war. From the sidelines he followed with consuming interest the rapid military and diplomatic developments of the summer of 1870, observing the French troop buildup in Lyon and studying the competence and organization of the armies of both sides. He was no longer in a position in which his government valued his military intelligence, at least on the record; there is no evidence in his official dispatches of the period that he sent any military information to the State Department, confining his reports to the economic impact of the war. That is not surprising, since President Grant had Phil Sheridan observing the German army and Ambrose Burnside going back and forth to Paris attempting to broker an armistice between the belligerents.[4]

The war began in July 1870, when Napoléon III, who had been emperor since the days of the German revolution of 1848, declared war on Prussia and the Northern German Confederation, ostensibly over a diplomatic slight. Historians suggest that then premier of Prussia, Otto von Bismarck, skillfully used the French aggression to finally spur the reluctant southern German duchies to join the confederation, thereby creating a German empire controlled by Prussia. Having anticipated this war since 1866, the Prussians, who had had universal conscription since before Osterhaus was born, quickly mobilized to meet Napoléon's attack. By contrast, Osterhaus observed that the French were hampered by fewer readily available soldiers in their aging army cadre, chaotic mobilization, and lack of a coherent strategic plan for conducting the attack. Not surprisingly, the war went Bismarck's way: in a period of only six weeks, Bismarck defeated more than half of the divided French army. He first captured and imprisoned Emperor Napoléon III along with 100,000 soldiers at Sedan, northeast of Paris, on September 1, shocking Paris. Another 133,000 besieged Frenchmen surrendered to the Prussians at Metz on October 27. Less than a week after Napoléon was imprisoned in Baden he was deposed by the Parisian citizens in a bloodless coup and the new republican provisional Government of National Defense was formed, quickly recognized by the United States on September 8.[5]

Now Prussian progress slowed as the Germans began a prolonged siege of Paris and its garrison of forty thousand French troops. Besides the siege that winter there were several more bloody battles in the Loire Valley and around Dijon as well, the French army continuing to falter. Finally, in February, after the last French army in the field fled over the border into Switzerland, a newly elected National Assembly agreed to a preliminary peace accord with Bismarck, granting Germany five billion francs, the province of Alsace, and part of Lorraine in reparations. But that was not the end of the bloodshed: a short but severe civil war followed the final signing of the peace accord in May. From March Paris had been under the chaotic control of radical Communards and National Guardsmen, who now refused to disarm or to recognize the new French government operating from Versailles. The government attacked, and after six days of fierce street-to-street fighting retook Paris on May 28.[6]

American and English diplomatic sympathies in this war sided initially with Germany, since France was the original aggressor. Only later did they switch to support the nascent republican government established in Paris. Meanwhile, the chaos of the war triggered frantic American consular activity on behalf of the thirty thousand or more German expatriates living in France, as the now belligerent country threatened to expel them all. From early summer on, both Washburne and Read in Paris concerned themselves almost exclusively with protecting German interests, and Read sent word to Osterhaus and the other consuls to do the same. There was much to do. To those thousands who swamped the consulates clamoring to leave, the U.S. staff issued border passes and money. The consulates also provided protection for the property of foreigners and refuge for those who chose to stay.[7]

Although threatened for a time, the city of Lyon was spared any damage in this relatively brief war, since most of the fighting occurred well to the north around Paris and in Alsace-Lorraine. The closest the fighting came to the city was in the vicinity of Dijon, some miles to the north, where several engagements were fought over the fall and winter. But there was great civil unrest in Lyon during the war as the more radical republicans seized control of the city. Osterhaus claimed that there was more dread of these Communards and their program to redistribute wealth than there was of invasion by the Germans. Lyon endured several severe riots, coming perilously close to anarchy at times and making the city dangerous for Osterhaus's family. After a tense winter, the Osterhauses were relieved when the final peace accords were signed the following May.[8]

As representative of a neutral American government in a country at war with his old homeland, Osterhaus was in a ticklish situation during hostilities, particularly as regards his charge to represent the American government favorably to the French people. He was under official orders from Chief Consul Read to assist the Germans in his district, which, while it meant that he could follow his own inclinations, flew in the face of keeping the French people happy with the United States. In response to his attention to the needs of the Germans, he was quite likely vilified by the French as a German sympathizer. The nervous Read wrote home that, in his experience in Paris at least, "when . . . one identifies himself so far with the Prussians as to become their representative, he incurs an amount of dislike and even hatred which may prove not only disagreeable, but actually dangerous to himself and his surroundings in the highly-excited state of the public mind." Osterhaus himself noted a "prevailing antipathy against all Germans and German interference." Once again, as it had in Mannheim and St. Louis, it seemed that Osterhaus's duty posed a potential threat to the well-being of his family. Fortunately, in this case nothing terrible happened, except, perhaps, for social snubbing, which should have been familiar to him from his experience in Mississippi after the American Civil War. As some consolation, after the Franco-Prussian War, Osterhaus was given special thanks by the German government for his efforts to help German citizens.[9]

Osterhaus's official reports to the State Department during and after the war focused on his analysis of the conflict's impact on French trade and finance. In a letter to Hamilton Fish, Osterhaus predicted that the French economy would be slow to recover, although the money market seemed firm and he could see signs of "industrial hyperproduction" that might speed recovery. He pointed out that since German vessels were not welcome in French ports, American shippers had a good opportunity to take on a larger share of sea traffic. He also rightly predicted that Germany would spend the bulk of its reparation money on military and naval expansion.[10]

Osterhaus saw much to criticize in the behavior of the Prussians toward France, specifically their excessive demand for reparations. He also criticized the conduct of both opposing armies and considered the valor, discipline, and moral excellence of the United States Army to be superior to either one, even though the Europeans had had much more training and a longer military tradition. Osterhaus very likely agreed with Friedrich Hecker and other old Forty-Eighters that Germany's unification was long overdue. Not until later would he find that far from being the German republic that he had fought to create in 1849, Bismarck's version of a constitutional empire was in fact a Prussian hegemony that left little control in the hands of the people. (A German republic would not emerge until after the First World War.)[11]

In the years following the Franco-Prussian War, the light, routine duties of the consulate were all Osterhaus could tolerate, as his health remained poor. He was constantly under medical care for chronic dysentery and other aftereffects of malaria, and his old leg wound pained him so much that he could not stand or sit comfortably for any length of time. Shortly after the conclusion of the Franco-Prussian War he spent three months in a little country town at a higher elevation in hopes of relief. Yet by 1873 he was so ill that his physician thought that his life was in danger and sent him to the Black Forest to recuperate. He continued to have relapses off and on until finally, in 1877, his physicians advised him to move permanently to a more northern climate, and Osterhaus concurred.[12]

Besides his own health, family factors also drove his decision to move: Amalie's health was also declining, and he was concerned about the anticipated costs of the children's higher education in France on a consul's salary. Osterhaus noted that the revenues of the consulate had declined for several years following the war; that might have impacted his salary. His oldest daughter, Anna, had married a German expatriate in France, but Emma, at twenty, was still at home, the four youngest children were still in grade school, and Karl, at eighteen, was more than ready for college or military training. Osterhaus longed to return to Mannheim, the home of his youth, recalling in a letter to his son Hugo that Mannheim was "where I married, where two of your sisters were born, one of whom [Eleanor] is buried there, and where the dearest recollections of the days of youth, when the hand and heart are full of hope, when everything seems to be within one's grasp, concentrate."[13]

Ideally, Osterhaus would have preferred another diplomatic mission in Germany, but that was not forthcoming. He found begging for such a position distasteful: "I am, thank God, a very poor hand for soliciting favors, and without this excellent democratic quality the American Civil Service is a barren Sahara even for a man who did honestly his work for sixteen years and carried his hide to the market for the safety of his adopted country," he wrote Hugo bitterly.[14]

As an alternative, some of his old American friends wanted him to come to Mannheim to be a director of their firm, the American Rubber Company, a manufacturer of rubber boots, shoes, and mackintoshes with plants in Mannheim and near Paris. After taking a leave from the consulate to try the new position for three months, he decided the job would work out, although it was not ideal, and he gave his notice to the Department of Civil Service. Surprising to him, they refused his first two resignation letters, begging him to reconsider. But by now he was deep into resettlement, shuttling between Paris, Mannheim, and Lyon in an effort to get his affairs settled; his family had already moved to Mannheim. Finally, in August 1877, the department accepted his third resignation notice, and he was free to go, a private American citizen again for the first time in years.[15]

For the next twenty-five years Osterhaus and his family lived in Mannheim. Shortly after settling in, he applied for Baden citizenship, which was granted on January 8, 1879. (He had already received amnesty years before for his part in the revolution of 1848–1849.) He also retained his U.S. citizenship and continued to have close ties with Americans beyond his family, corresponding with William T. Sherman and "Black Jack" Logan as well as other war cronies and old friends from St. Louis and Belleville.[16]

P. Jos. Osterhaus, businessman. Mannheim, 1882. (Courtesy of Dale Hargrave)

Apparently, his new position with the American Rubber Company was no more suitable than he had anticipated, because in 1880 Osterhaus wrote son Hugo's wife that his business was winding down and that the company was being reorganized. He left the company late the next year. Part of the reason for quitting had again to do with his health; a coworker described sudden attacks of dysentery that would occur sometimes in rapid succession: "He left our house greatly for the reason of his health, thereby undergoing considerable pecuniary losses."[17]

Osterhaus now energetically tried to promote himself as a candidate for another consulate in Germany, consular work appealing to him more than private employment. With just four children left at home, he thought that the family could now live comfortably on two thousand dollars a year. No longer too proud to lobby for a patronage position, he encouraged Hugo to contact William T. Sherman for a kind word, and wrote to Sherman, Logan, and other friends himself as well. But by late 1881 he still did not have a position. He figured that his application was delayed because President James A. Garfield had been assassinated and the department was slow to act on applications until his successor, Chester A. Arthur, had appointed a new secretary. In any case, no offer was made to him at this time. In 1883, still having found no satisfactory consular or private position, Osterhaus opened his own business in Mannheim, again specializing in the sale and shipment of coal, as he had at the beginning of his career. Twelve years later he made his son Alexander a partner, and they restructured the firm, "P. Jos. and Alex. Osterhaus," to deal only with coal sales.[18]

Since Osterhaus was aging but still had a large family to support, in 1885, at the age of sixty-two, he decided to apply for a disabled veteran's pension from the U.S. government. (The law had changed in 1879 to award soldiers retroactive lump sums for all of the postwar years prior to their applications.) To support his claim, he put together the required extensive affidavits to show that he had both chronic illness and disability from injury that impacted his ability to perform physical work. (Osterhaus's complaints mirrored the most common three conditions submitted by Civil War veterans in their applications: wounds, musculoskeletal impairments, and diarrhea.) For his pains he was awarded the princely sum of $7.50 a month for his malaria. Osterhaus reapplied three years later, and now his wound was taken into account. His stipend was increased to $30 per month, where it stayed until 1902, when Congress boosted it to $50.[19]

Osterhaus's wife, Amalie, died in 1896, but he continued his business in Mannheim for two more years, until, at the age of seventy-five, he finally received a much-hoped-for appointment as American vice counsel in Mannheim. Osterhaus gratefully turned his company over to Alexander, who subsequently sold out and moved to Southern California in 1904 with his German wife and family. After serving as vice consul in Mannheim just nineteen months, Osterhaus finally retired on his meager disability pension in late 1901. Since his last daughter at home, Teresa, was about to be married, he moved to Bonn to live with an older daughter, Mathilde, and her husband, Dr. Hermann Petersen, who was the director of the Bonn Polyclinic, a surgical center. Osterhaus spent his days in Bonn perusing American and European newspapers and corresponding with his many friends about world events. He was particularly interested in following the news as it touched the lives of his two sons who were career military officers, one in each of his countries.[20]

Son Karl was now an artillery major in the German army, stationed in China during and after the Boxer Rebellion in 1900–1901. (Kaiser Wilhelm II awarded

Karl the Order of the Red Eagle with crossed swords for his work in China.) In June 1904 Karl was posted to German Southwest Africa (now Namibia) with Gen. Lothar von Trotha, who also had been his commander in China, to reinforce a small colonial force facing a Herero tribal uprising. On August 11 the German troops encircled and attacked the Herero tribe in their encampment on the Waterberg plateau near the Kalahari Desert. Karl, commander of the First Field Artillery, an eight-gun battery, was wounded in this battle. The surviving Herero broke out and were pursued deeper into the desert, where most soon died of thirst. Of the survivors, von Trotha ordered the Germans to take no prisoners, even among nonwarriors. His openly professed policy of extermination shocked Europe at the time and resulted in the near annihilation of the Herero people, becoming the first genocide of the twentieth century.[21]

Historian Isabel Hull argues that the African genocide was a natural but disastrous consequence of the military culture ascendant in Germany after the Franco-Prussian War, in which victory was redefined as complete annihilation of the enemy, not just capture of the field, and citizens were considered part of the enemy and therefore dispensable. One wonders what Joseph Osterhaus thought of von Trotha's policy of extermination both in Africa and his previous brutality in China after the Boxer Rebellion. Could Osterhaus reconcile his own values of patriotism and duty with the new military culture condoning massacre that was burgeoning in his homeland?[22]

At the same time that Karl was in Southwest Africa, Osterhaus's eldest son, Hugo, was reaching the pinnacle of his military career in the United States Navy. Interestingly, Hugo had married a Southern belle, Mary Willoughby Wilson. She was from an old slaveholding Norfolk, Virginia, family; in fact, her father, George Riddick Wilson, had been pardoned by President Johnson in July 1865. Osterhaus had no problem embracing Mary warmly into the family; to him the Civil War was long over. As evidence, he invited Mary and his two grandsons to live with him and Amalie in Germany for a year while Hugo was at sea.[23]

Beginning his naval career at Annapolis at age fourteen, Hugo served at sea for a total of twenty-seven years, interspersed with shore stints as a mathematics instructor at Annapolis and much later as commander of the Mare Island Naval Shipyard and Twelfth Naval District in San Francisco. He was made captain in 1906 and commanded the battleship USS *Connecticut*, flagship of Theodore Roosevelt's Great White Fleet of sixteen battleships that made a world tour in 1907–1909. Hugo's final rank was rear admiral, awarded in 1910, and he was assigned to command the second division of the Atlantic Fleet, his flagship the battleship USS *Minnesota.* Then in 1911 Hugo was appointed commander in chief of the Atlantic Fleet, the largest fleet under single command in the history of the country. Not the most senior in line for the promotion, he won the assignment in part because he was thought to be the best to prepare the navy for the looming war in Europe. Much like his father had been, Hugo was known as an approachable leader who enjoyed developing his subordinates and excelled in drilling and war games. Although his was a peacetime command, one of his more spectacular feats was to lead his entire fleet (thirty-one battleships, four armored cruisers, and eighty-eight smaller ships and submarines manned by twenty-eight thousand men) flawlessly into New York Harbor for a nine-day celebration and review by President Taft in October 1912. Hugo held the position of commander in chief for two years before retiring in June 1913. Little wonder that his father followed his career with great interest.[24]

As time faded Osterhaus's memories of the painful aftermath of the Civil War, he looked back with satisfaction on his contributions: "When it was all done I admit that I felt in seeing the results of the war a feeling of great happiness. I had snatched at something from the sun." The year 1904 was a momentous one for the old soldier. At the urging of old army comrades, in the spring he sailed for a long and triumphal return visit to the United States, reveling in the belated recognition of his adopted country. The United States was at the height of post–Civil War nostalgia, and Osterhaus was one of the very few remaining Union major generals at that point. After being feted in New York, the general was greeted at the Washington rail station by crowds of members of the Grand Army of the Republic, a large veterans' organization. Osterhaus was surprised by all the attention: "I thought I was forgotten. I can scarcely understand this warmth of greeting," he commented.[25]

Shortly after he arrived in Washington he was invited to dinner at the White House with President Theodore Roosevelt and was honored at a reception and luncheon of the Whip-Poor-Wills, a Union veterans' organization. "Osterhaus was a grandly prominent figure in the war, and always doing the most effective service. . . . Wherever Osterhaus was needed, he was always there and on time, and stayed until he saw the disappearing backs of the last enemy," read the program. The president, cabinet, Supreme Court members, and members of Congress were on the guest list, and as he arrived at the hall Osterhaus was greeted by a five-minute standing ovation. Osterhaus's comments in response to all this outpouring epitomized his philosophy:

> I was a soldier. We were all soldiers. We tried with the best of our ability to execute the task that had been assigned to us. In the days of danger we tried to preserve the Union and the country. It was the duty of each and every one of us. And I believe we succeeded in the fulfillment of that duty. I know one thing that was particularly satisfactory to me. It was the surrender of the last army of the South after Appomattox.
>
> Now, gentlemen, as we look back on our military careers we can feel only patriotism. That was our excuse and our reason for desiring to protect the Union and the Flag. . . . Patriotism cannot be bought by money. It must come from the love of country, from love of the Starry Banner that floats on high as the insignia of the greatest country on earth. Right and justice, truth and

1904 portrait of Osterhaus flanked by Daniel Lindsey and James Keigwin from the Vicksburg campaign. (Courtesy of Vicksburg National Military Park, Mississippi)

> liberty, must and will always prevail. I am most happy to again be with my old comrades. Press onward and forward until the star of civilization shall be placed by the loyal sons of the United States where its effect can be felt by every nation, every country in the world.[26]

Other honors followed. While Osterhaus was in the Midwest staying with old friends in Belleville and St. Louis, he traveled to both Northwestern University and the University of Illinois, where he was awarded honorary doctorates. He and the governor of Iowa were guests of honor at the German Day celebration in Burlington, Iowa. Belleville made him an honorary citizen, and on June 23 he was invited to speak to the Republican National Convention being held in Chicago. During the fall he attended the great St. Louis World's Fair of 1904, where his old friend Carl Schurz was a featured speaker.[27]

One impetus for Osterhaus's visit was the surge of interest in improving the pensions of Civil War veterans, particularly by Republican politicians looking to win their votes during that presidential election year. Various proposals surfaced in Congress to reactivate the Civil War Volunteer veterans, promote them to regular army commissions, and then immediately retire them on improved pensions. Osterhaus and Joseph R. Hawley, a retired brigadier general of volunteers and now senator, were the poster boys for this idea.[28]

Late in the year, Congressman Richard Bartholdt of St. Louis introduced a bill in Congress to place Osterhaus on the retired list of the regular army with the rank and pension of a brigadier general, which was higher than the pension of a major general of volunteers. Hawley's name was added, and both men's appointments were approved by a special act of Congress in March 1905. One of the high points of Osterhaus's trip was another visit to the White House, where President Theodore Roosevelt officially congratulated him and told him he had never put his name to any government document with more pleasure. (Roosevelt, who said he considered Osterhaus an old friend, also knew and admired his son Rear Adm. Hugo Osterhaus, and had his grandson Lt. Hugo W. on the staff of his yacht, *Mayflower*.) For his part, Osterhaus was pleased with the honor, although he remarked much later that even though the pension was higher, "After having enjoyed the rank of Major General during the closing operations in the field I naturally felt it a diminution when I had to accept a lower grade." He was finally promoted to major general, Regular Army, in 1915.[29]

But in the midst of all the pleasantries, Osterhaus suffered a terrible blow: news reached him of the death of his son Karl on September 25, 1904. He had died of blood poisoning six weeks after being wounded in Africa during the battle at the Waterberg plateau. However philosophical about it Osterhaus tried to be, Karl's loss affected him greatly. Of all his sons, he seemed proudest of his two military professionals, who came closest to his ideals of what patriotism is about. Even two years later he was still feeling Karl's death greatly.[30]

When Osterhaus finally returned to Germany in 1905 after an eleven-month stay in America, he moved to Duisburg with daughter Mathilde and her family, where he lived quietly until his death. He made one more trip to the United States in 1906 to visit son Ludwig in Belleville, and in 1911 Hugo took a month's leave from his duties to visit his father in Duisburg, seeing him again two years later. In 1914 the old general was described by an American reporter as "witty, alert," with a comprehensive mind as well as a long white beard. The next year, although still mentally active, his uncertain health precluded another trip to America as honored guest of the Grand Army of the Republic for the fiftieth anniversary of the end of the war.[31]

Osterhaus had a small apartment in Duisburg, with a study "like an old Civil War museum," on his desk autographed photographs of Lincoln and Johnson and other memorabilia of the Civil War period. There he spent his time poring over international newspapers, closely following the events leading up to World War I, and frequently commenting on them to Hugo in his letters. He continued to support Germany's position, apparently willing to accept the increasingly harsh militaristic tone of the government. He did not agree with some of its military excesses, however, as witness his distaste for the behavior of Prussian soldiers in savaging civilians in the internationally decried Zabern incident of 1913.[32]

Historian Michael Howard has argued that the most damaging long-term effects of the Franco-Prussian War were subtle changes in thinking in Germany that evolved over the next generation, and Osterhaus seems to have been no exception. Howard said, "It was too easy to believe that only by a preservation and extension of military power could the new German Empire, with the magnificent cultural tradition which it enshrined and all it made possible in the way of scientific, commercial and industrial development, be guarded against the rivals and enemies who surrounded it." Osterhaus's letters eerily echoed this point of view as world war erupted in 1914. He wrote to Hugo of "the superiority of the German armies as well as of the spirit of the people, its highest state of culture, civilization and unanimous patriotism," predicting a triumph for German arms against the "envious and grabby nations who since 1907 tried to encircle this country."[33]

Osterhaus was contemptuous of Woodrow Wilson and tried vigorously to convince Hugo that the United States should join Germany against Great Britain in the war. He still believed that this was a possibility as late as March 1915. His reasons ranged from the wars America had previously fought against England to the "lying and misguiding" English anti-German propaganda, even bringing in the complicity of England in providing matériel to the Confederacy during the Civil War. He noted that the large number of German immigrants had forged strong ties over the years between the United States and Germany, while he ignored those between earlier settlers and England. He was so sure of America's moral duty to support Germany that he confidently urged Hugo to convince his brother Ludwig of Belleville to join the U.S. Army, even though the attorney was forty-nine at the time, and also pushed for Hugo's son Karl to join either the army or navy. He himself would "gladly slip on the uniform, if the government can use an old man as I am."[34]

Of his European family, at least three were actively involved on the German side of the Great War. Daughter Teresa became a Red Cross leader who ran a hospital caring for wounded soldiers of all nations, while her husband, Emil Buth, a former Prussian cavalry officer, was the German army commander of occupied Luxembourg. Hermann Petersen, husband of daughter Mathilde, was surgeon in chief in charge of German military hospitals. Thus, when America finally joined the war in 1917, Osterhaus's family truly became a house divided. (Ironically, had Karl lived, he and his brother Hugo would have been commanding on opposites sides, Hugo having been recalled to active duty three months after his father's death to command the U.S. merchant marine fleet in the Atlantic.)[35]

Throughout 1915 Osterhaus repeatedly and urgently tried to get Hugo and his wife, Mary, to come and visit, noting that behind the front lines, which were sixty miles to the west, life went on as usual. By 1916, however, he had become more wistful: "I wish you could come over" replaced his previous demands. In his ninety-third year, Osterhaus was still vitally interested in current events and had very strong opinions about how the war was being conducted by all antagonists. In a 1916 interview, "Maj. Gen. Osterhaus discussed many phases of the war with the greatest zeal. He is a great admirer of Field Marshal von Hindenburg and he believes the war would have been ended long ago if Hindenburg had been made Chief of the General Staff at the beginning. 'Hindenburg is the greatest general the world has produced,' he said. 'He would have defeated Napoleon the first day.'"[36] A month after this final interview, Peter Joseph Osterhaus died of pneumonia a few days before his ninety-fourth birthday, fortunately not living to see his son and his adopted homeland come into the war against Germany or to endure the subsequent defeat of his homeland.

Thus ended the long and interesting life of a man who had strong principles and lived by them to the end. He truly spanned the centuries, touching the lives of some of the most prominent characters of his age and seeing war change from a bloody affair conducted with rules of honor from horseback to a mechanized, impersonal horror. Despite his accomplishments on the field of battle, the fondest memories of Osterhaus came from those who served with him. Wrote one:

> I knew your father well, having served under him, at the close of the war, as his acting assistant adjutant general. As an officer under him I formed a very high estimate of him as a patriot and an eminent soldier. His services during our Civil War won for him high praise and he was held in high esteem by

> the American people, and particularly by the soldiers who knew him personally. . . . He recommended me for Brevet Major. . . . Coming from one so eminently a gentleman as was the General, I always prized his most generous words of commendation. He was privileged to live to a ripe old age and his name will be honored among the noble patriots of his time.[37]

Despite the fact that his grave site has been obliterated in Koblenz, a few tangible mementos of Peter Joseph Osterhaus survive that show the gratitude of his two countries. Among these are a bust erected in 1913 on the Vicksburg battlefield and several state historical markers in Georgia and Tennessee. In Koblenz the street Osterhausstrasse, named for him, still exists.

Notes

Abbreviations

GHS	Georgia Historical Society
MHS	Missouri Historical Society, St. Louis
NARA	National Archives and Records Administration, Washington, D.C.
OR	U.S. War Department. *The War of the Rebellion: A Compilation of the Official Records of the Union and Confederate Armies.* Series 1–3. Washington, D.C.: Government Printing Office, 1880–1901. All citations of *OR* refer to Series 1 unless otherwise indicated.
ORN	U.S. Naval War Records Office. *Official Records of the Union and Confederate Navies in the War of the Rebellion.* Series 1. Washington, D.C.: Government Printing Office, 1894–1922.
VNMP	Vicksburg National Military Park, Mississippi

Introduction

1. Peter J. Osterhaus, "What I Saw of the War," 23, Peter Joseph Osterhaus Papers; Ezra J. Warner, *Generals in Blue: Lives of the Union Commanders,* 352; George Hazzard, *Hazzard's History of Henry County, Indiana,* 438.

2. U.S. War Department, *The War of the Rebellion: A Compilation of the Official Records of the Union and Confederate Armies,* 3:56, 520; *OR,* 8:192, 203, 438; W. T. Sherman, *Memoirs of General William T. Sherman,* 399.

3. Lyman G. Bennett and William M. Haigh, *History of the Thirty-sixth Regiment Illinois Volunteers during the War of the Rebellion,* 168.

4. Murray Horowitz, "Ethnicity and Command: The Civil War Experience," 186.

5. Thomas J. Goss, *The War within the Union High Command: Politics and Generalship during the Civil War,* xiii–xv.

6. Martin W. Ofele, *German-Speaking Officers in the U.S. Colored Troops, 1863–1867,* 103.

Chapter 1. Before the War

1. Hans-Peter Kleber, "Peter Joseph Osterhaus, Ein Deutsch-Amerikanisches Leben," 88–9.

2. Philip Katcher with Richard Hook, illus., *American Civil War Commanders (3), Union Leaders in the West,* 62; Kleber, "Osterhaus," 89; Frank L. Byrne and Jean P.

Soman, eds., *Your True Marcus: The Civil War Letters of a Jewish Colonel,* 270; Viet Valentin, *1848: Chapters of German History,* 392.

3. Hugo Osterhaus memorandum, March 3, 1957, Osterhaus Papers; Kleber, "Osterhaus," 89; Gordon A. Craig, *The Politics of the Prussian Army, 1640–1945,* 77, 79; Hajo Holborn, *A History of Modern Germany, 1840–1945,* 136.

4. Kleber, "Osterhaus," 90; Geoffrey Wawro, *The Franco-Prussian War,* 43.

5. Christopher Clark, *Iron Kingdom: The Rise and Downfall of Prussia, 1600–1947,* 465; Craig, *Politics of the Prussian Army,* 90–91; Kleber, "Osterhaus," 90.

6. Charles T. Dahlinger, *The German Revolution of 1849,* 6, 26.

7. Kleber, "Osterhaus," 90–91.

8. Ibid., 90.

9. Dahlinger, *German Revolution,* 7, 10; C. Clark, *Iron Kingdom,* 468–69, 478.

10. Kleber, "Osterhaus," 91; Stephen D. Engle, *Yankee Dutchman: The Life of Franz Sigel,* 7.

11. Kleber, "Osterhaus," 91; Lloyd E. Lee, "Popular Militias."

12. Holborn, *History of Modern Germany,* 88; Dahlinger, *German Revolution,* 24.

13. Hugo W. Osterhaus memorandum, December 18, 1956, Osterhaus Papers; Engle, *Yankee Dutchman,* 12.

14. Kleber, "Osterhaus," 91; Peter Blastenbrei, "Mannheim in der Revolution 1848/49," 96, 99–100; Carl Wittke, *Refugees of Revolution: The German Forty-Eighters in America,* 22.

15. Blastenbrei, "Mannheim in der Revolution," 96.

16. Kleber, "Osterhaus," 92; Dahlinger, *German Revolution,* 112.

17. Dahlinger, *German Revolution,* 87, 108.

18. Ibid., 98.

19. Kleber, "Osterhaus," 92; Dahlinger, *German Revolution,* 141.

20. Kleber, "Osterhaus," 92; Engle, *Yankee Dutchman,* 13, 15–16.

21. Dahlinger, *German Revolution,* 112–13, 187, 175.

22. Ibid., 195; Holborn, *History of Modern Germany,* 88–89.

23. Dahlinger, *German Revolution,* 195–200.

24. Ibid., 199–201, 210.

25. Ibid., 211.

26. Ibid., 211–13.

27. Kleber, "Osterhaus," 90.

28. Engle, *Yankee Dutchman,* 19; Dahlinger, *German Revolution,* 222–24.

29. Dahlinger, *German Revolution,* 234; Kleber, "Osterhaus," 92.

30. Blastenbrei, "Mannheim in der Revolution," 118–19; Dahlinger, *German Revolution,* 268; Engle, *Yankee Dutchman,* 22.

31. Dahlinger, *German Revolution,* 269–70; Raymond E. Swing, "Osterhaus Great Man," *Chicago Daily News,* January 3, 1914, MHS; Kleber, "Osterhaus," 92.

32. Hugo W. Osterhaus memorandum, December 18, 1956, Osterhaus Papers; Kleber, "Osterhaus," 93.

33. Kleber, "Osterhaus," 93; *Argo* manifest.

34. *Argo* manifest; James F. Harris, "The Arrival of the Europamude: Germans in America after 1848," 27; Kleber, "Osterhaus," 94; Wittke, *Refugees of Revolution,* 45;

Blastenbrei, "Mannheim in der Revolution," 96.

35. Wittke, *Refugees of Revolution,* 39.

36. Gustave Koerner, *Memoirs of Gustave Koerner, 1809–1896,* 1:529.

37. Wittke, *Refugees of Revolution,* 64.

38. Koerner, *Memoirs of Gustave Koerner,* 1:529, 559–60; Horowitz, "Ethnicity and Command," 183.

39. Ernest Kirschten, *Catfish and Crystal,* 250; Wittke, *Refugees of Revolution,* 62–63; Engle, *Yankee Dutchman,* 34.

40. *Belleville (IL) Republican,* May 1, 1850, Osterhaus Papers; U.S. Bureau of the Census, Federal Census, 1850.

41. Peggy Lathrop Sapp, *St. Clair County, Illinois: A Register of Births and Deaths, 1843–1857, as Recorded by John Scheel, County Clerk,* 29, 80.

42. Kleber, "Osterhaus," 94–95; Emil Mannhardt, "General Peter Joseph Osterhaus," 54.

43. Bonnie J. Krause, "German Americans in the St. Louis Region, 1840–1860," 306–7; William L. Burton, *Melting Pot Soldiers: The Union's Ethnic Regiments,* 39; James Pickett Jones, *"Black Jack": John A. Logan and Southern Illinois in the Civil War Era,* 25–26, 28.

44. Kleber, "Osterhaus," 94; Swing, "Osterhaus Great Man"; Jacob Mueller, *Memories of a Forty-Eighter: Sketches from the German American Period of Storm and Stress in the 1850's,* 204.

45. *Belleville (Ill.) Advocate,* March 11, 1857, Osterhaus Papers; Kleber, "Osterhaus," 94; U.S. Bureau of the Census, Federal Census, 1860; Mannhardt, "Osterhaus," 54.

46. Christopher Phillips, *Damned Yankee: The Life of General Nathaniel Lyon,* 129; Michael Fellman, *Inside War,* 10.

47. R. V. Kennedy, ed., *St. Louis Directory for 1860,* 427; Ernst D. Kargau, *St. Louis in Former Years: A Commemorative History of the German Element,* 58, 124.

48. Phillips, *Damned Yankee,* 129; Swing, "Osterhaus Great Man."

49. Joseph R. Reinhart, trans. and ed., *August Willich's Gallant Dutchmen: Civil War Letters from the 32nd Indiana Infantry,* 8; Virgil C. Blum, "The Political and Military Activities of the German Element in St. Louis, 1859–1861," 108–9.

50. Reinhart, *Willich's Gallant Dutchmen,* 8; Krause, "German Americans in St. Louis," 307–8; Steven Rowan, ed. and trans., *Germans for a Free Missouri: Translations from the St. Louis Radical Press, 1857–1862,* 26–27.

51. Rowan, *Germans for a Free Missouri,* 38–40; Engle, *Yankee Dutchman,* 42–44.

52. Krause, "German Americans in St. Louis," 309–10; Horowitz, "Ethnicity and Command," 183.

53. Rowan, *Germans for a Free Missouri,* 14.

54. James Peckham, *General Nathaniel Lyon and Missouri in 1861,* 42.

55. James N. Primm, "Missouri, St. Louis, and the Secession Crisis," 14–15; Peckham, *Lyon and Missouri,* 38.

56. Engle, *Yankee Dutchman,* 245n; Robert J. Rombauer, *The Union Cause in St. Louis in 1861: An Historical Sketch,* 197.

57. Rombauer, *Union Cause in St. Louis,* 128, 193.

58. Blum, "German Element in St. Louis," 119.

59. Engle, *Yankee Dutchman,* 52–53; Rombauer, *Union Cause in St. Louis,* 141, 193.

60. *OR,* Series 3, 1, 67, 83; William E. Parrish, *Frank Blair: Lincoln's Conservative,* 99.

61. Rombauer, *Union Cause in St. Louis,* 195–99.

62. Osterhaus, "What I Saw," 1, Osterhaus Papers; Samuel P. Curtis, "Army of the South-West and the First Campaign in Arkansas," 684; Louis S. Gerteis, *Civil War St. Louis,* 97.

63. Rombauer, *Union Cause in St. Louis,* 195, 198; Rowan, *Germans for a Free Missouri,* 32; Wilhelm Kaufmann, *The Germans in the American Civil War,* 99; Horowitz, "Ethnicity and Command," 188.

64. Rombauer, *Union Cause in St. Louis,* 219; Peter Blanck and Chen Song, "'With Malice toward None; with Charity Toward All': Civil War Pensions for Native and Foreign-Born Union Army Veterans," 13; Swing, "Osterhaus Great Man."

65. Jay Monaghan, *Civil War on the Western Border, 1854–1865,* 144; Eugene F. Ware, *The Lyon Campaign in Missouri: Being a History of the First Iowa Infantry,* 155; Brent Nosworthy, *The Bloody Crucible of Courage: Fighting Methods and Combat Experience of the Civil War,* 79–83, 142–43.

66. William R. Brooksher, *Bloody Hill: The Civil War Battle of Wilson's Creek,* 50–51; Rombauer, *Union Cause in St. Louis,* 218; Gerteis, *Civil War St. Louis,* 103.

67. Peckham, *Lyon and Missouri,* 140–41, 32; Primm, "St. Louis and Secession," 17.

68. Phillips, *Damned Yankee,* 185–89.

69. Osterhaus, "What I Saw," 1, Osterhaus Papers; Osterhaus, "Generals' Reports," 7:402, RG 94, NARA.

70. Gerteis, *Civil War St. Louis,* 103; Rombauer, *Union Cause in St. Louis,* 230, 227.

71. Rombauer, *Union Cause in St. Louis,* 230, 208.

72. Phillips, *Damned Yankee,* 189–91; James W. Covington, "The Camp Jackson Affair: 1861," 207–8, 211.

73. Heinrich Boernstein, *Memoirs of a Nobody: The Missouri Years of an Austrian Radical, 1849–1866,* 309–10; Peckham, *Lyon and Missouri,* 154; Covington, "Camp Jackson," 209.

74. Boernstein, *Memoirs of a Nobody,* 309–10; Gerteis, *Civil War St. Louis,* 108; Otto C. Lademann, "The Capture of 'Camp Jackson,' St. Louis."

75. Boernstein, *Memoirs of a Nobody,* 310; Sherman, *Memoirs,* 191.

76. Gerteis, *Civil War St. Louis,* 109; Rombauer, *Union Cause in St. Louis,* 236.

77. Peckham, *Lyon and Missouri,* 156–58; Rombauer, *Union Cause in St. Louis,* 238–39; Lademann, "Capture of 'Camp Jackson,'" 75.

78. Swing, "Osterhaus Great Man."

79. Burton, *Melting Pot Soldiers,* 42; John C. Moore, *Missouri,* 35–36.

80. Gerteis, *Civil War St. Louis,* 119.

Chapter 2. The Trans-Mississippi Campaigns of 1861 and 1862

1. William G. Piston and Richard W. Hatcher III, *Wilson's Creek: The Second Battle of the Civil War and the Men Who Fought It,* 41–42; *OR,* 3:382; Brooksher, *Bloody Hill,* 92.

2. *OR,* 3:13; Rombauer, *Union Cause in St. Louis,* 270; Robert Dyer, *Boonville: An Illustrated History,* 110; Osterhaus, "What I Saw," 1, Osterhaus Papers; Brooksher, *Bloody Hill,* 88; Phillips, *Damned Yankee,* 119.

3. Brooksher, *Bloody Hill,* 90; Phillips, *Damned Yankee,* 219; Dyer, *Boonville: An Illustrated History,* 110, 112; Paul Rorvig, "The Significant Skirmish: The Battle of Boonville, June 17, 1861," 142.

4. *OR,* 3:13.

5. Piston and Hatcher, *Wilson's Creek,* 45.

6. Franc B. Wilkie, *The Iowa First: Letters from the War,* 74, 76.

7. Kaufmann, *Germans in the Civil War,* 259; Thomas L. Snead, "The First Year of the War in Missouri," 271.

8. "Speech by Gen. Osterhaus," *New York Times,* August 16, 1863; RG 393, pt. 2, 3221:3, NARA.

9. Engle, *Yankee Dutchman,* 66; Piston and Hatcher, *Wilson's Creek,* 104.

10. Wilkie, *Iowa First,* 81–82, 77; Phillips, *Damned Yankee,* 230; Brooksher, *Bloody Hill,* 128–29; Rombauer, *Union Cause in St. Louis,* 287; Ware, *Lyon Campaign,* 192–95.

11. Wilkie, *Iowa First,* 83; Snead, "First Year of the War," 268–69; Piston and Hatcher, *Wilson's Creek,* 105; William M. Wherry, "The Campaign in Missouri and the Battle of Wilson's Creek, 1861," 6; William W. Branson diary, July 29, 1861.

12. Branson diary, July 28 and July 27, 1861; *OR,* 3:394; Piston and Hatcher, *Wilson's Creek,* 132–33; Osterhaus, "Generals' Reports," 7:404, RG 94, NARA.

13. "Important Military Order," *St. Louis Daily Missouri Democrat,* August 1, 1861; Osterhaus, "Generals' Reports," 7:404, RG 94, NARA; John C. Frémont, "In Command in Missouri," 282; *St. Louis Daily Missouri Democrat,* August 24, 1861.

14. Piston and Hatcher, *Wilson's Creek,* 134–36.

15. *OR,* 3:47; "In the Ranks under General Lyon in Missouri, 1861: The Observations of a Private Soldier," pt. 2, 66; Return I. Holcombe and [unknown] Adams, *An Account of the Battle of Wilson's Creek, or Oak Hills,* 11–12, 15–16; Ware, *Lyon Campaign,* 301; Snead, "First Year of the War," 271.

16. John Schofield, *Forty-six Years in the Army,* 39–40; *OR,* 3:96; "In the Ranks," pt. 3, 142–43.

17. Rowan, *Germans for a Free Missouri,* 276.

18. Piston and Hatcher, *Wilson's Creek,* 186; Rombauer, *Union Cause in St. Louis,* 318.

19. Swing, "Osterhaus Great Man" (see chap. 1, n. 31).

20. *OR,* 3:60; Edwin C. Bearss, *The Battle of Wilson's Creek,* 56–57.

21. Thomas L. Snead, *The Fight for Missouri from the Election of Lincoln to the Death of Lyon,* 269–70; *OR,* 3:73, 65–66; "Report of Major Osterhaus," *St. Louis Daily Missouri Democrat,* August 24, 1861; *OR,* 53:427–28.

22. *OR,* 3:66; Albert R. Greene, "On the Battle of Wilson's Creek," 123; Bearss, *Wilson's Creek,* 66–67; *OR,* 3:105.

23. "Report of Major Osterhaus," *St. Louis Daily Missouri Democrat,* August 24, 1861; George E. Knapp, *The Wilson's Creek Staff Ride and Battlefield Tour,* 15–16.

24. *OR,* 3:76; Bearss, *Wilson's Creek,* 79; Piston and Hatcher, *Wilson's Creek,* 239–40; Peckham, *Lyon and Missouri,* 335; *OR,* 53:435.

25. Joyce Farlow and Louise Barry, eds., "Vincent B. Osborne's Civil War Experiences," 118; Ware, *Lyon Campaign,* 319; "In the Ranks," pt. 4, 200.

26. Bearss, *Wilson's Creek,* 102; Piston and Hatcher, *Wilson's Creek,* 262; *OR,* 3:67; "Report of Major Osterhaus," *St. Louis Daily Missouri Democrat,* August 24, 1861.

27. "Report of Major Osterhaus," *St. Louis Daily Missouri Democrat,* August 24, 1861.

28. Ibid.; Bearss, *Wilson's Creek,* 112; *OR,* 3:77; Osterhaus, "What I Saw," 2, Osterhaus Papers.

29. "Report of Major Osterhaus," *St. Louis Daily Missouri Democrat,* August 24, 1861; Jared C. Lobdell, "The Civil War Journal and Letters of Colonel John Van Deusen du Bois, April 2, 1861, to October 16, 1862," 30–31; Piston and Hatcher, *Wilson's Creek,* 275.

30. Schofield, *Forty-six Years,* 45; *OR,* 3:67–68.

31. *OR,* 3:62; Piston and Hatcher, *Wilson's Creek,* 282.

32. *OR,* 3:62–63, 68–69, 77.

33. "Report of Major Osterhaus," *St. Louis Daily Missouri Democrat,* August 24, 1861; *OR,* 3:63; Bearss, *Wilson's Creek,* 131–32; Otto C. Lademann, "The Battle of Wilson's Creek, August 10, 1861," 436–38; *OR,* 3:87.

34. Osterhaus, "What I Saw," 2, Osterhaus Papers; *OR,* 3:55, 100, 106.

35. Knapp, *Wilson's Creek Staff Ride,* 20; Christopher R. Gabel, *Staff Ride Handbook for the Vicksburg Campaign, December 1862–July 1863,* 35–37, 41–42.

36. *OR,* 3:94–98.

37. Gen. John Frémont to Osterhaus, August 16, 1861, RG 94, NARA; Osterhaus, "Generals' Reports," 7:404, RG 94, NARA.

38. Frémont, "In Command in Missouri," 282; Earl J. Hess, "The 12th Missouri Infantry: A Socio-Military Profile of a Union Regiment," 55; Earl J. Hess, "Osterhaus in Missouri: A Study of German-American Loyalty," 156; Osterhaus, "What I Saw," 3, Osterhaus Papers.

39. Hess, "12th Missouri," 60, 55, 57.

40. Ibid., 56–57; Mannhardt, "General Peter Joseph Osterhaus," 56, 55; Osterhaus, "What I Saw," 3, Osterhaus Papers.

41. Camille Ferri Pisani, *Prince Napoleon in America, 1861: Letters from His Aide-de-Camp,* 251–53; Jorg Nagler, "The Lincoln-Frémont Debate and the Forty-Eighters," 160.

42. Osterhaus, "Generals' Reports," 7:405, RG 94, NARA; Ella Lonn, *Foreigners in the Union Army and Navy,* 103; Kaufmann, *Germans in the Civil War,* 292.

43. William G. Bek, trans., "The Civil War Diary of John T. Buegel, Union Soldier," 316; Jay Monaghan, *Civil War on the Western Border, 1854–1865,* 205; Bek, "Diary of John Buegel," 317.

44. Koerner, *Memoirs of Gustave Koerner,* 2:190–91; Lobdell, "Journal of du Bois," 42; Hess, "Osterhaus in Missouri," 158.

45. Ethan S. Rafuse, "McClellan and Halleck at War: The Struggle for Control of the Union War Effort in the West, November 1861–March 1862," 35.

46. Engle, *Yankee Dutchman,* 89; Grenville M. Dodge, *The Battle of Atlanta and Other Campaigns, Addresses, etc.,* 13; Osterhaus, "What I Saw," 3, Osterhaus Papers; Bek, "Diary of John Buegel," 317; *OR,* 8:393.

47. Rafuse, "McClellan and Halleck," 35; *OR,* 8:438; Hess, "12th Missouri," 55.

48. *OR,* 8:462; Engle, *Yankee Dutchman,* 90–91; Hess, "Osterhaus in Missouri," 160; *OR,* 8:828–29.

49. Kenneth E. Colton, ed., "Frontier War Problems: Letters of Samuel Ryan Curtis," 310–11; Engle, *Yankee Dutchman,* 91–95.

50. Colton, "Frontier War Problems," 313; Curtis, "Army of the South-West," 675; William L. Shea and Earl J. Hess, *Pea Ridge: Civil War Campaign in the West,* 9–10.

51. *OR,* 8:504, 829.

52. Mary A. Livermore, *My Story of the War,* 643–45; RG 393, pt. 2, 3221:13, NARA; *OR,* 8:527.

53. Shea and Hess, *Pea Ridge,* 7–9, 14; Osterhaus, "Generals' Report," 7:406–7, RG 94, NARA; *OR,* 8:550.

54. L. Bennett and Haigh, *Thirty-sixth Illinois,* 110–12; *OR,* 8:549; Wallace P. Benson diary, February 9, 1862; R. V. Marshall, *Historical Sketch of the Twenty-second Regiment Indiana Volunteers,* 13.

55. *OR,* 8:757; L. Bennett and Haigh, *Thirty-sixth Illinois,* 116–7, 120; Shea and Hess, *Pea Ridge,* 42–43; Marshall, *Twenty-second Indiana,* 14; Benson diary, February 17, 1862; Shea and Hess, *Pea Ridge,* 46, 48; *OR,* 8:258, 561.

56. Shea and Hess, *Pea Ridge,* 51–52; Phil Gottschalk, *In Deadly Earnest: The History of the First Missouri Brigade, CSA,* 53–54; *OR,* 8:568, 196.

57. *OR,* 8:750, 283, 763; Gottschalk, *In Deadly Earnest,* 54–5.

58. *OR,* 8:763; W. H. Tunnard, *A Southern Record: The History of the Third Regiment Louisiana Infantry,* 136; L. Bennett and Haigh, *Thirty-sixth Illinois,* 129–31; Shea and Hess, *Pea Ridge,* 68–69.

59. *OR,* 8:210; Engle, *Yankee Dutchman,* 108–9; Franz Sigel, "The Pea Ridge Campaign," 320; Shea and Hess, *Pea Ridge,* 69–70; *OR,* 8:198, 216.

60. *OR,* 8:197–99; Shea and Hess, *Pea Ridge,* 82.

61. *OR,* 8:283; William L. Shea, "1862: 'A Continual Thunder,'" 30–31; *OR,* 8:283–84.

62. Dodge, *Battle of Atlanta,* 20; Shea and Hess, *Pea Ridge,* 90; *OR,* 8:199.

63. *OR,* 8:217; Shea and Hess, *Pea Ridge,* 104; James Grant Wilson, *Biographical Sketches of Illinois Officers in the Rebellion of 1861,* 41.

64. *OR,* 8:217–18; Shea and Hess, *Pea Ridge,* 94.

65. *OR,* 8:232–33; Osterhaus, "What I Saw," 4, Osterhaus Papers; *OR,* 8:217.

66. *OR,* 8:217, 233, 232, 194, 288; Tunnard, *Southern Record,* 133, 137; Henry Voelkner to family, March 18, 1862, Voelkner Papers; William S. Burns, *Recollections of the 4th Missouri Cavalry,* 29–30; *OR,* 8:236–37, 218.

67. *OR,* 8:217–18, 234; Nosworthy, *Bloody Crucible of Courage,* 424; *OR,* 8:236.

68. *OR,* 8:226, 288; Shea and Hess, *Pea Ridge,* 107; L. Bennett and Haigh, *Thirty-sixth Illinois,* 65, 133.

69. Shea and Hess, *Pea Ridge,* 102–3, 106–7, 109; Tunnard, *Southern Record,* 137–38.

70. *OR,* 8:226; Shea and Hess, *Pea Ridge,* 110, 113; *OR,* 8:218; Marshall, *Twenty-second Indiana,* 16; Shea and Hess, *Pea Ridge,* 114–15.

71. *OR,* 8:199; Shea and Hess, *Pea Ridge,* 119–20.

72. *OR,* 8:218–19, 247; Shea and Hess, *Pea Ridge,* 141–42; Tunnard, *Southern Record,*

138, 135; L. Bennett and Haigh, *Thirty-sixth Illinois,* 150–51; *OR,* 8:293–95, 289–90.

73. *OR,* 8:218, 247; L. Bennett and Haigh, *Thirty-sixth Illinois,* 151; *OR,* 8:289–90.

74. *OR,* 8:212, 219, 200–201.

75. Ibid., 284, 201; Henry Voelkner to family, March 18, 1862, Voelkner Papers; Shea and Hess, *Pea Ridge,* 219–20; Engle, *Yankee Dutchman,* 114.

76. L. Bennett and Haigh, *Thirty-sixth Illinois,* 162–63, 165; *OR,* 8:219, 214; Sigel, "The Pea Ridge Campaign," 327–28; Shea and Hess, *Pea Ridge,* 231; Marshall, *Twenty-second Indiana,* 19.

77. *OR,* 8:214; Sigel, "The Pea Ridge Campaign," 327–28; Osterhaus, "What I Saw," 5, Osterhaus Papers; L. Bennett and Haigh, *Thirty-sixth Illinois,* 166; *OR,* 8:202, 220; Sigel, "The Pea Ridge Campaign," 329.

78. Bek, "Diary of John Buegel," 321; *OR,* 8:220, 202; Burns, *4th Missouri Cavalry,* 34; Shea and Hess, *Pea Ridge,* 240; Marshall, *Twenty-second Indiana,* 20; L. Bennett and Haigh, *Thirty-sixth Illinois,* 168; *OR,* 8:220, 203, 199.

79. *OR,* 8:202, 290–91; Shea and Hess, *Pea Ridge,* 256–59; Curtis, "Army of the South-West," 158; *OR,* 8:598, 202–3.

80. *New York Herald,* March 11 and March 21, 1862; Curtis, "Army of the South-West," 155–56; Shea and Hess, *Pea Ridge,* 279–80, 314, 316; Engle, *Yankee Dutchman,* 118–19; *OR,* 8:204–5; Nosworthy, *Bloody Crucible of Courage,* 259.

81. Engle, *Yankee Dutchman,* 194.

82. Osterhaus, "What I Saw," 5, Osterhaus Papers.

83. *OR,* 13:85, 405, 380, 31, 33–34; Scott H. Akridge and Emmett E. Powers, *A Severe and Bloody Fight: The Battle of Whitney's Lane,* 106.

84. *OR,* 13:392, 70–71; *OR,* Series 2, 3:558–59; Akridge and Powers, *Severe and Bloody Fight,* 59; *OR,* 13:69, 416–17.

85. Osterhaus, "What I Saw," 6, Osterhaus Papers; Goss, *Union High Command,* 18–19; Koerner, *Memoirs of Gustave Koerner,* 2:210; Carl Schurz to Abraham Lincoln, April 23, 1862; Hess, "Osterhaus in Missouri," 165; *Senate Executive Journal,* May 2, 1862.

86. Bek, "Diary of John T. Buegel," 323; Burns, *4th Missouri Cavalry,* 42.

87. *OR,* 13:448; Shea and Hess, *Pea Ridge,* 300–301.

88. Edwin C. Bearss, "The White River Expedition, June 10–July 15, 1862," 358; Bek, "Diary of John T. Buegel," 323; Cyrus Bussey, "Civil War Reminiscences," 20–21; Curtis, "Army of the South-West," 215–16.

89. Isaac H. Elliott, *History of the Thirty-third Regiment Illinois Veteran Volunteer Infantry in the Civil War, 22nd August, 1861, to 7th December, 1865,* 29; Osterhaus, "What I Saw," 6, Osterhaus Papers.

90. Fred T. Ledergerber affidavit, July 26, 1886; Ferdinand von Steinburg affidavit, November 26, 1886; Adolph Wagner affidavit, October 27, 1887, all Osterhaus Pension File, RG 94, NARA; Osterhaus, "Generals' Report," 7:411, RG 94, NARA.

91. John Schenk affidavit, September 9, 1886; Wagner affidavit, October 27, 1887; Ledergerber affidavit, July 26, 1886, all Osterhaus Pension File, RG 94, NARA; Osterhaus, "Generals' Report," 7:411, RG 94, NARA.

92. *OR,* 22:852.

Chapter 3. The Vicksburg Campaign

1. U. S. Grant, *The Civil War Memoirs of Ulysses S. Grant,* 141–42.

2. James R. Arnold, *Grant Wins the War: Decision at Vicksburg,* 28–31, 36–38; Terrence J. Winschel, "Fighting Politician: John A. McClernand," 131, 136; James M. McPherson, *This Mighty Scourge: Perspectives on the Civil War,* 136–37.

3. Sherman, *Memoirs,* 318–20, 319; *OR,* vol. 17, 2:546; *OR,* vol. 17, 1:709; Richard L. Kiper, *Major General John Alexander McClernand, Politician in Uniform,* 165, 176; David D. Porter, *Incidents and Anecdotes of the Civil War,* 131.

4. Osterhaus, "Generals' Reports," 7:413, RG 94, NARA; Winschel, "McClernand," 131; Swing, "Osterhaus Great Man" (see chap. 1, n. 31); Daniel Webster and Don Cameron, *The History of the First Wisconsin Battery Light Artillery,* 110. Swing quotes Osterhaus as saying that he had his cold feet in an interview with Grant, but Grant was miles away at Holly Springs at the time, so more likely it was in his interview with McClernand.

5. *OR,* vol. 17, 2:537, 573; *OR,* vol. 17, 1:745–46.

6. *OR,* vol. 17, 1:746.

7. Ibid., 780–81, 711.

8. F. H. Mason, *The Forty-second Ohio Infantry: A History,* 173; *OR,* vol. 17, 1:706, 745–46.

9. *OR,* vol. 17, 1:705; Edwin C. Bearss, *Campaign for Vicksburg,* 1:350–51; Gabel, *Staff Ride Handbook,* 31.

10. *OR,* vol. 17, 1:705–6.

11. Ibid., 746, 706, 747; Webster and Cameron, *First Wisconsin Battery,* 114.

12. *OR,* vol. 17, 1:747; Webster and Cameron, *First Wisconsin Battery,* 112, 114; Mason, *Forty-second Ohio,* 176.

13. U.S. Naval War Records Office, *Official Records of the Union and Confederate Navies in the War of the Rebellion,* Series 1, 24:109; *OR,* vol. 17, 1:706, 747; Webster and Cameron, *First Wisconsin Battery,* 112, 115–16.

14. *OR,* vol. 17, 1:784, 747, 750; Sherman, *Memoirs,* 321; J. S. B. Matson to Friend Lyman, ca. January 18, 1863, on Raymond K. Moore, "They Were the 114th O.V.I."; Bek, "Diary of John Beugel," 505.

15. Mason, *Forty-second Ohio,* 176–77; *OR,* vol. 17, 1:785.

16. *OR,* vol. 17, 1:707–8; *ORN,* 24:107, 115; Porter, *Incidents and Anecdotes,* 131; Bearss, *Campaign for Vicksburg,* 1:371; Sherman, *Memoirs,* 322; Stella S. Coatsworth, *The Loyal People of the North-west: A Record of Prominent Persons, Places, and Events during Eight Years of Unparalleled American History.*

17. *OR,* vol. 17, 1:706, 723, 747, 749; Webster and Cameron, *First Wisconsin Battery,* 115, 116–18, 120; Mason, *Forty-second Ohio,* 176–77.

18. Gabel, *Staff Ride Handbook,* 41; *OR,* vol. 17, 1:747; Osterhaus, "What I Saw," 7, Osterhaus Papers.

19. General Orders Nos. 3 and 4, RG 393, pt. 2, 3230:11–12, NARA; B. F. Stevenson, *Letters from the Army,* 175–77; Kenneth Lyftogt, ed., *Left for Dixie: The Civil War Diary of John Rath,* 16; Swing, "Osterhaus Great Man."

20. Stevenson, *Letters from the Army,* 178; *OR,* vol. 24, 1:11; Kiper, *McClernand,* 192; *OR,* vol. 24, 3:250; John Y. Simon, ed., *The Papers of Ulysses S. Grant,* 7:453.

21. Osterhaus, "What I Saw," 8, Osterhaus Papers; *OR,* vol. 24, 3:74.

22. Terrence J. Winschel, ed., *The Civil War Diary of a Common Soldier,* 37–39; von Steinburg affidavit, November 26, 1886, Osterhaus Pension File, RG 94, NARA; Stevenson, *Letters from the Army,* 184–85; Charles F. Larimer, ed., *Love and Valor: The Intimate Civil War Letters between Captain Jacob and Emeline Ritner,* 114; Livermore, *My Story of the War,* 301–2; Special Orders No. 8, 15, and 21, RG 393, pt. 2, 3230:15–16, 19, 22, NARA; Byrne and Soman, *Your True Marcus,* 244–45; "Military Record of A. H. Clark."

23. Osterhaus diary, May 23, 1864, Osterhaus Pension File, RG 94, NARA; William G. Cutler, "Doniphan County, pt. 13," in *History of the State of Kansas,* ed. Cutler.

24. Larimer, *Love and Valor,* 126.

25. Webster and Cameron, *First Wisconsin Battery,* 125–26; General Order No. 26, March 22, 1862, RG 393, pt. 2, 3230:26, NARA; Larimer, *Love and Valor,* 126.

26. Byrne and Soman, *Your True Marcus,* 260; *OR,* vol. 24, 3:90; Special Orders No. 24 and 26, RG 393, pt. 2, 3230:25–26, NARA; Webster and Cameron, *First Wisconsin Battery,* 125; Larimer, *Love and Valor,* 133.

27. Grant, *Memoirs,* 149; *OR,* vol. 24, 1:22.

28. Warren E. Grabau, *Ninety-eight Days: A Geographer's View of the Vicksburg Campaign,* 18–20, 62; Otto F. Bond, ed., *Under the Flag of the Nation: Diaries and Letters of a Yankee Volunteer in the Civil War,* 50.

29. *OR,* vol. 24, 1:46–47; Grant, *Memoirs,* 192; Charles A. Dana, *Recollections of the Civil War,* 32–33; William L. Shea and Terrence J. Winschel, *Vicksburg Is the Key,* 91.

30. *OR,* vol. 24, 1:495; Dana, *Recollections,* 32–33; Hess, "Grant's Ethnic General," 216; Oran Perry, "The Entering Wedge," 364.

31. Gottschalk, *In Deadly Earnest,* 195; Grabau, *Ninety-eight Days,* 67; RG 393, pt. 2, 3221:111, NARA.

32. *OR,* vol. 24, 1:491; Janet B. Hewett, Noah Andre Trudeau, and Bryce A. Suderow, eds., *Supplement to the Official Records of the Union and Confederate Armies,* 4:353–54.

33. *OR,* vol. 24, 1:493 3:713–14, 724.

34. Ibid., 1:491–92; Bond, *Under the Flag,* 50; Paul H. Hass, ed., "The Vicksburg Diary of Henry Clay Warmoth," 336; Bearss, *Campaign for Vicksburg,* 2:31.

35. *OR,* vol. 24, 1:492; Byrne and Soman, *Your True Marcus,* 267.

36. *OR,* vol. 24, 1:140; Hass, "Diary of Henry Warmoth," 336–37.

37. Hass, "Diary of Henry Warmoth," 337–38; *OR,* vol. 24, 3:171; John A. Ritter to Margarett, April 8, 1863, "Civil War Letters of Captain John A. Ritter, M.D.," ed. Gerald W. Ritter.

38. *OR,* vol. 24, 1:492; Perry, "The Entering Wedge," 365–66; Bearss, *Campaign for Vicksburg,* 2:36.

39. Perry, "The Entering Wedge," 366–67; *OR,* vol. 24, 1:492.

40. *OR,* vol. 24, 1:490; John Ritter to Margarett, April 8, 1863, "Civil War Letters," ed. Ritter; Frank E. Everett, *Brierfield: Plantation Home of Jefferson Davis,* 18–19.

41. *OR,* vol. 24, 1:493.

42. Ibid., 490; Bearss, *Campaign for Vicksburg,* 2:38.

43. *OR,* vol. 24, 3:140, 186, 1:493; Perry, "The Entering Wedge," 372, 369; John Ritter to Margarett, April 8, 1863, in "Civil War Letters," ed. Ritter.

44. *OR,* vol. 24, 3:744, 1:494; RG 393, pt. 2, 3221:112, NARA; Hass, "Diary of Henry Warmoth," 341.

45. Gottschalk, *In Deadly Earnest,* 198; *OR,* vol. 24, 3:730, 737, 744.

46. Grant, *Memoirs,* 151; *OR,* vol. 24, 1:47; Perry, "The Entering Wedge," 373–75; John Ritter to Margarett, April 8, 1863, in "Civil War Letters," ed. Ritter; Mason, *Forty-second Ohio,* 187.

47. Porter, *Incidents and Anecdotes,* 179; *OR,* vol. 24, 3:200, 755, 211; *ORN,* 24:704; Theophilus T. Garrard, "General Garrard's Account of His Military Service."

48. *ORN,* 24:682; Grant, *Memoirs,* 153; Webster and Cameron, *First Wisconsin Battery,* 127; *OR,* vol. 24, 1:187, 220, 601, 3:220–21.

49. *ORN,* 24:603; *OR,* vol. 24, 3:221, 228.

50. *OR,* vol. 24, 3:225–26, 228–29; RG 393, pt. 2, 3221:123, NARA; Bearss, *Campaign for Vicksburg,* 2:281; *OR,* vol. 24, 1:79–80.

51. Simon, *Papers of U. S. Grant,* 8:113–14; *OR,* vol. 24, 3:239, 1:572–73; Bearss, *Campaign for Vicksburg,* 2:292.

52. *OR,* vol. 24, 1:80–81; Ofele, *German-Speaking Officers,* 48, 100, 103, 197; Hass, "Diary of Henry Warmoth," 347.

53. *OR,* vol. 24, 3:238–39; RG 393, pt. 2, 3221:125–26, NARA; *OR,* vol. 24, 1:81–82, 572–73, 142.

54. General Order [no number] April 27, 1863, RG 393, pt. 2, E3230:37, NARA.

55. *OR,* vol. 24, 1:142, 593; Stevenson, *Letters from the Army,* 217; Shea and Winschel, *Vicksburg Is the Key,* 103.

56. *OR,* vol. 24, 1:48; Henry S. Commager, ed., *The Civil War Archive,* 470.

57. James H. Wilson, *Under the Old Flag,* 169.

58. Hewett, Trudeau, and Suderow, *Supplement to the Official Records,* 4:369; Larimer, *Love and Valor,* 165; Grant, *Memoirs,* 164.

59. *OR,* vol. 24, 1:257; Arnold, *Grant Wins the War,* 94; Ephraim M. Anderson, *Memoirs: Historical and Personal; Including the Campaigns of the First Missouri Confederate Brigade,* 282.

60. Grant, *Memoirs,* 161; *OR,* vol. 24, 1:34; Grabau, *Ninety-eight Days,* 148; Bearss, *Campaign for Vicksburg,* 2:357.

61. *OR,* vol. 24, 1:672; James M. McPherson, *Battle Cry of Freedom,* 631; *OR,* vol. 24, 1:48; John Follett to wife, May 5, 1863, Ohio State University "ehistory" Web site.

62. Bearss, *Campaign for Vicksburg,* 2:359, 407n; *OR,* vol. 24, 1:661, 664.

63. *OR,* vol. 24, 1:615; John Follett to wife, May 5, 1863, Ohio State University "ehistory" Web site.

64. *OR,* vol. 24, 1:143, 678; Hewett, Trudeau, and Suderow, *Supplement to the Official Records,* 4:368; Bearss, *Campaign for Vicksburg,* 2:406.

65. Hewett, Trudeau, and Suderow, *Supplement to the Official Records,* 4:370; Calvin D. Cowles, comp., *Atlas to Accompany the Official Records of the Union and Confederate Armies,* plate 31.6.

66. *OR,* vol. 24, 1:679.

67. Ibid., 679–80.

68. Hewett, Trudeau, and Suderow, *Supplement to the Official Records,* 4:371–73; *OR,* vol. 24, 1:591–92, 679.

69. *OR,* vol. 24, 1:591; Webster and Cameron, *First Wisconsin Battery,* 133.

70. Webster and Cameron, *First Wisconsin Battery,* 133; *OR,* vol. 24, 1:679.

71. Hewett, Trudeau, and Suderow, *Supplement to the Official Records,* 4:372–73; *OR,* vol. 24, 1:590–91.

72. Ibid.

73. Hewett, Trudeau, and Suderow, *Supplement to the Official Records,* 4:373–74; *OR,* vol. 24, 1:590, 582; A. B. Hubbell to William Rigby, March 12 and April 30, 1908, file no. 480, VNMP; Joseph Bowker journal, May 1, 1863, file no. 480, VNMP.

74. Bearss, *Campaign for Vicksburg,* 1:362–63; Mason, *Forty-second Ohio,* 195; A. B. Hubbell to William Rigby, April 30, 1908, file no. 480, VNMP; *OR,* vol. 24, 1:590.

75. Hewett, Trudeau, and Suderow, *Supplement to the Official Records,* 4:374–75; *OR,* vol. 24, 1:49, 589; Webster and Cameron, *First Wisconsin Battery,* 133–34.

76. *OR,* vol. 24, 1:679–80; William M. Kelly, "A History of the Thirtieth Alabama Volunteers (Infantry), Confederate States of America," 137; *OR,* vol. 24, 1:664, 681–82.

77. Webster and Cameron, *First Wisconsin Battery,* 135; *OR,* vol. 24, 1:635, 643, 144; Hewett, Trudeau, and Suderow, *Supplement to the Official Records,* 4:375; Ira Blanchard, *I Marched with Sherman: Civil War Memoirs of the 20th Illinois Volunteer Infantry,* 86.

78. Grant, *Memoirs,* 163; Blanchard, *I Marched with Sherman,* 86; *OR,* vol. 24, 1:681; Webster and Cameron, *First Wisconsin Battery,* 135; Joseph Bowker journal, May 1, 1863, file 480, VNMP; Hewett, Trudeau, and Suderow, *Supplement to the Official Records,* 4:375.

79. *OR,* vol. 24, 1:670, 144, 627; John Follett to wife, May 8, 1863, Ohio State University "ehistory" Web site.

80. *OR,* vol. 24, 1:681; Hewett, Trudeau, and Suderow, *Supplement to the Official Records,* 4:375–76; Stevenson, *Letters from the Army,* 221; Kelly, "Thirtieth Alabama," 135; John Ritter to Margarett, April 8, 1863, "Civil War Letters," ed. Ritter; E. L. Hawk, "Port Gibson: From Another Participant," *National Tribune,* December 4, 1884, quoted in Steven E. Woodworth, *Nothing but Victory: The Army of the Tennessee, 1861–1865,* 346.

81. *OR,* vol. 24, 1:673, 587, 662, 146.

82. Ibid., 144, 635, 49; Osterhaus, "What I Saw," 9, Osterhaus Papers; Joel T. Headley, *The Great Rebellion,* 1:162.

83. Kiper, *McClernand,* 225; Michael B. Ballard, *Vicksburg: The Campaign That Opened the Mississippi,* 231; Bearss, *Campaign for Vicksburg,* 2:366; Arnold, *Grant Wins the War,* 106; Gabel, *Staff Ride Handbook,* 39; Grant, *Memoirs,* 163.

84. Hewett, Trudeau, and Suderow, *Supplement to the Official Records,* 4:374–75; Kiper, *McClernand,* 228.

85. *OR,* vol. 24, 1:666.

86. W. Maury Darst, ed., "The Vicksburg Diary of Mrs. Alfred Ingraham," 153–54.

87. Webster and Cameron, *First Wisconsin Battery,* 138; Stevenson, *Letters from the Army,* 247; Darst, "Diary of Mrs. Ingraham," 151, 159; George P. Clark, ed., "Remenecence of My Army Life," by Louis Bir, 28; Bond, *Under the Flag,* 60; Joseph Bowker journal, May 4, 1863, file 480, VNMP; Gordon A. Cotton, ed., *From the Pen of a She-Rebel:*

The Civil War Diary of Emilie Riley McKinley, 50.

88. *OR,* vol. 24, 3:270, 1:187, 2:12.

89. Ibid., vol. 24, 3:277, 2:12; RG 393, pt. 2, 3221:127, 205, 130, NARA; Byrne and Soman, *Your True Marcus,* 277; Simon, *Papers of U. S. Grant,* 8:177.

90. Bearss, *Campaign for Vicksburg,* 2:469; *OR,* vol. 24, 3:296–97, 300, 1:50.

91. *OR,* vol. 24, 1:147; Grant, *Memoirs,* 172; *OR,* vol. 24, 3:875.

92. *OR,* vol. 24, 1:239–40, 50–51, 2:12–13.

93. Ibid., vol. 24, 3:313; Elias Moore diary, May 15, 1863, file 499, VNMP; *OR,* vol. 24, 2:13–14.

94. *OR,* vol. 24, 3:876–78, 2:75, 125.

95. Simon, *Papers of U. S. Grant,* 8:224; *OR,* vol. 24, 1:51, 3:314, 2:125–26.

96. *OR,* vol. 24, 2:91; Bearss, *Campaign for Vicksburg,* 2:583–84.

97. Timothy B. Smith, *Champion Hill: Decisive Battle for Vicksburg,* 160–61; *OR,* vol. 24, 2:126.

98. *OR,* vol. 24, 1:148–49, 3:317–18; Kiper, *McClernand,* 244–45.

99. *OR,* vol. 24, 2:13–14.

100. Ibid., 14, 134; Bearss, *Campaign for Vicksburg,* 2:587.

101. *OR,* vol. 24, 2:15, 134, 3:317.

102. Ibid., vol. 24, 2:105; Bearss, *Campaign for Vicksburg,* 2:601, 610; T. Smith, *Champion Hill,* 288–90; *OR,* vol. 24, 1:149–50; Elliott, *Thirty-third Illinois,* 40; Mason, *Forty-second Ohio,* 207.

103. *OR,* vol. 24, 2:49–50; T. Smith, *Champion Hill,* 250, 269.

104. *OR,* vol. 24, 3:318, 1:149; Bearss, *Campaign for Vicksburg,* 2:625; *OR,* vol. 24, 2:15, 25–26; T. Smith, *Champion Hill,* 452n.

105. *OR,* vol. 24, 1:265, 2:15; T. Smith, *Champion Hill,* 309–10, 318; Hewett, Trudeau, and Suderow, *Supplement to the Official Records,* 4:265; Mason, *Forty-second Ohio,* 211.

106. Osterhaus, "What I Saw," 9, Osterhaus Papers; Gabel, *Staff Ride Handbook,* 149; Bearss, *Campaign for Vicksburg,* 2:617–18; Arnold, *Grant Wins the War,* 188; Mason, *Forty-second Ohio,* 207–8.

107. Grant, *Memoirs,* 181; Gabel, *Staff Ride Handbook,* 43.

108. Anderson, *Memoirs,* 314–16; *OR,* vol. 24, 2:16; James H. Wilson, "A Staff Officer's Journal of the Vicksburg Campaign, April 30 to July 4, 1863," 108.

109. *OR,* vol. 24, 1:151–52; Webster and Cameron, *First Wisconsin Battery,* 143–44, 146; Peter J. Osterhaus affidavit, 1885, Osterhaus Pension File, RG 94, NARA.

110. *OR,* vol. 24, 1:152; William H. Bentley, *History of the 77th Illinois Volunteer Infantry,* chap. 5, http://77illinois.homestead.com/files/77il/77ch05.html; Schenk affidavit, September 9, 1886, Osterhaus Pension File, RG 94, NARA; *OR,* vol. 24, 2:136–7; Bearss, *Campaign for Vicksburg,* 2:673–74; Osterhaus, "Generals' Report," 7:418, RG 94, NARA.

111. Webster and Cameron, *First Wisconsin Battery,* 147; *OR,* vol. 24, 2:17; Grant, *Memoirs,* 184–85.

112. *OR,* vol. 24, 3:329, 2:17, 343–44, 1:153.

113. Bearss, *Campaign for Vicksburg,* 3:742; Brig. Gen. (Ret.) Parker Hills, personal communication with author; *OR,* vol. 24, 1:153.

114. *OR,* vol. 24, 2:17–18, 1:154; Mason, *Forty-second Ohio,* 219; James Keigwin to William T. Rigby, March 5, 1902, file 345, VNMP; C. E. Henry to W. P. Gault, February 13, 1903, file 480, VNMP.

115. *OR,* vol. 24, 2:18.

116. Byrne and Soman, *Your True Marcus,* 281; *OR,* vol. 24, 2:19; Bond, *Under the Flag,* 64; Grant, *Memoirs,* 185; Bearss, *Campaign for Vicksburg,* 3:774–76, 766–67.

117. *OR,* vol. 24, 2:19; John Pickering to W. P. Gault, May 9, 1903, file 499, VNMP; G. Clark, "My Army Life," 31; Bond, *Under the Flag,* 65; A. B. Hubbell to William T. Rigby, May 22, 1908, file 480, VNMP; *OR,* vol. 24, 1:55.

118. *OR,* vol. 24, 2:20; RG 393, pt. 2, 3221:135, NARA; *OR,* vol. 24, 2:240, 344; Bearss, *Campaign for Vicksburg,* 3:823.

119. *OR,* vol. 24, 2:344, 1:154; Mason, *Forty-second Ohio,* 221–22.

120. Bond, *Under the Flag,* 65; *OR,* vol. 24, 2:28; Mason, *Forty-second Ohio,* 224; John Pickering to W. P. Gault, May 9, 1903, file 499, VNMP.

121. C. R. Davisson, letter to the editor, *National Tribune,* September 10, 1914; M. M. Lacey to James Keigwin, February 27, 1902, file 345, VNMP.

122. *OR,* vol. 24, 2:20; James Keigwin to William T. Rigby, March 5, 1902, file 345, VNMP; C. E. Henry to W. P. Gault, February 13, 1903, file 480, VNMP; *OR,* vol. 24, 2:232; E. L. Hawk to W. T. Rigby, April 21, 1914, file 499, VNMP.

123. *OR,* vol. 24, 1:155; Bearss, *Campaign for Vicksburg,* 3:836–37; *OR,* vol. 24, 3:340, 2:240; Grant, *Memoirs,* 186.

124. *OR,* vol. 24, 1:776–77, 732; Kiper, *McClernand,* 263; RG 393, pt. 2, 3221:136, NARA; *OR,* vol. 24, 2:160–65.

125. Osterhaus to McClernand, May 22, 1863, RG 393, pt. 2, 3221, NARA.

126. Osterhaus, "Generals' Report," 7:418, RG 94, NARA; Byrne and Soman, *Your True Marcus,* 282; Webster and Cameron, *First Wisconsin Battery,* 172.

127. Dana, *Recollections,* 64; *OR,* vol. 24, 3:351, 362; Grant, *Memoirs,* 193.

128. *OR,* vol. 24, 2:209–10; RG 393, pt. 2, 3221:208–9, NARA; *OR,* vol. 24, 3:393–94.

129. *OR,* vol. 24, 2:210–15; Osterhaus to Lt. Col. Walter B. Scates, June 1, 1863, RG 393, pt. 2, 3221:154, NARA.

130. *OR,* vol. 24, 2:210–13, 224; Simon, *Papers of U. S. Grant,* 8:314, 336–37; *OR,* vol. 52, 1:360.

131. Hewett, Trudeau, and Suderow, *Supplement to the Official Records,* 4:290, 383; *OR,* vol. 24, 2:217–24, 226; Wagner affidavit, October 27, 1887, Osterhaus Pension File, RG 94, NARA; Simon, *Papers of U. S. Grant,* 8:566; Ofele, *German-Speaking Officers,* 101; *OR,* vol. 24, 3:962; Cowles, *Atlas,* plate 57.6.

132. Hewett, Trudeau, and Suderow, *Supplement to the Official Records,* 4:291; William B. Feis, *Grant's Secret Service: The Intelligence War from Belmont to Appomattox,* 165.

133. Jacob Snyder diary, June 7–July 3, 1863, file 345, VNMP; Bond, *Under the Flag,* 72; William C. Davis, ed., *Diary of a Confederate Soldier: John S. Jackman of the Orphan Brigade,* 77; *OR,* vol. 24, 3:379, 2:220, 223–24; Hess, "Grant's Ethnic General," 212.

134. *OR,* vol. 24, 2:223–24, 226; Simon, *Papers of U. S. Grant,* 8:371.

135. Grant, *Memoirs,* 195; Osterhaus diary, January 28 and February 3, 1864, Osterhaus Papers.

136. Stevenson, *Letters from the Army,* 247; Cotton, *Pen of a She-Rebel,* 18–19, 23, 35, 48, 50; Sallie Brock Putnam, *Richmond during the War: Four Years of Personal Observation,* 230; Gary L. Scheel, *Rain, Mud, and Swamps: 31st Missouri Volunteer Infantry Regiment,* 166.

137. *OR,* vol. 24, 2:225–26, 228, 3:428, 458, 1:244–45, 281.

138. *OR,* vol. 24, 2:228; W. Davis, *Diary of a Confederate Soldier,* 77–78; *OR,* vol. 24, 1:244–45.

139. *OR,* vol. 24, 3:474–75; Hess, "Grant's Ethnic General," 216; *OR,* vol. 24, 2:575.

140. *OR,* vol. 24, 2:580–81, 3:473–75; Bond, *Under the Flag,* 74; Webster and Cameron, *First Wisconsin Battery,* 158; Stevenson, *Letters from the Army,* 250.

141. Clifford K. Reese, letter to the editor, *New York Times,* January 16, 1898; Webster and Cameron, *First Wisconsin Battery,* 158, 156, 167.

142. *OR,* vol. 24, 2:581–82.

143. Stevenson, *Letters from the Army,* 247; Thomas Linn to father, July 28, 1863.

144. Hewett, Trudeau, and Suderow, *Supplement to the Official Records,* 4:294; *OR,* vol. 24, 3:508; Webster and Cameron, *First Wisconsin Battery,* 160–61; Bentley, *77th Illinois,* 188–89.

145. *OR,* vol. 24, 2:582–83; G. Clark, "My Army Life," 33; Bond, *Under the Flag,* 77; RG 393, pt. 2, 3221:212, NARA; Webster and Cameron, *First Wisconsin Battery,* 166.

146. *OR,* vol. 24, 3:581, 563; Grant, *Memoirs,* 214; John C. Entrekin, letter to the editor, *National Tribune,* April 2, 1903; "Speech by Gen. Osterhaus," *New York Times,* August 16, 1863; Osterhaus, "What I Saw," 10, Osterhaus Papers.

147. Wagner affidavit, October 27, 1887, Osterhaus Pension File, RG 94, NARA; *New York Times,* May 17, 1863, in *Most Fearful Ordeal: Original Coverage of the Civil War by Writers and Reporters of the "New York Times,"* 241; Thomas Linn to mother, August 9, 1863; "Rear Admiral Hugo Osterhaus," *St. Louis Daily Globe-Democrat,* November 12, 1911.

Chapter 4. The Chattanooga Campaign

1. *OR,* vol. 30, 3:97, 160, 719–20, 747; vol. 24, 1:156; Larimer, *Love and Valor,* 209.

2. Osterhaus, "Generals' Reports," 7:419–20, RG 94, NARA; *OR,* vol. 32, 3:326; Joseph T. Glatthaar, *The March to the Sea and Beyond,* 27; Stewert Bennett and Barbara Tillery, eds., *The Struggle for the Life of the Republic: A Civil War Narrative by Brevet Major Charles Dana Miller, 76th Ohio Volunteer Infantry,* 81.

3. Osterhaus, "Generals' Reports," 7:419–20, RG 94, NARA; U.S. Army Center of Military History, "Civil War Medal of Honor Recipients," Web site; Bearss, *Campaign for Vicksburg,* 3:768.

4. Osterhaus, "What I Saw," 10, Osterhaus Papers; Swing, "Osterhaus Great Man" (see chap. 1, n. 31).

5. Osterhaus, "What I Saw," 10, Osterhaus Papers; Grant, *Memoirs,* 215; *OR,* vol. 30, 1:161–62, 3:772–73, 787–88, 841; Earl J. Hess, ed., *A German in the Yankee Fatherland: The Civil War Letters of Henry A. Kircher,* 125.

6. Osterhaus, "What I Saw," 10–11, Osterhaus Papers; Osterhaus, "Generals' Reports," 7:420–22, RG 94, NARA; *OR,* vol. 31, 1:17–18.

7. *OR,* 31:19–22; Hess, *German in the Yankee Fatherland,* 134, 136; Calvin Ainsworth diary, 66.

8. *OR,* vol. 31, 1:22; Hess, *German in the Yankee Fatherland,* 137; Matilda Osterhaus Death Certificate, Osterhaus Papers.

9. Hess, *German in the Yankee Fatherland,* 137; Matilda Osterhaus Cemetery Certificate, Osterhaus Papers; "Rear Admiral Hugo Osterhaus," *St. Louis Daily Globe-Democrat,* November 12, 1911.

10. Hess, *German in the Yankee Fatherland,* 139; Osterhaus diary, February 2, 1864, Osterhaus Papers.

11. Steve Meyer, *Iowa Valor: A Compilation of Civil War Combat Experiences from Soldiers of the State Distinguished as Most Patriotic of the Patriotic,* 267; Charles A. Willison, *Reminiscences of a Boy's Service with the 76th Ohio in the Fifteenth Army Corps, under General Sherman,* 72; Ainsworth diary, 72–73; Hess, *German in the Yankee Fatherland,* 141–42; *OR,* vol. 31, 2:41, 39; H. T. Noble et al., *Military History and Reminiscences of the Thirteenth Regiment of Illinois Volunteer Infantry in the Civil War in the United States, 1861–1865,* 365.

12. Grant, *Memoirs,* 223–24, 232; Peter Cozzens, *The Shipwreck of Their Hopes: The Battles for Chattanooga,* 143; Thomas Lawrence Connelly, *Autumn of Glory,* 270–75; Grant, *Memoirs,* 232, 235–37; Sherman, *Memoirs,* 387; *OR,* vol. 31, 2:64, 31–32.

13. *OR,* vol. 31, 3:231; Osterhaus, "What I Saw," 11, Osterhaus Papers; *OR,* vol. 31, 2:106–7, 314; Walter H. Hebert, *Fighting Joe Hooker,* 166, 226, 262–63.

14. David Donald, ed., *Inside Lincoln's Cabinet: The Civil War Diaries of Salmon P. Chase,* 154; William F. Smith, "An Historical Sketch of the Military Operations around Chattanooga, Tennessee, September 22 to November 27, 1863," 174–5; *OR,* vol. 31, 2:345; Osterhaus, "What I Saw," 11, Osterhaus Papers; *OR,* vol. 31, 2:390, 143.

15. J. W. A. Wright, "The Battles of Lookout Mountain and Missionary Ridge," 146; *OR,* vol. 31, 2:718–19, 685; Cozzens, *Shipwreck of Their Hopes,* 117; *OR,* vol. 31, 2:687; John C. Moore, "Battle of Lookout Mountain," 426–27.

16. J. Moore, "Battle of Lookout Mountain," 426; *OR,* vol. 31, 2:728, 725–26, 718–19.

17. *OR,* vol. 31, 2:599.

18. Swing, "Osterhaus Great Man"; Wright, "Lookout Mountain," 145.

19. Noble et al., *Thirteenth Illinois,* 373; *OR,* vol. 31, 2:599, 693, 698; Cozzens, *Shipwreck of Their Hopes,* 163.

20. *OR,* vol. 31, 2:599, 170, 728; Arnold Gates, *The Rough Side of War: The Civil War Journal of Chesly A. Mosman,* 124; Osterhaus, "What I Saw," 12, Osterhaus Papers.

21. *OR,* vol. 31, 2:391–92; John G. Langguth, letter to the editor, *National Tribune,* August 25, 1898; E. C. Mount, letter to the editor, *National Tribune,* February 10, 1887; *OR,* vol. 31, 2:599, 693; Osterhaus, "What I Saw," 12, Osterhaus Papers; Noble et al., *Thirteenth Illinois,* 373; Kelly, "Thirtieth Alabama," 148; H. M. Woodson, "Battle on the Side of Lookout Mountain," 34; Grant, *Memoirs,* 228.

22. *OR,* vol. 31, 2:599–600, 693, 699; John G. Langguth, letter to the editor, *National Tribune,* August 25, 1898; Ainsworth diary, 73–74.

23. Gates, *Rough Side of War,* 125; *OR,* vol. 31, 2:600.

24. *OR,* vol. 31, 2:607; E. C. Walthall, "Walthall on the Battle of Lookout Mountain," 563.

25. *OR,* vol. 31, 2:613–14, 607, 600, 705; Meyer, *Iowa Valor,* 268; Cozzens, *Shipwreck of Their Hopes,* 175.

26. J. Moore, "Battle of Lookout Mountain," 428; *OR,* vol. 31, 2:720–21.

27. L. Bennett and Haigh, *Thirty-sixth Illinois,* 522; Grant, *Memoirs,* 245; Commager, *The Civil War Archive,* 687; Wright, "Lookout Mountain," 146.

28. *OR,* vol. 31, 2:316–17, 600; J. Moore, "Battle of Lookout Mountain," 428; Charles A. Partridge, ed., *History of the Ninety-sixth Regiment Illinois Volunteer Infantry,* 271; *OR,* vol. 21, 2:721.

29. Gates, *Rough Side of War,* 127; Wright, "Lookout Mountain," 146.

30. Kaufmann, *Germans in the Civil War,* 232.

31. *OR,* vol. 31, 2:44, 115, 317–18; Cozzens, *Shipwreck of Their Hopes,* 201; W. F. Smith, "Operations around Chattanooga," 210, 215; Osterhaus, "What I Saw," 12, Osterhaus Papers; Cowles, *Atlas,* plate 123, views 3 and 4; Cozzens, *Shipwreck of Their Hopes,* 195–96; A. P. Stewart report, December 14, 1863, GHS.

32. *OR,* vol. 31, 2:664–66; Cozzens, *Shipwreck of Their Hopes,* 250–51; Larry J. Daniel, *Cannoneers in Gray: The Field Artillery of the Army of Tennessee, 1861–1865,* 112; Wright, "Lookout Mountain," 147.

33. *OR,* vol. 31, 2:318, 610; R. J. Henderson report, December 12, 1863, GHS.

34. *OR,* vol. 31, 2:601, 615; Henderson report, GHS.

35. Hewett, Trudeau, and Suderow, *Supplement to the Official Records,* 6:106–7.

36. Cozzens, *Shipwreck of Their Hopes,* 314; *OR,* vol. 31, 2:601, 147; Noble et al., *Thirteenth Illinois,* 379; Ainsworth diary, 75; *OR,* vol. 31, 2:615.

37. *OR,* vol. 31, 2:318, 601–2, 665, 740; Hewett, Trudeau, and Suderow, *Supplement to the Official Records,* 6:156–57; Wright, "Lookout Mountain," 149; Abraham Jefferson Seay, *Civil War Diary as Written on the Battlefields,* 63.

38. *OR,* vol. 31, 2:602; Hewett, Trudeau, and Suderow, *Supplement to the Official Records,* 6:157–58; Willison, *76th Ohio,* 77; Gates, *Rough Side of War,* 129.

39. Wright, "Lookout Mountain," 149–50; William C. Davis, *Breckinridge: Statesman, Soldier, Symbol,* 390; Hewett, Trudeau, and Suderow, *Supplement to the Official Records,* 6:157–58; Willison, *76th Ohio,* 77; Osterhaus, "What I Saw," 13, Osterhaus Papers; *OR,* vol. 31, 2:602; Hewett, Trudeau, and Suderow, *Supplement to the Official Records,* 6:163.

40. W. F. Smith, "Operations around Chattanooga," 221, 215; J. H. Wilson, *Under the Old Flag,* 1:297–98; Hewett, Trudeau, and Suderow, *Supplement to the Official Records,* 6:120, 116–17; *OR,* vol. 31, 2:401, 147.

41. Hewett, Trudeau, and Suderow, *Supplement to the Official Records,* 6:158, 121; Benjamin F. Scribner, *How Soldiers Were Made; or, The War as I Saw It under Buell, Rosecrans, Thomas, Grant, and Sherman,* 182–83; Noble et al., *Thirteenth Illinois,* 380.

42. Hewett, Trudeau, and Suderow, *Supplement to the Official Records,* 6:109, 129; *OR,* vol. 31, 3:801; W. F. Smith, "Operations around Chattanooga," 245.

43. Scribner, *How Soldiers Were Made,* 183; Angus L. Waddle, *Three Years with the Armies of the Ohio and the Cumberland,* 62; *OR,* vol. 31, 2:341.

44. Lyftogt, *Left for Dixie,* 35.

45. Cozzens, *Shipwreck of Their Hopes,* 364–65; *OR,* 31:2, 603, 608.

46. *OR,* 31:2, 680, 754–55; Keith S. Bohannon, "Preservation Plan for the Ringgold Gap, Ga., Battlefield," 10–11.

47. *OR,* vol. 31, 2:754–55; Cozzens, *Shipwreck of Their Hopes,* 369.

48. *OR,* vol. 31, 2:754–55; Bohannon, "Ringgold Gap," 12.

49. *OR,* vol. 31, 2:754–55, 759.

50. Ibid., 603–4, 320–21; Osterhaus, "What I Saw," 13, Osterhaus Papers.

51. Larimer, *Love and Valor,* 256; *OR,* vol. 31, 2:608, 776, 755–56.

52. Noble et al., *Thirteenth Illinois,* 384; *OR,* vol. 31, 2:608, 759.

53. *OR,* vol. 31, 2:759–60, 756–57; Noble et al., *Thirteenth Illinois,* 384; Willison, *76th Ohio,* 79.

54. *OR,* vol. 31, 2:756–57, 759–60.

55. Ibid., 611, 604, 756.

56. Bohannon, "Ringgold Gap," 21, 23; *OR,* vol. 31, 2:604, 616, 611–12, 619, 756; Andrew G. Henderson, letter to family, March 29, 1864, 2–4; Ainsworth diary, 76; Charles H. Kibler, "The 76th O.V.I. at Ringgold, Georgia," 4–5.

57. *OR,* vol. 31, 2:616, 619, 769–70, 772–73, 756, 761–65; Ainsworth diary, 76.

58. Cozzens, *Shipwreck of Their Hopes,* 382–83; Osterhaus, "What I Saw," 13, Osterhaus Papers.

59. *OR,* vol. 31, 2:403–4, 438. One account has Hooker asking Geary, "Have you any regiments that will not run?" but this is from one of Geary's units so may be a bit biased. In any case, they, too, ran (George K. Collins, *Memoirs of the 149th New York Infantry,* 207).

60. *OR,* vol. 31, 2:616–17, 623.

61. Ibid., 756, 616, 623, 404, 86, 122; Ainsworth diary, 76–77.

62. *OR,* vol. 31, 2:423, 415–16, 626, 120–21, 404–5; Bohannon, "Ringgold Gap," 31–32.

63. *OR,* vol. 31, 2:757, 769; William W. Smith, "Holocaust Holiday: The Journal of a Strange Vacation to the War-Torn South and a Visit with U.S. Grant," 39.

64. Noble et al., *Thirteenth Illinois,* 388; *OR,* vol. 31, 2:454, 438, 617, 619, 621, 625.

65. Hewett, Trudeau, and Suderow, *Supplement to the Official Records,* 1:6, 62–63; Noble et al., *Thirteenth Illinois,* 387; *OR,* vol. 31, 2:83, 122, 757; W. W. Smith, "Holocaust Holiday," 39; Koerner, *Memoirs of Gustave Koerner,* 2:397; *OR,* vol. 31, 2:605; Osterhaus diary, July 16, 1864, Osterhaus Papers.

66. Scheel, *Rain, Mud, and Swamps,* 221; Larimer, *Love and Valor,* 256; Lyftogt, *Left for Dixie,* 35.

67. Grant, *Memoirs,* 255; *OR,* vol. 31, 2:70, 469; Bohannon, "Ringgold Gap," 44; Cozzens, *Shipwreck of Their Hopes,* 386.

68. William Hyde and Howard L. Conard, eds. *Encyclopedia of the History of St. Louis,* 4:218; Gates, *Rough Side of War,* 134; *OR,* vol. 31, 2:124, 3:306, 543; Willison, *76th Ohio,* 81–82; RG 393, pt. 2, 5904:123, NARA; Ainsworth diary, 80; Willison, *76th Ohio,* 81–82; Noble et al., *Thirteenth Illinois,* 405.

Chapter 5. The Atlanta Campaign and the March to the Sea

1. *OR,* vol. 31, 3:543; Osterhaus diary, January 2–8, 1864, Osterhaus Papers.

2. *OR,* vol. 31, 2:345, vol. 24, 1:156; John H. Eicher and David J. Eicher, *Civil War High Commands,* 772–75; Horowitz, "Ethnicity and Command," 183–85.

3. Osterhaus diary, January 8–12, 1864, Osterhaus Papers; Schurz to Lincoln, April 23, 1862.

4. Goss, *Union High Command,* 174–75.

5. Ibid., 127, 172, 182–83; John F. Marszalek, *Commander of All of Lincoln's Armies: A Life of Henry W. Halleck,* 21, 150.

6. Osterhaus diary, January 12–19, 1864, Osterhaus Papers; Walter B. Stevens, *Missouri, the Center State, 1821–1915,* 462; Edward C. Kirkland, *The Peacemakers of 1864,* 189.

7. Swing, "Osterhaus Great Man" (see chap. 1, n. 31); *OR,* vol. 32, 1:73; Osterhaus diary, January 17–18, 1864, Osterhaus Papers; J. G. Randall and Richard N. Current, *Lincoln the President: Last Full Measure,* 92, 98.

8. *OR,* vol. 31, 2:568.

9. Osterhaus diary, January 26–29, 1864, Osterhaus Papers; James S. Brisbin, *The Campaign Lives of Ulysses S. Grant and Schuyler Colfax,* 245–46.

10. Osterhaus diary, January 30, 1864, Osterhaus Papers.

11. Ibid., February 18, 1864; Kleber, "Osterhaus," 98.

12. J. Jones, *"Black Jack,"* xvi–xvii; Osterhaus diary, March 13, 16, April 3, 5, 19, 20, 1864, Osterhaus Papers.

13. Osterhaus diary, March 15, April 21, 26, 29, Osterhaus Papers; *OR,* vol. 38, 3: 124; Kaufmann, *Germans in the Civil War,* 249; Waddle, *Three Years with the Armies,* 66.

14. Sherman, *Memoirs,* 488–89, 496.

15. Osterhaus diary, May 8–9, 1864, Osterhaus Papers; *OR,* vol. 38, 4:85.

16. Albert Castel, *Decision in the West: The Atlanta Campaign of 1864,* 139; Osterhaus diary, May 8–12, 1964, Osterhaus Papers; Charles W. Wills, *Army Life of an Illinois Soldier,* 239–40.

17. *OR,* vol. 38, 3:176, 125, 722.

18. Ibid., 141, 125–26; Osterhaus diary, May 13, 1864, Osterhaus Papers; Castel, *Decision in the West,* 152.

19. Richard M. McMurry, *Atlanta, 1864: Last Chance for the Confederacy,* 69; Castel, *Decision in the West,* 154; Joseph E. Johnston, "Opposing Sherman's Advance to Atlanta," 589–90; *OR,* vol. 38, 3:126, 141, 92.

20. *OR,* vol. 38, 3:141–43, 177, 93, 126–27; Cowles, *Atlas,* plate 58.1.

21. *OR,* vol. 38, 3:142, 191, 377; Castel, *Decision in the West,* 167.

22. Wills, *Illinois Soldier,* 242; Philip L. Secrist, *The Battle of Resaca: Atlanta Campaign, 1864,* 43; Castel, *Decision in the West,* 181.

23. Johnston, "Opposing Sherman's Advance," 589–90; *OR,* vol. 38, 3:615, 142–43, 127; Castel, *Decision in the West,* 188, 167.

24. Osterhaus diary, May 23, 1864, Osterhaus Papers; S. Bennett and Tillery, *Struggle for the Life,* 167; Jacob D. Cox, *Sherman's Battle for Atlanta,* 60; James A. Angle,

ed., *Three Years in the Army of the Cumberland: The Letters and Diary of Major James A. Connolly,* 224.

25. Sherman, *Memoirs,* 511–12; *OR,* vol. 38, 3:616.

26. Osterhaus diary, May 25, 1864, Osterhaus Papers, *OR,* vol. 38, 2:14; Sherman, *Memoirs,* 513; Castel, *Decision in the West,* 229.

27. *OR,* vol. 38, 3:129, 153–54; Larry M. Strayer and Richard A. Baumgartner, eds., *Echoes of Battle: The Atlanta Campaign, an Illustrated Collection of Union and Confederate Narratives,* 126; Meyer, *Iowa Valor,* 307;

28. *OR,* vol. 38, 3:129–30, 154, 161.

29. Sherman, *Memoirs,* 514; *OR,* vol. 38, 3:34, 706; Castel, *Decision in the West,* 243–4.

30. Castel, *Decision in the West,* 244–46; Meyer, *Iowa Valor,* 313.

31. *OR,* vol. 38, 3:131, 155; Wills, *Illinois Soldier,* 250–51; "Served the Union Well," *Brookfield (Mo.) Gazette,* June 4, 1904, Hulston Library, Wilson's Creek National Battlefield, Missouri.

32. Donald Allendorf, *Long Road to Liberty: The Odyssey of a German Regiment in the Yankee Army,* xxii; Strayer and Baumgartner, *Echoes of Battle,* 153.

33. W. Davis, *Diary of a Confederate Soldier,* 132; *OR,* vol. 38, 3:131, 146.

34. Sherman, *Memoirs,* 514–15; Castel, *Decision in the West,* 272; Swing, "Osterhaus Great Man"; McMurry, *Atlanta, 1864,* 49–52.

35. *OR,* vol. 38, 3:131–32; Osterhaus diary, June 13, 15, 1864, Osterhaus Papers; Bek, "Diary of John Buegel," 520; S. Bennett and Tillery, *Struggle for the Life,* 167, 171; Wills, *Illinois Soldier,* 264.

36. Gottschalk, *In Deadly Earnest,* 363; Bek, "Diary of John Buegel," 521; *OR,* vol. 38, 3:132; Osterhaus, "What I Saw," 16, Osterhaus Papers.

37. *OR,* vol. 38, 3:98, 617; Osterhaus diary, June 24, 1864, Osterhaus Papers; Albert Castel, *Tom Taylor's Civil War,* 131–32.

38. Osterhaus diary, June 25–29, 1864, Osterhaus Papers; William R. Scaife, *The Campaign for Atlanta,* plate before p. 66.

39. Sherman, *Memoirs,* 530–31; *OR,* vol. 38, 4:588, 3:84–85; Osterhaus diary, June 27, 1864, Osterhaus Papers; Strayer and Baumgartner, *Echoes of Battle,* 161.

40. Osterhaus, "What I Saw," 16, Osterhaus Papers; *OR,* vol. 38, 3:84–85; Meyer, *Iowa Valor,* 315; Cox, *Sherman's Battle for Atlanta,* 126; Janet C. Ellison, ed., *On to Atlanta: The Civil War Diaries of John Hill Ferguson, Illinois Tenth Regiment of Volunteers,* 54–55; Osterhaus diary, June 27, 1864, Osterhaus Papers; *OR,* vol. 38, 1:151.

41. *OR,* vol. 38, 3:133; Wills, *Illinois Soldier,* 273; Osterhaus diary, July 7–8, 1864, Osterhaus Papers; J. Jones, *"Black Jack,"* 210; Osterhaus, "What I Saw," 17, Osterhaus Papers; S. Bennett and Tillery, *Struggle for the Life,* 177.

42. *OR,* vol. 38, 3:133, 156; Osterhaus, "Generals' Report," 8:231, RG 94, NARA; Osterhaus diary, July 3–16, 1864, Osterhaus Papers.

43. Osterhaus diary, July 12, 1864, Osterhaus Papers; Osterhaus, "What I Saw," 17–18, Osterhaus Papers.

44. John F. Marszalek, *Sherman: A Soldier's Passion for Order,* 278–79; J. Jones, *"Black Jack,"* 193, 219; Sherman, *Memoirs,* 558–60.

45. Wills, *Illinois Soldier,* 281; Justin McCarthy, "Sherman's Memoirs," 463; *OR,* vol. 38, 5:241.

46. Sherman, *Memoirs,* 568; *OR,* vol. 38, 5:247.

47. Earl J. Hess, "Alvin P. Hovey and Abraham Lincoln's 'Broken Promises': The Politics of Promotion," 38–45; Sherman, *Memoirs,* 568; *OR,* vol. 38, 5:259–60.

48. *OR,* vol. 38, 5:271.

49. Hess, "Lincoln's 'Broken Promises,'" 45; Eicher and Eicher, *Civil War High Commands,* 774; Kerry Webb, "U.S. Civil War Generals" Web site.

50. Eicher and Eicher, *Civil War High Commands,* 704, 31; Goss, *Union High Command,* 183.

51. Walter D. Kamphoefner and Wolfgang Helbich, eds., *Germans in the Civil War: The Letters They Wrote Home,* 12; Randall and Current, *Lincoln the President,* 114; Horowitz, "Ethnicity and Command," 185; Hess, "Lincoln's 'Broken Promises,'" 42–43, 47.

52. Wagner affidavit, October 27, 1887, Osterhaus Pension File, RG 94, NARA; Angle, *Army of the Cumberland,* 252; Osterhaus diary, August 25, 1864, Osterhaus Papers.

53. *OR,* vol. 38, 5:505; vol. 39, 2:440; vol. 38, 3:42; Gen. W. B. Hazen, *A Narrative of Military Service,* 280.

54. Sherman, *Memoirs,* 576–79; *OR,* vol. 38, 3:106.

55. *OR,* vol. 38, 3:107–8; Castel, *Decision in the West,* 495, 502; Gottschalk, *In Deadly Earnest,* 396.

56. *OR,* vol. 38, 3:108–9, 135; Strayer and Baumgartner, *Echoes of Battle,* 294–95; Oliver O. Howard, *Autobiography,* 2:37.

57. *OR,* vol. 38, 3:700, 109, 727.

58. Ibid., 135, 158; Strayer and Baumgartner, *Echoes of Battle,* 295.

59. *OR,* vol. 38, 3:136, 702, 762; Castel, *Decision in the West,* 502–3.

60. Sherman, *Memoirs,* 580–81, 584; *OR,* vol. 38, 1:82; Castel, *Decision in the West,* 530–33.

61. McMurry, *Atlanta, 1864,* 163; Larimer, *Love and Valor,* 367–68, 360–61; General Order No. 72, RG 393, pt. 2, 5906:73, NARA.

62. Fred T. Ledergerber affidavit, July 26, 1886, Osterhaus Pension File, RG 94, NARA; Hess, "12th Missouri," 76; Bek, "Diary of John Buegel," 528; Randall and Current, *Lincoln the President,* 240; Sherman, *Memoirs,* 620–21; *OR,* vol. 39, 2:426.

63. Osterhaus, "Generals' Reports," 8:237–41, RG 94, NARA; Parrish, *Frank Blair: Lincoln's Conservative,* 205.

64. J. Jones, *"Black Jack,"* 233; Glatthaar, *March to the Sea,* 22–26.

65. *OR,* vol. 39, 2:448–49, 554; Osterhaus, "Generals' Reports," 8:241–42, RG 94, NARA; Hazen, *Narrative of Military Service,* 313.

66. Glenn V. Longacre and John E. Hass, eds., *To Battle for God and the Right: The Civil War Letterbooks of Emerson Opdyke,* 163; Swing, "Osterhaus Great Man."

67. Anne J. Bailey, *Chessboard of War: Sherman and Hood in the Autumn Campaigns of 1864,* 19, 26; Wills, *Illinois Soldier,* 308–10; Hazen, *Narrative of Military Service,* 299; Scheel, *Rain, Mud, and Swamps,* 421–22; Larimer, *Love and Valor,* 404.

68. Bailey, *Chessboard of War,* 33–34; Osterhaus, "Generals' Reports," 8:243–45, RG 94, NARA; Osterhaus diary, October 16, 1864, Osterhaus Papers.

69. Osterhaus, "What I Saw," 19, Osterhaus Papers; Osterhaus diary, October 18, 1864, Osterhaus Papers; Scheel, *Rain, Mud, and Swamps,* 443; Wills, *Illinois Soldier,* 313–15.

70. *OR,* vol. 39, 3:418, 445; Sherman, *Memoirs,* 631–36; Osterhaus, "Generals' Reports," 8:245–47, RG 94, NARA; Osterhaus diary, October 23–28, 1864; Osterhaus Papers.

71. Osterhaus diary, November 5–8 and October 22–23, 1864, Osterhaus Papers; *OR,* 44:465; Sherman, *Memoirs,* 651–53.

72. *OR,* vol. 39, 3:702; O. Howard, *Autobiography,* 1:349, 375.

73. Osterhaus, "Generals' Reports," 8:249, RG 94, NARA; Sherman, *Memoirs,* 652, 656, 650; Osterhaus, "What I Saw," 20, Osterhaus Papers; Osterhaus diary, November 15, 1864, Osterhaus Papers.

74. Osterhaus, "What I Saw," 20, Osterhaus Papers; Osterhaus diary, November 21, 1864, Osterhaus Papers; *OR,* 44:406–7, 82.

75. Osterhaus diary, November 17–24, 1864, Osterhaus Papers; *OR,* 44:466, 565, 82; O. Howard, *Autobiography,* 2:71, 74; John N. Morton, letter to the editor, *National Tribune,* March 26, 1903.

76. Wills, *Illinois Soldier,* 322; *OR,* 44:82; Osterhaus, "Generals' Reports," 8:251, RG 94, NARA.

77. Osterhaus diary, November 21, 1864, Osterhaus Papers; Charles C. Jones Jr., *The Siege of Savannah in December, 1864,* 24–25; *OR,* 44:82–83; Sherman, *Memoirs,* 664; Osterhaus, "Generals' Reports," 8:253, RG 94, NARA.

78. Wills, *Illinois Soldier,* 322–24; Osterhaus, "Generals' Reports," 8:255, RG 94, NARA; *OR,* 44:83, 414, 53:41–42; C. Jones, *Siege of Savannah,* 27.

79. *OR,* 44:522; John N. Morton, letter to the editor, *National Tribune,* March 26, 1903.

80. *OR,* 44:68, 147; Osterhaus diary, November 25, 1864, Osterhaus Papers; O. Howard, *Autobiography,* 2:80.

81. *OR,* 44:521, 594, 605, 412; Castel, *Tom Taylor's Civil War,* 198–99, 201; Wills, *Illinois Soldier,* 326; Larimer, *Love and Valor,* 392; Meyer, *Iowa Valor,* 402; Glatthaar, *March to the Sea,* 120, 151; Anne J. Bailey, *War and Ruin: William T. Sherman and the Savannah Campaign,* xiv, 78; Osterhaus, "What I Saw," 20, Osterhaus Papers.

82. Jefferson Moses diary, December 1–5, 1864, "The Memoirs, Diary, and Life of Private Jefferson Moses, Company G, 93rd Illinois Volunteers"; *OR,* 44:84–86, 73.

83. Larimer, *Love and Valor,* 390–91; Osterhaus diary, December 9–12, 1864, Osterhaus Papers; *OR,* 44:87–88; Cowles, *Atlas,* plates 69.4, 70.1, 70.2; Glatthaar, *March to the Sea,* 167; C. Jones, *Siege of Savannah,* 79–80, 88.

84. *OR,* 44:88; Cornelius C. Platter diary, December 12, 1864; Burke Davis, *Sherman's March,* 104, 97–98.

85. Sherman, *Memoirs,* 671; O. Howard, *Autobiography,* 2:86–87; C. Jones, *Siege of Savannah,* 120; Osterhaus diary, December 13, 1864, Osterhaus Papers.

86. Osterhaus diary, December 13, 1864, Osterhaus Papers; *OR,* 44:88; Hazen, *Nar-*

rative of Military Service, 330; O. Howard, *Autobiography,* 2:87; George Ward Nichols, *The Story of the Great March,* 88.

87. Sherman, *Memoirs,* 672; Osterhaus diary, December 14, 1864, Osterhaus Papers; C. Jones, *Siege of Savannah,* 125; Hazen, *Narrative of Military Service,* 333; Sherman, *Memoirs,* 673–74.

88. *OR,* 44:767; Osterhaus, "What I Saw," 22, Osterhaus Papers.

89. Lyftogt, *Left for Dixie,* 64; *OR,* 44:783, 794–95; Osterhaus, "What I Saw," 22, Osterhaus Papers.

90. Glatthaar, *March to the Sea,* 316; Nichols, *Great March,* 46; B. Davis, *Sherman's March,* 43, 54; R. W. Burt, *War Songs, Poems, and Odes.*

Chapter 6. Mobile Bay and Reconstruction

1. *OR,* vol. 39, 3:702; Osterhaus, "What I Saw," 23, Osterhaus Papers.

2. Hazen, *Narrative of Military Service,* 335; *OR,* vol. 47, 2:25.

3. *OR,* vol. 48, 1:867; Swing, "Osterhaus Great Man" (see chap. 1, n. 31).

4. Max L. Heyman Jr., *Prudent Soldier: A Biography of Major General E. R. S. Canby,* 62–63, 180, 195–97, 208–10; *OR,* vol. 38, 4:70; vol. 39, 3:702.

5. McPherson, *Battle Cry of Freedom,* 826–28; Sean M. O'Brien, *Mobile, 1865: Last Stand of the Confederacy,* 1–2.

6. *OR,* vol. 48, 1:580; Sherman, *Memoirs,* 737, 740; Grant, *Memoirs,* 432; *OR,* vol. 49, 1:781, 593, 92, 856–57, 875, 907.

7. C. Clark, *Iron Kingdom,* 373; Jack Coggins, *Arms and Equipment of the Civil War,* 11; Gabel, *Staff Ride Handbook,* 9; *OR,* vol. 48, 1:1092.

8. Grant, *Memoirs,* 432; *OR,* vol. 48, 1:580.

9. Shelby Foote, *The Civil War: A Narrative,* 74–77.

10. O'Brien, *Mobile, 1865,* 2–3.

11. *OR,* vol. 48, 1:1111; Chester G. Hearn, *Mobile Bay and the Mobile Campaign: The Last Great Battles of the Civil War,* 148–49.

12. Hearn, *Mobile Bay,* 147; Osterhaus, "What I Saw," 23, Osterhaus Papers.

13. Christopher C. Andrews, *History of the Campaign of Mobile,* 26; *OR,* vol. 49, 1:857; G. Clark, "My Army Life," 52.

14. *OR,* vol. 49, 1:93, 2:48; Osterhaus, "What I Saw," 23, Osterhaus Papers; *ORN,* 22:65.

15. Grant, *Memoirs,* 436, 489–90.

16. *OR,* vol. 49, 1:94–95; Osterhaus, "What I Saw," 23, Osterhaus Papers; *OR,* vol. 49, 2:95, 158, 248, 251, 263.

17. See Canby to Steele and Osterhaus to Steele, *OR,* vol. 49, 2:233, 295.

18. Meyer, *Iowa Valor,* 450; Andrews, *Campaign of Mobile,* 143; Hearn, *Mobile Bay,* 186.

19. *OR,* vol. 49, 1:96; O'Brien, *Mobile, 1865,* 178–79.

20. Andrews, *Campaign of Mobile,* 191; Elias Moore to mother, April 10, 1865, on Raymond Moore, "They Were the 114th O.V.I."

21. *OR,* vol. 49, 1:98, 289; Henry C. Merriam, "The Capture of Mobile," 245–46; Andrews, *Campaign of Mobile,* 195.

22. Merriam, "The Capture of Mobile," 246; Camille Corte, "History of the 73rd USCT."

23. Andrews, *Campaign of Mobile,* 192, 221; *OR,* vol. 49, 1:289; Merriam, "The Capture of Mobile," 246–47; Gottschalk, *In Deadly Earnest,* 519.

24. *OR,* vol. 49, 1:283; Andrews, *Campaign of Mobile,* 192, 221; Hearn, *Mobile Bay,* 179, 199; Gottschalk, *In Deadly Earnest,* 521, 523–25.

25. Hearn, *Mobile Bay,* 206; Osterhaus, "Generals' Reports," 8:265, RG 94, NARA.

26. *OR,* vol. 49, 1:98–99; Andrews, *Campaign of Mobile,* 259; *OR,* vol. 49, 2:341, 371; vol. 48, 2:299.

27. *OR,* vol. 47, 3:221; vol. 48, 2:136; vol. 49, 2:558, 563.

28. Richard Taylor, "The Last Confederate Surrender," 68–69; Richard Taylor, *Destruction and Reconstruction: Personal Experiences of the Late War in the United States,* 225.

29. Taylor, *Destruction and Reconstruction,* 250.

30. *OR,* vol. 49, 2:559; vol. 48, 2:311; Taylor, *Destruction and Reconstruction,* 226; *ORN,* 22:176; Osterhaus, "What I Saw," 24, Osterhaus Papers.

31. Arndt M. Stickles, *Simon Bolivar Buckner, Borderland Knight,* 268–69; Taylor, *Destruction and Reconstruction,* 229; *OR,* vol. 48, 2:502.

32. Heyman, *Prudent Soldier,* 235; Brad R. Clampitt, "The Breakup: The Collapse of the Confederate Trans-Mississippi Army in Texas, 1865," 500, 510–12, 528; *ORN,* 27:219; Osterhaus, "What I Saw," 25, Osterhaus Papers.

33. *OR,* vol. 48, 2:608, 730.

34. Carl Schurz, "Report to Andrew Johnson, President of the United States, on the Condition of the South," 60, 75; William C. Harris, *Presidential Reconstruction in Mississippi,* 63–67, 8–9, 26, 32–33.

35. Thomas Adams Upchurch, "Speaking on Behalf of the Vagabond Rebels: The Mississippi Press on Race and Reconstruction in 1865," 351; W. Harris, *Presidential Reconstruction in Mississippi,* 30–31; Carl Schurz, "Report to Andrew Johnson, President of the United States, on the Condition of the South," 16; *OR,* vol. 48, 2:878.

36. W. Harris, *Presidential Reconstruction in Mississippi,* 69, 35–36, 38; Schurz, "Condition of the South," 18–20; *OR,* vol. 48, 2:878.

37. Eric Foner, *Reconstruction: America's Unfinished Revolution, 1863–1877,* 124–40; Schurz, "Condition of the South," 60.

38. W. Harris, *Presidential Reconstruction in Mississippi,* 61, 82; William Blair, "The Use of Military Force to Protect the Gains of Reconstruction," 391, 393–94.

39. Claude H. Nolen, *African American Southerners in Slavery, Civil War, and Reconstruction,* 146; James Wilford Garner, *Reconstruction in Mississippi,* 97; Dan T. Carter, *When the War Was Over: The Failure of Self-Reconstruction in the South, 1865–1867,* 214.

40. *OR,* vol. 48, 2:878, 792, 855, 832; William C. Davis, *Look Away! A History of the Confederate States of America,* 423; Schurz, "Condition of the South," 60–61; Blair, "Use of Military Force," 393.

41. Carter, *When the War Was Over,* 179–80; *OR,* vol. 48, 2:958, 919; Osterhaus, "What I Saw," 25, Osterhaus Papers.

42. Heather Cox Richardson, *The Death of Reconstruction: Race, Labor, and Politics in the Post–Civil War,* 20; Swing, "Osterhaus Great Man"; *OR,* vol. 48, 2:919.

43. Schurz, "Condition of the South," 60–61.

44. Garner, *Reconstruction in Mississippi,* 62, 77; Carter, *When the War Was Over,* 25.

45. Foner, *Reconstruction,* 183–84, 189; *OR,* vol. 48, 2:919.

46. Garner, *Reconstruction in Mississippi,* 97–98, 99n.

47. *OR,* vol. 48, 2:1003–4; Carter, *When the War Was Over,* 212; Schurz, "Condition of the South," 61.

48. W. Harris, *Presidential Reconstruction in Mississippi,* 46–47, 50–51.

49. Mississippi State Constitutional Convention, *Journal of the Proceedings and Debates in the Constitutional Convention of the State of Mississippi, August 1865: By Order of the Convention,* 25, 43; Garner, *Reconstruction in Mississippi,* 90; Carter, *When the War Was Over,* 84–85.

50. Garner, *Reconstruction in Mississippi,* 78, 100; Chad L. Williams, "Symbols of Freedom and Defeat," 221; W. Harris, *Presidential Reconstruction in Mississippi,* 72.

51. Schurz, "Condition of the South," 102–4, 62; Garner, *Reconstruction in Mississippi,* 101; W. Harris, *Presidential Reconstruction in Mississippi,* 73.

52. Garner, *Reconstruction in Mississippi,* 102–5; W. Harris, *Presidential Reconstruction in Mississippi,* 74–75; *OR,* vol. 48, 2:1234; J. S. McNeely, "War and Reconstruction in Mississippi, 1863–1890," 340.

53. Schurz, "Condition of the South," 78–80, 97; Carter, *When the War Was Over,* 217, 231, 219, 224; Garner, *Reconstruction in Mississippi,* 265; W. Harris, *Presidential Reconstruction in Mississippi,* 87.

54. W. Harris, *Presidential Reconstruction in Mississippi,* 83, 76; Garner, *Reconstruction in Mississippi,* 266.

55. Foner, *Reconstruction,* 119, 148–49; Garner, *Reconstruction in Mississippi,* 104; Taylor, *Destruction and Reconstruction,* 250; Schurz, "Condition of the South," 69–70.

56. Ofele, *German-Speaking Officers,* 199, 201; Garner, *Reconstruction in Mississippi,* 106, 104n; Carter, *When the War Was Over,* 198; W. Harris, *Presidential Reconstruction in Mississippi,* 67, 70–71.

57. Schurz, "Condition of the South," 8, 60, 69; Carter, *When the War Was Over,* 215–17, 192; Upchurch, "Vagabond Rebels," 356; Nolen, *African American Southerners,* 151–52; Garner, *Reconstruction in Mississippi,* 106–7; Williams, "Symbols of Freedom and Defeat," 218–19, 222.

58. Garner, *Reconstruction in Mississippi,* 107; Osterhaus, "Generals' Report," 8:267, RG 94, NARA.

59. Carter, *When the War Was Over,* 229; Blair, "Use of Military Force," 388; Swing, "Osterhaus Great Man."

60. Von Steinburg affidavit, November 26, 1886; Ledergerber affidavit, July 26, 1886, both in Osterhaus Pension File, RG 94 NARA; U.S. Congress, *Journal of the House of Representatives,* 255.

61. Emerson O. Stevens, "The National Soldiers' Home," 412; U.S. Department of Veterans Affairs, "National Home for Disabled Volunteer Soldiers."

62. *Ft. Wayne Daily Gazette,* May 19, 1866; Osterhaus to son Hugo, November 28,

1881, Osterhaus Papers; Kleber, "Osterhaus," 98; U.S. Congress, *Senate Executive Journal,* 39th Cong.; Swing, "Osterhaus Great Man."

63. "Rear Admiral Hugo Osterhaus," *St. Louis Daily Globe-Democrat,* November 12, 1911.

Epilogue

1. Kleber, "Osterhaus," 99; RG 393, pt. 2, 5904:78, NARA; "Attorney Osterhaus Dies," *Belleville (Ill.) Daily Advocate,* June 10, 1929.

2. David N. Camp, ed., *The American Year Book and National Register for 1869,* 83–87; Henry Clay Conrad, *History of the State of Delaware.*

861; Patricia Dougherty, O.P., *American Diplomats and the Franco-Prussian War,* v, 1–4, 35–37.

3. Osterhaus to son Hugo, July 28, 1877, Osterhaus Papers; Edward Young, *Labor in Europe and America: A Special Report on the Rates of Wages, the Cost of Subsistence, and the Working Classes,* 472–73, 483, 487; "Despatches from United States Consuls in Lyons, 1829–1906," T169 Roll 5, RG 59.2.2, NARA; Hugo W. Osterhaus memorandum, March 3, 1957, Osterhaus Papers.

4. Osterhaus, "Generals' Reports," 8:269–71, RG 94, NARA; Despatches from Lyon (NARA); Moritz Busch, *Bismarck: Some Secret Pages of His History,* 90, 98, 215–16, 269.

5. John Breuilly, "Revolution to Unification," 153; Wawro, *The Franco-Prussian War,* 42–43, 66, 74–75, 80, 233; U.S. Department of State, *Papers Relating to Foreign Relations of the United States, 1870,* 67–68, 111.

6. Wawro, *The Franco-Prussian War,* 283, 296–98, 301; Michael Howard, *The Franco-Prussian War,* 446–53; Elihu B. Washburne, *Recollections of a Minister to France, 1869–1877,* 34–35, 161.

7. Peter F. Krogh, foreword to *American Diplomats and the Franco-Prussian War,* vi; M. Howard, *The Franco-Prussian War,* 454; U.S. Department of State, *Foreign Relations,* 86, 106–7, 110, 145, 94, 124.

8. M. Howard, *The Franco-Prussian War,* 291, 409–11, 226, 234, 236; Osterhaus, "Despatches from Lyons," 4th quarter, 1870, NARA.

9. U.S. Department of State, *Foreign Relations,* 145; Osterhaus, "Despatches from Lyons," 4th quarter, 1870, NARA; Kaufmann, *Germans in the Civil War,* 259.

10. Osterhaus, "Despatches from Lyons," 4th quarter, 1870, NARA.

11. Osterhaus, "Generals' Reports," 8:270, RG 94, NARA; "People Met in Hotel Lobbies," *Washington Post,* January 7, 1905; Wawro, *The Franco-Prussian War,* 302–3; C. Clark, *Iron Kingdom,* 558; Ofele, *German-Speaking Officers,* 209–10; Holborn, *History of Modern Germany,* 223.

12. Wilhelm Brussel affidavit, January 21, 1888; William Hilbert affidavit, n.d.; Dr. Berg affidavit, March 6, 1888, all from Osterhaus Pension File, RG 94, NARA.

13. Osterhaus to son Hugo, July 28, 1877, Osterhaus Papers.

14. Ibid.

15. Charles L. Johnson, "American Rubber Manufacture," 502–3; Osterhaus to son Hugo, July 28, 1877, Osterhaus Papers.

16. Kleber, "Osterhaus," 101, 94; Osterhaus to son Hugo, November 28, 1881, Osterhaus Papers.

17. Osterhaus to Mary, 1880, n.d., and Osterhaus to son Hugo, November 28, 1881, Osterhaus Papers; William Keim affidavit, n.d., Osterhaus Pension File, RG 94, NARA.

18. Osterhaus to son Hugo, November 28, 1881, Osterhaus Papers; Kleber, "Osterhaus," 101.

19. Blanck and Song, "Civil War Pensions," 7, 30; Taliaferro, "Report No. 1412," and von Steinburg affidavit, November 26, 1886, Osterhaus Pension File, RG 94, NARA.

20. Kleber, "Osterhaus," 101; Taliaferro, "Report No. 1412," Osterhaus Pension File, RG 94, NARA; Emma Kamp memorandum, Osterhaus Papers.

21. Osterhaus to son Hugo, January 28, 1901, Osterhaus Papers; Kleber, "Osterhaus," 102; Isabel V. Hull, "The Military Campaign in German Southwest Africa, 1904–1907," 40, 41–43.

22. Hull, "Campaign in South-West Africa," 42–43; Trutz von Trotha, "'The Fellows Can Just Starve': On Wars of 'Pacification' in the African Colonies of Imperial Germany and the Concept of 'Total War,'" 429–30; Sabine Dabringhaus, "An Army on Vacation? The German War in China, 1900–1901," 463–65.

23. Elizabeth Osterhaus Bobbitt, personal communication with author.

24. "Fleet Ceremonies Will Begin Today," *New York Times,* October 12, 1912; "American Naval Commanders in the War," 21; J. Walter McSpadden, ed., *The American Statesman's Yearbook from Official Reports of the United States Government,* 870.

25. Swing, "Osterhaus Great Man" (see chap. 1, n. 31); *National Tribune,* "Maj. Gen. Osterhaus," May 5, 1904.

26. *U.S. Intelligencer,* Reception Program, April 29, 1904, MHS; "Maj. Gen. Osterhaus," *National Tribune,* May 5, 1904.

27. Swing, "Osterhaus Great Man"; Kleber, "Osterhaus," 102; *New York Times,* June 23, 1904; *Stevens Point (Wis.) Journal,* October 15, 1904; Paul Michael Lutzeler, "The St. Louis World's Fair of 1904 as a Site of Cultural Transfer: German and German-American Participation," 50, 75.

28. Jeremiah E. Goulka, ed., *The Grand Old Man of Maine: Selected Letters of Joshua Lawrence Chamberlain, 1865–1914,* xxiv, 213.

29. *Washington Post,* December 14, 1904, January 27, February 24, and March 25, 1905; Swing, "Osterhaus Great Man"; Osterhaus to son Hugo, April 9, 1915, Osterhaus Papers; *Washington Post,* March 9, 1916.

30. Osterhaus to son Hugo, October 22, 1906, Osterhaus Papers.

31. *Oakland Tribune,* March 25, 1905; *Belleville (Ill.) Daily Advocate,* May 14, 1906, MHS; "Osterhaus to Visit Abroad," *Washington Post,* November 19, 1911; "Heroes of '61 Coming," *Washington Post,* July 11, 1915; "New York Passenger Lists, 1820–1957"; Osterhaus to son Hugo, August 4, 1915, Osterhaus Papers.

32. Carl W. Ackerman, "Gen. Osterhaus of Civil War Fame Is Detained in Germany"; Susannah U. Bruce, "Liberty Is without Nationality: Major General Peter Joseph Osterhaus and the Civil War," 114.

33. M. Howard, *The Franco-Prussian War,* 456; Osterhaus to son Hugo, April 9 and August 4, 1915, Osterhaus Papers.

34. Osterhaus to son Hugo, February 25, March 4, and December 1915, Osterhaus Papers.

35. Osterhaus to Hugo, February 25, 1915, Osterhaus Papers.

36. Ackerman, "Gen. Osterhaus."

37. Major Charles W. Snyder to Hugo Osterhaus, January 5, 1917, Osterhaus Papers.

Bibliography

Ackerman, Carl W. "Gen. Osterhaus of Civil War Fame Is Detained in Germany." Newspaper clipping, source unknown, December 8, 1916. Osterhaus Papers, Missouri Historical Society.

Ainsworth, Calvin. Diary. Photocopy of typescript. Bentley Historical Library, University of Michigan, Ann Arbor.

Akridge, Scott H., and Emmett E. Powers. *A Severe and Bloody Fight: The Battle of Whitney's Lane.* Searcy, Ark.: White County Historical Museum, 1996.

Allendorf, Donald. *Long Road to Liberty: The Odyssey of a German Regiment in the Yankee Army.* Kent: Kent State University Press, 2006.

"American Naval Commanders in the War." *Sea Power,* January 1918.

Anderson, Ephraim M. *Memoirs: Historical and Personal; Including the Campaigns of the First Missouri Confederate Brigade.* 2nd ed. St. Louis, 1868. Reprinted with notes and foreword by Edwin C. Bearss. Dayton: Morningside Bookshop, 1972.

Andrews, Christopher C. *History of the Campaign of Mobile.* New York, 1889. Available at http://books.google.com/books?id=lOSHxLOy-8QC&dq andrews+christopher.

Angle, James A., ed. *Three Years in the Army of the Cumberland: The Letters and Diary of Major James A. Connolly.* Bloomington: Indiana University Press, 1959.

Argo manifest. November 6, 1849. M237, Roll 85. National Archives and Records Administration, Washington, D.C.

Arnold, James R. *Grant Wins the War: Decision at Vicksburg.* New York: Wiley, 1997.

Bailey, Anne J. *Chessboard of War: Sherman and Hood in the Autumn Campaigns of 1864.* Great Campaigns of the Civil War Series. Lincoln: University of Nebraska Press, 2000.

———. *War and Ruin: William T. Sherman and the Savannah Campaign.* American Crisis Series 10. Wilmington, Del.: Scholarly Resources, 2003.

Ballard, Michael B. *Vicksburg: The Campaign That Opened the Mississippi.* Chapel Hill: University of North Carolina Press, 2004.

Bearss, Edwin C. *The Battle of Wilson's Creek.* St. Louis: George Washington Carver Birthplace District Association, 1975.

——. *Campaign for Vicksburg.* Vols. 1–3. Dayton: Morningside Bookshop, 1986.

——. "The White River Expedition, June 10–July 15, 1862." *Arkansas Historical Quarterly* 21 (1962): 305–62.

Bek, William G., trans. "The Civil War Diary of John T. Buegel, Union Soldier." Pts. 1 and 2. *Missouri Historical Review* 7, no. 40 (April 1946): 307–29; (July 1946): 503–30.

Bennett, Lyman G., and William M. Haigh. *History of the Thirty-sixth Regiment Illinois Volunteers During the War of the Rebellion.* Aurora, Illinois, 1876. Reprint, Marengo, Ill.: Prairie State Press, 1997. Page references are to reprint.

Bennett, Stewart, and Barbara Tillery, eds. *The Struggle for the Life of the Republic: A Civil War Narrative by Brevet Major Charles Dana Miller, 76th Ohio Volunteer Infantry.* Kent: Kent State University Press, 2004.

Benson, Wallace P. Diary. Pea Ridge National Military Park archives, Missouri.

Bentley, William H. *History of the 77th Illinois Volunteer Infantry.* Peoria, 1883.

Blair, William. "The Use of Military Force to Protect the Gains of Reconstruction." *Civil War History* 51, no. 4 (2005): 388–402.

Blanchard, Ira. *I Marched with Sherman: Civil War Memoirs of the 20th Illinois Volunteer Infantry.* San Francisco: J. D. Huff, 1992.

Blanck, Peter, and Chen Song. "'With Malice toward None; with Charity Toward All': Civil War Pensions for Native and Foreign-Born Union Army Veterans." *Transnational Law and Contemporary Problems* 11 (Spring 2001): 1–75.

Blastenbrei, Peter. "Mannheim in der Revolution 1848/49." In *Vorwarts! Ist Der Ruf Der Zeit,* ed. Thomas Hagen and Hans-Joachim Hirsch. Mannheim: Verlagsburo v. Brandt, 1997.

Blum, Virgil C. "The Political and Military Activities of the German Element in St. Louis, 1859–1861." *Missouri Historical Review* 42 (January 1948): 103–27.

Boernstein, Heinrich. *Memoirs of a Nobody: The Missouri Years of an Austrian Radical, 1849–1866.* Trans. Steven Rowan. St. Louis: Missouri Historical Society Press, 1997.

Bohannon, Keith S. "Preservation Plan for the Ringgold Gap, Ga., Battlefield." Prepared for the American Battlefield Protection Program and the Catoosa County, Ga. Historical Society, October 1997. Held at Chickamauga and Chattanooga National Military Park, Georgia.

Bond, Otto F., ed. *Under the Flag of the Nation: Diaries and Letters of a Yankee Volunteer in the Civil War.* Columbus: Ohio State University Press, 1961.

Brancaforte, Charlotte L., ed. *The German Forty-Eighters in the United States.* New York: Peter Lang, 1989.

Branson, William W. Diary. Western Historical Manuscript Collection, University of Missouri, Columbia.

Breuilly, John. "Revolution to Unification." In *Nineteenth Century Germany: Politics, Culture, and Society, 1780–1918.* Ed. John Breuilly. New York: Oxford University Press, 2001.

Brisbin, James S. *The Campaign Lives of Ulysses S. Grant and Schuyler Colfax.* Chicago, 1868. Available at the University of Michigan's "Making of America" Web site, http://quod.lib.umich.edu/m/moagrp/.

Brooksher, William R. *Bloody Hill: The Civil War Battle of Wilson's Creek.* Washington, D.C.: Brassey's, 1995.

Bruce, Susannah U. "Liberty Is without Nationality: Major General Peter Joseph Osterhaus and the Civil War." Master's thesis, Kansas State University, 1997.

Burns, William S. *Recollections of the 4th Missouri Cavalry.* Ed. Frank Allen Dennis. Dayton: Morningside, 1988.

Burt, R. W. *War Songs, Poems, and Odes.* Peoria, Ill.: J. W. Franks, 1909.

Burton, William L. *Melting Pot Soldiers: The Union's Ethnic Regiments.* New York: Fordham University Press, 1998.

Busch, Moritz. *Bismarck: Some Secret Pages of His History.* Vol. 1. New York, 1898. Transcript available at http://www.questia.com/read/9977273. Page references are to the Web transcript.

Bussey, Cyrus. "Civil War Reminiscences." Special Collections, MS 606. Iowa State University Library, Ames.

Byrne, Frank L., and Jean P. Soman, eds. *Your True Marcus: The Civil War Letters of a Jewish Colonel.* Kent: Kent State University Press, 1985.

Camp, David N., ed. *The American Year Book and National Register for 1869.* Vol. 1. Hartford, 1869.

Carter, Dan T. *When the War Was Over: The Failure of Self-Reconstruction in the South, 1865–1867.* Baton Rouge: Louisiana State University Press, 1985.

Castel, Albert. *Decision in the West: The Atlanta Campaign of 1864.* Lawrence: University Press of Kansas, 1992.

——. *Tom Taylor's Civil War.* Lawrence: University Press of Kansas, 2000.

Clampitt, Brad R. "The Breakup: The Collapse of the Confederate Trans-Mississippi Army in Texas, 1865." *Southwestern Historical Quarterly* 108, no. 4 (April 2005): 499–534.

Clark, Christopher. *Iron Kingdom: The Rise and Downfall of Prussia, 1600–1947.* Cambridge: Belknap, 2006.

Clark, George P., ed. "Remenecence of My Army Life," by Louis Bir. *Indiana Magazine of History* 101, no. 1 (March 2005): 27–56.

Coatsworth, Stella S. *The Loyal People of the North-west: A Record of Prominent Persons, Places, and Events during Eight Years of Unparalleled American History.* Chicago, 1869. On the University of Michigan's "Making of America" Web site, http://www.hti.umich.edu/cgi/t/text/.

Coggins, Jack. *Arms and Equipment of the Civil War.* New York: Dover Publishing, 2004.

Collins, George K. *Memoirs of the 149th New York Infantry.* Syracuse, 1891. Copy at Chickamauga and Chattanooga National Military Park, Georgia.

Colton, Kenneth E., ed. "Frontier War Problems: Letters of Samuel Ryan Curtis." *Annals of Iowa,* 3rd ser., 24 (April 1943): 298–315.

Commager, Henry S., ed. *The Civil War Archive.* New York: Black Dog and Leventhal, 2000.

Connelly, Thomas Lawrence. *Autumn of Glory.* Baton Rouge: Louisiana State University Press, 1971.

Conrad, Henry Clay. *History of the State of Delaware.* Vol. 3. Lancaster, Pa.: Wickersham, 1908. Available at http://books.google.com/books?id=XKsGZAtHlDIC&printsec=frontcover&dq=conrad+delaware.

Corte, Camille. "History of the 73rd USCT." Available at http://www.siteone.com/tourist/blakeley/73rdUSCT.htm.

Cotton, Gordon A., ed. *From the Pen of a She-Rebel: The Civil War Diary of Emilie Riley McKinley.* Columbia: University of South Carolina Press, 2001.

Covington, James W. "The Camp Jackson Affair: 1861." *Missouri Historical Review* 55 (April 1961): 197–212.

Cowles, Calvin D., comp. *Atlas to Accompany the Official Records of the Union and Confederate Armies.* Washington, D.C.: Government Printing Office, 1891–1895. Reissued as *The Official Military Atlas of the Civil War.* New York: Barnes and Noble, 2003. References are to the later edition.

Cox, Jacob D. *Sherman's Battle for Atlanta.* Republication of Cox's *Atlanta,* published in 1882, with a new introduction by Brooks D. Simpson. New York: Da Capo, 1994. References are to the new edition.

Cozzens, Peter. *The Shipwreck of Their Hopes: The Battles for Chattanooga.* Urbana: University of Illinois Press, 1994.

Craig, Gordon A. *The Politics of the Prussian Army, 1640–1945.* London: Oxford University Press, 1955.

Curtis, Samuel P. "The Army of the South-West and the First Campaign in Arkansas." Pts. 1–4. *Annals of Iowa* 4, no. 3 (July 1866): 673–89; 6, no. 3 (July 1868): 141–60; 7, no. 2 (April 1869): 118–32; 7, no. 3 (July 1869): 209–25.

Cutler, William G., ed. *History of the State of Kansas.* Chicago, 1883. Reprint, Atchison: Atchison County Historical Society, Kansas, in cooperation with the Kansas State Historical Society, Topeka, 1976. Available at http://www.kancoll.org/books/cutler/. Page references are to the Web site.

Dabringhaus, Sabine. "An Army on Vacation? The German War in China, 1900–1901." In *Anticipating Total War: The German and American Experiences, 1871–1914,* ed. Manfred F. Boemeke, Roger Chickering, and Stig Forster, 459–76. Washington, D.C.: German Historical Institute, 1999.

Dahlinger, Charles T. *The German Revolution of 1849.* New York: Putnam, 1903.

Dana, Charles A. *Recollections of the Civil War.* New York, 1898.

Daniel, Larry J. *Cannoneers in Gray: The Field Artillery of the Army of Tennessee, 1861–1865.* Tuscaloosa: University of Alabama Press, 1984.

Darst, W. Maury, ed. "The Vicksburg Diary of Mrs. Alfred Ingraham." *Journal of Mississippi History* 44 (May 1982): 148–79.

Davis, Burke. *Sherman's March.* New York: Vintage Books, 1980.

Davis, William C. *Breckinridge: Statesman, Soldier, Symbol.* Baton Rouge: Louisiana State University Press, 1974.

———. *Look Away! A History of the Confederate States of America.* New York: Simon and Schuster, 2003.

———, ed. *Diary of a Confederate Soldier: John S. Jackman of the Orphan Brigade.* Columbia: University of South Carolina Press, 1990.

Dodge, Grenville M. *The Battle of Atlanta and Other Campaigns, Addresses, etc.* 2nd ed. Denver: Sage Books, 1982.

Donald, David, ed. *Inside Lincoln's Cabinet: The Civil War Diaries of Salmon P. Chase.* New York: Longmans, Green, 1954.

Dougherty, Patricia, O.P. *American Diplomats and the Franco-Prussian War.* Washington, D.C.: Georgetown University, 1980.

Dyer, Robert. *Boonville: An Illustrated History.* Boonville, Mo.: Pekitanoui Publications, 1987.

Eicher, John H., and David J. Eicher. *Civil War High Commands.* Stanford: Stanford University Press, 2001.

Elliott, Isaac H. *History of the Thirty-third Regiment Illinois Veteran Volunteer Infantry in the Civil War, 22nd August, 1861, to 7th December, 1865.* Gibson City, Ill.: Thirty-third Regimental Association, 1902.

Ellison, Janet C., ed. *On to Atlanta: The Civil War Diaries of John Hill Ferguson, Illinois Tenth Regiment of Volunteers.* Lincoln: University of Nebraska Press, 2001.

Engle, Stephen D. *Yankee Dutchman: The Life of Franz Sigel.* Baton Rouge: Louisiana State University Press, 1999.

Everett, Frank E. *Brierfield: Plantation Home of Jefferson Davis.* Hattiesburg: University and College Press of Mississippi, 1971.

Farlow, Joyce, and Louise Barry, eds. "Vincent B. Osborne's Civil War Experiences." *Kansas Historical Quarterly* 20 (May 1952): 108–33.

Feis, William B. *Grant's Secret Service: The Intelligence War from Belmont to Appomattox.* Lincoln: University of Nebraska Press, 2002.

Fellman, Michael. *Inside War: The Guerilla Conflict in Missouri during the American Civil War.* New York: Oxford University Press, 1989.

Ferri Pisani, Camille. *Prince Napoleon in America, 1861: Letters from His Aide-de-Camp.* Trans. Georges J. Joyaux. Bloomington: Indiana University Press, 1959.

Foner, Eric. *Reconstruction: America's Unfinished Revolution, 1863–1877.* New York: Harper, Row, 1988.

Foote, Shelby. *The Civil War: A Narrative.* Vol. 3, *Red River to Appomattox.* New York: Random House, 1974.

Frémont, John C. "In Command in Missouri." In *Battles and Leaders of the Civil War,* ed. Robert U. Johnson and C. C. Buel, 1:278–88. New York, 1887.

Gabel, Christopher R. *Staff Ride Handbook for the Vicksburg Campaign, December 1862–July 1863.* Fort Leavenworth: Combat Studies Institute, 2001.

Garner, James Wilford. *Reconstruction in Mississippi.* New York: Macmillan, 1901. Available at http://books.google.com/books?id=kpnodaJMJlsC&pg=PR3&dq=%22thomas+j+wood%22+mississippi#PPR3,M1.

Garrard, Theophilus T. "General Garrard's Account of His Military Service." Available at http://www.geocities.com/Pentagon/Base/1408/account.html.

Gates, Arnold. *The Rough Side of War: The Civil War Journal of Chesly A. Mosman.* New York: Basin, 1987.

Gerteis, Louis S. *Civil War St. Louis.* Lawrence: University Press of Kansas, 2001.

Glatthaar, Joseph T. *The March to the Sea and Beyond.* New York: New York University Press, 1985.

Goss, Thomas J. *The War within the Union High Command: Politics and Generalship during the Civil War.* Lawrence: University Press of Kansas, 2003.

Gottschalk, Phil. *In Deadly Earnest: The History of the First Missouri Brigade, CSA.* Columbia: Missouri River, 1991.

Goulka, Jeremiah E., ed. *The Grand Old Man of Maine: Selected Letters of Joshua Lawrence Chamberlain, 1865–1914.* Chapel Hill: University of North Carolina Press, 2004.

Grabau, Warren E. *Ninety-eight Days: A Geographer's View of the Vicksburg Campaign.* Knoxville: University of Tennessee Press, 2000.

Grant, U. S. *The Civil War Memoirs of Ulysses S. Grant.* Abridged single-volume edition covering war years only. Edited by Brian M. Thomsen. New York: Tom Doherty Associates, 1999.

Greene, Albert R. "On the Battle of Wilson's Creek." In vol. 5 of *Transactions of the Kansas State Historical Society 1889–96.* Topeka, 1896.

Harris, James F. "The Arrival of the Europamude: Germans in America after 1848." In *The German Forty-Eighters in the United States,* ed. Charlotte L. Brancaforte, 1–18. New York: Peter Lang, 1989.

Harris, William C. *Presidential Reconstruction in Mississippi.* Baton Rouge: Louisiana State University Press, 1967.

Hass, Paul H., ed. "The Vicksburg Diary of Henry Clay Warmoth." Pts. 1 and 2. *Journal of Mississippi History* 31, no. 4 (November 1969): 334–47; 32 (1970): 60–74.

Hazen, Gen. W. B. *A Narrative of Military Service.* Boston, 1885.

Hazzard, George. *Hazzard's History of Henry County, Indiana.* New Castle, Ind.: G. Hazzard, 1906. Available at http://books.google.com/books?id=uySoLuDJxxsC&printsec=frontcover&source=gbs_v2_summary_r&cad=0#v=onepage&q=&f=false.

Headley, Joel T. *The Great Rebellion.* Vol. 1. Hartford, 1863. On the University of Michigan's "Making of America" Web site, http://quod.lib.umich.edu/cgi/t/text/pageviewer-idx?c=moa;cc=moa;g=moagrp;xc=1;q1=headley;rgn=full%20text;idno=AAW9632.0002.001;didno=AAW9632.0002.001;view=image;seq=00000005.

Hearn, Chester G. *Mobile Bay and the Mobile Campaign: The Last Great Battles of the Civil War.* Jefferson, N.C.: McFarland, 1993.

Hebert, Walter H. *Fighting Joe Hooker.* New York: Bobbs-Merrill, 1944.

Henderson, Andrew G. Letter to family, March 29, 1864. Typescript copy, 31st Iowa file, Chickamauga and Chattanooga National Military Park, Georgia. Original in Henderson Papers, Iowa State Historical Society, Des Moines.

Hess, Earl J. "Alvin P. Hovey and Abraham Lincoln's 'Broken Promises': The Politics of Promotion." *Indiana Magazine of History* 80, no. 1 (March 1984): 35–49.

———. "Osterhaus in Missouri: A Study of German-American Loyalty." *Missouri Historical Review* 78, no. 2 (January 1984): 144–65.

———. "Peter J. Osterhaus, Grant's Ethnic General." In *Grant's Lieutenants from Cairo to Vicksburg,* ed. Steven E. Woodworth, 199–216. Lawrence: University Press of Kansas, 2001.

———. "The 12th Missouri Infantry: A Socio-Military Profile of a Union Regiment." *Missouri Historical Review* 6 (October 1981): 53–77.

———, ed. *A German in the Yankee Fatherland: The Civil War Letters of Henry A. Kircher.* Kent: Kent State University Press, 1983.

Hewett, Janet B., Noah Andre Trudeau, and Bryce A. Suderow, eds. *Supplement to the Official Records of the Union and Confederate Armies.* Part 1, *Reports.* Vol. 4, no. 4; vol. 6, no. 6. Wilmington, Del.: Broadfoot, 1995.

Heyman, Max L., Jr. *Prudent Soldier: A Biography of Major General E. R. S. Canby.* Glendale, Calif.: Arthur H. Clark, 1959.

Holborn, Hajo. *A History of Modern Germany, 1840–1945.* New York: Alfred A. Knopf, 1969.

Holcombe, Return I., and [unknown] Adams. *An Account of the Battle of Wilson's Creek, or Oak Hills.* Springfield, Mo., 1883.

Horowitz, Murray. "Ethnicity and Command: The Civil War Experience." *Military Affairs* 42 (December 1978): 182–89.

Howard, Michael. *The Franco-Prussian War.* London: Routledge, 2001.

Howard, Oliver O. *Autobiography.* 2 vols. New York: Baker and Taylor, 1907.

Hull, Isabel V. "The Military Campaign in German Southwest Africa, 1904–1907." *German Historical Institute Bulletin,* no. 37 (Fall 2005): 39–44. Available at http://www.ghi-dc.org/publications/ghipubs/bu/037/6hull.pdf.

Hyde, William, and Howard L. Conard, eds. *Encyclopedia of the History of St. Louis.* 4 vols. New York, 1899.

"In the Ranks under General Lyon in Missouri, 1861: The Observations of a Private Soldier." Pts. 1–4. *Blue and Gray Magazine* 4 (September 1894): 142–47; 5 (February 1895): 66–70; 5: 141–47; 5: 199–203.

Johnson, Charles L. "American Rubber Manufacture." In *1795–1895: One Hundred Years of American Commerce,* ed. Charles M. Depew, 2:498–504. New York, 1895. Available at http://books.google.com/books?id=z8gJAAAAIAAJ&pg=PA500&dq=johnson+rubber+hundred#PPP12,M1.

Johnston, Joseph E. "Opposing Sherman's Advance to Atlanta." *Century* 34, no. 4 (August 1887): 585–97. Available at Cornell University's "Making of America" Web site, http://cdl.library.cornell.edu/moa/moa_browse.html.

Jones, Charles C., Jr. *The Siege of Savannah in December, 1864.* Albany, 1874. Available at http://docsouth.unc.edu/fpn/jonescharles/jones.html.

Jones, James Pickett. *"Black Jack": John A. Logan and Southern Illinois in the Civil War Era.* Carbondale: Southern Illinois University Press, 1967.

Kamphoefner, Walter D., and Wolfgang Helbich, eds. *Germans in the Civil War: The Letters They Wrote Home.* Chapel Hill: University of North Carolina Press, 2006.

Kargau, Ernst D. *St. Louis in Former Years: A Commemorative History of the German Element.* St. Louis, 1893. Reissued as *The German Element in St. Louis,* ed. Don Heinrich Tolzmann and trans. William G. Bek. Baltimore: Clearfield, 2000.

Katcher, Philip, with Richard Hook, illus. *American Civil War Commanders (3): Union Leaders in the West.* Elite Series 89. Oxford: Osprey, 2003.

Kaufmann, Wilhelm. *The Germans in the American Civil War.* Trans. Steven Rowan. Ed. Don Heinrich Tolzmann, with Werner E. Mueller and Robert E. Ward. Carlisle, Pa.: John Kallmann, 1999.

Kelly, William M. "A History of the Thirtieth Alabama Volunteers (Infantry), Confederate States of America." *Alabama Historical Quarterly* 9, no. 1 (Spring 1947): 115–67.

Kennedy, R. V., ed. *St. Louis Directory for 1860.* St. Louis, 1860.

Kibler, Charles H. "The 76th O.V.I. at Ringgold, Georgia." N.p., n.d. Photocopy of book excerpt or pamphlet at Chickamauga and Chattanooga National Military Park, Georgia.

Kiper, Richard L. *Major General John Alexander McClernand, Politician in Uniform.* Kent: Kent State University Press, 1999.

Kirkland, Edward C. *The Peacemakers of 1864.* New York: Macmillan, 1927.

Kirschten, Ernest. *Catfish and Crystal.* Garden City, N.Y.: Doubleday, 1960.

Kleber, Hans-Peter. "Peter Joseph Osterhaus, Ein Deutsch-Amerikanisches Leben." *Koblenzer Beitraege zur Geschichte und Kulter,* n.s., 2 (1992): 87–109. Unofficial translation by Axel Steuerwald.

Knapp, George E. *The Wilson's Creek Staff Ride and Battlefield Tour.* Fort Leavenworth: U.S. Army Combat Studies Institute, 1993.

Koerner, Gustave. *Memoirs of Gustave Koerner, 1809–1896.* 2 vols. Cedar Rapids, Iowa: Torch Press, 1909.

Krause, Bonnie J. "German Americans in the St. Louis Region, 1840–1860." *Missouri Historical Review* 83, no. 3 (April 1989): 295–310.

Krogh, Peter F. Foreword to *American Diplomats and the Franco-Prussian War,* by Sister Patricia Dougherty, O.P. Washington, D.C.: Georgetown University, 1980.

Lademann, Otto C. "The Battle of Wilson's Creek, August 10, 1861." In *War Papers Read before the Commandery of the State of Wisconsin, MOLLUS,* 4:435–39. Milwaukee: Burdick and Allen, 1914.

——. "The Capture of 'Camp Jackson,' St. Louis." In vol. 4 of *War Papers Read before the Commandery of the State of Wisconsin, MOLLUS.* Transcribed by Douglas R. Niermeyer. Available at http://suvcw.org/mollus/warpapers/Wiv4p069.htm.

Larimer, Charles F., ed. *Love and Valor: The Intimate Civil War Letters between Captain Jacob and Emeline Ritner.* Western Spring, Ill.: Sigourney, 2000.

Lee, Loyd E. "Baden." In *Encyclopedia of 1848 Revolutions,* ed. James Chastain. Athens: Ohio University, 1997. Available at http://www.ohiou.edu/~chastain/ip/military.htm.

——. "Military Reform." In *Encyclopedia of 1848 Revolutions,* ed. James Chastain. Athens: Ohio University, 1997. Available at http://www.ohiou.edu/~chastain/ip/military.htm.

——. "Popular Militias." In *Encyclopedia of 1848 Revolutions,* ed. James Chastain. Athens: Ohio University, 1997. Available at http://www.ohiou.edu/~chastain/ip/military.htm.

Linn, Thomas. "Diary and Letters of Thomas Buchanan Linn, Drummer, 16th OVI August, 1863 through January, 1864." Transcribed by Mary Bavender. http://www.mkwe.com/ohio/pages/Linn-00.htm.

Livermore, Mary A. *My Story of the War.* New York: Arno Press, 1972.

Lobdell, Jared C. "The Civil War Journal and Letters of Colonel John Van Deusen du Bois, April 2, 1861, to October 16, 1862." Pt. 2. *Missouri Historical Review* 61 (October 1966): 21–50.

Longacre, Glenn V., and John E. Hass, eds. *To Battle for God and the Right:*

The Civil War Letterbooks of Emerson Opdyke. Urbana: University of Illinois Press, 2003.

Lonn, Ella. *Foreigners in the Union Army and Navy.* New York: Columbia University Press, 1969.

Lutzeler, Paul Michael. "The St. Louis World's Fair of 1904 as a Site of Cultural Transfer: German and German-American Participation." In *German Culture in Nineteenth-Century America,* ed. Lynne Tatlock and Matt Erlin, 60–79. Rochester, N.Y.: Camden House, 2005.

Lyftogt, Kenneth, ed. *Left for Dixie: The Civil War Diary of John Rath.* Parkersburg, Iowa: Mid-Prairie Books, 1991.

Mannhardt, Emil. "General Peter Joseph Osterhaus." Unknown translator. *Deutch-Amerikanische Geshcichtblatte* 4 (July 1904): 54–62.

Marshall, R. V. *An Historical Sketch of the Twenty-second Regiment Indiana Volunteers.* Madison, Ind., 1877.

Marszalek, John F. *Commander of All of Lincoln's Armies: A Life of Henry W. Halleck.* Cambridge, Mass.: Belknap, 2004.

——. *Sherman: A Soldier's Passion for Order.* New York: Macmillan, 1993.

Mason, F. H. *The Forty-second Ohio Infantry: A History.* Cleveland, 1876.

McCarthy, Justin. "Sherman's Memoirs." *Galaxy* 20, no. 4 (October 1875): 450–86. Available at Cornell University's "Making of America" Web site, http://cdl.library.cornell.edu/moa/moa_browse.html.

McMurry, Richard M. *Atlanta, 1864: Last Chance for the Confederacy.* Lincoln: University of Nebraska Press, 2000.

McNeely, J. S. "War and Reconstruction in Mississippi, 1863–1890." In *Publications of the Mississippi Historical Society.* Centenary Series 2. Jackson: Mississippi Historical Society, 1918. Available at http://books.google.com/books?id=4nQOAAAAIAAJ&pg=PA1&dq=osterhaus+mississippi+reconstruction#PPP7,M1.

McPherson, James M. *Battle Cry of Freedom.* New York: Oxford University Press, 1988.

——. *This Mighty Scourge: Perspectives on the Civil War.* Oxford: Oxford University Press, 2007.

McSpadden, J. Walker, ed. *The American Statesman's Yearbook from Official Reports of the United States Government.* New York: McBride Nast, 1912. Available at http://books.google.com/books?id=JUoBAAAAYAAJ&printsec=frontcover&dq=mcspadden+yearbook.

Merriam, Henry C. "The Capture of Mobile." In *War Papers Read before the Commandery of the State of Maine, MOLLUS,* 3:230–50. Wilmington, Del.: Broadfoot, 1992.

Meyer, Steve. *Iowa Valor: A Compilation of Civil War Combat Experiences from Soldiers of the State Distinguished as Most Patriotic of the Patriotic.* Garrison, Iowa: Meyer Publishing, 1994.

"Military Record of A. H. Clark." http://www.kentuckyregiments.org/milrec.php?id=2045.

Mississippi State Constitutional Convention. *Journal of the Proceedings and Debates in the Constitutional Convention of the State of Mississippi, August 1865: By Order of the Convention.* Jackson, 1865.

Monaghan, Jay. *Civil War on the Western Border, 1854–1865.* New York: Bonanza Books, 1985.

Moore, John C. "Battle of Lookout Mountain." *Confederate Veteran* 6, no. 9 (September 1898): 426–29. Photocopy at Chickamauga/Chattanooga Military Park.

——. *Missouri.* In vol. 9 of *Confederate Military History,* edited by Clement A. Evans. Atlanta, 1895. Reprinted by Secaucus, N.J.: Blue and Gray Press, n.d.

Moore, Raymond K. "They Were the 114th O.V.I." http://www.fortunecity.com/westwood/makeover/347/id192.htm.

Moses, Jefferson. "The Memoirs, Diary, and Life of Private Jefferson Moses, Company G, 93rd Illinois Volunteers." Available at "Civil War: A Soldier's Diary," http://www.ioweb.com/civilwar/.

Most Fearful Ordeal: Original Coverage of the Civil War by Writers and Reporters of the "New York Times." New York: St. Martin's Press, 2004.

Mueller, Jacob. *Memories of a Forty-Eighter: Sketches from the German American Period of Storm and Stress in the 1850's.* Trans. Steven Rowan. Cleveland, Ohio: Western Reserve Historical Society, 1996.

Nagler, Jorg. "The Lincoln-Frémont Debate and the Forty-Eighters." In *The German Forty-Eighters in the United States,* ed. Charlotte L. Brancaforte, 157–78. New York: Peter Lang, 1989.

National Archives. Central files for the Department of State, 1779–1963. Consular correspondence. RG 59.2.2.

——. Orders, muster rolls, and returns. Records relating to volunteers. Records relating to wars. RG 94.

"New York Passenger Lists, 1820–1957." November 1, 1849, and January 12, 1850. M237–85, National Archives and Records Administration, Washington, D.C.

Nichols, George Ward. *The Story of the Great March.* New York, 1865. Reprint, Williamstown, Mass.: Corner House, 1972. Page references are to the reprint.

Noble, H. T., S. C. Plummer, H. D. Dement, and C. E. Bolles. *Military History and Reminiscences of the Thirteenth Regiment of Illinois Volunteer Infantry in the Civil War in the United States, 1861–1865.* Chicago, 1892.

Nolen, Claude H. *African American Southerners in Slavery, Civil War, and Reconstruction.* Jefferson, N.C.: McFarland, 2001.

Nosworthy, Brent. *The Bloody Crucible of Courage: Fighting Methods and Combat Experience of the Civil War.* New York: Carroll and Graf, 2003.

O'Brien, Sean M. *Mobile, 1865: Last Stand of the Confederacy.* Westport, Conn.: Praeger, 2001.

Ofele, Martin W. *German-Speaking Officers in the U.S. Colored Troops, 1863–1867.* Gainesville: University Press of Florida, 2004.

Ohio State University "ehistory" Web site. Primary Sources Section. Follett letters. http://ehistory.osu.edu/osu/sources/letters/follett_brothers/follett_letters.cfm.

Osterhaus, Peter Joseph. Papers. Missouri Historical Society, St. Louis.

Parrish, William E. *Frank Blair: Lincoln's Conservative.* Columbia: University of Missouri Press, 1998.

Partridge, Charles A., ed. *History of the Ninety-sixth Regiment Illinois Volunteer Infantry.* Chicago, 1887.

Peckham, James. *General Nathaniel Lyon and Missouri in 1861.* New York, 1866.

Perry, Oran. "The Entering Wedge." In *War Papers Read before the Commandery of the State of Indiana, MOLLUS,* 359–76. Wilmington, Del.: Broadfoot, 1992.

Phillips, Christopher. *Damned Yankee: The Life of General Nathaniel Lyon.* Columbia: University of Missouri Press, 1990.

Piston, William G., and Richard W. Hatcher III. *Wilson's Creek: The Second Battle of the Civil War and the Men Who Fought It.* Chapel Hill: University of North Carolina Press, 2000.

Platter, Cornelius C. Diary. Hargrett Library. Available at the Digital Library of Georgia, http://dlg.galileo.usg.edu/hargrett/platter/004.php#18641123.

Porter, David D. *Incidents and Anecdotes of the Civil War.* New York, 1886.

Primm, James N. "Missouri, St. Louis, and the Secession Crisis." Introduction to *Germans for a Free Missouri: Translations from the St. Louis Radical Press, 1857–1862,* ed. and trans. Steven Rowan, 3–22. Columbia: University of Missouri Press, 1983.

Putnam, Sallie Brock. *Richmond during the War: Four Years of Personal Observation.* New York: G. W. Carelton, 1867. Reprint, Lincoln: University of Nebraska Press, 1996. References are to the reprint.

Rafuse, Ethan S. "McClellan and Halleck at War: The Struggle for Control of the Union War Effort in the West, November 1861–March 1862." *Civil War History* 49, no. 1 (March 2003): 32–51.

Randall, J. G., and Richard N. Current. *Lincoln the President: Last Full Measure.* Urbana: University of Illinois Press, 2000.

Reinhart, Joseph R., trans. and ed. *August Willich's Gallant Dutchmen: Civil War Letters from the 32nd Indiana Infantry.* Kent: Kent State University Press, 2006.

Richardson, Heather Cox. *The Death of Reconstruction: Race, Labor, and Politics in the Post–Civil War.* Cambridge: Harvard University Press, 2001.

Ritter, Gerald W., ed. "Civil War Letters of Captain John A. Ritter, M.D." http://gwillritter.tripod.com/jarletters3.htm.

Rombauer, Robert J. *The Union Cause in St. Louis in 1861: An Historical Sketch.* St. Louis: Nixon-Jones Printing, 1909.

Rorvig, Paul. "The Significant Skirmish: The Battle of Boonville, June 17, 1861." *Missouri Historical Review* 86 (January 1992): 127–48.

Rowan, Steven, ed. and trans. *Germans for a Free Missouri: Translations from the St. Louis Radical Press, 1857–1862.* Columbia: University of Missouri Press, 1983.

Sapp, Peggy Lathrop. *St. Clair County, Illinois: A Register of Births and Deaths, 1843–1857, as Recorded by John Scheel, County Clerk.* Springfield, Ill.: Folk-Works Research, 1993.

Scaife, William R. *The Campaign for Atlanta.* Cartersville, Ga.: Scaife Publications, 1993.

Scheel, Gary L. *Rain, Mud, and Swamps: 31st Missouri Volunteer Infantry Regiment.* St. Louis: Plus Communications, 1998.

Schofield, John. *Forty-six Years in the Army.* New York, 1887.

Schurz, Carl, to Abraham Lincoln, April 23, 1862. Abraham Lincoln Papers. Library of Congress. Available at http://memory.loc.gov/ammem/alhtml/malhome.html.

———. "Report to Andrew Johnson, President of the United States, on the Condition of the South." In *Message of the President of the United States to the 39th Congress,* by Andrew Johnson. December 19, 1865. Washington, D.C.: Government Printing Office.

Scribner, Benjamin F. *How Soldiers Were Made; or, The War as I Saw It under Buell, Rosecrans, Thomas, Grant, and Sherman.* Chicago, 1887.

Seay, Abraham Jefferson. *Civil War Diary as Written on the Battlefields.* N.p.: Sigler and Sigler, 1968. Photocopy at Chickamauga and Chattanooga National Military Park, Georgia. Original at Chisholm Trail Museum, Kingfisher, Okla.

Secrist, Philip L. *The Battle of Resaca: Atlanta Campaign, 1864.* Macon: Mercer University Press, 1998.

Shea, William L. "1862: 'A Continual Thunder.'" In *Rugged and Sublime: The Civil War in Arkansas,* ed. Mark K. Christ, 21–58. Fayetteville: University of Arkansas Press, 1994.

Shea, William L., and Earl J. Hess. *Pea Ridge: Civil War Campaign in the West.* Chapel Hill: University of North Carolina Press, 1992.

Shea, William L., and Terrence J. Winschel. *Vicksburg Is the Key.* Lincoln: University of Nebraska Press, 2003.

Sherman, W. T. *Memoirs of General William T. Sherman.* 2 vols. Second edition published in 1886. Single-volume reprint, New York: Literary Classics, 1990. Page references are to the reprint.

Sigel, Franz. "The Pea Ridge Campaign." In *Battles and Leaders of the Civil War,* ed. Robert U. Johnson and C. C. Buel, 1:313–34. New York, 1887–1888.

Simon, John Y., ed. *The Papers of Ulysses S. Grant.* Vols. 7–8. Carbondale: Southern Illinois University Press, 1979.

Smith, Timothy B. *Champion Hill: Decisive Battle for Vicksburg.* New York: Savas Beatie, 2004.

Smith, William F. "An Historical Sketch of the Military Operations around Chattanooga, Tennessee, September 22 to November 27, 1863." In *Papers of the Military Historical Society of Massachusetts.* Vol. 8, *The Mississippi Valley, Tennessee, Georgia, Alabama, 1861–1864,* 149–245. Boston: Military Historical Society of Massachusetts, 1910.

Smith, William W. "Holocaust Holiday: The Journal of a Strange Vacation to the War-Torn South and a Visit with U.S. Grant." *Civil War Times Illustrated* 18 (October 1979): 28–40.

Snead, Thomas L. *The Fight for Missouri from the Election of Lincoln to the Death of Lyon.* New York, 1886.

——. "The First Year of the War in Missouri." In *Battles and Leaders of the Civil War,* ed. Robert U. Johnson and C. C. Buel, 1:262–77. New York, 1887–1888. Reprint, New York: Thomas Yoseloff, 1957. References are to the reprint.

Stevens, Emerson O. "The National Soldiers' Home." In *The Making of America.* Vol. 9, *Army and Navy,* ed. Robert Marion La Follette, 411–28. Chicago: Making of America, 1906. Available at http://books.google.com/books?id=2FiuZqXrnOcC&pg=PA411&dq=stevens+national+soldiers+home#PPP14,M1.

Stevens, Walter B. *Missouri, the Center State, 1821–1915.* Vol. 2. Chicago: J. S. Clark, 1915.

Stevenson, B. F. *Letters from the Army.* Cincinnati, 1884.

Stickles, Arndt M. *Simon Bolivar Buckner, Borderland Knight.* Chapel Hill: University of North Carolina Press, 1940.

Strayer, Larry M., and Richard A. Baumgartner, eds. *Echoes of Battle: The Atlanta Campaign, an Illustrated Collection of Union and Confederate Narratives.* Huntington, W.Va.: Blue Acorn Press, 1991.

Swing, Raymond E. "Osterhaus Great Man." *Chicago Daily News,* January 3, 1914. Photocopy in Osterhaus Papers, Missouri Historical Society, St. Louis.

Taylor, Richard. *Destruction and Reconstruction: Personal Experiences of the Late War in the United States.* Edinburgh, 1879. Available at http://books.google.com/

books?id=IIZZrgnnfXkC&printsec=frontcover&dq=taylor+destruction+reconstruction.

——. "The Last Confederate Surrender." In *Annals of the War Written by Leading Participants North and South,* 67–71. 1879. Reprint, Secaucus, N.J.: Blue and Gray Press, 1996. References are to the reprint.

Trotha, Trutz von. "'The Fellows Can Just Starve': On Wars of 'Pacification' in the African Colonies of Imperial Germany and the Concept of 'Total War.'" In *Anticipating Total War: The German and American Experiences, 1871–1914,* ed. Manfred F. Boemeke, Roger Chickering, and Stig Forster, 415–36. Washington, D.C.: German Historical Institute, 1999.

Tunnard, W. H. *A Southern Record: The History of the Third Regiment Louisiana Infantry.* Baton Rouge, 1866.

Upchurch, Thomas Adams. "Speaking on Behalf of the Vagabond Rebels: The Mississippi Press on Race and Reconstruction in 1865." *Journal of Mississippi History* 61 (Winter 1999): 351–70.

U.S. Army Center of Military History. "Civil War Medal of Honor Recipients" Web site, http://www.army.mil/cmh/html/moh/civwarmz.html.

U.S. Bureau of the Census. Federal Census, 1850 and 1860. Available at Ancestry.com.

U.S. Congress. *Journal of the House of Representatives.* 39th Cong., 1st sess., February 9, 1866. Library of Congress. Available at http://memory.loc.gov/cgi-bin/query/r?ammem/hlaw:@field(DOCID+@lit(hj06341)).

——. "Report to Andrew Johnson, President of the United States, on the Condition of the South," by Carl Schurz. In *Message of the President of the United States to the 39th Congress,* by Andrew Johnson. Washington, D.C., 1865.

——. *Senate Executive Journal.* 37th Cong., 2nd sess., May 2, 1862; 39th Cong., 1st sess., May 18, June 11, and June 18, 1866. Library of Congress. Available at http://memory.loc.gov/ammem/amlaw/lwejlink.html#anchor37.

U.S. Department of State. *Papers Relating to Foreign Relations of the United States, 1870.* Transmitted to Congress with the Annual Message of the President, December 5, 1870. Washington, D.C., 1870.

U.S. Department of Veterans Affairs. "National Home for Disabled Volunteer Soldiers." http://www.va.gov/FACMGT/HISTORIC/NHDVS.ASP.

U.S. Naval War Records Office. *Official Records of the Union and Confederate Navies in the War of the Rebellion.* Series 1. Washington, D.C.: Government Printing Office, 1894–1922. On Cornell University's "Making of America" Web site, http://cdl.library.cornell.edu/moa/moa_browse.html.

U.S. War Department. *The War of the Rebellion: A Compilation of the Official Records of the Union and Confederate Armies.* Series 1–3. Washington, D.C.: Government Printing Office, 1880–1901. On Cornell University's "Making of America" Web site, http://cdl.library.cornell.edu/moa/moa_browse.html.

Valentin, Viet. *1848: Chapters of German History.* Hamden, Conn.: Archon Books, 1965.

Vicksburg National Military Park. Regimental Files 480 (42nd Ohio), 345 (49th Indiana), 499 (114th Ohio).

Voelkner, Henry. Papers. Western Historical Manuscript Collection, University of Missouri, Columbia.

Waddle, Angus L. *Three Years with the Armies of the Ohio and the Cumberland.* Chillicothe, Ohio, 1889. Available at the Library of Congress, http://lcweb2.loc.gov/cgi-bin/ampage?collId=gdc3&fileName=scd0001_20020321002typage.db&recNum=62.

Walthall, E. C. "Walthall on the Battle of Lookout Mountain." *Confederate Veteran* 6, no. 12 (December 1898): 562–64.

Ware, Eugene F. *The Lyon Campaign in Missouri: Being a History of the First Iowa Infantry.* Topeka, 1907. Reprint, Iowa City: Press of the Camp Pope Bookshop, 1991. Page references are to the original.

Warner, Ezra J. *Generals in Blue: Lives of the Union Commanders.* Baton Rouge: Louisiana State University Press, 1964.

Washburne, Elihu B. *Recollections of a Minister to France, 1869–1877.* Vol. 2. New York, 1889.

Wawro, Geoffrey. *The Franco-Prussian War.* New York: Cambridge University Press, 2003.

Webb, Kerry. "U.S. Civil War Generals" Web site, http://sunsite.utk.edu/civil-war/generals.html.

Webster, Daniel, and Don Cameron. *The History of the First Wisconsin Battery Light Artillery.* Washington, D.C.: National Tribune, 1907.

Wherry, William M. "The Campaign in Missouri and the Battle of Wilson's Creek, 1861." In *Missouri Historical Society Collections,* 1:1–19. St. Louis, 1880.

Wilkie, Franc B. *The Iowa First: Letters from the War.* Dubuque, 1861.

Williams, Chad L. "Symbols of Freedom and Defeat." In *Black Flag over Dixie: Racial Atrocities and Reprisals in the Civil War,* ed. Gregory J. W. Urwin, 210–30. Carbondale: Southern Illinois University Press, 2004.

Willison, Charles A. *Reminiscences of a Boy's Service with the 76th Ohio in the Fifteenth Army Corps, under General Sherman.* Minasha, Wis.: G. Banta, 1908. Reprint, Huntington, W.Va.: Blue Acorn Press, 1995. References are to the reprint.

Wills, Charles W. *Army Life of an Illinois Soldier.* Comp. Mary E. Kellogg. Washington, D.C.: Globe Printing, 1906. Available at http://books.google.com/books?id=s349lI7F_H8C&printsec=frontcover&dq=wills+%22army+life%22#PPA3,M1.

Wilson, James Grant. *Biographical Sketches of Illinois Officers in the Rebellion of 1861.* Chicago, 1863. Available at http://books.google.com/books?id=-SNmKurg-sIC&printsec=frontcover&dq=James+wilson+%22illinois+officers%22.

Wilson, James H. "A Staff Officer's Journal of the Vicksburg Campaign, April 30 to July 4, 1863." *Journal of the Military Institution of the United States* 43 (1908): 93–109.

——. *Under the Old Flag.* Vol. 1. New York: D. Appleton, 1912.

Winschel, Terrence J. "Fighting Politician: John A. McClernand." In *Grant's Lieutenants from Cairo to Vicksburg,* ed. Steven E. Woodworth, 129–50. Lawrence: University Press of Kansas, 2001.

——, ed. *The Civil War Diary of a Common Soldier.* Transcribed by Mike Edwards. Baton Rouge: Louisiana State University Press, 2001.

Wittke, Carl. *Refugees of Revolution: The German Forty-Eighters in America.* Philadelphia: University of Pennsylvania Press, 1952.

Woodson, H. M. "Battle on the Side of Lookout Mountain." *Confederate Veteran* 6, no. 1 (January 1898). Typescript excerpt in Lookout Mountain file at Chickamauga and Chattanooga National Military Park.

Woodworth, Steven E. *Nothing but Victory: The Army of the Tennessee, 1861–1865.* New York: Alfred A. Knopf, 2005.

——, ed. *Grant's Lieutenants from Cairo to Vicksburg.* Lawrence: University Press of Kansas, 2001.

Wright, J. W. A. "The Battles of Lookout Mountain and Missionary Ridge." *Overland Monthly and Out West Magazine* 6, no. 32 (August 1885): 138–52. Available at the University of Michigan's "Making of America" Web site, http://www.hti.umich.edu/cgi/t/text/.

Young, Edward. *Labor in Europe and America: A Special Report on the Rates of Wages, the Cost of Subsistence, and the Working Classes.* Washington, 1875. On the University of Michigan's "Making of America" Web site, http://www.hti.umich.edu/cgi/t/text/.

Index